TO MAKE THE
WOUNDED WHOLE

TO MAKE THE WOUNDED WHOLE

THE CULTURAL LEGACY OF

MARTIN LUTHER KING, JR.

Lewis V. Baldwin

FORTRESS PRESS   MINNEAPOLIS

TO MAKE THE WOUNDED WHOLE
The Cultural Legacy of Martin Luther King, Jr.

Scripture quotations unless otherwise noted are from the Revised Standard
Version of the Bible, copyright © 1946, 1952, and 1971 by the Division of
Christian Education of the National Council of Churches.

Interior and cover design: Jim Gerhard
Cover photo: Martin Luther King, Jr. in Freedom March 1961. Copyright ©
Flip Schulke.

Library of Congress Cataloging-in-Publication Data

Baldwin, Lewis V., 1949–
    To make the wounded whole : the cultural legacy of Martin Luther
King, Jr. / Lewis V. Baldwin.
        p.   cm.
    Includes bibliographical references and index.
    ISBN 0-8006-2543-9
    1. King, Martin Luther, Jr., 1929–1968. 2. King, Martin Luther,
Jr., 1929–1968—Philosophy. 3. Black theology. I. Title.
E185.97.K5B353   1992
323'.092—dc20   91-34739
                                                                  CIP

The paper used in this publication meets the minimum requirements of
American National Standard for Information Sciences—Permanence of
Paper for Printed Library Materials, ANSI Z329.48-1984.   ∞™

Manufactured in the U.S.A.   AF 1-2543

96   95   94   93   92   1   2   3   4   5   6   7   8   9   10

In memory of
George M. "Mickey" Leland
and for all people
who are engaged in the search
for human wholeness

There is a balm in Gilead,
To make the wounded whole.
There is a balm in Gilead,
To heal the sin-sick soul.

—Slave Spiritual

ACKNOWLEDGMENTS

Excerpts from *Why We Can't Wait* by Martin Luther King, Jr. Copyright © 1963, 1964 by Martin Luther King, Jr. Reprinted by permission of Harper-Collins, Publishers, Inc. and the Joan Daves Agency.

Excerpts from *My Life with Martin Luther King, Jr.* by Coretta Scott King. Copyright © 1969 by Coretta Scott King. Reprinted by permission of Harcourt Brace Jovanovich, Inc. and the Joan Daves Agency.

Excerpts from *Where Do We Go From Here? Chaos or Community* by Martin Luther King, Jr. Copyright © 1967 by Martin Luther King, Jr. Reprinted by permission of HarperCollins, Publishers, Inc. and the Joan Daves Agency.

Excerpts from *Malcom X Speaks: Selected Speeches and Statements* by Malcom X, ed. George Breitman. Copyright © 1965, 1989 by Betty Shabazz and Pathfinder Press. Reprinted by permission of Pathfinder Press.

Excerpt from "Precious Lord, Take My Hand," words and music by Thomas A. Dorsey, copyright © 1938 by Hill & Range Songs, Inc. Copyright renewed, assigned to Unichappell Music, Inc. (Rightsong Music, Publisher). International copyright secured. All rights reserved. Unauthorized copying, arranging, adapting, recording or puplic performance is an infringement of copyright. Infringers are liable under the law. Reprinted by permission of Hal Leonard Publishing Corporation.

Excerpts from *Black and White Power Subreption* by Joseph R. Washington, Jr. Copyright © 1969 by Joseph R. Washington, Jr. Reprinted by permission.

Excerpts from *Liberation and Reconciliation: A Black Theology* by J. Deotis Roberts. Copyright © 1971 by J. Deotis Roberts. Reprinted by permission.

Excerpts from *Four Decades of Concern: Martin Luther King, Jr.* Copyright © 1986 by The Martin Luther King, Jr. Center for Nonviolent Social Change, Inc. Reprinted by permission of the Joan Daves Agency.

Excerpts from *The Trumpet of Conscience* by Martin Luther King, Jr. Copyright © 1967 by Martin Luther King, Jr. Reprinted by permission of Harper-Collins, Publishers, Inc. and the Joan Daves Agency.

Letters between George Houser and Martin Luther King, Jr. reprinted by permission of George Houser, Executive Director Emeritus, American Committee on Africa.

Selected documents of the American Negro Leadership Conference on Africa reprinted by permission of James Farmer.

CONTENTS

ACRONYMS

A.C.O.A.	American Committee on Africa
A.D.A.	Americans for Democratic Action
A.D.A.F.	African Defense and Aid Fund
A.F.L.C.I.O.	American Federation of Labor and Congress of Industrial Organizations
A.I.C.	Atlanta Intercollegiate Council
A.I.D.	Agency for International Development
A.M.E.	African Methodist Episcopal Church
A.M.E.Z.	African Methodist Episcopal Zion Church
A.N.C.	African National Congress
A.N.C.	African National Council
A.N.L.C.A.	American Negro Leadership Conference on Africa
A.S.F.	Anglican Students' Federation
B.B.C.	Black Business Council
B.C.N.	Black Christian Nationalist Church
B.P.	Balubakat Party
B.S.C.P.	Brotherhood of Sleeping Car Porters
C.A.F.	Central African Federation

C.B.C.	Congressional Black Caucus
C.E.A.F.	Church Emergency Aid Fund
C.M.E.	Christian Methodist Episcopal Church
C.O.G.I.C.	Church of God in Christ
C.O.N.A.K.A.T.	Confederation of Ktanga Tribal Associations
CORE	Congress of Racial Equality
F.C.C.	Federal Council of Churches
F.M.G.	Federal Military Government
F.O.R.	Fellowship of Reconciliation
F.S.A.M.	Free South Africa Movement
I.D.A.F.	International Defense and Aid Fund
I.O.C.	International Olympic Committee
L.W.F.	Lutheran World Federation
M.L.K.C.	Martin Luther King, Jr. Center for Nonviolent Social Change, Inc.
NAACP	National Association for the Advancement of Colored People
N.B.C.	National Baptist Convention of America
N.B.C.	National Baptist Convention, U.S.A.
N.C.C.C.	National Council of the Churches of Christ
N.C.M.	National Congolese Movement
N.C.N.W.	National Council of Negro Women
N.C.R.M.	National Civil Rights Museum
N.L.F.	National Liberation Front
N.O.W.	National Organization of Women
N.U.L.	National Urban League

N.U.S.A.S.	National Union of South African Students
O.A.S.	Organization of African States
O.A.U.	Organization of African Unity
O.C.A.	Operation Crossroads Africa
O.I.C.	Opportunities Industrialization Centers
P.A.O.C.C.	Pan African Orthodox Christian Church
P.A.S.O.A.	Pan-African Students' Organization in the Americas, Inc.
P.N.B.C.	Progressive National Baptist Convention of America
P.U.S.H.	People United to Save Humanity
R.N.A.	Republic of New Africa
S.A.E.C.	South Africa Emergency Committee
S.A.D.F.	South Africa Defense Fund
S.A.P.O.	Southwest Africa Peoples Organization
S.B.M.	Shrines of the Black Madonna
S.C.L.C.	Southern Christian Leadership Conference
S.N.C.C.	Student Nonviolent Coordinating Committee
U.N.I.A.	Universal Negro Improvement Association
U.P.C.E.M.R.	United Presbyterian Commission on Ecumenical Missions and Relations
U.S.G.A.I.D.	United States Government Agency for International Development
W.A.R.C.	World Alliance of Reformed Churches

W.C.C.	World Council of Churches
W.C.F.C.C.	Wilgespruit Christian Fellowship and Conference Center
W.I.L.P.F.	Women's International League for Peace and Freedom
W.S.P.	Women's Strike for Peace
Z.A.P.U.	Zimbabwe African Peoples' Union

PREFACE

This book is largely the product of a collective effort. It was brought to completion with the support and encouragement of many scholars, librarians, archivists, students, and friends. These persons are too numerous to name individually, but I cannot resist the need to recognize some of them.

I owe an enormous intellectual debt to Professor James H. Cone of Union Theological Seminary in New York. Dr. Cone willingly shared the products of his own research on Martin Luther King, Jr., with me, and we exchanged ideas that stimulated my thinking and helped me to conceptualize this work. Although Dr. Cone and I have not always agreed in our perceptions of King's life, thought, and legacy, we have nevertheless made each other's work pleasant and richer. I share with him the wish to preserve King's life and legacy from the fate of obscurity and of misunderstanding that often befalls great black men and women.

Dr. Sterling Stuckey, a former teacher at Northwestern University, influenced this study in profound ways. I have benefited immensely from Dr. Stuckey's treatments of black nationalist theory, particularly as they relate to the ties between African-Americans and Africans. Dr. Stuckey has always shown interest in and support for my work.

Dr. Jimmie L. Franklin and Dr. Walter E. Fluker, colleagues at Vanderbilt University, read parts of the manuscript and offered many important substantive and stylistic suggestions. They provided me with meticulous editing and incisive criticism, and whatever errors I have made in this work are due largely to my inability to follow their fine scholarly advice.

I also acknowledge the support of archivists, librarians, and other staff persons at the Martin Luther King, Jr. Center for Nonviolent Social Change, Inc., and at Boston University's Mugar Memorial Library. These persons led me to important documents, provided a pleasant atmosphere for my research, and performed other tasks that made my work easier and more enriching and rewarding.

I would like to thank the many students who have taken my courses on Dr. King at Colgate University and Vanderbilt University over the last decade. They often challenged my facile generalizations and rescued me from some of my biases and misconceptions. They made the manuscript much better in every way than it would otherwise have been.

I must offer a special word of gratitude to the editors of Fortress Press, who worked closely with me in making this an attractive volume. The late Dr. John A. Hollar developed a strong interest in my research in 1985, and was a tremendous source of inspiration and support until his death in the fall of 1989. Michael West, senior editor at Fortress Press, provided excellent editorial advice and suggestions that significantly improved the manuscript.

Some of my most meaningful support came from my wife Jacqueline, who read the entire manuscript. As my familial colleague, she assisted me with proofreading and called my attention to important omissions. Jacqueline's affirmation of my life and work has motivated and inspired me to reach for higher goals in the world of scholarship.

Finally, I want to thank Pat Mundy, our department secretary, for her painstaking typing of this and many other manuscripts in the past. Pat helped make this a worthy endeavor.

Lewis V. Baldwin
Nashville, Tennessee

INTRODUCTION

To Make the Wounded Whole is my second major treatment of Martin Luther King, Jr., as a product and an exemplar of black culture and folk tradition. In *There Is a Balm in Gilead*, issued recently by Fortress Press, I examined King's roots in the black family and church traditions in the South, noting particularly how those sources shaped his personality, his thought, his vision, and his activities as a preacher and social activist. Here King was treated as a perfect illustration of how black intellectual life or literary culture has traditionally found continuity with the folk culture and experiences of the black masses.[1] *To Make the Wounded Whole* is a more conscious effort to explore the dimensions of King's cultural legacy, and it should therefore be considered a companion volume to my book, *There Is a Balm in Gilead*. The two volumes are essentially one in that they, when considered jointly, demonstrate how King's vision gradually transcended southern particularism to assume national and international implications.[2]

While focusing specifically on King's rich legacy of thought and activism and its meaning for black America,

1. See Lewis V. Baldwin, *There Is a Balm in Gilead: The Cultural Roots of Martin Luther King, Jr.* (Minneapolis, Minn.: Fortress Press, 1991), 1–14.
2. *Ibid.*

1

this study also examines the meaning and significance of that legacy for the world. It shows that King's legacy is essentially as rich and as broad as the range of experiential and intellectual sources from which he benefited.[3] It highlights King's role in reviving, reaffirming, and reshaping a past, and suggests that from him a stream still flows, seeking to express, in changing contexts, his concern for peace, justice, and human community.

The most prominent theme coursing through *To Make the Wounded Whole* is *community*. This work suggests that King's greatest legacy was revealed in his understanding and articulation of the communitarian ideal and also in his serious and persistent quest for human community. King envisioned and struggled for an American society and a world that would not be fragmented on the basis of race, sex, class, religion, nationality, and other artificial human categories. A central contention here is that ethical dialogue with King, around his vision of "the world house" or the "worldwide neighborhood," can, as Walter E. Fluker puts it, "yield fruitful insight into the conception, character, and actualization of human community."[4]

Chapter 1 concentrates on King's critiques of and dialogues with other historic black leaders and thinkers who proposed fundamentally different prescriptions for and offered essentially different diagnoses of the afflictions of their people. Using Robert M. Franklin's typology of

3. The breadth of King's experiential and intellectual sources is examined in *Ibid.*, 1–10, 15–336. Here it is noted that King drew heavily on the ideals and values of family and church, and on the Bible, Gandhian ideas and methods, the principles of American participatory democracy, Western philosophy, Niebuhrian Christian realism, and Personalistic and Social Gospel concepts. King's family and church background taught him to read widely and critically, but it was largely through his own creativity that he achieved a dynamic complementarity of so many diverse sources and themes.

4. See Walter E. Fluker, *They Looked for a City: A Comparative Analysis of the Ideal of Community in the Thought of Howard Thurman and Martin Luther King, Jr.* (Lanham, Md.: University Press of America, Inc., 1989), 1–50. This contention is also strongly implied, if not specifically stated, in Lewis V. Baldwin, ed., *Toward the Beloved Community: Martin Luther King, Jr. and South African Apartheid* (Unpublished manuscript, 1991), 1–22 and 320–360.

black religious communities as a guide, careful consideration is given to King's critiques of and dialogues with the *progressive accommodationism* of Booker T. Washington and Joseph H. Jackson, the *redemptive nationalism* of Marcus Garvey and Malcolm X, the *grassroots revivalism* of conservative black churches, and the *prosperity positivism* of the Reverend Dr. Frederick J. Eikerenkoetter (Reverend Ike) and the Reverend Roosevelt Franklin.[5] The discussion demonstrates that King's dialogues with representatives of these thought and protest traditions accounted in large measure for his growth and maturation as a leader and thinker. Although King shared ideas with all of these traditionally black approaches to the black condition, and constantly engaged in dialogue with them, he identified primarily with the tradition of *prophetic radicalism* that stemmed from figures like Richard Allen, Harriet Tubman, and Frederick Douglass.[6] The importance of this chapter lies in its treatment of King's responses to the panorama of perspectives on the race problem presented by African-American leaders before and during his time.

Chapter 2 examines how major black theologians and ethicists have treated Martin Luther King, Jr., in their works. Of particular significance are the images of King reflected in the writings of theologians like James H. Cone, Gayraud S. Wilmore, Albert B. Cleage, Jr., Joseph R. Washington, Jr., Major J. Jones, J. Deotis Roberts, and James H. Evans, Jr., and in the works of ethicists such as Preston N. Williams, John H. Cartwright, Peter J. Paris, Ervin Smith, Enoch H. Oglesby, William D. Watley, Robert M. Franklin, Jr., Walter E. Fluker, and Katie G.

---

5. This systematic classification of black religious communities, which identifies dominant attitudes toward the political establishment in America, was developed in Robert M. Franklin, "Religious Belief and Political Activism in Black America: An Essay," *The Journal of Religious Thought* 43, no. 2 (Fall-Winter, 1986–87): 63–72.

6. *Ibid.* Franklin's association of King with prophetic radicalism in the black Christian tradition finds support in Peter J. Paris, "The Bible and the Black Churches," in *The Bible and Social Reform*, ed. Ernest R. Sandeen (Philadelphia: Fortress Press, 1982): 140–44.

Cannon. The primary focus is on the extent to which the emerging disciplines of black theology and ethics have drawn on the insights and vision of King. The whole question of how King's thought relates to contemporary black theology and ethics, and to the black theological tradition generally, is essential to any serious consideration of his cultural heritage as an African-American.[7]

In Chapter 3, King's perception of how the black American struggle related to the struggles of other peoples of African descent is discussed. Much of the focus is on how King dealt with the broad issue of universal black liberation. The analogies he drew between the racist oppression of African-Americans and the colonial domination of other peoples of African ancestry, particularly at the point of what he called "politico-economic forces," provide a key to understanding why he stressed the need for cooperation between black peoples throughout the world. The argument here is that King's interest in bonds and obligations between persons of African descent everywhere, whom he considered related by blood and condition, was not necessarily inconsistent with his beloved community vision, which embraced all persons irrespective of race, creed, or nationality.[8]

Chapter 4 assesses the relevance and implications of King's life, thought, and legacy for the continuing struggle against various forms of oppression in the world. The focus is on King as an international symbol of community, with special attention to how he employed the metaphor of "the great world house" as an expression

7. Unfortunately, there are no serious studies that treat King as a connecting link between the folk theology of his slave forebears and the more contemporary expressions of black theology as an intellectual discipline. This pattern of omission is reflected to some extent even in seminal essays by the black theologian James H. Cone. See James H. Cone, "Martin Luther King, Jr., Black Theology-Black Church," *Theology Today* 40, no. 4 (January 1984): 409–20; and James H. Cone, "The Theology of Martin Luther King, Jr.," *Union Seminary Quarterly Review* 40, no. 4 (January 1986), 21–39.

8. Baldwin, ed., *Toward the Beloved Community*, 1–22 and Lewis V. Baldwin, "Martin Luther King, Jr.'s 'Beloved Community' Ideal and the Apartheid System in South Africa," *The Western Journal of Black Studies* 10, no. 4 (Winter 1986): 214.

of his vision of world community.[9] Some discussion of
the degree to which this vision has been pursued since
King's death by the Southern Christian Leadership Conference and the Martin Luther King, Jr. Center for Nonviolent Social Change, Inc., both headquartered in Atlanta,
Georgia, is also provided. The findings in this chapter
suggest that King speaks more relevantly about the
meaning, practice, and significance of human community than most contemporary social activists and theorists, and that ethical dialogue with him around the
beloved community concept can be enormously benefi-
cial to the search for a universal human fellowship
grounded in love and justice.[10]

As was the case with my book *There Is a Balm in
Gilead*, this work relies heavily upon King's published
books and essays and his largely unpublished, sponta-
neously delivered sermons and mass meeting speeches.
Information from King's personal letters and interviews
has also been used. These sources together provide the
angle from which to view King's cultural legacy in its
wholeness.[11]

This is not the final word on King's cultural legacy. My
purpose was to produce a book that can serve as a good
introduction to the subject. My hope is that scholars, students, and others will read *To Make the Wounded Whole*
with a critical eye and then build on its content with
their own research and reflections. Furthermore, I hope
this study will lead to a greater appreciation of King's
cultural legacy and to more determined efforts to fulfill
his dream for humankind as a whole.

9. See Martin Luther King, Jr., *Where Do We Go from Here: Chaos
or Community?* (Boston: Beacon Press, 1967), 167–191.
10. Baldwin, ed., *Toward the Beloved Community*, 1–22 and 320–60;
and Fluker, *They Looked for a City*, 155–89.
11. I have already alluded to David J. Garrow's and James H. Cone's
arguments concerning the unreliability of King's largely ghostwritten,
published books and essays. I do not agree with their arguments, and
contend that there are no important discrepancies between the content
of King's published essays and books and that of his largely unpublished
sermons, speeches, interviews, and personal letters. See Baldwin, *There
Is a Balm in Gilead*, 11–14.

LIFT EVERY VOICE
BLACK PERSPECTIVES IN DIALOGUE

1

. . . the voice of my race thus tortured and outraged is stifled or ignored wherever it is lifted in America in a demand for justice.

Ida B. Wells, 1893[1]

Lift every voice and sing,
Till earth and heaven ring,
Ring with the harmonies of liberty. . . .

The Negro National Anthem, 1900[2]

All of our people have the same goals, the same objective. That objective is freedom, justice, equality. . . . Integration is only a method that is used by some groups to obtain freedom, justice, equality and respect as human beings. Separation is only a method that is used by other groups to obtain freedom, justice, equality or human dignity.

Malcolm X, 1964[3]

I began thinking about the fact that I stand in the middle of two opposing forces in the Negro community. One is a force of complacency. . . . The other force is one of bitterness and hatred, and it comes perilously close to advocating violence.

Martin Luther King, Jr., 1964[4]

Black Americans have always been united by their common desire to achieve freedom, justice, equality, and human dignity. However, they have differed historically in their responses to racism and oppression, and also in their perceptions of what constitutes the ideal society.

1. Ida B. Wells, *Crusade for Justice: The Autobiography of Ida B. Wells*, ed. John Hope Franklin (Chicago: The University of Chicago Press, 1970), 100.

2. Quoted in *The New National Baptist Hymnal* (Nashville: The National Baptist Publishing Board, 1977), 477.

3. Malcolm X, *Malcolm X Speaks: Selected Speeches and Statements*, ed. with Prefatory Notes by George Breitman (New York: Merit Publishers, 1965), 51.

4. Martin Luther King, Jr., *Why We Can't Wait* (New York: The New American Library, 1964), 86–87.

This diversity has resulted in what Robert M. Franklin calls "five basic modes of orientation to the political realm," namely, progressive accommodationism, redemptive nationalism, grassroots revivalism, prosperity positivism, and prophetic radicalism.[5] This typology reflects the complex and diverse responses of black Americans to the existing social, political, and economic order. As a prophetic radical, one who criticized and confronted the status quo with nonviolent methods to achieve social justice, Martin Luther King, Jr., engaged in much conflict and dialogue with the progressive accommodationism of Booker T. Washington and Joseph H. Jackson, the redemptive nationalism of Marcus M. Garvey and Malcolm X, the grassroots revivalism of conservative black churches, and the prosperity positivism of excessively materialistic black preachers.[6]

This chapter highlights the nature and extent of that conflict and dialogue, particularly as related to the whole question of what should be the response of blacks to racism and oppression as social evils. The discussion will

5. Robert M. Franklin, "Charisma and Conflict in Religious Belief and Political Activism in Black America," a lecture given at Vanderbilt University (April 7, 1986), 1ff.; and Robert M. Franklin, "Religious Belief and Political Activism in Black America: An Essay," *The Journal of Religious Thought* 43, no. 2 (Fall-Winter 1986–87): 63–72. Peter Paris takes a different approach by identifying four strands in the black Christian tradition—pastoral, prophetic, reformist, and nationalist. See Peter J. Paris, "The Bible and the Black Churches," in Ernest R. Sandeen, ed., *The Bible and Social Reform* (Philadelphia: Fortress Press, 1982), 135–52. Although I am indebted to Robert M. Franklin for these categories, my analysis is somewhat different from his. For an excellent study of visions of the moral and just society as held by progressive accommodationists, redemptive nationalists, and prophetic radicals, see Robert M. Franklin, *Liberating Visions: Human Fulfillment and Social Justice in African American Thought* (Minneapolis: Fortress Press, 1990), 11–158.

6. Franklin, "Religious Belief and Political Activism," 65; Franklin, "Charisma and Conflict," 1ff.; and Paris, "The Bible and the Black Churches," 140–44. Some studies emphasize King's conflicts and disagreements with groups like the accommodationists and the nationalists, with little attention to how he had dialogue with and shared ideas with such groups. Such studies stress *conflict* rather than *dialogue* between various traditions of thought among black leaders. See Peter J. Paris, *Black Leaders in Conflict: Martin Luther King, Jr., Malcolm X, Joseph H. Jackson, Adam Clayton Powell, Jr.* (New York and Philadelphia: Pilgrim Press, 1978), 15–226; and John J. Ansbro, *Martin Luther King, Jr.: The Making of a Mind* (Maryknoll, N.Y.: Orbis Books, 1982), 198–230.

develop in the following manner: (1) King and the progressive accommodationists; (2) King and the redemptive nationalists; (3) King and other black responses to collective evil; and (4) King as the great synthesizer.

KING AND THE PROGRESSIVE ACCOMMODATIONISTS

Progressive accommodationists have historically emphasized cooperating with the sociopolitical and economic order with the intention of creating a just and peaceful society for everyone. This stream of thought dates at least as far back as Jupiter Hammon (1702–1786), the black preacher/poet who counseled his people to adjust to their enslavement while awaiting gradual emancipation. It found its fullest expression with Booker T. Washington in the late nineteenth century, and has been advanced most recently by nationally-known black preachers such as Joseph H. Jackson and E. V. Hill.[7] Robert M. Franklin has written the following about such proponents of progressive accommodationism:

> Their central political-ethical goal is a harmonious, conflict-free society in which blacks can freely pursue their economic and political interests. Progressive accommodationist religious communities are able to cooperate with the political status quo because both the religious leaders and politicians understand themselves to share the values of social order, economic prosperity, and political freedom and individualism.[8]

Martin Luther King, Jr., raised critical questions about progressive accommodationism as a moral and practical response to racism, and as an effective approach to the creation of a just and peaceful society. Much of his critique was directed at Booker T. Washington, the chief proponent of the progressive accommodationist philosophy.

7. Franklin, "Religious Belief and Political Activism," 64, and Milton C. Sernett, ed., *Afro-American Religious History: A Documentary Witness* (Durham, N.C.: Duke University Press, 1985), 33–42.
8. *Ibid.*

Born a slave in Virginia around 1858, Washington successfully employed this philosophy in building Tuskegee Normal and Industrial Institute in Alabama from a
dilapidated shanty with forty students to a world-famous
institution.[9] He emphasized the need for black people to
be independent, the importance of industrial education
and the acquisition of manual skills as the prerequisite to
black economic independence, and the need for his people
to reject social intercourse with whites as a path to their
advancement, ideas that became key aspects of progressive accommodationism.[10] The dimensions of Washington's philosophy and program were revealed in his famous
address at the Cotton States Exposition in Atlanta in 1895.
In this address, perhaps the most celebrated given by a
black leader prior to King's "I Have a Dream" speech
decades later, Washington urged his people, "Cast down
your bucket where you are":

> Cast it down in agriculture, mechanics, in commerce,
> in domestic service, in all the professions. And in this
> connection it is well to bear in mind that whatever
> other sins the South may be called to bear, when it
> comes to business, pure and simple, it is in the South
> that the Negro is given a man's chance in the commer-
> cial world, and in nothing is this exposition more elo-
> quent than in emphasizing this chance. Our greatest
> danger is that in the great leap from slavery to free-
> dom we may overlook the fact that the masses of us
> are to live by the productions of our hands, and fail to
> keep in mind that we shall prosper in proportion as
> we learn to dignify and glorify common labor and put
> brains and skill into the common occupations of life;
> shall prosper in proportion as we learn to draw the
> line between the superficial and the substantial, the
> ornamental gewgaws of life and the useful. No race

9. Philip S. Foner, ed., *The Voice of Black America: Major Speeches
by Blacks in the United States, 1797–1973*, Vol. I (New York: Capricorn
Books, 1975), 607–8; and Ansbro, *Martin Luther King, Jr.*, 198–202.
    10. Franklin, "Religious Belief and Political Activism," 64; and
Gayraud S. Wilmore, *Black Religion and Black Radicalism: An Interpre-
tation of the Religious History of Afro-American People* (Maryknoll, N.Y.:
Orbis Books, 1983), 136–37.

can prosper till it learns that there is as much dignity
in tilling a field as in writing a poem. It is at the
bottom of life we must begin, and not at the top.[11]

Washington assured whites that "the wisest among my
race understand that the agitation of questions of social
equality is the extremist folly, and that progress in the
enjoyment of all the privileges that will come to us must
be the result of severe and constant struggle rather than
of artificial forcing." He predicted that if white southerners would make use of black labor instead of European
immigrants, they and their "families will be surrounded
by the most patient, faithful, law-abiding, and unresent-
ful people that the world has ever seen." "In all things
that are purely social we can be as separate as the fin-
gers," Washington concluded, "yet one as the hand in all
things essential to mutual progress."[12]

Martin Luther King, Jr., dismissed Washington's progressive accommodationism as "pressureless persuasion," "passive acceptance," "passive resignation," or
"passive acquiescence," and suggested that this path "had
too little freedom in its present and too little promise in
its future."[13] He accused Washington of appeasing whites
and of reinforcing their deeply ingrained prejudices toward black people:

> He said just what the whites wanted to hear. He
> didn't feel that pressure was necessary. He was hon-
> ored and heralded everywhere as a responsible
> leader. I always get a little disturbed when I'm re-
> ferred to as a responsible leader because I have come
> to see that all too often that means that you are not a
> leader who is willing to tell the truth about the situa-
> tion. It may mean that you are more concerned with
> saying what the white power structure *wants* to hear

11. Quoted in Foner, ed., *The Voice of Black America* 1: 609–12.
12. *Ibid*.
13. King, *Why We Can't Wait*, 33; Martin Luther King, Jr., *Where Do
We Go from Here: Chaos or Community?* (Boston: Beacon Press, 1967),
128–29; and Martin Luther King, Jr., "Transforming a Neighborhood," a
sermon (The Archives of the Martin Luther King, Jr., Center for Nonviolent Social Change, Inc., Atlanta, Ga., 10 August 1967), 5–6.

instead of what the white power structure *needs* to
hear. Booker Washington went on to discover that
this kind of pressureless persuasion causes the forces
of reaction to dive deeper into bonds of oppression
and injustice.[14]

The basis for King's critique of Washington was his
belief that nonviolent direct action, in conjunction with
education, political action, religious persuasion, and liti-
gation, was the only moral and practical way of overcoming black oppression, and of moving blacks into the
mainstream of American social, political, and economic
life.[15] In his view, Washington had essentially surrendered black rights and, at least tacitly, accepted second-
class citizenship in return for economic opportunity in
menial functions and white support for black industrial
training. King believed that "Washington's error was that
he underestimated the structures of evil," as evidenced
by his belief that "if the South was not pushed too hard,
that if the South was not forced to do something that it
did not for the moment want to do, it would voluntarily
rally in the end to the Negro's cause." Furthermore, King
held that Washington's progressive accommodationism
ignored the moral obligation of the oppressed to resist
evil and unjust systems.[16]

King echoed the criticisms of many of Washington's
black contemporaries, who believed that progressive accommodationism was an inadequate response to the
ruthless oppression of their people. William Monroe
Trotter, who began the publication of the black-owned
Boston Guardian in 1901, rejected Washington's program
and demanded full and unqualified justice through the
mechanisms of equal educational and political and civil
rights, a position not unlike King's. However, King did

14. King, "Transforming a Neighborhood," 5–6. King held that "the
tragedy is that you have to plague Pharaoh," rather than appeasing him
as Booker Washington did. See Martin Luther King, Jr., "Address at a
Mass Meeting," Maggie Street Baptist Church, Montgomery, Ala. (The
King Center Archives, 16 February 1968), 5.
15. Ansbro, *Martin Luther King, Jr.*, 198.
16. King, *Where Do We Go from Here?* 129.

not make the claim, consistently advanced by Trotter and others, that Washington was an "Uncle Tom" or a black Benedict Arnold who sold his people's political rights in exchange for peace and for power for himself.[17] King praised W. E. B. Du Bois for counteracting "the apparent resignation of Booker T. Washington's philosophy."[18] In his essay, "Of Mr. Booker T. Washington and Others," issued as a part of his *The Souls of Black Folk* (1903), Du Bois accused Washington of preaching "a gospel of Work and Money to such an extent as apparently almost completely to overshadow the higher aims of life." In an essay entitled "The Talented Tenth" (1903), Du Bois carried his critique of Washington a bit further:

> If we make money the object of man-training, we shall develop money-makers but not necessarily men; if we make technical skill the object of education, we may possess artisans but not, in nature, men. Men we have only as we make manhood the object of the work of the schools—intelligence, broad sympathy, knowledge of the world that was and is, and of the relation of men to it—this is the curriculum of that Higher Education which must underlie true life.[19]

Du Bois charged that Washington—by asking his people to give up political power, insistence on civil rights, and higher education of black youth—had helped create the climate that led to (1) the disfranchisement of blacks, (2) the legal creation of a distinct status of civil inferiority for black people, and (3) the steady withdrawal of aid from institutions for the higher training of blacks.[20] King

17. *Ibid.*; and "Monroe Trotter Denounces Booker T. Washington as a Traitor to the Race," *Boston Guardian* (December 20, 1902) and quoted in *Negro Protest Thought in the Twentieth Century*, Francis L. Broderick, ed. (New York: The Bobbs-Merrill Company, Inc., 1965), 25–30.
18. King, *Why We Can't Wait*, 33; and Ansbro, *Martin Luther King, Jr.*, 201.
19. John Hope Franklin, ed., *The Souls of Black Folk in Three Negro Classics* (New York: Avon Books, 1965), 240–52; and John Hope Franklin, *From Slavery to Freedom: A History of Negro Americans* (New York: Alfred A. Knopf, Inc., 1974), 287.
20. Franklin, ed., *The Souls of Black Folk in Three Negro Classics*, 246–47.

recognized this flaw in Washington's approach decades later. While agreeing with much of Du Bois's critique of Washington, King did not accept his notion of the "Talented Tenth" as a more viable path to black freedom. Du Bois' theory of the "Talented Tenth," reminiscent of a view held earlier by the black Episcopal leader Alexander Crummell, proposed that the exceptional among black people, those blessed with education and native endowment, should lead in the salvation of the race.[21] King opposed this idea because it provided "no role for the whole people" to play in their liberation. "It was a tactic for an aristocratic elite," King argued, "who would themselves be benefited while leaving behind the 'untalented' 90 per cent."[22]

There was a certain irony about Booker T. Washington's ideas and activities that King would have found highly improper for any black leader. Washington urged his people to abandon dreams of a higher education but availed his own children to the very best training in the liberal arts. He implicitly accepted segregation in the South but moved in northern circles that were even closed to most white people. He told his people that Jim Crow was irrelevant but violated the law by riding first-class in Pullman cars with southern whites. Moreover, Washington advised his people to forget about politics but wielded more political power than any other black man in his time.[23] King desperately sought to avoid such inconsistencies in his own thought and activities. Unlike Washington, he constantly encouraged blacks to pursue higher, liberal arts education; social intercourse

---

21. King, *Why We Can't Wait*, 33; Wilmore, *Black Religion and Black Radicalism*, 113; and Sterling Stuckey, *Slave Culture: Nationalist Theory and the Foundations of Black America* (New York: Oxford University Press, 1987), 187, 268–69 and 293–94. The idea that educated blacks have a special responsibility to raise the masses of their people to greater heights of freedom and human dignity was also promoted by Henry H. Garnet in the nineteenth century and Paul Robeson in the twentieth century.

22. King, *Why We Can't Wait*, 33.

23. Lerone Bennett, Jr., "From Booker T. to Martin L.," *Ebony* 18 (November 1962): 152.

with whites; and political power. On this point, he was
more in line with that tradition represented by Frederick
Douglass.[24]

Despite his quarrel with certain aspects of Washington's philosophy and program, King expressed respect
and admiration for the leader of the so-called Tuskegee
Machine. He admitted that his own leadership philosophy had been greatly influenced by men like Washington
and Du Bois.[25] He subscribed to Washington's view that
hating whites was not the moral and practical way for
oppressed blacks. King also agreed with "a certain aspect" of Washington's "lift yourself by your own bootstraps" idea, but believed that, in the case of blacks,
government assistance was necessary as well.[26] Furthermore, King accepted Washington's view that all labor
that uplifts persons has dignity and worth, and should be
pursued with respect for excellence. In a real sense, King
built on the contributions of Washington, but this does
not mean that he, as Eldridge Cleaver allegedly claimed,
was " a more modern Booker T. Washington."[27]

Joseph H. Jackson, who became president of the
National Baptist Convention, U. S. A., Inc. (N.B.C.) in 1953
confronted King with a far more progressive form of
accommodationism than that advocated by Washington
at the turn of the century. Unlike Washington, Jackson

24. Wilmore, *Black Religion and Black Radicalism*, 137; and James
H. Cone, "The Theology of Martin Luther King, Jr.," *Union Seminary
Quarterly Review* 40, no. 4 (January 1986): 22.

25. Bennett, "From Booker T. to Martin L.," 153 and 161–62; and
Joseph Carpenter, Jr., "The Leadership Philosophy of Dr. Martin Luther
King, Jr.: Its Educational Implications" (Ph.D. diss., Marquette Univer-
sity, 1970), 164–65.

26. Martin Luther King, Jr., *Stride Toward Freedom: The Montgomery
Story* (New York: Harper and Row, 1958), 62; Martin Luther King, Jr.,
Where Do We Go from Here? (Unpublished draft from the King Center
Archives, n.d. circa 1967), 1–9; and Martin Luther King, Jr., "A Speech at
the Operation Breadbasket Meeting," Chicago Theological Seminary,
Chicago, Ill. (25 March 1967), The King Center Archives, 5–6.

27. King, *Where Do We Go from Here?*, 127–28; and Foner, ed., *The
Voice of Black America* 1: 609–10. For an interesting study of black leadership styles in Alabama from Washington to ·King, see Peter C. Moore,
"Journey Out of Egypt: The Development of Negro Leadership in Alabama
from Booker T. Washington to Martin Luther King" (B.A. thesis, Prince-
ton University, 1958).

expressed the belief that black Americans should pursue civil rights, political power, and higher, liberal arts education.[28] In conformity with this view, he supported King's activities in the Montgomery Bus Boycott in 1955 and 1956. However, when King's popularity began to increase significantly in the National Baptist Convention in the late 1950s, posing a threat to established leadership, Jackson gradually ceased support for the civil rights movement and became one of its most consistent and passionate critics. His opposition to King and the nonviolent direct action technique first came to public attention in 1960 to 1961, when he condemned the sit-in demonstrations, a move that surprised even his most loyal supporters.[29] Throughout the 1960s, Jackson accused King and the Southern Christian Leadership Conference (S.C.L.C.) of exciting racial tension and of creating an atmosphere of confusion and lawlessness with their nonviolent demonstrations. In a tone strikingly reminiscent of Booker Washington, Jackson repeatedly warned blacks that "cooperation will take you farther than confrontation."[30] As a progressive accommodationist, he made this saying his rallying cry.

Faced with a growing progressive movement in his convention, Jackson vehemently denied that he was against all forms of social protest. What he was really saying, he argued, was not that protest was wrong, but that "protest was not enough!" In June, 1961, he amplified this position in a famous address called "The American Struggle in the American Way," an address that many blacks denounced as "a masterpiece of Tomism."[31]

28. Franklin, "Religious Belief and Political Activism," 64; Leon Colvin, "Christian Activism and the National Baptist Convention," *Dollars and Sense* 7, no. 2 (June–July 1981): 37–38; and J. H. Jackson, *A Story of Christian Activism: The History of the National Baptist Convention, U.S.A., Inc.* (Nashville: Townsend Press, 1980), 5–551.

29. Charles H. King, "Quest and Conflict: The Untold Story of the Power Struggle Between King and Jackson," *Negro Digest* (May 1967): 6–10 and 71–79.

30. Colvin, "Christian Activism and the National Baptist Convention," 38.

31. King, "Quest and Conflict," 73.

By the fall of 1961, Jackson was advocating what he termed "both protest and production," a program that for him was more sweeping than that offered by King.[32] He approached the National Baptist Convention with a plan to purchase farmland in Tennessee to aid black sharecroppers in gaining independence from white landowners. Progressives in the convention dismissed this effort as simply another version of Booker T. Washington's "Let down your buckets where you are" approach. "Old man Jackson has a farm," they sang. It was absurd and ironic, they declared, that in an age of sit-ins and stand-ins, Jackson dared to propose a "farm-in."[33]

Another phase of Jackson's "protest is not enough" policy involved exporting black families to Liberia to teach the people of that country how to live and farm as Christians.[34] As he increasingly focused his attention on the agricultural arts, his followers deserted him in droves. In trying to revive aspects of the old Booker Washington program, Jackson exhibited a masterful flair for bad timing.[35] King believed that Jackson, like Washington many years earlier, had chosen the wrong side of the black revolution. Jackson's attacks on the confrontational methods of the civil rights movement struck King as absurd.

The basis for King's critique of Jackson was his conviction that the old Booker T. Washington philosophy was far more irrelevant in the 1960s than it had been at the turn of the century. In King's view, Jackson was either politically naive or unconcerned about the mobility of his people, especially given his belief that

---

32. "Dr. Jackson Explains to Martin Luther King: Calls Self Victim of Press," *New York Amsterdam News* (October 14, 1961), 1 and 13.

33. King, "Quest and Conflict," 73; and Colvin, "Christian Activism and the National Baptist Convention," 38. Concerning Jackson's farm program, one supporter wrote: "It is my belief that this act of purchasing a farm and encouraging self-help and self-reliance is one of the greatest forward steps among the people of your race since Booker T. Washington launched his program at Tuskegee Institute." See Jackson, *A Story of Christian Activism*, 570.

34. King, "Quest and Conflict," 73.

35. *Ibid.*

"pressureless persuasion" was an effective way of gaining freedom and justice. But Jackson never ceased preaching progressive accommodationism. In a statement remindful of Washington, he contended "that no government or social group lifts a people—they must climb themselves, and it takes patience and courage."[36] Like Washington, Jackson stressed the importance of economic independence for blacks, a policy King saw as desirable but one-sided. "The biggest handicap for Negroes as a race," Jackson suggested, "is our inability, or refusal, to organize money and use it as an economic tool for self-promotion and for opening new doors of opportunity." He further noted that "In future years, we should learn how money can be hired to work and make a wise and more creative use of it."[37]

Jackson used the National Baptist Convention as a base of operation to launch his "lift yourself by your own bootstraps" philosophy on a practical level, thus making it impossible for King to successfully draw on the full resources of that organization for his campaigns. In effect, Jackson combined sound business procedures with strong religious leadership to solidify the convention's financial base. He set up several committees and commissions to govern the convention's operations regarding theological education, church-supported colleges, labor and management, and current civic issues. In 1962, the convention established the Church Emergency Aid Fund (C.E.A.F.) to assist congregations with building programs. More than one million dollars from the tax-exempt fund was invested in certificates of deposits at banks throughout the country.[38] At the same time, Jackson urged members of the convention to move beyond street demonstrations to build black institutions.[39]

---

36. Quoted in a letter from Alfred A. Abbott to Martin Luther King, Jr., 2 January 1961, The King Papers, Boston University, Boston, Mass.
37. Colvin, "Christian Activism and the National Baptist Convention," 37.
38. *Ibid.*
39. *Ibid.*, 38; and Jackson, *A Story of Christian Activism*, 556–70.

He and King became essentially one in their conviction that economic power must undergird all efforts of blacks to establish themselves. This conviction united the two men on a philosophical level with Booker T. Washington.

The progressive accommodationism of both Washington and Jackson was noticeably affected by the challenges they confronted in their times. Before his death in November, 1915, Washington had moved considerably toward the position of Trotter, Du Bois, and other critics of his philosophy. His final magazine article, issued after his death, was a strong and open attack on racism and segregation.[40] Because of the challenge represented by King, Jackson became more assertive in his demand for civil rights for his people. Before the delegates at the 1980 National Baptist Convention in Birmingham, Alabama, he seemingly affirmed the importance of King's direct action approach while maintaining his belief in black self-help as a high priority:

> It is true that we have a right to demand equality, justice, and fair play, but we must not accept for ourselves an easy way out. Let us put at least as much time into teaching, tutoring, correcting and lifting our own race as we have spent trying to make other races and people honest, just and good.[41]

KING AND THE REDEMPTIVE NATIONALISTS

Redemptive nationalists have traditionally held that the political status quo in America is inherently evil, and have denied any love, loyalty, or obligation for the society that enslaved and continues to oppress black people.[42] This mode of thought can be traced back to Paul Cuffee, David Walker, and Robert A. Young in the early nineteenth century, and it has been consistently espoused in

40. Bennett, "From Booker T. to Martin L.," 154.
41. Quoted in Colvin, "Christian Activism and the National Baptist Convention," 38.
42. Franklin, "Religious Belief and Political Activism," 65– 66.

this century by Henry M. Turner, Marcus Garvey, Elijah Muhammad, Malcolm X, Louis Farrakhan, and countless others. Redemptive nationalists have always called for the destruction of the existing sociopolitical order, and many, especially political nationalists, have advocated the establishment of a separate black nation.[43] Ideas of this nature brought Martin Luther King, Jr., into conflict and dialogue with black nationalists in the 1950s and 1960s.

Much of King's thought on redemptive nationalism in the black community was formulated on the basis of his reading of Marcus Garvey. He grew up at a time when memories of Garvey's life and work were still strong among blacks in Atlanta, especially since that controversial black nationalist had spent almost three years in prison there before eventually dying in exile in London in 1940. Born in Jamaica in 1887, Garvey came to the United States in 1916 and organized one of the most phenomenal social movements in modern history—a movement built around race pride, black solidarity and self-help, and a desire to reclaim Africa for all people of African origin.[44] African independence and Pan-Africanism became his rallying cry, the principles on which he developed his Universal Negro Improvement Association (U.N.I.A.).

43. Robert M. Franklin and Peter J. Paris give the erroneous impression that the goal of all black nationalists has always been a separate black nation. This perception must be challenged, particularly in light of Sterling Stuckey's persuasive claim that "the desire for a separate and wholly sovereign black nation has not necessarily formed the burden of Afro-American thought on nationalism." David Walker, the author of the 1829 *Appeal to the Coloured Citizens of the World*, was representative of those black nationalists who have rejected the concept of a separate black nation. See Franklin, "Religious Belief and Political Activism," 65–66; Paris, "The Bible and the Black Churches," 148; Stuckey, *Slave Culture*, 126–27; Ples Sterling Stuckey, "The Spell of Africa: The Development of Black Nationalist Theory, 1829–1945" (Ph.D. diss., Northwestern University, June, 1973), ix; and Sterling Stuckey, ed., *The Ideological Origins of Black Nationalism* (Boston: Beacon Press, 1972), 27–29.
44. Amy Jacques-Garvey, ed., *Philosophy and Opinions of Marcus Garvey*, 2 Vols. (New York: Atheneum, 1973), Preface; and John Henrik Clarke, ed., *Marcus Garvey and the Vision of Africa* (New York: Vintage Books, a Division of Random House, 1974), xv–xxxii.

From 1916 until his arrest for allegedly using the mail to defraud in 1923, Garvey consistently proclaimed:

> We are the descendants of a suffering people; we are the descendants of a people determined to suffer no longer. . . . We Shall organize the . . . Negroes of the world into a vast organization to plant the banner of freedom on the great continent of Africa. . . . If Europe is for the Europeans, then Africa is for the black peoples of the world.[45]

Convinced that blacks and whites could never live together in peace and harmony, Garvey urged his people to free Africa of the chains of European colonialism. "We shall not ask England or France or Italy or Belgium, 'Why are you here [in Africa]?,'" he declared. "We shall only command them, 'Get out of here.'"[46] In Garvey's opinion, those black Americans who struggled to achieve complete assimilation into the white world were grossly unrealistic:

> The white man of America will not, to any organized extent, assimilate the Negro, because in so doing, he feels that he will be committing racial suicide. This he is not prepared to do. It is true he illegitimately carries on a system of assimilation; but such assimilation, as practised, is one that he is not prepared to support because he becomes prejudiced against his own offspring, if that offspring is the product of black and white; hence, to the white man the question of racial differences is eternal.[47]

Garvey scoffed at those black "brainless intellectuals" who spread rumors of "African fever," "African bad climate," "African mosquitos," and "African savages" as "a scare against our people in America and the West Indies taking a kindly interest in the new program of building a racial empire of our own in our Motherland."[48] His

45. Garvey, ed., *Philosophy and Opinions*, Preface.
46. *Ibid.*
47. *Ibid.*, 26.
48. *Ibid.*, 68.

faith in his people's ability to overcome feelings of inferiority and to govern themselves and plan their own destiny was as strong as that of Martin Delany, John E. Bruce, Henry M. Turner, Edward W. Blyden, and other proponents of African emigration before him. Garvey's leading role in establishing the Negro Factory Corporation, the Black Star Shipping Line, a black paramilitary group, the *Negro World* publication, and numerous other agencies, rituals, and practices in connection with the U.N.I.A., may be taken as a true measure of that faith. Like scores of black leaders before and after him, Garvey had the capacity to excoriate his people for their apathy and cowardice while, at the same time, praising them for their strength of body and spirit, and "for their loyalty and sacrificial service to the nations of the world that had so misunderstood and misused them."[49]

Martin Luther King, Jr., found Garvey's "Back to Africa" plan both unrealistic and undesirable. According to King, the "plan was doomed because an exodus to Africa in the twentieth century by a people who had struck roots for three and a half centuries in the New World did not have the ring of progress."[50] Furthermore, the plan represented "a dashing of hope, a conviction of the inability of the Negro to win and a belief in the infinitude of the ghetto."[51] In 1964, King denounced the very idea that black Americans should return to Africa as an exercise in nonsense:

> The Negro is an American. We know nothing about Africa, although our roots are there in terms of our forebears. But I mean as far as the average Negro

---

49. *Ibid.*, Preface; and Wilmore, *Black Religion and Black Radicalism*, 148. Interestingly enough, it was not Garvey's Pan-African predecessors—Paul Cuffee, David Walker, Robert A. Young, Martin Delany, Edward Wilmot Blyden, John E. Bruce, and Henry M. Turner—who set him on the path of Pan-Africanism, but the progressive accommodationist Booker T. Washington. Garvey read Washington's classic work *Up from Slavery* (1900), which, by his own admission, influenced him profoundly.
50. King, *Why We Can't Wait*, 33.
51. King, *Where Do We Go from Here?* 47.

today, he knows nothing about Africa. I think he's got to face the fact that he is an American, his culture is basically American, and one becomes adjusted to this when he realizes what he is. He's got to know what he is. Our destiny is tied up with the destiny of America.[52]

By 1967 King, perhaps under the impact of the growing black power movement, had begun to take into serious account both the African and American sides of his people's heritage:

The Negro's greatest dilemma is that in order to be healthy he must accept his ambivalence. The Negro is the child of two cultures—Africa and America. The problem is that in the search for wholeness all too many Negroes seek to embrace only one side of their natures. Some, seeking to reject their heritage, are ashamed of their color, ashamed of black art and music, and determine what is beautiful and good by the standards of white society. They end up frustrated and without cultural roots. Others seek to reject everything American and to identify totally with Africa, even to the point of wearing African clothes. But this approach leads also to frustration because the American Negro is not an African. . . . The American Negro is neither totally African nor totally Western. He is Afro-American, a true hybrid, a combination of two cultures.[53]

King's rejection of Garvey's "Back to Africa" strategy was rooted in his belief in the essential "oneness" of humanity. In other words, racial separatism was inconsistent with his beloved community vision. While he recognized that there was much grounding in past experiences for Garvey's cynicism and disenchantment with white America, he was not willing to abandon all hope in

52. Robert P. Warren, "An Interview with Martin Luther King, Jr.," in *Who Speaks for the Negro?* (Unpublished manuscript from the King Center Archives, 18 May 1964), 15–16.
53. King, *Where Do We Go from Here?* 53; and Martin Luther King, Jr., "See you in Washington," a speech delivered at the S.C.L.C. Staff Retreat, Ebenezer Baptist Church, Atlanta, Ga. (The King Center Archives, 17 January 1968), 3–4.

the possibility of blacks and whites coexisting on terms of peace and community. Moreover, King was convinced that black and white Americans, because of the very nature of their situations, needed each other. "The Negro needs the white man to free him from his fears," he explained. "The white man needs the Negro to free him from his guilt. Any approach that overlooks this need for 'a coalition of conscience' is unwise and misguided."[54]

King's analysis of Garvey's philosophy and program was not as perceptive as it appeared at first glance. He failed to see that Garvey's idea of a black nation was characterized more by feelings of confidence and hope than by a spirit of cynicism and disenchantment. The driving force for Garvey was not so much his disillusionment with whites and white Western society, but, rather, his faith in his people's capacity for self-elevation and self-government. More importantly, perhaps, was King's failure to recognize that his belief in integration and the American dream was no more realistic than Garvey's desire for a totally separate and independent black nation, especially considering the depth of white America's racism.[55]

Even so, King recognized that Garvey, though unrealistic in some of his goals, stirred hope and race pride among black Americans at a time when many were mercilessly lynched and deprived of basic civil and human rights. In his *Why We Can't Wait*, King wrote:

> After the First World War, Marcus Garvey made an appeal to the race that had the virtue of rejecting concepts of inferiority. He called for a return to

54. King, *Where Do We Go from Here?* 47–48; and Martin Luther King, Jr., "Address at the Chicago Freedom Movement Rally," Soldier Field, Chicago, Ill. (The King Center Archives, 10 July 1966), 10–11.
55. A common but erroneous viewpoint is that black nationalists have been more prone to feelings of cynicism and disillusionment than blacks who tend more toward integrationist and assimilationist views. Sterling Stuckey challenges this notion and also the view that believers in integration and the American dream are somehow more realistic than nationalistic separatists. See Paris, "The Bible and the Black Churches," 148; and Stuckey, ed., *The Ideological Origins of Black Nationalism*, 1–29.

Africa and a resurgence of race pride. His movement attained mass dimensions, and released a powerful emotional response because it touched a truth which had long been dormant in the mind of the Negro. There was reason to be proud of their heritage as well as of their bitterly won achievements in America.[56]

While visiting Jamaica in 1965, King laid a wreath at the Garvey memorial shrine in a Kingston public park. On that occasion, he implied that Garvey had paved the way for his leadership and for the success of the civil rights movement. King said:

> Marcus Garvey was the first man of color in the history of the United States to lead and develop a mass movement. He was the first man on a mass scale and level to give millions of Negroes a sense of dignity and destiny and make the Negro feel he was somebody.[57]

Despite their differences—philosophically, religiously, organizationally, and otherwise—King and Garvey agreed on many points. Garvey's insistence on racial pride, black solidarity and self-help, and bonds and obligations between people of African descent everywhere was largely embraced by King after 1965, the King who bore the influence of the black power movement. The two men also shared a belief in the messianic role of black Americans, a belief that led them to insist that their people struggle for peace and social justice even at the risk of their lives.[58]

In the 1950s and 1960s King confronted the challenge posed by another redemptive nationalist named

56. King, *Why We Can't Wait*, 33.
57. Quoted in Randall K. Burkett, *Garveyism as a Religious Movement: The Institutionalization of a Black Civil Religion* (Metuchen, N.J.: The Scarecrow Press, Inc. and The American Theological Library Association, 1978), xv; and David J. Garrow, *Bearing the Cross: Martin Luther King, Jr. and the Southern Christian Leadership Conference* (New York: William Morrow and Company, Inc., 1986), 428.
58. For a brief but interesting discussion of similarities and differences between King and Garvey, see Ansbro, *Martin Luther King, Jr.*, 206–11.

Malcolm X, who was profoundly inspired by Garvey. Born the son of a Garveyite Baptist preacher in Omaha, Nebraska in 1925, Malcolm became King's "ideological nemesis."[59] The two men are often referred to as the most significant black leaders in America in the 1950s and 1960s. They are perceived as having stood at opposite extremes on the spectrum of black leadership, representing different organizations and political-religious perspectives. Their public disagreements on various matters pertaining to civil rights not only prevented them from becoming closely connected by friendship and

---

59. David L. Lewis, *King: A Critical Biography* (New York: Praeger Publishers, 1970), 258; and Lewis V. Baldwin, "The Great Confrontation: A Reassessment of the Relationship Between Malcolm X and Martin Luther King, Jr.," *The Western Journal of Black Studies* 13, no. 2 (Summer, 1989): 103–13. The differences between the philosophies and methods of King and Malcolm have received extensive coverage in James H. Cone, *Martin and Malcolm and America: A Dream or Nightmare?* (Maryknoll, N.Y.: Orbis Books, 1991): 1–358. Also see Allan Boesak, *Coming Out of the Wilderness: A Comparative Interpretation of the Ethics of Martin Luther King, Jr. and Malcolm X* (Kampen, Holland: J. H. Kok, 1976), 4–80. King's dialogue with Malcolm and other nationalists is treated at various levels in Robert L. Shelton, "Black Revolution: The Definition and Meaning of 'Revolution' in the Writings and Speeches of Selected Nationally Prominent Negro Americans, 1963–1968" (Ph.D. diss., Boston University, 1970); Brygida I. Rudzka-Ostyn, "The Oratory of Martin Luther King and Malcolm X: A Study in Linguistic Stylistics" (Ph.D. diss., University of Rochester, 1972); David E. Luellen, "Ministers and Martyrs: Malcolm X and Martin Luther King, Jr." (Ph.D. diss., Ball State University, July, 1972); William W. Morris, "Strategies for Liberation: A Critical Comparison of Martin Luther King, Jr. and Albert B. Cleage, Jr." (D.Min. diss., Vanderbilt University, June, 1973); James C. Payne, "A Content Analysis of Speeches and Written Documents of Six Black Spokesmen" (Ph.D. diss., Florida State University, 1973); Otis Turner, "Toward an Ethic of Black Liberation Based on the Philosophy of Martin Luther King, Jr., and Stokely Carmichael's Concept of Black Power" (Ph.D. diss., Emory University, Spring, 1974); Chukwuemeka Onwubu, "Black Ideologies and the Sociology of Knowledge: The Public Response to the Protest Thoughts and Teachings of Martin Luther King, Jr. and Malcolm X" (Ph.D. diss., Michigan State University, 1975); Emilie Schmeidler, "Shaping Ideas and Actions: CORE, S.C.L.C., and S.N.C.C. in the Struggle for Equality, 1960–1966" (Ph.D. diss., University of Michigan, 1980); Gaye Todd Adegbalola, "A Conversation with Martin and Malcolm," *The Black Collegian* 8, no. 3 (January/February 1978): 4, 6, 8, and 83; and James H. Cone, "Martin Luther King, Jr. and Malcolm X: Speaking the Truth about America," *Sojourners* 15, no. 1 (January 1986): 26–30.

association, but were also of considerable importance in determining how they viewed and related to each other.[60] The relationship between King and Malcolm passed through two important stages. The first stage covered the period from 1957 to March, 1964. During most of this time, Malcolm was a minister in Elijah Muhammad's Black Muslim Movement (also called Nation of Islam), based in Harlem, and King was the president of the S.C.L.C. and a co-pastor at his father's church in Atlanta. The second stage began on March 26, 1964, when Malcolm and King met briefly in Washington, D. C., and ended with Malcolm's death on February 21, 1965. In both periods they often reached out to each other in public, in private, and in rather unorthodox ways. The difference between the two periods is suggested by the manner in which the two men softened their criticism of each other in the last eleven months of Malcolm's life, and also by the ways in which they moved closer together, personally and philosophically, within that same period.[61]

During that first stage the religious, philosophical, and political differences between Malcolm and King became very clear. In 1957, Malcolm and the Black Muslims tried unsuccessfully to start a dialogue with King and the S.C.L.C. concerning strategies and goals for the black movement.[62] In March, 1958, Elijah Muhammad sent a letter to King, inviting him to appear before the Muslims and other citizens "in a free rally in our great Temple #2 in Chicago's exclusive Hyde Park District." King expressed deep gratitude for the invitation but declined it because of his busy schedule.[63] In July, 1960, Malcolm

---

60. Baldwin, "The Great Confrontation," 1ff.; and Lewis V. Baldwin, "Malcolm X and Martin Luther King, Jr.: What They Thought about Each Other," *Islamic Studies* 25, no. 4 (October/December 1986): 395–416.
61. Baldwin, "The Great Confrontation," 2.
62. Lewis, *King*, 125.
63. A letter from Elijah Muhammad to Martin Luther King, Jr., 19 March 1958, The King Papers, Boston University; and a letter from Martin Luther King, Jr., to Elijah Muhammad, 9 April 1958, The King Papers, Boston University.

personally invited King to attend an "Education Rally" in
Harlem, noting that:

> Since so much controversy has been spoken and writ-
> ten about Mr. Muhammad and his 'Black Muslims,' we
> invite you as a spokesman and fellow leader of our
> people to be among our invited guests, so you can see
> and hear Mr. Muhammad for yourself and then make a
> more intelligent appraisal of his teachings, his meth-
> ods, and his program.[64]

The letter arrived at the S.C.L.C.'s headquarters after the
program was held, and again King escaped an opportunity to meet and speak with Malcolm and his fellow Muslims.[65] During the next three years, King essentially
ignored numerous challenges from Malcolm to "come to
Harlem and prove that 'peaceful suffering' is the solution to the atrocities suffered daily by Negroes throughout America."[66] Malcolm calmly ignored the avoidances
and constantly urged black leaders to forget their "petty
differences" and to "reason together and keep open
minds." He was convinced that King and other moderate
civil rights leaders were avoiding him out of a fear "of
irking their white bosses (or) embarrassing their white
liberal friends."[67] But there was a larger issue involved,
namely, that Malcolm and the Black Muslims were so
radically different in philosophy and methods from King
and the S.C.L.C. that a meeting between the two forces
offered little prospect of a constructive meeting of the
minds. The major issues that separated them included
love and hate, violence and nonviolence, separatism and
integration, and the relevancy of the Christian faith to
the black freedom struggle.[68]

64. A letter from Malcolm X to Martin Luther King, Jr., 21 July 1960,
The King Papers, Boston University.

65. A letter from Maude L. W. Ballou, Secretary to Dr. Martin
Luther King, Jr., to Malcolm X, 10 August, 1960, The King Papers,
Boston University.

66. *The New York Courier* (July 22, 1960), 1ff.; and C. Eric Lincoln,
The Black Muslims in America (Boston: Beacon Press, 1973), 163.

67. Baldwin, "The Great Confrontation," 3; Lincoln, *The Black
Muslims in America*, 146; and Malcolm X, *Malcolm X Speaks*, 4.

68. Baldwin, "The Great Confrontation," 1 and 3.

The problem the Muslims had with King's love ethic (agape) was constantly and consistently expressed in bold terms by Malcolm X. Malcolm emphasized the importance of black self-love in a manner similar to Marcus Garvey and other black nationalists who preceded him:

> Mr. Muhammad teaches us love for our own kind. The white man has taught the black people in this country to hate themselves as inferior, to hate each other, to be divided against each other. Messenger Muhammad restores our love for our own kind, which enables us to work together in unity and harmony.[69]

King's concept of a universal love, which included white people, struck Malcolm the Black Muslim as particularly absurd, mainly because it involved blacks loving whites before they learned to love themselves. In a statement directed at followers of King, Malcolm insisted that "Most of the Negroes you see running around here talking about 'love everybody'—they don't have any love whatsoever for their own kind. When they say, 'Love everybody,' what they are doing is setting up a situation for us to love white people."[70] Malcolm's essential point was that love, like any human emotion and virtue, must begin at home before it can be authentically extended abroad. He believed that there was a sound ethical basis for black people to love themselves first because collectively they were victims of a system created by whites, supported by whites, condoned by whites, and from which all whites benefited. Malcolm argued that his conception of love had nothing to do with being antiwhite or anti-Christian, and everything to do with being "anti-evil, anti-oppression, and anti-lynching." For him, black self-love amounted to an affirmation of the dignity and worth of black people.[71]

69. "Playboy Interview: Malcolm X," *Playboy* 10, no. 53 (May 1963): 54; Malcolm X, *Malcolm X on Afro-American History* (New York: Pathfinder Press, Inc., 1970), 15ff.; and Kenneth B. Clark, ed., *King, Malcolm, Baldwin: Three Interviews* (Middletown, Conn.: Wesleyan University Press, 1985), 41–42.
70. Clark, ed., *King, Malcolm, Baldwin*, 41–42.
71. "Playboy Interview: Malcolm X," 56.

Indeed, he pushed his analysis further to assert that anything short of a mutual love between blacks and whites would be unhealthy and unproductive. It was Malcolm's challenge, coupled with that of the later black power movement, that compelled King to place more emphasis on the need for black self-love and black solidarity after 1965.[72]

Nothing rankled Malcolm more than King's insistence that nonviolence was the only moral and practical method for blacks in their struggle against racism and oppression. Malcolm described nonviolence as "a begging hat-in-hand, compromising approach"—a device for disarming and unmanning blacks.[73] Considering the extent to which blacks used violence against each other, he found it almost unbelievable that King would advise them to "turn the other cheek" to racists who "brutalized and spat upon them" in the "worst fashion imaginable":

> Any Negro who teaches other Negroes to turn the other cheek is disarming that Negro. Any Negro who teaches Negroes to turn the other cheek in the face of attack is disarming that Negro of his God-given right, of his moral right, of his natural right, of his intelligent right to defend himself. Everything in nature can defend itself, and is right in defending itself except the American Negro. And men like King—their job is to go among Negroes and teach Negroes "Don't fight back." He doesn't tell them, "Don't fight each other." "Don't fight the white man" is what he's saying in essence, because the followers of Martin Luther King will cut each other from head to foot, but they will not do anything to defend themselves against the attacks of the white man.[74]

72. Malcolm X, *Malcolm X Speaks*, 145. King talked extensively about the need for black self-love and black solidarity in King, *Where Do We Go from Here?*, 23–166.

73. Malcolm X, *Malcolm X Speaks*, 52; and Peter Goldman, *The Death and Life of Malcolm X* (New York: Harper and Row, 1973), 6.

74. Malcolm X, *Malcolm X Speaks*, 34 and 93; Malcolm X, *The End of White World Supremacy: Four Speeches by Malcolm X*, ed. Imam Benjamin Karim (New York: Seaver Books, 1971), 116; and Clark, *King, Malcolm, Baldwin*, 42. For an excellent critique of King's nonviolent

Malcolm rejected King's claim that Christian-Gandhian principles constituted a moral philosophy, arguing instead that such principles amounted to "a criminal philosophy."[75] In his opinion, nonviolence was not the most practical approach for blacks in view of the long history of white violence against people of color. In fact, Malcolm seriously doubted the capacity of whites to respond morally and sympathetically to nonviolence on the part of blacks. Like David Walker more than a century earlier, he characterized whites as "bloodthirsty"—a people who "love to see the flow of other people's blood, not their own."[76] To those who argued that a violent response by black Americans would only lead to their destruction at the hands of a more powerful white majority, Malcolm, whose faith in the physical prowess of his people was as strong as that of Walker and other nationalists before him, rejoined:

> Don't let anybody tell you anything about the odds are against you. If they draft you, they send you to Korea and make you face 800 million Chinese. If you can be brave over there, you can be brave right here. These odds aren't as great as those odds. And if you fight here, you will at least know what you're fighting for.[77]

Malcolm urged his people to move beyond the idea of "nonviolence as the only way" to embrace the concept of "freedom by any means necessary," a slogan used by the black nationalist Henry H. Garnet in the 1840s.[78] Although King agreed with Malcolm's notion that blacks should not confine themselves to a single methodological approach in their struggle, he had serious problems with

ethic and of the challenge presented to it by Malcolm's analysis, see William R. Jones, "Liberation Strategies in Black Theology: Mao, Martin or Malcolm?," *Chicago Theological Seminary Register* 73 (Winter, 1983): 38–48.

75. Malcolm X, *By Any Means Necessary: Speeches, Interviews and a Letter by Malcolm X* (New York: Pathfinder Press, Inc., 1970), 8–9.

76. Malcolm X, *Malcolm X on Afro-American History*, 28.

77. Malcolm X, *Malcolm X Speaks*, 25, 32, and 52.

78. Malcolm X, *By Any Means Necessary*, 37. See Henry H. Garnet's "Address to the Slaves" (1843) in *The Voice of Black America*, ed. Foner, 1: 107–11.

the Muslim minister's thoughts on nonviolence. He portrayed Malcolm and the Black Muslims as a "hate group" who engaged in "an unconscious advocacy of violence."[79] At the same time, King understood the kind of frustration that created the Muslims. Malcolm and the Muslims were for him symbolic of the evils of a white-dominated, oppressive society—a society that foolishly and unrealistically talked "about nonviolence without creating the climate of justice which allows nonviolence to operate."[80]

The differences between Malcolm and King centered ultimately on their visions of community. King's idea of a completely integrated society based on love and justice appeared both unrealistic and undesirable to Malcolm and the Black Muslims. Malcolm often castigated King in speeches, magazine and newspaper interviews, and on radio and television as "a fool," "a chump," "a traitor," "a false shepherd," "a clown," "a Rev. Dr. Chickenwing," and "a twentieth century Uncle Tom," who, through a consistent advocacy of integration, had "sold out to the white devils." In his opinion, King and other black integrationists did not speak for the masses of the folk:

> These Uncle Tom leaders do not speak for the Negro majority; they don't speak for the black masses. They speak for the "black bourgeoisie," the brainwashed, white-minded, middle-class minority who are ashamed of black, and don't want to be identified with the black masses, and are therefore seeking to lose their "black identity" by mixing, mingling, intermarrying, and integrating with the white man.[81]

79. King, *Why We Can't Wait*, 87; a letter from Martin Luther King, Jr., to Mr. Kivie Kaplan, 6 March 1961, The King Papers, Boston University; and Martin Luther King, Jr., "Address at the National Bar Association Meeting," Milwaukee, Wis. (The King Center Archives, 20 August 1959), 9.

80. King, *Why We Can't Wait*, 35 and 87; and Martin Luther King, Jr., "A Speech on Pre-Election Day Moratorium: Youngsters and Jobs," New York, N.Y. (The King Center Archives, 6 November 1964), 1.

81. Baldwin, "The Great Confrontation," 4; Malcolm X, *The End of White World Supremacy*, 135; and Baldwin, "Malcolm X and Martin Luther King, Jr.," 399 and 431, n. 21.

Malcolm charged that King failed to seriously consider the question: "Integration for *whose sake* and on *whose terms?*" Malcolm clearly recognized that integration in the American context did not mean an exchange of values and cultural elements between blacks and whites as equals, but rather race-mixing for black people's sake on white people's terms. In other words, integration essentially meant continued white dominance. Convinced that integration promised nothing but frustration and destruction for his people, Malcolm called for a permanent separation of the races:

> The 22 million so-called Negroes should be separated completely from America and should be permitted to go back home to our African homeland, which is a long range program. So the short-range program is that we must eat while we're still here, we must have a place to sleep, we must have clothes to wear, we must have better jobs, we must have better education. So that although our long-range political philosophy is to migrate back to our African homeland, our short range program must involve that which is necessary to enable us to live a better life while we are still here. We must be in complete control of the politics of the so-called Negro community; we must gain complete control over the politicians in the so-called Negro community, so that no outsider will have any voice in the so-called Negro community.[82]

Malcolm's vision of a separate black nation, influenced strongly by Marcus Garvey and Elijah Muhammad, was not always consistent. In the 1950s and early 1960s, he subscribed to the Black Muslims' view of African emigrationism, and later, to their belief that black separation could be achieved in America without a long sea voyage to Africa. By late 1964, Malcolm had begun to

82. Malcolm X, *By Any Means Necessary*, 5–6. Malcolm, unlike King, identified the "enemy" as white people. In every movement, there is an "enemy." King's desire to attract support from whites led him to identify racism and segregation as the "enemy," and not white people.

envision a cultural, psychological, philosophical, and spiritual return to Africa for his people, a vision held by the black nationalist Paul Robeson a generation earlier.[83] This vision grew out of Malcolm's conviction that black Americans were essentially *Africans*, a belief not shared by King.[84]

King called Malcolm's concept of a completely separate and independent black nation "a strange dream," and sometimes used terms like "crazy," "tragic," "irresponsible," and "demagogic" in reference to the Black Muslim leader. Although King's and Malcolm's attacks against each other did not surge up from a deep hatred, they were indicative of the two leaders' strong dislike for each other's philosophy and methods.[85] The nature of their differences was such that King refused to debate Malcolm on radio and television, believing that

83. *Ibid.*; Malcolm X, *Malcolm X Speaks*, 210–11; Louis E. Lomax, *When the Word Is Given: A Report on Elijah Muhammad, Malcolm X, and the Black Muslim World* (Westport, Conn.: Greenwood Press, 1963), 74ff.; King, *Why We Can't Wait*, 35; and Stuckey, *Slave Culture*, 344ff.

84. Malcolm X, *Malcolm X Speaks*, 36, 48, 72–87, and 210–11; and King, *Where Do We Go from Here?* 53. This notion that black Americans are essentially *Africans* and should form a separate society based on that identity is at least as old as Paul Cuffee and as recent as the Republic of New Africa. See Wilmore, *Black Religion and Black Radicalism*, 100–1; and Lewis H. Wilson, "The Hawkish Doves: A History of the Republic of New Africa" (M.A. thesis, Mississippi College, December, 1986), 1ff. Malcolm's vision of a separate and independent black nation reflected his belief that whites were unredeemable and that blacks would never be accepted fully into the American society. He attacked white liberals for expressing a belief in integration on the one hand while using every excuse to avoid it on the other. "When a Negro moves into a white neighborhood, who are the first to flee?," asked Malcolm X. "The white liberals everytime. Negroes who think otherwise are blinding themselves to the facts." According to William R. Miller, King "wanted fervently, even if the effect seemed quixotic, to refute the growing insistence of people like Malcolm X that whitey was unredeemable." Albert B. Southwick, "Malcolm X: Charismatic Demagogue," *The Christian Century* (June 5, 1963): 740; and William R. Miller, *Martin Luther King, Jr.: His Life, Martyrdom and Meaning for the World* (New York: Weybright and Talley, Inc., 1968), 186.

85. Jim Bishop, *The Days of Martin Luther King, Jr.* (New York: G. P. Putnam's Sons, 1971), 4 and 379; "King Views Malcolm as Tragic," *New York Amsterdam News* (March 28, 1964): 1ff.; James M. Washington, ed., *A Testament of Hope: The Essential Writings of Martin Luther King, Jr.* (San Francisco: Harper and Row, Publishers, 1986), 365; and Baldwin, "The Great Confrontation," 4.

such a public appearance would only amuse white people and further divide the black community. King insisted that their quarrel was with the oppressive society and not with each other, a view with which Malcolm fully agreed. Both understood that they were involved in a protracted life-and-death struggle against the same enemy, white racism, and that this struggle alone demanded all the time, energy, and resources they could muster.[86]

The inability of King and Malcolm to cooperate in their areas of mutual concern was due largely to their radically different religious faiths. King's deep roots in the Christian religion, combined with his wide exposure to Christian theology and philosophy, made it impossible for him to come to terms with the teachings of Black Muslimism. He believed that Christianity, as practiced in and through the black church, provided the most solid ethical and theological foundation for the liberation, survival, and future advancement of his people, a belief sharply different from Malcolm's claim that Islam held the key to black self-understanding and freedom.[87] Malcolm insisted that Christianity—with its white God, white Jesus, white angels, and otherworldly orientation—only promised the continued enslavement of black bodies and minds.[88] This perspective clearly

86. Malcolm was always amused by the fact that King and others in the S.C.L.C. refused to debate him. Despite his lack of formal education, he was known as a sharp and clever debater. King once threatened to decline an invitation to appear on the David Susskind television panel if Malcolm was invited. See Goldman, *The Death and Life of Malcolm X,* 16–17; *Harper's Magazine* (June 1964): 57; a letter from Miss Dora McDonald, Secretary to Dr. Martin Luther King, Jr., to Mr. Frank Clarke, 26 November 1962, The King Papers, Boston University; and a letter from Frank Clarke to Martin Luther King, Jr., 4 December 1962, The King Papers, Boston University.

87. Lincoln, *The Black Muslims in America,* 78; "Playboy Interview: Malcolm X," 54; and Ansbro, *Martin Luther King, Jr.,* 178.

88. "Playboy Interview: Malcolm X," 54. Although critical of the black church, Malcolm came to see that there were those in its history who reflected a radical and socially conscious point of view. He praised the slave preacher Nat Turner, who led a rebellion in Southampton County, Virginia, in 1831, as one "who put the fear of God into the white slavemaster." "Nat Turner wasn't going around preaching pie-in-the-sky

reflected the kind of wisdom and critical insight he developed as a result of his experiences in prison, in the ghetto, and in the Black Muslim movement. The fact that Malcolm was self-taught, with only an eighth grade formal education, made his insights into the nature of Christianity all the more searching and interesting.

A second phase in the relationship between Malcolm and King began on March 26, 1964, when the two men met face-to-face in Washington, D. C. Malcolm had announced his split with Elijah Muhammad some three weeks earlier, and was beginning to chart a new course for himself in the black struggle. Peter Goldman, one of Malcolm's biographers, has described the circumstances under which the meeting occurred:

> In March, 1964, just after Malcolm quit the nation, he visited the U. S. Senate to take in a day of the civil rights filibuster and later slipped into the back row of a King news conference off the floor. King afterward left by one door; Malcolm popped out another into his path. "Well, Malcolm, good to see you," King said. "Good to see you," Malcolm grinned. Reporters crowded around. Flash bulbs flared. "Now you're going to get investigated," Malcolm teased, and then they parted.[89]

---

and 'nonviolent freedom' for the black man," Malcolm declared. Malcolm established friendships with several radical black Christian preachers, among them Adam Clayton Powell, Jr., Albert B. Cleage, Jr., of Detroit, and Franklin Florence of Rochester, New York. Malcolm referred to Powell, the Harlem congressman and pastor of the Abyssinian Baptist Church, as "the only real independent Negro politician in this country." See Malcolm X, *Malcolm X on Afro-American History*, 54 and 65; and Malcolm X, *By Any Means Necessary*, 72–73.

89. Goldman, *The Death and Life of Malcolm X*, 95. This chance encounter between King and Malcolm caused some alarm among white liberals who needed assurance that the two men were not forming an alliance. See a letter from Martin Luther King, Jr., to Mr. Abram Eisenman, 3 April 1964, The King Papers, Boston University; and a letter from Mr. Abram Eisenman to Martin Luther King, Jr., 9 April 1964, The King Papers, Boston University. James Cone is essentially right in contending that white liberals were largely responsible for preventing Malcolm and King from working together. See James H. Cone, *Speaking the Truth: Ecumenism, Liberation, and Black Theology* (Grand Rapids, Mich.: William B. Eerdmans Publishing Company, 1986), 167.

"The civil rights propaganda value of this meeting was considerable," wrote David L. Lewis, "as both men pledged to concert their efforts to pressure Congress into passing the pending civil rights legislation."[90] The meeting was even more significant in terms of changing the personal relationship between Malcolm and King. The two men showed that they could touch, smile at, and even tease each other. They actually greeted each other in the ancient tradition of hospitality, and the playful manner in which they related to each other must have diffused any anxiety they may have felt. Malcolm, who initiated the chance encounter, was actually reaching out to King in a public way. After the brief meeting, Malcolm ceased his constant, public denouncements of King as a traitor and an Uncle Tom, and the two men increasingly began to reevaluate their feelings toward each other.[91]

Malcolm's travels abroad in the spring and summer of 1964 helped bring him and King closer together ideologically. After visiting Egypt, Lebanon, Saudi Arabia, Nigeria, Ghana, Morocco, and Algeria, Malcolm made the pilgrimage to Mecca and met many orthodox Muslims whom he considered white but not racist, an experience that led him to embrace orthodox Islam (becoming El Hajj Malik El Shabazz). From that point, he moved beyond a simple skin-racism to a more enlightened, complex, and inclusive view of the world. As Malcolm and King graduated to a higher level of analysis of the economic roots of racism and classism, they stimulated

90. Lewis, *King*, 125 and 271–72. Lewis suggests that this agreement on the part of King and Malcolm "represented little in the way of intrinsic collaboration," a suggestion supported by a statement King issued concerning Malcolm's split with Muhammad. King had predicted the split but noted that it held "no particular significance to the present civil rights efforts of the American Negro." See Goldman, *The Death and Life of Malcolm X*, 142; and Martin Luther King, Jr., "A Statement on Malcolm X" (unpublished document, 16 March 1964, The King Papers, Boston University), 1.

91. Baldwin, "The Great Confrontation," 11–12; and Baldwin, "Malcolm X and Martin Luther King, Jr.," 397.

each other's increasing sophistication and radicalness.[92]
King helped make Malcolm more receptive to intermar-
riage and to the possibility of blacks and progressive-
minded whites working together for the improvement of
the human condition. In response to Malcolm's challenge, King moved beyond integration as a panacea for
racial problems to stress economic justice, became more
critical of white liberals, became less cautious about
making positive references to black power, and increasingly denounced black middle-class attitudes and bour-
geois organizations as barriers to black unity.[93] Coretta
Scott King recalled how her husband moved toward

92. Baldwin, "The Great Confrontation," 14–15. One author suggests that it is possible that during Malcolm's trips abroad, he was
"misled by the fictitious picture of colorless Islamic brotherhood,
waved constantly before his eyes by white Arabs who obtain thousands
of Black slaves from Africa every year." See Shawna Maglangbayan,
Garvey, Lumumba and Malcolm: National-Separatists (Chicago: Third
World Press, 1972), 71. The view that Malcolm and King were moving
closer together is widely accepted in scholarly circles. See Wilson J.
Moses, *Black Messiahs and Uncle Toms: Social and Literary Manipula-
tions of a Religious Myth* (University Park, Pa.: The Pennsylvania State
University Press, 1982), 212, 224, and 229; Clark, *King, Malcolm, Bald-
win*, 12–13; James Baldwin, "Malcolm and Martin," *Esquire* 67 (April
1972): 94 and 201; Lewis, *King*, 272; Art Sears, Jr., "Eulogize Malcolm X
as the Negroes' 'Black Prince'," *Jet* 27, no. 22 (March 11, 1965): 18–21;
Louis E. Lomax, *To Kill a Black Man* (Los Angeles: Holloway House
Publishing Company, 1968), 11–12 and 131; and John Morgan,
"Malcolm X's Murder," *New Statesman* (February 26, 1965): 310.
Harold Cruse argues that "no matter how nationalistic Malcolm X remained after his break (with Muhammad), he was forced by circumstances to swing closer to the civil rights–integrationist forces in order
to participate more fully in the broad struggle." Charles Hamilton contends that "Malcolm's entire life was one of constant transition." It is
better to say that both Malcolm and King experienced constant growth
during the periods of their leadership in the black freedom struggle.
See Harold Cruse, *The Crisis of the Negro Intellectual* (New York:
William Morrow and Company, Inc., 1967), 563–64; and Charles V.
Hamilton, *The Black Preacher in America* (New York: William Morrow
and Company, Inc., 1972), 87.
    93. Baldwin, "The Great Confrontation," 14–15; Baldwin,
"Malcolm X and Martin Luther King, Jr.," 411; and Moses, *Black Messiahs and Uncle Toms*, 212. Some have held that King was losing faith in
nonviolence toward the end of his life, which suggests that he was moving closer to Malcolm in terms of his philosophy. See "Hint Dr. King was
Losing Faith in Non-Violence," *New York Amsterdam News* (April 5,
1969): 1.

solidarity with Malcolm and the nationalists on many
pressing issues and concerns:

> Martin firmly agreed with certain aspects of the pro-
> gram that Malcolm X advocated. For example, he
> shared with Malcolm the fierce desire that the black
> American reclaim his racial pride, his joy in himself
> and his race in a physical, a cultural, and a spiritual
> rebirth. He shared with the nationalists the sure
> knowledge that "black is beautiful" and that in so
> many respects, the quality of the black people's scale
> of values was far superior to that of the white culture
> which attempted to enslave us. Martin too had a close
> attachment to our African brothers and to our com-
> mon heritage. . . . And, on the other side, Martin
> too believed that *white* Christianity had failed to act
> in accordance with its teachings. . . . Martin also
> believed in . . . Black Power. He believed that we
> must have our share of the economy, of education,
> of jobs, of free choice. We must have the same quality
> and quantity of power that other ethnic groups
> possess, so that blacks, as a group, can hold their
> own in a society where, instead of a melting pot,
> separate peoples function beside each other, ex-
> changing the power they control for the power the
> other fellow has.[94]

94. Coretta Scott King, *My Life with Martin Luther King, Jr.* (New
York: Avon Books, 1969), 260. Harold Cruse seems to suggest that King
was the pure black integrationist and Malcolm the pure black nationalist,
a suggestion not borne out by the evidence. Indeed, there was something
of the integrationist in Malcolm and a bit of the nationalist in King. See
Lewis V. Baldwin, "A Letter to the Editor: Concerning Elements of Black
Nationalism in the Thought of Martin Luther King, Jr. and Malcolm X,"
The Vanderbilt Hustler (Vanderbilt University) (February 20, 1987):
16–17. Further evidence of how King shared ideas with black nationalists was revealed in his plan to set up "freedom schools" and "black
cultural events" as a part of his Poor People's Campaign in early 1968.
Convinced that both blacks and whites should study intensely the contributions made by blacks to culture, history, and civilization, King believed that these events would educate the whole nation concerning
great poets like Countee Cullen and Langston Hughes, outstanding
philosophers such as W. E. B. Du Bois and Alaine Locke, important scientists like George Washington Carver, and "the great jazz, blues," and
other forms of "music that's made America beautiful." For King,
"freedom schools" and "black cultural events" were important ways of

One of the best indications of the growing unity between Malcolm and King occurred during the S.C.L.C.'s
Selma campaign in early February, 1965, some three
weeks before Malcolm's death. Malcolm visited Selma
while the movement was in full swing, addressed the
S.C.L.C. and an enthusiastic crowd of Student Nonviolent
Coordinating Committee (S.N.C.C.) supporters at the
Brown Chapel A.M.E., and spoke personally with Coretta
Scott King about his desire "to work with Dr. King and
not against him." King was confined in a Selma jail at that
time. "I want Dr. King to know that I didn't come to
Selma to make his job difficult," Malcolm explained to
Coretta Scott King. "I really did come thinking that I
could make it easier. If the white people realize what the
alternative is, perhaps they will be more willing to hear
Dr. King."[95] Both King and his wife were impressed and
moved by Malcolm's sincerity on that occasion but were
convinced that "he was not yet able to renounce violence
and overcome the bitterness which life had invested in
him."[96] Even so, the spirit and attitude Malcolm reflected

---

countering the arguments of those who "have made us feel that we
haven't done anything for the history and the culture of the world." See
Martin Luther King, Jr., "Address at a Mass Meeting," Clarksdale, Miss.
(The King Center Archives, 19 March 1968), 7; and Martin Luther King,
Jr., "Address at a Mass Meeting," Eutaw, Ala. (The King Center Archives,
20 March 1968), 3–4.

95. King, *My Life with Martin Luther King, Jr.*, 259–60; Baldwin,
"The Great Confrontation," 18–19; and Martin Luther King, Jr., "The
Nightmare of Violence: Regarding the Death of Malcolm X" (unpublished document, The King Center Archives, 26 February 1965), 1–3.
Early in February, 1965, Malcolm sent a telegram to George L. Rockwell,
head of the American Nazi Party, warning that any racist attacks against
King and other nonviolent demonstrators would be met with "maximum
physical retaliation" from "those of us who are not handcuffed by the
disarming philosophy of nonviolence." Back in June, 1964, he had sent a
telegram to King in St. Augustine, Florida, offering protection to nonviolent demonstrators. See a telegram from Malcolm X to Martin Luther
King, Jr., St. Augustine, Fla., 30 June 1964, The King Papers, Boston
University; Malcolm X, *Malcolm X on Afro-American History*, 43–44;
"Rockwell Gets Warning from Malcolm X," *The Militant* (February 1,
1965): 8; and Baldwin, "Malcolm X and Martin Luther King, Jr.," 406 and
415 n. 50–52.

96. King, "The Nightmare of Violence," 2. John A. Williams reported
that in a conversation he had with Malcolm X in Lagos, Nigeria early in
1964, "it was apparent that the distance between himself and King was
small indeed, although he never gave up the idea of self-defense for

in Selma made King more receptive to the possibility of meeting with him. Ralph Abernathy of the S.C.L.C. has said that he and King had planned to go to New York to meet with Malcolm after the conclusion of the Selma movement, mainly because they saw him as someone who could be useful to them when they moved their crusade to the northern ghettoes.[97] "We were trying to build a coalition," Abernathy reported. "We knew he wanted to be supportive of our movement, and, although we did not agree with his total philosophy, we thought it would be good to talk with him. Before we were able to arrange the trip to New York, Malcolm X was killed."[98] According to the black psychologist Kenneth B. Clark, Malcolm, too, was seeking an opportunity to meet face to face with King for a frank and friendly discussion of the future course of the black movement:

> He began to express his respect for the point of view of Martin Luther King. He stated to me his growing belief that black racism and white racism were practically one and the same. He wanted the opportunity to be able to talk with Martin face to face. . . . He asked if I could arrange for him to speak with Martin Luther King and James Baldwin. I told him I

blacks. Malcolm was even willing to sing 'We Shall Overcome,' just as long as all who were singing had .45's firmly in hand." See John A. Williams, *The King God Didn't Save: Reflections on the Life and Death of Martin Luther King, Jr.* (New York: Coward-McCann, Inc., 1970), 77. James Cone develops at great length the view that King's and Malcolm's ideas and visions were converging at the time of their deaths, a view set forth as early as 1965 by John Morgan. See Cone, *Martin and Malcolm and America*, 253–59; and Morgan, "Malcolm X's Murder," 310.

97. Goldman, *The Death and Life of Malcolm X*, 391; and a private interview with the Rev. Ralph D. Abernathy, Atlanta, Ga., 7 May 1987. Many scholars suggest that Malcolm's appeal to blacks in the ghetto was far stronger than that of King. See Miller, *Martin Luther King, Jr.*, 82; Norman Coombs, *The Black Experience in America* (New York: Twayne Publishers, Inc., 1972), 211; and Mercer Cook and Stephen E. Henderson, *The Militant Black Writer in Africa and the United States* (Madison, Wis.: The University of Wisconsin Press, 1969), 110–14. Cook and Henderson assert that "in some ways, his (Malcolm) death was more tragic than King's, for the Movement had moved North and he had the potential of unifying elements in the black community that King could not reach."

98. A private interview with the Rev. Ralph D. Abernathy, 7 May 1987.

would do my best to arrange for such a meeting. We agreed that prior to such a meeting, we would have a personal talk at my office at City College. It was arranged for a certain Tuesday. The Sunday before that Tuesday, Malcolm X was assassinated.[99]

Very little has been said in the literature about how Malcolm and King reached out to each other even as they disagreed on many issues and concerns. Malcolm, on business trips to Atlanta, sometimes visited the S.C.L.C.'s main office on Auburn Avenue to chat privately with King, but King was never in on such occasions.[100] Wyatt T. Walker tells how once the two men happened to meet in an airport, and Malcolm told King of his interest in advancing the cause of civil rights.[101] Coretta Scott King recounts how her husband and Malcolm "had talked together on occasion and had discussed their philosophies in a friendly way." "I know that, though he never said so publicly, Malcolm X had deep respect for Martin," she wrote. "He recognized that Martin was unique, not alone in talent or eloquence, but in fearlessness and courage. Malcolm admired manhood and he knew how supremely Martin exemplified it."[102]

There remained enormous differences between Malcolm and King in education, status, methods, philosophy, and achievements. However, they were drawn together in a dialectic of social activism by the roots they shared in the black folk tradition, by their common devotion to the liberation of the oppressed, by the ideas and convictions they shared, by the personal admiration and respect they had for each other, and by the impelling moral, spiritual, and intellectual power each received from the other.[103] Owing to "their reciprocally stimulated growth," writes Wilson J. Moses, Malcolm and King presented "a greater

99. Clark, *King, Malcolm, Baldwin*, 12–13.
100. Goldman, *The Death and Life of Malcolm X*, 95; and Wilmore, *Black Religion and Black Radicalism*, 189.
101. Wilmore, *Black Religion and Black Radicalism*, 189.
102. King, *My Life with Martin Luther King, Jr.*, 261–62.
103. Baldwin, "The Great Confrontation," 2 and 24 n. 4.

threat to American conservatives—black and white—and each experienced some erosion of his power base." This was particularly true as the two of them found common ground on international issues on which they could both agree, such as world poverty, South African apartheid, and American imperialism as revealed most prominently in the Vietnam War.[104]

Black America needed both Malcolm X and Martin Luther King, Jr., and both were conscious of the reciprocal roles they played in their people's quest for freedom, justice, and equality of opportunity. Malcolm occasionally mentioned the very important role he and the nationalists played in making King, Roy Wilkins, Whitney Young, and other moderate civil rights leaders more radical and more acceptable to white Americans.[105] Similarly, King spoke of the significance of the alternative roles presented by himself and the nationalists, indicating how each articulated different dimensions of the anguish and goals of black Americans.[106] The fates of both Malcolm and King were sealed "the moment they attempted to release the black American struggle from the domestic context and relate it to the struggles of the poor and the nonwhite all over the world."[107]

104. Moses, *Black Messiahs and Uncle Toms*, 212. Malcolm's critique of America's domestic and foreign policies was far more scathing than that of King. This is understandable because King relied more on the support of the federal government.

105. Baldwin, "The Great Confrontation," 9–10; and Malcolm X, *Malcolm X Speaks*, 172. Lerone Bennett concludes that "Malcolm X in sum, prepared the way for Martin Luther King's rebellion. Only time will tell if King, in turn, prepared the way of Malcolm X's succession." Colin Morris argues that "American Negroes needed both Martin Luther King and Malcolm X, just as India had to have both Gandhi and Nehru." See Lerone Bennett, Jr., *Confrontation: Black and White* (Chicago: Johnson Publishing Company, 1965), 205–07, 211–13, 216, 276, 278, 290, and 294; and Colin Morris, *Unyoung, Uncolored, Unpoor* (Nashville and New York: Abingdon Press, 1969), 90–91.

106. King, *Why We Can't Wait*, 86–87; and King, "A Statement on Malcolm X," 1.

107. James Baldwin, "Malcolm and Martin," 201. Malcolm always insisted, to a greater extent than King, that the African-American problem be viewed within an international context. He constantly raised the need to "internationalize" the plight of black Americans, or to take the issue before the United Nations General Assembly in search of a resolution. He

King's reaction to the assassination of Malcolm X in February, 1965, provides more evidence against the claim that the two men were bitter "adversaries in a great Manichaean contest, the forces of light against the forces of darkness, with the future course of black protest at stake."[108] At press conferences and in newspaper and radio interviews, King admitted that "I had a deep affection for Malcolm X, and I am very sorry about this whole thing."[109] In a telegram to Betty Shabazz, Malcolm's widow, King spoke of Malcolm's "great ability to put his finger on the existence and root of the problem." "He was an eloquent spokesman for his point of view and no one can honestly doubt that Malcolm had a great concern for the problems that we face as a race," King continued.[110] Convinced that Malcolm, "like so many of our number, was a victim of the despair that inevitably derives from the conditions of oppression, poverty, and injustice which engulf the masses of our race," King observed:

> The American Negro cannot afford to destroy its leadership any more than the Congo can. Men of talent are too scarce to be destroyed by envy, greed and tribal rivalry before they reach their full maturity. Like the murder of Lumumba, the murder of Malcolm X deprives the world of a potentially great leader. I could not agree with either of these men, but I could see in

---

also spoke of expanding "the civil rights struggle to the level of human rights." See Malcolm X, *Malcolm X Speaks*, 34–35; and Malcolm X, *By Any Means Necessary*, 86–88.

108. Goldman, *The Death and Life of Malcolm X*, 74. This image of King and Malcolm as bitter enemies has been created in the public imagination by the American mass media and reinforced in the writings of misinformed scholars, and therefore, must not be taken seriously by those who wish to understand the true nature of Malcolm's and King's relationship, as well as their meaning and significance for the black freedom struggle. Baldwin, "The Great Confrontation," 1–2.

109. Baldwin, "The Great Confrontation," 19; Baldwin, "Malcolm X and Martin Luther King, Jr.," 408; Martin Luther King, Jr., "Transcript of a Press Conference," Los Angeles, Ca. (The King Center Archives, 24 February 1965), 1–2 and 6; and "King and Roy on Malcolm's Death," *New York Amsterdam News* (February 27, 1965): 27.

110. A telegram from Martin Luther King, Jr., to Mrs. Malcolm X, Faith Temple Church, Harlem, N.Y., 26 February 1965, The King Center Archives.

them a capacity for leadership which I could respect, and which was only beginning to mature in judgement and statesmanship.[111]

On February 26, 1965, King wrote a three-page statement on the life and death of Malcolm X, called "The Nightmare of Violence." Here he discussed Malcolm's bout with white racism as a child and a teenager, his involvement in the criminal activities of the underworld, and his final emergence as a leader of his people. In King's view, Malcolm was one who "possessed a native intelligence and drive which demanded an outlet and means of expression." "It is a testimony to Malcolm's personal depth and integrity," King wrote, "that he could not become an underworld Czar, but turned again and again to religion for meaning and destiny."[112] King's perceptive and sensitive view of Malcolm's life and work supports Coretta Scott King's contention that her husband "did not have a one-dimensional, negative view of black nationalism."[113]

KING AND OTHER BLACK
RESPONSES TO COLLECTIVE EVIL

Some responses by black Americans to the social evils of racism and oppression have traditionally fallen into the categories of grassroots revivalism and prosperity positivism. Grassroots revivalism, almost as old as the black Christian tradition in America, has often emphasized personal salvation and abstinence from worldly

111. King, "The Nightmare of Violence," 1–3; and King, *My Life with Martin Luther King, Jr.,* 261–62. King apparently accepted reports that Malcolm was killed by fellow blacks.

112. King, "The Nightmare of Violence," 1–3; Baldwin, "The Great Confrontation," 21–22; and Baldwin, "Malcolm X and Martin Luther King, Jr.," 408–12. Apparently, King had carefully studied Malcolm X's life, using a week-long documentary series on the Black Muslims, produced in the early 1960s by Mike Wallace of CBS News under the title, "The Hate that Hate Produced," as a source. It is highly unlikely that King had had a chance at this point to read Malcolm's *Autobiography,* which was issued sometime after the black nationalist's death.

113. King, *My Life with Martin Luther King, Jr.,* 276.

social, economic, political, legal, and educational matters. In other words, grassroots revivalists tend to denounce evil "in the world" in order to compel their flocks
into strict isolation from it. Known for its assertion that
"churches should stay out of politics," this group is currently represented by many black Holiness and Pentecostal movements.[114] Unlike the grassroots revivalists,
prosperity positivists have customarily embraced con-
spicuous consumption while placing little emphasis,
comparatively speaking, on saving the souls of all humanity. For prosperity positivists, the most direct and
acceptable way of attaining socially desired ends is not by
attacking and avoiding contact with the status quo but
rather by using it to secure financial prosperity, prestige,
and health. This approach was common among black
spiritualist groups early in this century, and is used today by the Reverend Frederick J. Eikerenkoetter II (better known as Reverend Ike) of the United Church and
Science of Living Institute and the Reverend Roosevelt
Franklin of Macon, Georgia.[115] Martin Luther King, Jr.,
did not directly attack specific adherents to grassroots
revivalism and prosperity positivism, but he did critique
many of the principles and values on which these groups
were based.

Because King believed that oppressed people have a
moral obligation to resist any system that disrespects
their dignity and worth as persons, he could not accept
the grassroots revivalists' belief in nonresistance to social evil. Those conservative black churches that stressed
indifference toward the worldly, sociopolitical order
while encouraging their constituents to cultivate personal virtues and exemplary lives for salvation in heaven

114. Franklin, "Religious Belief and Political Activism," 66; and
Franklin, "Charisma and Conflict," 1ff.
115. See Hans A. Baer, *The Black Spiritual Movement: A Religious
Response to Racism* (Knoxville: The University of Tennessee Press,
1984), 9ff.; Joseph R. Washington, Jr., *Black Sects and Cults* (Lanham,
Md.: University Press of America, Inc., 1984), 112–16, 121, and 123–24;
and Franklin, "Religious Belief and Political Activism," 66–67.

struck King as unrealistic and self-defeating. His critique of such churches and their leadership was almost as scathing as that of Booker T. Washington and Malcolm X, both of whom were not religious in the usual sense of black Christian commitment.[116] In King's estimation, many grassroots revivalist–type churches and their leadership had become imbued with the idea of making black people satisfied with life under white domination, thereby diverting considerable numbers from agitation and from resistance to white racist values and institutions. Religion makes persons whole, he counseled, only by bringing together the proximate and ultimate concerns of life—by combining the joys of heavenly salvation with the concern for freedom, justice, and equality of opportunity on this earth:

> It's all right to talk about "silver slippers over yonder," but men need shoes to wear down here. It's all right to talk about streets flowing with "milk and honey" over yonder, but let's get some food to eat for people down here in Asia and Africa and South America and in our own nation who go to bed hungry at night. It's all right to talk about "mansions in the sky," but I'm thinking about these ghettoes and slums right down here.[117]

Over against the complacency and escapism of certain conservative, grassroots revivalist–type churches and preachers, King emphasized what might be called "Holistic evangelism"—an evangelism that connected preaching the word and saving souls with the critical events, problems, and questions that shaped the context in which his people lived and functioned. For King, the scope of the church's ministry had to be at least as

---

116. King, *Stride Toward Freedom*, 35–36; Martin Luther King, Jr., "Answer to a Perplexing Question," a sermon delivered at the Ebenezer Baptist Church, Atlanta, Ga. (The King Center Archives, 3 March 1963), 7–8; "Playboy Interview: Malcolm X," 54ff.; Malcolm X, *The End of White World Supremacy*, 25, 71, and 77; and Hart M. Nelsen, et al., eds., *The Black Church in America* (New York: Basic Books, Inc., Publishers, 1971), 40–43.

117. King, "Answer to a Perplexing Question," 8.

pervasive as the power of sin and evil in order to be a force in the actualization of the Kingdom of God, which is both present and future, earthly and heavenly. Through his life and work, he affirmed the idea that God's Kingdom is not merely "beyond you" but "among you" and "within you," and that it cannot be a social order unless it is first within the hearts of human beings.[118]

Despite the problems King had with the orientation of conservative, grassroots revivalism, he appreciated and respected the deep spirituality and the rich emotional heritage associated with that expression of black religion. This attitude made it possible for him to relate to the mass of black church folk with great ease and comfort.[119]

The principles and values associated with prosperity positivism received little approval from King. The Reverend Ike, as earlier indicated, became the chief proponent of this type of religion. Born the son of a Baptist minister and a schoolteacher in Ridgeland, South Carolina in the 1930s, "just one step from slavery," Ike borrowed liberally from the thinking and writings of Norman Vincent Peale, the widely-known self-motivation author-lecturer and former minister at Marble Collegiate Church in New York. Ike's pilgrimage took him from the United Church of Jesus Christ for All People, in Charleston, South Carolina, to the Miracle Temple, which he organized in Boston in 1964, and finally to his United Church and Science of Living Institute, which he started in New York in 1969.[120] His prosperity positivism, or what he calls "Positive Self-Image Psychology," has resulted from a lifetime of study and reexamination of the Bible, and of what he describes as "a determination 'to be and to

118. For the term "Holistic evangelism," I am indebted to Harvie M. Conn, *Evangelism: Doing Justice and.Preaching Grace* (Grand Rapids, Mich.: Zondervan Publishing House, 1982), 9ff.

119. King, *Stride Toward Freedom*, 178.

120. Charles L. Sanders, "The Gospel According to Rev. Ike," *Ebony*, 32, no. 2 (December 1976): 151 and 154.

do and to have.'"[121] Concerning his drive toward material prosperity, Ike once remarked that he used to believe he had to suffer and sacrifice so he could have milk and honey some day. "But I got tired of being poor, while God sat up in Heaven, behind the pearly gates, with streets of gold and walls of precious jewels." Ike said he thought, "What kind of God is that sitting up in Heaven while I'm down here catching hell?" He surmised that any God who delights in the suffering of His people is sadistic. Ike decided not to pray to a "sadistic God," but to the "Presence and Power of God-in-me." He taught people that the "God-in-me" that everyone possesses is "the power they can utilize to heal anything, to be anything, to do anything and have anything they want."[122]

In a statement that clearly revealed his political stance, Ike declared in 1976: "I'm not trying to save the world. Everybody who ever tried that ended up being crucified."[123] His primary concern has been, and continues to be, teaching people how to appreciate and secure success, wealth, prestige, and good health. "Jesus said 'I have come that you might have life and that you might have it more abundantly,'" he proclaims. "I like the part about '*more abundantly*,' and if Jesus wants us to have it that way, well, why not? He wants us to have plenty in life and enjoy it—*abundantly!*" Rejecting the Biblical injunction that "the love of money is the root of all evil," Ike insists that "It's the *lack* of money that's the root of all evil. What's more evil than not having money to pay your rent that's 90 days past due, and not having money to get a decent meal?"[124] In his opinion, many of the social and economic problems in the black community stem from the failure of black preachers to proclaim a relevant and motivating gospel, a view expressed in various ways by

121. *Ibid.*, 154; and Mark Edwards, "Rev. Ike," *Sepia* 30, no. 4 (April 1981): 47.
122. Sanders, "The Gospel According to Rev. Ike," 148, 150, and 154.
123. *Ibid.*, 150.
124. *Ibid.*, 154; and Edwards, "Rev. Ike," 47.

King. In a 1976 interview, Ike commented that the failures of black preachers were due to their practice of teaching "slavery time religion" to the masses of black people. He expressed that although many of the preachers, the educated ones especially, knew better, they continued this practice because of its convenience. "[It's] very easy to keep people happy by telling them all that pie in the sky by and by stuff." He said that those preachers "know that when the white man took blacks off the boats from Africa they taught them religion but they didn't teach them how to *think*. Blacks were taught to use their behinds, not their minds." Ike remarked that he was "trying to reverse that tired old psychology."[125]

Ike's prosperity positivism has won only a few converts in the black community since the early 1970s. A few black preachers, such as Roosevelt Franklin, have borrowed from and promoted Ike's gospel. Franklin's "prosperity plan" is designed to make his listeners believe that "if you can believe it, you can achieve it." This gospel strikes at the heart of apathy and self-doubt in the black community.[126]

The prosperity positivists' apolitical posture and lack of interest in social reform activities stood in sharp contrast to King's notion of nonviolent direct action. King's rejection of the values associated with prosperity positivism hinged on his conviction that an excessively materialistic orientation could only lead to selfish ambition and cutthroat competition, thus undercutting the possibility of black solidarity and a collective role on the part of blacks for their liberation. King believed that it was the responsibility of the black preachers to raise the masses of their people to greater heights rather than to focus on self-aggrandizement. Hence, he had little patience for ministers who used the pulpit as a sacred opportunity for exhibitionism and for exploiting rather than empowering black people. He lashed out at "Negro

125. Sanders, "The Gospel According to Rev. Ike," 154.
126. *Ibid.*, 148–54; and Edwards, "Rev. Ike," 47.

preachers who are really more concerned about the size of the wheel base on their automobile and how much money they are getting than they are about the size of their service to humanity."[127] He further declared:

> And I'm sick and tired of seeing Negro preachers riding around in big cars and living in big houses and not concerned about the problems of the people who made it possible for them to get these things. It seems that I can hear the Almighty God say—"Stop preaching your loud sermons and whooping your irrelevant mess in my face, for your hands are full of tar for the people that I sent you to serve, . . . and you are doing nothing but being concerned about yourself."[128]

Because his perspective was diametrically opposed to that advanced today by the Reverends Ike and Roosevelt Franklin, King simply refused to build a fortune for himself and his family.[129] He consciously chose not to buy Cadillac cars and at times refused to ride in them because of the stereotypical image they attached to black preachers. "I won't have any money to leave behind," he cried in his last sermon at Atlanta's Ebenezer Baptist Church in February, 1968. "I won't have the fine and luxurious things of life to leave behind. But I just want to leave a committed life behind." With words that became his life's motto, he exclaimed:

> If I can help somebody as I pass along,
> If I can cheer somebody with a song,
> If I can show somebody he's traveling wrong,
> Then my living will not be in vain.

127. King, *Where Do We Go from Here?* 102–66; King, "Answer to a Perplexing Question," 7–8; and Martin Luther King, Jr., "The Good Samaritan," a sermon delivered at the Ebenezer Baptist Church, Atlanta, Ga. (The King Center Archives, 28 August 1966), 7.
128. King, "Answer to a Perplexing Question," 7–8.
129. King, *My Life with Martin Luther King, Jr.,* 91. The Reverend Michael E. Haynes said of King: "During that latter period, he (Martin) knew there was a penalty on his head, and that he had four little children. He could have withdrawn for the sake of being able to be with his kids, but he was willing to pay that price. He knew his days were limited." A private interview with the Rev. Michael E. Haynes, Boston, Mass., 25 June 1987.

If I can do my duty as a Christian ought,
If I can bring salvation to a world once wrought,
If I can spread the messages as the master taught,
Then my living will not be in vain.[130]

Despite all his attacks on individualism and unbridled materialism, King agreed with certain principles that prosperity positivists have consistently preached in the black community. The idea that blacks should believe in themselves and strive to achieve the very best in life, an idea closely associated with prosperity positivism, was a persistent theme in King's sermons, speeches, and writings. The principles of black self-help and black self-sufficiency, which still hold a prominent place in the teachings of the Reverend Ike, also found acceptance with King.[131]

THE GREAT SYNTHESIZER

Martin Luther King, Jr., was a prophetic radical who stood in the tradition of Richard Allen, Sojourner Truth, Frederick Douglass, Harriet Tubman, Ida B. Wells, and many other black thinkers and leaders.[132] Like his prophetic predecessors, King not only challenged evil and unjust systems with words but with militant and sustained action as well. More specifically, he subjected the dominant institutions, values, and practices in America to scrutiny and criticism in order to expose their racist, classist, and imperialistic tendencies, and then confronted the system nonviolently in an effort to make it more just and responsive to the needs of the poor and oppressed.[133] King's place in the black tradition of prophetic radicalism takes on new meaning when considered against the background of Richard

130. John H. Johnson, et al., compilers, *Martin Luther King, Jr., 1929–1968: An Ebony Picture Biography* (Chicago: Johnson Publishing Company, Inc., 1968), 8–9.
131. King, *Where Do We Go from Here?* 102–66.
132. Franklin, "Religious Belief and Political Activism," 65; and Franklin, "Charisma and Conflict," 1ff.
133. Franklin, "Religious Belief and Political Activism," 65; and Paris, "The Bible and the Black Churches," 140–44.

Allen's contributions to the independent black church movement, Sojourner Truth's agitation on behalf of black and women's rights, Frederick Douglass' militant abolitionism, Harriet Tubman's courageous activities on the Underground Railroad, and Ida B. Wells' persistent and militant stands against lynchings.[134]

As a prophetic radical who preached and practiced nonviolent direct action, King saw himself standing between the force of complacency and the force of bitterness and hatred in the black community.[135] It is more correct to say that King represented one of many forces on the spectrum of black leadership and action—forces that included prophetic radicalism, progressive accommodationism, grassroots revivalism, and prosperity positivism. Categorizing these various types is not easy because, as Robert M. Franklin has stated, none of them "is a pure type." A single leader commonly operated "from several of these modes, employing their symbols and rhetoric, while maintaining his or her primary identity in the designated tradition."[136]

King is an excellent example of this. Although essentially a prophetic radical, he affirmed and appropriated ideas and limited truths usually associated with progressive accommodationists, redemptive nationalists, grassroots revivalists, and prosperity positivists, while, at the same time, avoiding their extremes and pitfalls. King reflected the spirit of progressive accommodationism by stressing the importance of exercising restraint when

134. John Hope Franklin, "The Forerunners," *American Visions: The Magazine of Afro-American Culture* 1, no. 1 (January/February 1986): 26–35. Another black leader and thinker who expressed views later adopted by King was William Whipper of Pennsylvania. Whipper was an integrationist who opposed racial separatism and racial designations in the 1830s and early 1840s. However, he was more of an integrationist than the post-1963 King because Whipper called for the dissolution of every all-black and all-white institution, and was seemingly opposed to all efforts to promote black identity and black cultural expression and understanding. See "Opposition to Black Separatism: Three Letters by William Whipper," in Stuckey, ed., *The Ideological Origins of Black Nationalism*, 252–60; and Stuckey, *Slave Culture*, 203–4, 206–7, 210–11, and 231.

135. King, *Stride Toward Freedom*, 211–14; and King, *Why We Can't Wait*, 86–87.

136. Franklin, "Religious Belief and Political Activism," 67.

necessary and of working with the system as much as possible. He accepted the redemptive nationalists' appeal for black unity and militant, assertive action. He combined these elements with the spirituality he inherited from the grassroots revivalists and the self-confidence and desire for achievement so typical of prosperity positivists. King combined partial truths from all of these traditions to fashion a creative, meaningful, and effective synthesis to achieve social justice. To achieve this, he relied on the dialectical approach of the German philosopher Georg Wilhelm Friedrich Hegel, who had concluded in the nineteenth century that truth is found neither in the *thesis* nor in the *antithesis* but in the resulting *synthesis*, which reconciles both. The synthesis in Hegelian philosophy led King to look for truth in polarities.[137] Many times he purposely called together several of his aides and advisors who had different points of view, listened carefully to their opinions, and then made a final judgment, which brought together the limited truths expressed in all the opinions.[138]

As the struggle for human dignity and equality of opportunity moves toward the twenty-first century, black Americans should give serious consideration to the moral reflections and social criticisms of prophetic radicals like King, progressive accommodationists such as Booker Washington and Joseph Jackson, redemptive nationalists like Marcus Garvey and Malcolm X, prosperity positivists such as Reverend Ike and Roosevelt Franklin, and grassroots revivalists like the Holiness and Pentecostal groups. The limitations of King's thought and methods must be considered in the light of the perspectives of these various groups. The representatives of these groups have provided us with markedly different responses to the social evils of racism and oppression, but they have all shared ideas in common and have been in search of the goal of freedom, justice, and equality for

137. Ansbro, *Martin Luther King, Jr.*, 123–26.
138. Bernard Lafayette, "Martin Luther King, Jr.: A Lecture," Vanderbilt University, Nashville, Tenn., 21 April 1989, 1ff. Lafayette was an active member of the S.C.L.C. in King's final years.

their people. They have all left us bits and pieces of truth that together may increase our understanding of the nature and effects of racism and provide a much-needed synthesis for a black liberation ethic. Because their contributions and legacies complement one another, they should not be evaluated and appreciated separately. We cannot honor one group without honoring the others. Their combined ideas and strategies could possibly give new integrity, vitality, and direction to the continuing black struggle, especially since they offer so much on how to relate the theoretical to the practical in matters of race relations.[139] King's dialectical approach affords an ideal model for black Americans who seek to reconcile the values and truths embodied in prophetic radicalism, progressive accommodationism, redemptive nationalism, grassroots revivalism, and prosperity positivism.

It is only through our study of King as a great synthesizer of ideas that we can best understand the broad contours of his thought, the credibility of his vision, and the relevance of his principles for black America in this last decade of the twentieth century. King was not a disciple of any one particular school of thought or methodological approach. Yet he achieved coherence in his thinking and an amazing pattern of consistency in his praxis.[140] This level of achievement will become more evident in the following discussion of King in relation to black theology and ethics.

139. Peter Paris makes a similar argument in his study of King, Malcolm X, Joseph H. Jackson, and Adam Clayton Powell, Jr. He argues that "a comprehensive view of racism requires all the conceptions and that the several understandings and their implied activities are complementary and could form the basis for cooperative action." See Paris, *Black Leaders in Conflict*, 9 ff. The contents of this chapter and Paris's reflections show that the search for a viable liberation ethic must transcend the legacies of King and Malcolm X, as discussed by James Cone, to embrace the positive elements of other resistance traditions in the African-American community. See Cone, *Martin and Malcolm and America*, 288–314. The ideas and insights from the black womanist tradition should not be ignored in this search. See Katie G. Cannon, *Black Womanist Ethics* (Atlanta: Scholars Press, 1988), 31–175.

140. Peter J. Paris, *Black Religious Leaders: Conflict and Unity — Insights from Martin Luther King, Jr., Malcolm X, Joseph H. Jackson, and Adam Clayton Powell, Jr.* (Louisville: Westminster/John Knox Press, 1991), 100–101.

TAKE MY HAND, PRECIOUS LORD
A LEGACY FOR BLACK THEOLOGY
AND ETHICS

2

Precious Lord, take my hand,
Lead me on, let me stand,
I am tired, I am weak, I am worn;
Thru the storm, thru the night,
Lead me on to the Light,
Take my hand, precious Lord,
Lead me home.

Black Gospel Song[1]

We have the power to make the church that institution that
even young people, who feel temporarily separated from it,
can respect. . . . We can even get them to have a new loyalty, because they'll know that we are on the battle line for
them. And they'll come to see that Jesus Christ was not a
white man. Christianity is not just a Western religion. We can
make the church recapture its authentic ring. We have the
power to change America, and give a kind of new vitality to
the religion of Jesus Christ.

Martin Luther King, Jr., 1968[2]

The task of Black Theology is to inform black people that
because of God's act in Christ they need not offer anyone an
apology for being black.

James H. Cone, 1969[3]

As long as the white-male experience continues to be established as the ethical norm, Black women, Black men and
others will suffer unequivocal oppression.

Katie G. Cannon, 1988[4]

1. *The New National Baptist Hymnal* (Nashville: The National Baptist Publishing Board, 1977), 339. Minutes before his tragic death, King
requested the noted musician Ben Branch to give a musical rendition of
"Take My Hand, Precious Lord" on saxophone at the meeting he was to
attend in Memphis on the night of April 4, 1968. This song, born out of the
wisdom and suffering of the black musical genius Thomas Dorsey, was
among King's favorite gospel songs.
2. Martin Luther King, Jr., "An Address at the Ministers' Leadership Training Program," Miami, Fla. (The Archives of the Martin Luther
King, Jr. Center for Nonviolent Social Change, Inc., Atlanta, Georgia, 19
and 23 February 1968), 5.
3. James H. Cone, *Black Theology and Black Power* (New York: The
Seabury Press, 1969), 149.
4. Katie G. Cannon, *Black Womanist Ethics* (Atlanta: Scholars
Press, 1988), 3.

Martin Luther King, Jr., was perhaps the most creative
theologian and ethicist to grace the American scene in
this century.[5] As such, he interpreted and appropriated
the liberative, redemptive essence of the Christian faith
in light of the human struggle for freedom, peace, and
community. King has been characterized theologically
as an Evangelical Liberal, and ethically as a Personalist,
and many have assumed that his social concern and nonviolent activism were rooted in liberal Christian theology and ethics.[6] Such views are well taken, but they do
not take into full account the eclectic and synthetic nature of King's theological and ethical method. Although
influenced by liberal Christian theologians and ethicists,
King's basic theological and ethical perspectives were
rooted primarily in the faith of the black church and

5. The significance of King's contributions as a theologian and
ethicist is still not sufficiently recognized. However, an increasing number of books and articles on the subject have appeared in the last two
decades. See Herbert W. Richardson, "Martin Luther King—Unsung
Theologian," in *New Theology*, no. 6, ed. Martin E. Marty and Dean G.
Peerman (New York: The Macmillan Company, 1969), 178–84; Paul R.
Garber, "Martin Luther King, Jr.: Theologian and Precursor of Black
Theology" (Ph.D. diss., Florida State University, December, 1973), 10–
442; John Colin Harris, "The Theology of Martin Luther King, Jr." (Ph.D.
diss., Duke University, April, 1974), 1ff; L. Harold DeWolf, "Martin
Luther King, Jr., as Theologian," *The Journal of the Interdenominational
Theological Center* 4, no. 2 (Spring 1977): 1–11; Joseph M. Thompson,
"Martin Luther King, Jr. and Christian Witness: An Interpretation of
King Based on a Theological Model of Prophetic Witness" (Ph.D. diss.,
Fordham University, April, 1981), 1ff; James H. Cone, "The Theology of
Martin Luther King, Jr.," *Union Seminary Quarterly Review* 40, no. 4
(January 1986): 21–39; Charles P. Henry, "Delivering Daniel: The Dialec-
tic of Ideology and Theology in the Thought of Martin Luther King, Jr.,"
Journal of Black Studies 17, no. 3 (March 1987): 327–45; Ervin Smith,
The Ethics of Martin Luther King, Jr. (Lewiston, N.Y.: The Edwin Mellen
Press, 1981),1–160; and William D. Watley, *Roots of Resistance: The Non-
violent Ethic of Martin Luther King, Jr.* (Valley Forge, Pa.: Judson Press,
1985), 17–128. One source contends that King was perhaps "self-con-
sciously neither strictly an ethicist nor a theologian. For example, he
wrote no systematic exposition of the principles of the Christian faith."
See Lonnie Edmondson and Archie Logan, "Martin Luther King, Jr.:
Theology in Context," *Duke Divinity Review* 40 (Spring 1975): 126.
6. Watley, *Roots of Resistance*, 18; Kenneth L. Smith and Ira G.
Zepp, Jr., *Search for the Beloved Community: The Thinking of Martin
Luther King, Jr.* (Valley Forge, Pa.: Judson Press, 1974), 11; Smith, *The
Ethics of Martin Luther King, Jr.*, 11–23; and John J. Ansbro, *Martin
Luther King, Jr.: The Making of a Mind* (Maryknoll, N.Y.: Orbis Books,
1982), 1–162.

were afforded practical application in the movement he led in and through that institution.[7] Therefore, any serious attempt to understand King as a theologian and an ethicist must begin with his background in the black church, and then move toward a consideration of the intellectual categories he borrowed from a variety of other Christian and non-Christian sources.

This chapter establishes King's relationship to the black theological tradition, with special attention to his influence on contemporary black theology and ethics. It is divided into four sections: (1) King as a black theologian and ethicist; (2) King and contemporary black theologians; (3) King and contemporary black ethicists; and (4) King and the future of black theology and ethics.

KING AS A BLACK THEOLOGIAN AND ETHICIST

Martin Luther King, Jr., provided an important link between the theological tradition of his forebears and the more systematic expressions of black theology that have developed since the late 1960s.[8] One must take this point seriously to understand the religious, intellectual, cultural, and political significance of King and the civil rights movement of the 1950s and 1960s. As a black theologian, King did not have the leisure to develop theology as carefully formulated, systematic discourses on Christian creeds and doctrines. As Paul R. Garber states, "King, of course, was not a formal, or systematic, theologian, but there is certainly an implicit theology in his sermons and other writings and indeed in his actions that can be made explicit. It is a Black theology." King's

7. Cone, "The Theology of Martin Luther King, Jr.," 21; and Watley, *Roots of Resistance*, 15.

8. Paul R. Garber, "Black Theology: The Latter Day Legacy of Martin Luther King, Jr.," *The Journal of the Interdenominational Theological Center* 2, no. 2 (Spring 1975): 100–13; and Paul R. Garber, "King Was a Black Theologian," *The Journal of Religious Thought* 31, no. 2 (Fall/Winter 1974–75): 16–32. Garber has written more about King as a black theologian than any other scholar.

theology was largely shaped and expressed in the course of conflict and action, and was, therefore, an existential appropriation of the Christian faith as interpreted in the black church. King was, in the words of Garber,

> literally a theologian on the run, spending more time in airports and aboard planes than in office or study. He wrote his sermons and books not in a comfortable solitude, but rather in the context of a profoundly restless people who were (or who at least thought they were) on the move, straining from oppression toward freedom.[9]

Although King did not ignore common theological themes such as the parenthood of God, sin, the finitude of humanity, and salvation, his primary focus as a black theologian was on the theme of *liberation*. This theme permeated his prayers, speeches, sermons, and books, and provided the thread that connected him theologically with his slave foreparents and with black theologians who emerged after him. King often expressed the conviction that racism and oppression contradicted God and that God would therefore liberate both blacks and whites. For him, the liberation of the poor and oppressed constituted the essential core of the Christian faith and of the entire Biblical revelation.[10] This explains why the Bible's Exodus theme and symbolism

9. Cone, "The Theology of Martin Luther King, Jr.," 21; Paul R. Garber, "Too Much Taming of Martin Luther King?," *The Christian Century* (June 5, 1974): 616; and Garber, "King was a Black Theologian," 22. The power of Garber's statement is revealed when one considers, for example, the business and hurry of King as opposed to the stillness and contemplation of great black thinkers like Howard Thurman. Black theology has always been an existential or experience-oriented theology, dating back to slavery. The only work King produced that leaned in the direction of a systematic theology was his dissertation, which is scheduled to appear in published form at some point. See Martin Luther King, Jr., "A Comparison of the Conceptions of God in the Thinking of Paul Tillich and Henry N. Wieman" (Ph.D. diss., Boston University, 1955), 1–320.

10. Garber, "King Was a Black Theologian," 16, 22, and 24–25; Garber, "Black Theology: The Latter Day Legacy," 112–13; James H. Cone, *A Black Theology of Liberation* (Philadelphia and New York: J. B. Lippincott Company, 1970), 77–79; and Jon M. Temme, "Jesus as Trailblazer: The Christology of Martin Luther King, Jr.," *The Journal of Religious Thought* 42, no. 1 (Spring-Summer 1985): 80.

held such a prominent place in his theology.[11] King rejected all concepts of God and of ultimate reality that
did not speak in a liberating way to the historical experiences and struggles of his people.

The person, work, and message of Jesus Christ were
central to King's understanding and analysis of the liberation motif. In his view, Jesus Christ was the human face
of God—the flesh through whom God revealed Himself
and His liberating concern and purpose for humanity:

> Where do we find this God? In a test tube? Where else
> except in Jesus Christ, the Lord of our lives? By know-
> ing him we know God. Christ is not only Godlike but
> God is Christlike. Christ is the word made flesh. He is
> the language of eternity translated into words of time.
> If we are to know what God is like and understand his
> purposes for mankind, we must turn to Christ. By
> committing ourselves absolutely to Christ and his
> way, we will participate in the marvelous act of faith
> that will bring us to the true knowledge of God.[12]

King regarded Jesus as a co-sufferer with and liberator
of the poor and oppressed—as one who brought healing
and a sense of unity to humanity through his identification with outsiders:

> A voice out of Bethlehem 2000 years ago said that all
> men are equal. It said that right would triumph. Jesus
> of Nazareth wrote no books. He owned no property to
> endow him with influence. He had no friends in the
> courts of the powerful. But he changed the course of
> mankind with only the poor and the despised.[13]

In Jesus Christ, King found an example of love in
its highest form (agape)—that love which transcends

11. Martin Luther King, Jr., "A Speech at the Ford Hall Forum,"
Boston, Mass. (The King Papers, Boston University, Boston, Mass., 11
December 1960), 1; and James H. Smylie, "On Jesus, Pharaohs, and the
Chosen People: Martin Luther King as Biblical Interpreter and Human-
ist," *Interpretation* 24 (January 1970): 74–91.
12. Quoted in Temme, "Jesus as Trailblazer," 76–77.
13. *Ibid.*, 77–78; and Coretta Scott King, "The Legacy of Martin
Luther King, Jr.," *Theology Today* 27 (July 1970): 139.

human differences and which, when combined with non-violent activism, provided the necessary formula for social reform and uplift:

> In our quest to make neighborly love a reality, we have in addition to the inspiring example of the Good Samaritan, the magnanimous life of our Christ to guide us. His altruism was universal, for he thought of all men, even publicans and sinners, as brothers. His altruism was dangerous, for he willingly travelled hazardous roads in a cause he knew was right. His altruism was excessive, for he chose to die on Calvary, history's most magnificent expression of obedience to the unenforceable.[14]

The Cross of Jesus Christ was for King, the black theologian, a symbol of suffering and salvation, of subjugation and liberation. It showed that Jesus "was an extremist for love, truth, and goodness," thereby rising "above his environment." It symbolized God's power to overcome sin and evil through suffering. King held that the task of truly moral and committed persons involved suffering with Christ for human redemption and transformation.[15] At this point, conviction and experience merged in his understanding of the Cross. In this sense, King was similar to his slave foreparents who, as Sterling Brown has observed, "fused belief and experience" in their "picturing of Calvary":

> Dey whupped him up de hill . . .
> Dey crowned his head with thorns . . .
> Dey pierced him in de side,
> An' de blood came a-twinklin' down;
> But he never said a mumbalin' word;
> Not a word; not a word.[16]

14. Martin Luther King, Jr., *Strength to Love* (Philadelphia: Fortress Press, 1981), 35.
15. Martin Luther King, Jr., *Why We Can't Wait* (New York: The New American Library, Inc., 1964), 88–89.
16. August Meier and Elliot Rudwick, eds., *The Making of Black America: Essays in Negro Life and History*, vol. 2 (New York: Atheneum, 1974), 212–13.

King's Christology reflected a combination of traditional Western christological concepts mixed with a heavy emphasis on the life and ministry of Jesus as understood in the black Christian experience.[17] Although his Christology clearly revealed his nurture within southern black Baptist Protestantism, King moved beyond particularistic notions of Christ's relevance to the black experience to embrace the universal implications of his person and message for the liberation and wholeness of all human beings. This is why the color of Jesus' skin did not become as important for King as it did for black theologians who followed him. King understood the white Christ symbol not as a depiction of reality but as a cultural definition.[18]

One important aspect of King's theology was his merging of the themes of liberation and reconciliation. As Paul R. Garber points out, these themes were inseparable or dynamically related for King, whose goal, in both theory and practice, was liberation as well as redemption and reconciliation:

> King was arguing that liberation and reconciliation are in fact bound up together, and that you cannot have one without the other. Liberation is never, in King's view, only *from* oppression; it is *for* community. This is the reason that love and nonviolence were essential to the quest for freedom. Violence might indeed achieve freedom *from* oppressors if there were some place to go away from them. But suppose you must live in the same house with your enemy after the battle is ended, as indeed you must in our world house. King understood nonviolence as the way of liberation not only *from* oppression but also *for* community. . . . Liberation was, for King, both the overcoming of

17. Temme, "Jesus as Trailblazer," 76.
18. King, "An Address at the Ministers' Leadership Training Program," 5. By refusing to confine Jesus Christ to a particular experience and by de-emphasizing his skin color, King stood solidly in the tradition of the slaves. See Lewis V. Baldwin, "'Deliverance to the Captives': Images of Jesus Christ in the Minds of Afro-American Slaves," *Journal of Religious Studies* 12, no. 2 (Fall 1986): 43.

oppression and the achieving of a new positive peace
between former enemies.[19]

King's theology embraced a Christian optimism and
hope that evolved out of his black cultural experience.
Because his theology was grounded in the conviction
that God will ultimately triumph over evil and sin, it can
be reasonably classified as a *theology of hope.* King understood how paradoxical notions of pessimism and optimism, of apathy and hope, of pain and affirmation had
always existed side by side in black art and thought. In
the many versions of his sermon, "A Knock at Midnight,"
he often mentioned how his slave ancestors combined
heartache and hope in their songs:

> Our slave foreparents taught us so much in their beau-
> tiful sorrow songs. . . . They looked at the midnight
> surrounding their days. They knew that there were
> sorrow and agony and hurt all around. When they
> thought about midnight they would sing:
>
> > Nobody knows the trouble I see,
> > Nobody knows but Jesus.
>
> But pretty soon something reminded them that morn-
> ing would come, and they would sing:
>
> > I'm so glad,
> > Trouble don't last always.[20]

Drawing on the insight of the black theologian Howard
Thurman, King continued with a probing remark about

19. Garber, "King Was a Black Theologian," 28–29. Garber aptly
refers to King's theology as "a community-oriented theology."
20. Martin Luther King, Jr., "The Meaning of Hope," a sermon delivered at the Dexter Avenue Baptist Church, Montgomery, Ala. (The King
Center Archives, 10 December 1967), 16–17; Martin Luther King, Jr., "A
Knock at Midnight," a sermon delivered at the All Saints Community
Church, Los Angeles, Cal. (The King Center Archives, 25 June 1967),
16–17; and Martin Luther King, Jr., "A Knock at Midnight," a record
album of a sermon delivered at Mt. Zion Baptist Church, Cincinnati,
Ohio, LP 3008-A (Nashville: Nashboro Record Company, c. 1967).

how the slaves captured the mood of tragedy and hope, of discontent and triumph, in the Prophet Jeremiah:

> Centuries ago Jeremiah, the great prophet, raised a very profound question. He looked at the inequities around and he noticed a lot of things. He noticed the good people so often suffering, and the evil people so often prospering. Jeremiah raised the question: "Is there no balm in Gilead? Is no physician there?" Centuries later our slave forefathers came along, and they too were confronted with the problems of life. They had nothing to look forward to morning after morning but the sizzling heat—the rawhide whip of the overseer—long rows of cotton. But they did an amazing thing. They looked back across the centuries, and they took Jeremiah's question mark and straightened it into an exclamation point. And they could sing:

> There is a balm in Gilead,
> To make the wounded whole.
> There is a balm in Gilead,
> To heal the sin-sick soul.

Then they came with another verse—

> Sometimes I feel discouraged,
> and feel my work's in vain.
> But then the Holy Spirit,
> Revives my soul again.[21]

King frequently ended this message with explanations of how his own faith, optimism, and vision arose out of a similar insight. His theology affirmed his people's capacity, as he put it, to "hope against hope."[22]

21. King, "The Meaning of Hope," 16–17; and King, "A Knock at Midnight," a record album. Interestingly enough, King never specifically mentioned Howard Thurman in his references to Jeremiah's question. Here again we can see how King borrowed from Thurman's idioms and insight. He apparently read many of Thurman's books. King took the references to Jeremiah and black slaves from Howard Thurman, *Deep River and the Negro Spiritual Speaks of Life and Death* (Richmond, In.: Friends United Press, 1975; originally published in 1945 and 1947), 59–60.

22. King, "The Meaning of Hope," 13–18; and Martin Luther King, Jr., *Where Do We Go from Here: Chaos or Community?* (Boston: Beacon ress, 1967), 113.

Much of King's theology can be gleaned from the songs he loved so dearly. He frequently quoted from slave spirituals like "Free at Last," "There is a Balm in Gilead," "Climbin' Jacob's Ladder," "Swing Low, Sweet Chariot," "Before I'll Be a Slave," "Bye and Bye, I'm Gonna Lay Down My Heavy Load," and "All God's Chillun' Got Wings"—songs that revealed a sense of freedom and a hope for liberation ultimately grounded in God. King's frequent references to black gospel songs—such as "How I Got Over," "Take My Hand, Precious Lord," and "Thank You Lord, You Brought Me from a Mighty, Mighty Long Way"—reflected his sense of his own human limitations as well as his faith in and desire for divine guidance. These and other black spirituals and gospel songs, which permeated King's sermons and speeches, affirmed such beliefs as the justice and providence of God, the goodness of creation, and the equality and uniqueness of humans. Indeed, they established King's rootedness in a folk theology, that had found full expression among generations of his ancestors.[23]

Though trained in philosophical theology, King was also a Christian ethicist who used the black experience as a point of departure for his reflections on morality and the ethical task. As a black ethicist, he focused much attention on the following questions: What is the correct analysis of the contemporary black condition and of the human situation as a whole? What is the goal of the civil rights movement? What are the best strategies and/or means for achieving human freedom, peace, and community? These questions led King to set forth an essentially black ethic—an ethic that embraced black liberation as a particular problem, and total human liberation as a

---

23. Scholars who have treated King as a theologian have failed to emphasize the rich, life-giving affirmations of the black oral tradition, particularly as expressed in black songs and tales, as a source of his theology. For examples, see Richardson, "Martin Luther King—Unsung Theologian," 178–84; Harris, "The Theology of Martin Luther King, Jr.," 1ff; Garber, "Martin Luther King, Jr.: Theologian and Precursor of Black Theology," 10–431; and Cone, "The Theology of Martin Luther King, Jr.," 21–39.

broader issue and concern. Although his ethic of liberation was decisively influenced by Boston Personalism, it
was his experiences and perspective as a black American that gave that ethic cogency and credibility.[24]

A proper understanding of King's ethic of liberation
must begin with his analysis of the racial situation in
America. He described racism and segregation as America's most pressing problems because they denied black
people access to public accommodations, decent housing, good education, voting rights, and other basic social
freedoms. "For King," writes Ervin Smith, "the immorality of segregation is that it restrains Blacks from
deliberating upon, deciding upon, and achieving these
basic social freedoms, thereby distorting their psychological and moral freedom as well."[25] King characterized racism and segregation as social evils caused by
human folly, ignorance, and an abuse of freedom, and
which denied the essential worth and dignity of human
personality, the unity of the universe, and the existence
of a moral order. He applied this same analysis to the
global problems of racism, poverty, and war—problems
that, in his view, were symptomatic of a deeper moral
and spiritual malady.[26]

This analysis of social or collective evil undergirded
King's quest for the ethical ideal of the beloved community. For him, the beloved community was the goal of the
civil rights movement and of the human struggle as a
whole. His oft-repeated phrase "I Have a Dream" best
symbolized his hunger for this ethical ideal. King insisted that humans, as creatures reflecting the divine
image, were morally obligated to work toward this ideal
through the practice of *agapaic* love and nonviolence. In

24. The influence of black sources on the development of King's
ethics is alluded to in Smith, *The Ethics of Martin Luther King, Jr.*, 1–10.
25. *Ibid.*, 84; and Otis Turner, "Toward an Ethic of Black Liberation
Based on the Philosophy of Martin Luther King, Jr., and Stokely
Carmichael's Concept of Black Power" (Ph.D. diss., Emory University,
Spring, 1974), 114–22.
26. Smith, *The Ethics of Martin Luther King, Jr.*, 84–85 and 158–59.

other words, he considered humans moral agents who, in partnership with God, held the key to the realization of God's kingdom on earth.[27]

King's greatest contribution as an ethicist was his application of the concepts of love, power, and justice to America's social problems. He saw love, particularly as expressed through nonviolence and unearned suffering, as the "moral ideal" and "the norm of ethical action."[28] Influenced by Paul Tillich's conclusions on the relationship between love, power, and justice, King insisted that "Power at its best is love implementing the demands of justice. Justice at its best is love correcting everything that stands against love."[29] He discovered the basis for community in that love that is expressed through justice and a sharing of power.

Also as an ethicist, King challenged America to live up to her moral principles and ideals. His contribution to ethics at this point has not been properly recognized and appreciated. King consistently declared that America could not truly be "the land of the free and the home of the brave" as long as her practices contradicted the noble human ideals embodied in her Constitution, her Declaration of Independence, and her Judeo-Christian faith. The power of this message moved white America toward a broader vision of human equality and of the rights of all persons to life, liberty, and the pursuit of happiness.[30] In a real sense, King's moral analysis of the society, coupled with his efforts to translate moral vision into practical reality, brought all Americans closer to the beloved community.

King's most obvious weakness as an ethicist was revealed in his conception and practice of nonviolence as an absolute moral principle. He largely ignored the fact that nonviolence, like every social ethic, is tainted with

27. Walter E. Fluker, *They Looked for a City: A Comparative Analysis of the Ideal of Community in the Thought of Howard Thurman and Martin Luther King, Jr.* (Lanham, Md.: University Press of America, 1989), 137–43.

28. Smith, *The Ethics of Martin Luther King, Jr.*, 61–62, and 90.

29. King, *Where Do We Go from Here?* 37; and Ansbro, *Martin Luther King, Jr.*, 8.

30. Smith, *The Ethics of Martin Luther King, Jr.*, 151 and 158–59.

sin.[31] This was clearly illustrated by the many persons who were hurt or killed during and after King's nonviolent campaigns. Furthermore, King failed to emphatically point out that his nonviolent demonstrations were politically potent and significant because they were staged against a background of widespread, institutionalized violence. He lived and functioned within, and benefited from, a social and political system that was based on force and that employed force to prohibit significant revolutionary change.[32] King's refusal to emphasize the inherent weaknesses of the nonviolent approach, at both the moral and practical levels, was not surprising, especially considering his persistent efforts to keep his people devoted to the idea of peaceful change.

King's roles as black theologian and ethicist ultimately involved a search for *truth*—that *truth* that allows one to break through illusions and human barriers to attain liberation and a grasp of the deeper meaning of life. Concerning King's innate passion for truth, Philip Lenud has remarked: "Martin was interested in anybody who had intellect, or who could *think*. He was always grasping for understanding and for a handle on ideas and truth."[33]

KING AND CONTEMPORARY BLACK THEOLOGIANS

The idea of black theology as an intellectual discipline began in the late 1960s when a small group of black

31. King did admit in his "Pilgrimage to Nonviolence" that "I see the pacifist position not as sinless but as the lesser evil in the circumstances. Therefore I do not claim to be free from the moral dilemmas that the Christian nonpacifist confronts." However, at other points in his writings and speeches he appears to prescribe an absolute stand on nonviolence—to view it as the only moral and practical approach to social evil. See James M. Washington, ed., *A Testament of Hope: The Essential Writings of Martin Luther King, Jr.* (San Francisco: Harper and Row, 1986), 39; and Martin Luther King, Jr., *Stride Toward Freedom: The Montgomery Story* (New York: Harper and Row, 1958), 212–22.

32. See Colin Morris, *Unyoung, Uncolored, Unpoor* (Nashville: Abingdon Press, 1959), 90–91.

33. A private interview with Dr. Philip Lenud, Nashville, Tenn., 7 April 1987.

clergy began to relate the Christian faith and Biblical revelation to the black liberation struggle.[34] Martin Luther King, Jr., inspired this development, and his writings and activities provided a point of departure for black theologians who followed him.[35] King's perspective on black theology is difficult to assess, especially because he died before the idea found expression in a major work. However, there is reason to believe that he would have had the same reservations about the term "black theology" that he had concerning the slogan "black power." Both phrases carried the implications of separatism, and were therefore inconsistent with King's philosophy as well as his desire to maintain white support for the movement. It is also conceivable that the radicalization of King in the period from 1965 to 1968 would have eventually led him to accept black theology as a unique and authentic black way of interpreting and responding to the Christian faith.[36]

Contemporary black theologians have discussed King extensively in their writings. James H. Cone, a pioneer in the black theology movement, has acknowledged the influence of King on his theological perspective. Cone describes King's life, message, and leadership in the civil rights movement as one of the major contexts of the origin of black theology.[37] King's greatest gift to black

34. James H. Cone, *For My People—Black Theology and the Black Church: Where Have We Been and Where Are We Going?* (Maryknoll, N.Y.: Orbis Books, 1984), 5.
35. Garber, "Black Theology: The Latter Day Legacy," 106–07.
36. King's father, Martin Luther King, Sr., never really supported the black theology movement. However, young Martin, who disagreed with his father on many points of theology, would have most likely embraced the concept. Ralph Abernathy declares that Martin Luther King, Jr., "would have been supportive of black theology, a theology that speaks to the needs of black people. He greatly inspired the black theology movement. Dr. Cone and all of the black theologians were inspired by Dr. King." A private interview with the Rev. Ralph D. Abernathy, Atlanta, Ga., 7 May 1987.
37. Cone, *For My People*, 6 and 31–32; James H. Cone, *Speaking the Truth: Ecumenism, Liberation, and Black Theology* (Grand Rapids, Mich.: William B. Eerdmans Publishing Company, 1986), 71 and 110; and Garber, "Black Theology: the Latter Day Legacy," 100, 105–07, and 112–13. Garber calls radical contemporary black theologians King's "strange disciples."

theology, according to Cone, was his insistence that the gospel of Jesus Christ was consistent with the political struggle of black people. "As a prophet, with a charisma never before witnessed in this century," Cone declares, "King preached black liberation in the light of Jesus Christ and thus aroused the spirit of freedom among black people."[38] "To justify his fight against injustice," Cone continues, "Martin Luther King, Jr., referred not only to the Exodus and Jesus Christ but especially to the prophets of the Old Testament."[39] In Cone's opinion, King's life and message demonstrated "that the 'soul' of the black community is inseparable from liberation, but always liberation grounded in Jesus Christ."[40]

Since the late 1960s, Cone has devoted considerable attention to King's place in the history of black struggle. King's leadership and the civil rights movement repre-sented for Cone a resurgence of the spirit of resistance that existed among pre–Civil War black preachers such as Richard Allen and Henry Highland Garnet:

> At least during its early stages this movement was a return to the spirit of the pre–Civil War black preach-ers with the emphasis being on freedom and equality in the present political structure. King saw clearly the meaning of the gospel with its social implications and sought to instill its true spirit in the hearts and minds of black and white in this land.[41]

Cone characterizes King as one of "the best examples in the black community of the creative role that religion can play in the transformation of society."[42] In his view,

---

38. Cone, *A Black Theology of Liberation*, 77–78; James H. Cone, *God of the Oppressed* (New York: The Seabury Press, 1975), 31 and 153–54; James H. Cone, "The Black Church and Marxism: What Do They Have to Say to Each Other" (an occasional paper from the Institute for Demo-cratic Socialism, April, 1980), 7; James H. Cone, *My Soul Looks Back* (Nashville: Abingdon Press, 1982), 133; Cone, *For My People*, 204; and Cone, *Speaking the Truth*, 15, 37, and 102.
39. Cone, *God of the Oppressed*, 154.
40. Cone, *A Black Theology of Liberation*, 78.
41. Cone, *Black Theology and Black Power*, 108–09. This point is also made by Garber, "King Was a Black Theologian," 18.
42. Cone, *For My People*, 204.

the creative potential of black religion was reflected in King's impact on the development of the black power movement. "He may not have endorsed the concept of Black Power," Cone observes, "but its existence is a result of his work. Black Power advocates are men who were inspired by his zeal for freedom, and Black Power is their attempt to make his dream a reality."[43]

Equally important for Cone was the challenge King put before white America, a challenge not unlike that presented by his slave forebears: "It was a black man, Martin Luther King, Jr., who challenged the conscience of this nation by his unselfish giving of his time and eventually his life for the poor blacks and whites of America."[44] King "proclaimed God's judgment against America," Cone declares, "and insisted that God would break the backbone of American power if this nation did not bring justice to the poor and peace to the world." Cone insists that King "was an integrationist and a Christian minister who, during most of his ministry, saw America as 'essentially a dream . . . as yet unfulfilled,' 'a dream of a land where [people] of all races, of all nationalities and of all creeds can live together as brothers [and sisters].'"[45] King's challenge to whites, as Cone states, centered on this idea of the American Dream and the urgent need to make that dream a concrete reality for every citizen.[46]

Cone has given special attention to what he considers key concepts in King's theology and ethics. He concludes that the basic content of King's thought hinges on the notion of *liberation*. Although he accepts King's idea of liberation and of Jesus as the liberator, Cone opposes the

43. Cone, *Black Theology and Black Power,* 109. Cone's suggestion that King rejected the concept of black power is not supported by the evidence. King at first rejected the slogan "black power" because of its "wrong connotations," but he embraced the concept. See King, *Where Do We Go from Here?* 30.

44. Cone, *Black Theology and Black Power,* 79.

45. James H. Cone, "Martin Luther King, Jr. and Malcolm X: Speaking the Truth about America," *Sojourners* 15, no. 1 (January 20, 1986): 27; and James H. Cone, "Black Theology in American Religion," *Theology Today* 43, no. 1 (April 1986): 14.

46. Cone, "Martin Luther King, Jr. and Malcolm X," 27–28.

civil rights leader's view that liberation from and reconciliation with white America must occur simultaneously. Cone insists that the demands of liberation must be met as a precondition for reconciliation. Genuine reconciliation for him will be attainable only after black people are liberated from white oppression and granted full equality in the society, a view that appears, at least on the surface, to be more logical than King's.[47] This is why Cone, in contrast to King, devotes very little attention to the reconciliation theme in his theology, particularly as it relates to black-white relations. Also unlike King, Cone holds that black people must be reconciled to themselves and each other before they can truly experience reconciliation with whites.[48]

Cone's de-emphasis on reconciliation between blacks and whites is also reflected in his critique of King's concept of the beloved community. While recognizing that the Christian understanding of God and humanity demands a quest for community, Cone nevertheless dismisses King's idea of a beloved community in America as naive and unrealistic:

> Regarding my views of M. L. King's concept of the "Beloved Community," I would say that I fully believe in the ideal but reject his optimism regarding its realization. While I think Martin's goal of the beloved community with love at its center is fully identical with the Christian idea of the Kingdom of God; yet I think that he failed to see that whites were not as open to the ideal as he apparently assumed, especially among liberal whites. It was Malcolm X who analyzed white people correctly and thus needs to be read alongside of Martin King.[49]

47. Cone, *A Black Theology of Liberation*, 77–78; Garber, "King Was a Black Theologian," 26–27; and Garber, "Black Theology: The Latter Day Legacy," 109–10. Some would argue that King's moral vision of reconciliation/community is more teleological than Cone's because King talked a great deal about how the oppressed should relate to the oppressor after the oppressed are liberated and empowered, a subject about which Cone says very little.

48. Cone, *Black Theology and Black Power*, 143–52.

49. A letter from James H. Cone to Lewis V. Baldwin, 23 June 1982.

King's powerful emphasis on love, forgiveness, and reconciliation as essential ingredients of the beloved community ideal has led Cone to classify him as an integrationist who stood over against the nationalist Malcolm X.[50] Such a classification seems to ignore how King, confronted with the powerlessness of his people in a complex and hypocritical society, was forced to combine both integrationist and nationalist perspectives in his quest for black liberation. The ambivalent nature of the racial situation in America drove him toward such a flexible liberation strategy. In fact, this union of integrationist and nationalist elements was inevitable for King, as it was for Malcolm, and it helps explain the tension he felt as a result of his efforts to embrace whites while, at the same time, stressing black unity and addressing the peculiar needs and interests of his people. This deep tension, this need to choose between two equally balanced, ever-present alternatives, prevented King from conforming to the rigid category of *integrationist* as described by Cone.[51]

50. Cone, "Martin Luther King, Jr. and Malcolm X," 27. Cone includes King in what he calls "The Black Integrationist Tradition"—a tradition that for him was exemplified in Frederick Douglass, the NAACP, and the National Urban League. See Cone, "The Theology of Martin Luther King, Jr.," 22.

51. James H. Cone, *Martin and Malcolm and America: A Dream or a Nightmare* (Maryknoll, N.Y.: Orbis Books, 1991), 1–17, 33, 247, 272, 287, 310. Cone's characterization of King as an "integrationist" who stood over against the "nationalist" Malcolm X is as much a rank oversimplification as James and Lois Horton's contention that King and Malcolm symbolized the sharp polarities of "class" and "race" in the black freedom struggle. See Lewis V. Baldwin, "A Letter to the Editor: Concerning Elements of Black Nationalism in the Thought of Martin Luther King, Jr. and Malcolm X," *The Vanderbilt Hustler,* Vanderbilt University (February 20, 1987): 16–17; Coretta Scott King, *My Life with Martin Luther King, Jr.* (New York: Avon Books, 1969), 260; and James O. Horton and Lois E. Horton, "Race and Class," *American Quarterly* 35, nos. 1 and 2 (Spring/Summer 1983): 156–68. Cone makes other mistakes in his analysis of King and Malcolm. He emphasizes King's love for European education and culture to the point of suggesting that the civil rights leader was at one time a complete assimilationist, thus failing to demonstrate properly that King's love for elements of European culture always existed side-by-side with his deep appreciation for African-American culture. Cone also errs in implying that King's and Malcolm's influences were primarily regional, with King being more influential in the South and Malcolm in the North. This view is misleading, and it comes close to

Cone's sharpest critique of King has been directed at the civil rights leader's commitment to and theological interpretation of nonviolence and unmerited suffering. He concludes that King's method of nonviolent protest, much like his "integrationist philosophy," was informed by his middle class background.[52] This claim is partly true. However, Cone's analysis is slightly marred by his failure to recognize the ways in which King transcended the middle class ethos and mentality. Cone's assessment of King's nonviolent absolutism is much more insightful and searching. In Cone's view, King, in an effort to uphold the morality and practicality of nonviolence and redemptive suffering, sidestepped and failed to examine objectively the question of violence. Cone asks: "Can we then, by any strength of the imagination or clever exegesis, interpret" Jesus' commandment "to turn the other cheek to mean a turning of the gun?"[53] He asserts that because black people are the constant victims of violence in a racist society, they should not analyze nonviolence and violence on the basis of the Western distinction between right and wrong. Unlike King, Cone declares that it is not so much a question of choosing between violence and nonviolence, but rather a question of embracing the method most likely to win black freedom:

> The Christian does not decide between violence and nonviolence, evil and good. He decides between the less and the greater evil. He must ponder whether

---

minimizing the national impact of both men. Moreover, Cone exaggerates the extent to which both men failed to address classism and erroneously suggests that King's sexism was such that he saw marriage as a male-dominated partnership instead of a shared relationship.

52. Garber, "Black Theology: The Latter Day Legacy," 106; and Fluker, *They Looked for a City,* 85.

53. Cone, *Black Theology and Black Power,* 139; Cone, *My Soul Looks Back,* 46 and 221; and Cone, *Speaking the Truth,* 76–77. Cone argues that King's "dependence on the analysis of love found in liberal theology and his confidence that 'the universe is on the side of justice' seem not to take seriously white violence in America." "I disagreed with his conceptual analysis of violence versus nonviolence," Cone continues, "because his distinctions between these terms did not appear to face head-on the historical and sociological complexities of human existence in a racist society." See Cone, *God of the Oppressed,* 221.

revolutionary violence is less or more deplorable than the violence perpetuated by the system. There are no absolute rules which can decide the answer with certainty. But he must make a choice. If he decides to take the "nonviolent" way, then he is saying that revolutionary violence is more detrimental to man in the long run than systemic violence. But if the system is evil, then revolutionary violence is both justified and necessary.[54]

Cone maintains that it was King's commitment to nonviolence, and not his efforts to liberate his people, that made him more acceptable to white America than radicals like Malcolm X, Rap Brown, and Stokely Carmichael:

One cannot help but think that most whites "loved" Martin Luther King, Jr., not because of his attempt to free his people, but because his approach was the least threatening to the white power structure. Thus, churchmen and theologians grasped at the opportunity to identify with him so that they could keep blacks powerless and simultaneously appease their own guilt about white oppression.[55]

The radicalization of King after the Selma campaign in 1965 is not sufficiently treated in Cone's writings. Only in a few places has he mentioned the King who moved beyond integration as a panacea, who criticized America for her violence and imperialism, who called for economic justice and an end to the Vietnam War, and who used radical labels like Marxism and Democratic Socialism to describe his idea of "the new economic structure."[56] Cone's de-emphasis on the "radical King" is

54. Cone, *Black Theology and Black Power*, 141 and 143.
55. *Ibid.*, 56 and 79; and Cone, *A Black Theology of Liberation*, 79. This suggestion is also made in Morris, *Unyoung, Uncolored, Unpoor*, 90–91.
56. One of Cone's strongest statements on the "radical King" appears in Cone, *Speaking the Truth*, 75–76 and 100–01. Cone largely corrects this pattern of omission in *Martin and Malcolm and America*, 253–71.

directly related to his need to preserve King's image as an "integrationist."

Significantly, Cone has been more perceptive than most black theologians in his treatment of the message of *hope* in King's theology. He identifies hope as a central theme in King's theology—that theme that linked the nonviolence activist to the theological tradition of the slaves and to contemporary black theology:

> King combined the exodus-liberation and cross-love themes with the message of hope found in the resurrection of Jesus. He derived hope not from the optimism of liberal protestant theology but from his belief in the righteousness of God as defined by his reading of the Bible through the eyes of his slave forerunners. The result was the most powerful expression in black history of the essential themes of black religious thought from the integrationist viewpoint.[57]

Since 1983, Cone has focused primarily on the black sources of King's theological perspective in his works. He insists that "the source for King's courage to face death, from Montgomery (1955) to Memphis (1968), was the faith and theology of the Black Church."[58] Cone attacks

57. Cone skillfully analyzes "King's emphasis on the eschatalogical hope of freedom," or his "hope in God's coming eschatalogical freedom." See Cone, *Speaking the Truth*, 102; James H. Cone, "Martin Luther King: The Source for His Courage to Face Death," *Concilium* (March, 1983): 77–79; and Cone, *A Black Theology of Liberation*, 264.

58. Cone made a fleeting reference to King's "black church heritage" in Cone, *God of the Oppressed*, 221–22. Since 1983, Cone has given considerably more attention to this subject in books and articles. See Cone, "Martin Luther King: The Source," 74–79; Cone, "The Theology of Martin Luther King, Jr.," 21–39; Cone, *Speaking the Truth*, 99–100; James H. Cone, "A Review of John J. Ansbro's *Martin Luther King, Jr.: The Making of a Mind (1982)*," *Fellowship* 50, no. 1 (January/February 1984): 32– 33; James H. Cone, "Martin Luther King, Jr., Black Theology-Black Church," *Theology Today* XL, no. 4 (January 1984), 409–20; James H. Cone, "Martin Luther King, Jr.: The Black Church and Black Theology," *The Western Journal of Black Studies* 8, no. 2 (Summer 1984): 92–98; James H. Cone, "Martin Luther King, Jr., Black Theology and the Black Church," *The Drew Gateway* 56, no. 2 (Winter 1985): 1–16; Cone, "Black Theology in American Religion," 11–17; James H. Cone, "Martin Luther King, Jr., Black Theology, and the Black Church," *The A.M.E. Zion Quarterly Review* 97, no. 2 (July 1986): 2– 17; and Cone, *For My People*, 6–7. John J. Ansbro, a white King scholar, has responded to Cone's critical review of

major white theologians and ethicists for ignoring King's roots in what he calls "the black church tradition"—that tradition from which King's "faith was derived and to which he returned for strength and courage in the context of crisis during his ministry."[59] According to Cone, Protestant Liberalism and the dissenting traditions of Mohandas K. Gandhi and Henry David Thoreau were also important sources of King's theology, but they were not as significant as "The Black Integrationist Tradition" and "The Faith of the Black Church."[60]

Cone boldly claims that King stands as perhaps the most important theologian in American history. While recognizing the significant contributions of Jonathan Edwards, Walter Rauschenbusch, and others to American theology, Cone asserts nevertheless that:

> No thinker has made a greater impact upon black religious thought or even upon American society and religion as a whole than Martin Luther King, Jr. The fact that many white theologians can write about American religion and theology with no reference to him reveals both the persistence of racism in the academy and the tendency to limit theology narrowly to the academic discourse of seminary and university professors.[61]

Cone's assessment of King's unique importance as an American theologian is based on three criteria. First, King skillfully interpreted the meaning of the gospel for the present time and related it in a profound way to the plight of the poor and oppressed. If this is the purpose of theology as "a disciplined endeavor," writes Cone, "then I would claim that no one has articulated the Christian message of freedom more effectively, prophetically, and

---

his book. See John J. Ansbro, "An Author Responds," *Fellowship* 50, no. 3 (March 1984): 21.

59. Cone, "A Review of John J. Ansbro's *Martin Luther King, Jr. (1982),*" 33.

60. Cone, "The Theology of Martin Luther King, Jr.," 22–28.

61. *Ibid.*, 35–36; and Cone, "Black Theology in American Religion," 11. Cone suggests that the making of King's birthday a national holiday is symbolic of his unique importance as an American theologian.

creatively in America than Martin Luther King, Jr."[62] Second, Cone notes that King's "theological perspective achieved its creativity by engaging uniquely American issues." In other words, King, unlike so many American theologians, did not "look toward Europe in order to identify theological problems which require disciplined reflection." Consequently, King "was truly an *American* theologian and not simply a theologian who happened to live in the United States."[63] Finally, Cone declares that King, in contrast to most white theologians, "did not limit his theological reflections to the problems of one group," nor did he practice theology as if his definition of it was universal and final. "While he began with a focus on the racial oppression of blacks," says Cone of King, "his theological vision was universal":

> He was as concerned about the liberation of whites from their *oppression as oppressors* as he was in eliminating the racial oppression of blacks. He was as concerned about the life-chances of brown children in Vietnam as he was about black children in America's cities. King's vision was truly international, embracing all humanity. That is why his name is invoked by the oppressed around the world who are fighting for freedom.[64]

King's image as a theologian is treated in a similar manner in the writings of Gayraud S. Wilmore, who has been recognized as both a black theologian and ethicist. Wilmore describes King as "an essentially liberal theologian" who "summoned the resources of theological liberalism to undergird the successful nonviolent campaign that he waged in the name of the dignity of the human personality and the power of love."[65] In Wilmore's opinion, King's liberal thought and activism were problematic in the sense that they did not lead him to embrace

62. Cone, "The Theology of Martin Luther King, Jr.," 35.
63. *Ibid.*
64. *Ibid.*, 36.
65. See Choan Seng-Song and Gayraud S. Wilmore, *Asians and Blacks* (Bangkok, Thailand: East Asian Christian Conference, 1972), 69.

the new black theology that was beginning to sprout toward the end of his life. King studiously avoided
Wilmore, Albert B. Cleage, Jr., and other emerging black
theologians, mainly because of their close collaboration
with the young militants of the black power movement.[66]
Although King "never sought to draw the Southern
Christian Leadership Conference into the Black Theology movement," Wilmore observes, "many of his close
associates did, including Ralph Abernathy, Bernard Lee,
Wyatt T. Walker, Andrew Young, and Hosea Williams."[67]

Like James Cone, Wilmore locates the significance of
King's thought for black theology and ethics in three areas. First, King represented a tradition of protest and
social action for liberation that characterized the black
church in America during slavery—a tradition forged by
Denmark Vesey, Harriet Tubman, Martin Delany, and
others. Concerning King's tie with that tradition,
Wilmore comments:

> From Denmark Vesey's insurrection in 1822 to Martin
> Luther King's civil rights movement in 1955, black
> people have used their churches in politics, economic
> boycotts, marches, and in both violent and nonviolent
> direct action to fight for freedom, not only for them-
> selves, but for all oppressed people.[68]

Second, Wilmore credits King with "reawakening
militancy and discontent in the black church"—

66. Gayraud S. Wilmore, "Our Heritage and Our Hope," (Unpublished paper, 1977), 1.

67. Gayraud S. Wilmore and James H. Cone, eds., *Black Theology: A
Documentary History, 1966–1979* (Maryknoll, N.Y.: Orbis Books, 1979),
11 n. 1. Interestingly enough, King's name did not appear among the
notable black clergymen who signed the "Black Power Statement" of
the National Committee of Negro Churchmen in July, 1966. See C. Eric
Lincoln, *The Black Church Since Frazier* (New York: Schocken Books,
Inc., 1974), 168–78.

68. Gayraud S. Wilmore, "The Gifts and Tasks of the Black Church"
(Unpublished paper, n.d.), 4 and 12; Gayraud S. Wilmore, *Black Religion
and Black Radicalism: An Examination of the Black Experience in Religion* (New York: Doubleday and Company, 1973), 70–71; and Seng-Song
and Wilmore, *Asians and Blacks*, 64, 67–68, and 70–71.

characteristics that "the older leadership of the black church during the 1940s and 50s had tacitly repudiated."[69] According to Wilmore, "The black church, by 1950, was in a defensive, accommodating mood and young black people were abandoning it by the thousands."[70] A reversal of this trend occurred in the mid-1950s when King "gave new vitality and relevance to black Christianity in the United States" through his "Christian witness," his "creative religious extremism," and his "quasi-religious movement":

> King's contribution to the black revolution gave the lie to the allegation that black preachers were nothing but Uncle Toms and that Christianity was hopelessly out of tune with the times. Despite the fact that he was never able to muster the full power of the churches and received only token support from many of the most prestigious ministers, King nevertheless projected a new image of the church upon the nation and a new awareness of the radical possibilities inherent in black religion.[71]

Wilmore, however, like other black theologians, fails to emphasize properly how King rediscovered in a powerful way his slave forebears' image of the black church as *the Old Israel*—as that institution called and commissioned to be a comforting, transforming, redemptive, and liberating force for blacks as well as others. More attention to this image would have strengthened Wilmore's claim that the black church provides rich and vital resources

69. Seng-Song and Wilmore, *Asians and Blacks*, 68 and 71; Gayraud S. Wilmore, *Black and Presbyterian: The Heritage and the Hope* (Philadelphia: The Geneva Press, 1983), 45; and Gayraud S. Wilmore, *Last Things First* (Philadelphia: The Westminster Press, 1982), 63–64 and 89–90.
70. Seng-Song and Wilmore, *Asians and Blacks*, 71.
71. Gayraud S. Wilmore, *The Secular Relevance of the Church* (Philadelphia: The Westminster Press, 1962), 28–29; Gayraud S. Wilmore, *Black Religion and Black Radicalism: An Interpretation of the Religious History of Afro-American People* (Maryknoll, N.Y.: Orbis Books, 1983), 174; Wilmore, "The Gifts and Tasks of the Black Church," 3; and Gayraud S. Wilmore, "The New Challenge of Black Religion to American Christianity" (Unpublished paper, 1976), 10.

for ecclesial reflection, and for reshaping and revitalizing visions of the Christian church as a whole.[72]

Finally, Wilmore suggests that King's significance for black theology was evident in the way he affected Western theological and ethical perspectives. He explains how King "permitted the seeds of nonconformity in American black religion to germinate and blossom forth as something new in the garden of Western Christian theologies and ethics," thereby challenging theologians and ethicists across the world with a new sense of the universal implications of the Biblical revelation and the Christian faith.[73]

Wilmore essentially agrees with James Cone's insistence on *liberation* as the central theme in King's theology and ethics. He describes King's vision as "an eschatological vision of the Kingdom of God as liberation from sin, slavery, and second-class citizenship," and "as freedom from bigotry, hatred, and the alienation of people from one another in the land of their birth and common destiny."[74] Wilmore views liberation and reconciliation as inseparable in King's theology, but he seems at odds with King's idea that black liberation and reconciliation with whites must occur simultaneously. Like Cone, Wilmore insists that black Americans' "first task is to be reconciled to ourselves, to black people everywhere," as a precondition for liberation and ultimately for reconciliation with whites:

> The black church, gifted with love, should lead the way toward reconciliation and solidarity among black people everywhere—for everywhere we have been victimized by the "divide and conquer" strategy of

72. See Wilmore, "The Gifts and Tasks of the Black Church," 1ff.; and Gayraud S. Wilmore's foreword in Lewis V. Baldwin, *The Mark of a Man: Peter Spencer and the African Union Methodist Tradition* (Lanham, Md.: University Press of America, 1987), xiii–xv.

73. Seng-Song and Wilmore, *Asians and Blacks*, 64.

74. Wilmore, *Last Things First*, 89; and Gayraud S. Wilmore, "The Black Church in Search of a New Theology," in *Will the Church Lose the City*, ed. Kendig Brubaker Cully and F. Nile Harper (New York and Cleveland: The World Publishing Company, 1969), 130.

our oppressors. But because the gift of love has been given to the black church by Christ himself, the task of reconciliation and cooperation must take us beyond our own people, beyond our own communities, to the white people and churches and communities from which we have been alienated for so long.[75]

Wilmore identifies love, nonviolence, forgiveness, reconciliation, and integration as vital elements in King's theology of community and in his beloved community ideal. Here again he is in essential agreement with Cone. Both Wilmore and Cone seem to believe that King's devotion to the fulfillment of the communitarian ideal, and specifically to integration and the assimilationist position, accounted for his initial reluctance to concede that power, and especially black power, was the critical issue.[76] However, Wilmore goes further than Cone in asserting how King eventually recognized "that racial integration, for its own sake, was an inadequate goal for the black people of America":

> As the cry for Black Power began to rise up all around him in the ghettoes of the great cities of the North and West, King began to sense that black pride, solidarity and self-determination were the necessary conditions for racial justice and that the old, one-sided emphasis upon integration would neither satisfy the people nor achieve that manhood which Malcolm X and the Black Nationalist movement was all about.[77]

For Wilmore, as for Cone, *hope* was a significant component of King's theology of liberation. Both theologians have noted how Christian hope found supreme expression in the eschatology of King's "I Have a Dream" speech—a speech that "envisioned a new society in which black and white would walk hand in hand." Moreover, both Wilmore and Cone are mindful of how the Christian hope theme relates to King's black messianism.

75. Wilmore, "The Gifts and Tasks of the Black Church," 12–13.
76. Wilmore and Cone, eds., *Black Theology*, 17.
77. Seng-Song and Wilmore, *Asians and Blacks*, 74.

King was convinced, they argue, that God had called black Americans to redeem this country through their suffering love and their spirit of brotherhood. Wilmore regards King as one who, "as high priest of the civil rights movement," not only comforted his people in the midst of tragedy and struggle but also directed their Christian hope and their sense of messianic vocation toward the promise and the ultimate realization of a new order and a new humanity:

> King represented the historic tradition of black Christianity at its best—the faith of another eschatalogical people who had come to these shores in chains, but who had not given up hope, a people for whom the promises of "a new heaven and a new earth" were to be taken as both spiritual and material possibilities in the present. For this tradition to say that "Jesus is coming" was to make an eschatological statement that was both religious and secular, and it was within the competence of believers to experience both the spirit and the substance of this eschatology in the world in which they lived.[78]

Wilmore preceded Cone and other contemporary black theologians in emphasizing the black cultural roots of King's theological perspective. Wilmore contends that the power of King's civil rights campaigns resulted from his ability to combine dexterously the theological substance and the activist ethic of black folk religion with the sophistication of philosophical and theological liberalism.[79] He suggests that King's roots in "the black puritanism of Atlanta's Negro middle class" made it possible for him to forge such a creative synthesis:

> His middle class Negro background . . . led him to bring together the black folk religion of his Baptist forebears and the Social Gospel of the white middle

---

78. Wilmore, "The New Challenge of Black Religion to American Christianity," 11; Wilmore, "The Gifts and Tasks of the Black Church," 1; and Cone, "The Theology of Martin Luther King, Jr.," 26.; Wilmore, "The Black Church in Search of a New Theology," 130; and Wilmore, *Last Things First*, 90.
79. Seng-Song and Wilmore, *Asians and Blacks*, 64, 68–70, and 74.

class theologians of Europe and America. He added to this synthesis the philosophy of Gandhi and the social strategy of the Fellowship of Reconciliation. But it was precisely the middle class liberalism of King which made it impossible for him to assimilate and champion another more strident, but equally important motif of black folk religion—the motif of black survival and separatism as represented in the anti-Christian radicalism of the man known as Malcolm X.[80]

Wilmore was also the first theologian to emphasize the importance of the combined legacies of King and Malcolm X for contemporary black theology. As far back as 1972, Wilmore declared that "one cannot fully understand the contemporary black revolution in the United States and its religious foundations without grasping the complementary functions of independence and interdependence between Martin and Malcolm," a point also made by James Cone a decade later.[81] Wilmore explains how King and Malcolm represented "two dialectical themes in black religion in America which historically were never completely disjoined—liberation and survival, integration and separatism, white neo-orthodoxy and black heterodoxy"—themes that have determined the basic outlines of black theological discourse since the late 1960s.[82] Concerning the dialectic of social action that bound King and Malcolm together, Wilmore remarks:

> Little has been written about how they actually reacted to one another in private, or whether they were really conscious of their reciprocal roles, but it seems incontrovertible that their contributions cannot be evaluated separately. These two young men, both of whom were struck down by assassins' bullets, approached the

80. *Ibid.*, 64 and 68.

81. *Ibid.*, 64–65 and 71–75; Wilmore, *Black Religion and Black Radicalism* (1973 edition), 260; and "James Cone Interview: Liberation, Black Theology, and the Church," *Radix Magazine* (September/October 1982), 9–11.

82. Seng-Song and Wilmore, *Asians and Blacks*, 65 and 71–74. Wilmore's treatment of the Martin-Malcolm dialectic and how it had an impact on the black revolution and contemporary black theology, a treatment that appeared in *Asians and Blacks* in 1972, was brilliant and perceptive for that time.

vocation of black liberation from two profoundly politico-religious perspectives which had been growing silently, side by side, in the fecund soil of the black folk tradition. They shared the nourishment of that religious tradition together and received tremendous moral and spiritual power by calling forth from each other, perhaps unconsciously, the single, full-orbed interpretation of black reality which caught and held in tension the antimonies of the centuries-old yearning for black manhood and liberation.[83]

James Cone's current efforts to demonstrate how the faiths and contributions of King and Malcolm coalesced to affect Black theology and political radicalism bear the marks of Wilmore's influence. Both theologians have much to tell us about how King and Malcolm took black America beyond the boundaries of *liberation thought* to *liberation praxis*.[84]

The appraisal of King's thought, methods, and significance for black liberation by Albert B. Cleage is by far the harshest leveled by a contemporary black theologian. As the National Chairman of the Pan African Orthodox Christian Church (also called the Black Christian Nationalist Church), Cleage (now Jaramogi Abebe Agyeman) has developed a theology and a strategy for black liberation similar to Malcolm's and radically different from King's. Theologically speaking, Cleage and King agree only on the contention that the liberation of the poor and oppressed is consistent with the promises of God, with the spirit and teachings of Jesus Christ, and with the demands of the Christian faith.[85] The sharp

83. Seng-Song and Wilmore, *Asians and Blacks*, 73–74. Wilmore speaks of the "DeChristianization of the radical movement King initiated" toward the end of the 1960s, a development influenced by Malcolm X and the black power movement. See Wilmore, *Black Religion and Black Radicalism* (1983 edition), 183.

84. Seng-Song and Wilmore, *Asians and Blacks*, 65 and 71–74; "James Cone Interview," 9–11; Cone, "Martin Luther King, Jr. and Malcolm X," 26–30; and James H. Cone, *Martin and Malcolm and America*, 1–355.

85. *The Articles of Association, Constitution and By-Laws of the Pan-African Orthodox Christian Church*, adopted by the Pan-African Synod, Houston, Texas (July 3, 1978), 1–25; "A Tribute to the Founder," in *The*

differences between Cleage's and King's theologies of liberation are highlighted when one considers dialectical themes such as black self-love and universal agapaic love, separatism and integration, and counterviolence and nonviolence.[86]

Influenced strongly by Malcolm X, Cleage emphasizes the importance of black self-love and repudiates King's notion of a universal agapaic love that embraces white people. In this sense, his view of the practical aspect of the love ethic is close to that of James Cone. Cleage believes that "to love your oppressor and seek to persuade him to love you is certainly the acceptance of inferiority."[87] King's idea of an unselfish, universal, redemptive love strikes Cleage as another form of the old slave theology:

> Try to love everybody and you will probably be beaten to death before the week is over. We must cleanse our minds of this old slave theology. If we are engaged in a struggle for survival we must recognize the nature of that struggle. We must not say a word without realizing that struggle means confrontation and conflict. It means that we pit ourselves against others.[88]

Cleage is convinced that his concept of black self-love is supported by Scripture and tradition. Jesus was the Black Messiah, he argues, who confined his love to the Black Israelite Nation, and who led his people against

Shrines of the Black Madonna of the Pan-African Orthodox Christian Church: 25 Years of Christian Service (October 29, 1978), 2–11; and Garber, "Black Theology: The Latter Day Legacy," 109. Paul Garber concludes that William R. Jones' attack on King is "perhaps the harshest that has been leveled by a black theologian. . . ." I reject this conclusion on two grounds. First, Jones is a philosopher of religion, not a theologian in the precise sense of that discipline. Second, Jones' perspective on King is not as harsh as that of Albert Cleage. See Garber, "Martin Luther King, Jr.: Theologian and Precursor of Black Theology," 407.

86. William W. Morris, "Strategies for Liberation: A Critical Comparison of Martin Luther King, Jr. and Albert B. Cleage, Jr." (D.Min. diss., Vanderbilt University, June, 1973), 106–41.

87. Albert B. Cleage, Jr., *Black Christian Nationalism: New Directions for the Black Church* (New York: William Morrow and Company, Inc., 1972), 150.

88. *Ibid.*, 139.

white Roman domination.[89] Instead of teaching his people to love their white oppressors, Cleage explains, Jesus
sought to turn them against the individualism and the
identification with whiteness that had corrupted them.[90]
This perspective contrasts sharply with King's Christology, and it shows that Cleage's and King's theologies were
based on entirely different hermeneutical principles.

The doctrine of humanity is at the center of Cleage's
rejection of King's integrationism. Both men have affirmed the idea of humans made in the image of God, but
the reality and depth of white racism and oppression
prevent Cleage from embracing King's notion that blacks
and whites are brothers and sisters, and are therefore
involved in a single process and a common destiny.[91]
King's stress on integration between blacks and whites
is, for Cleage, an affirmation of black inferiority and self-
hatred—indeed, another example of slave theology. "To
seek integration with someone who hates and despises
you and has declared you to be inferior is certainly some
strange kind of group insanity," Cleage asserts. "We cannot engage realistically in a Black Liberation Struggle
thinking that Black liberation means integration."[92]
Cleage claims, rather excessively, that "Dr. King's struggle was not against this white definition of Black inferiority, but rather an attempt to persuade the white man to
accept us, to let us into his world."[93]

It is obvious, then, that Cleage does not subscribe to
King's concept of the inseparability of liberation and
reconciliation. For Cleage, reconciliation between
blacks and whites is impossible and therefore has no
relationship to black liberation. To the contrary, liberation involves blacks being reconciled to themselves, to

89. Albert B. Cleage, Jr., *The Black Messiah* (New York: Sheed and
Ward, Inc., 1969), 3–4; and *Program of the B.C.N. National Convention*,
Atlanta, Ga. (April 1–6, 1975), 11 ff.
90. Cleage, *The Black Messiah*, 3.
91. Morris, "Strategies for Liberation," 112–13.
92. Cleage, *Black Christian Nationalism*, 150–51.
93. *Ibid.*, 224.

each other, and to the Black God and the Black Christ.[94]
Cleage has moved beyond a mere theological analysis of
this concept to materialize it through his all-black
Shrines of the Black Madonna, which currently exist in
cities like Detroit, Chicago, Atlanta, and Houston.[95]
These Shrines have been established on the premise that
black separatism and institution building must become
the fundamental thrust for the future if blacks are to
preserve their African heritage and achieve power and
self-determination. Unlike King, Cleage does not envision black power and black destiny intersecting with
white power and white destiny.[96]

Cleage shares James Cone's view that King did not analyze intelligently and objectively the dialectic between violence and nonviolence. Both men believe that violence is
inherent to the oppressive system, a situation that ren-
ders unwise any tendency toward nonviolent absolutism
on the part of black people. Cleage writes disparagingly
of "the absurd nonviolent and redemptive-love tactics
that Dr. King used," and he insists that "If Dr. King's
death proved anything beyond the shadow of a doubt, it
proved that nonviolence will never work in a violent
white racist society."[97] In a manner similar to Cone and
Malcolm X, Cleage advocates freedom by any means necessary, and stresses black counterviolence as an alternative to King's nonviolent absolutism.

Cleage appears opposed to the idea, held by Cone and
other contemporary black theologians, that King was
authentically a *black* theologian of liberation—one who
proclaimed liberation in the light of Jesus Christ.
In Cleage's opinion, King was essentially a modern

94. *Ibid.*, chapters 1–3 and 11–14; and Cleage, *The Black Messiah*, 3–9 and 48–59.
95. Cleage, *Black Christian Nationalism*, 173–248; Cleage, *The Black Messiah*, 48–59; and *The Shrines of the Black Madonna*, 2–11.
96. Morris, "Strategies for Liberation," 109; Cleage, *The Black Messiah*, 85–99; and Cleage, *Black Christian Nationalism*, 11–14 and 44–66.
97. Cleage, *Black Christian Nationalism*, 26; and Cleage, *The Black Messiah*, 202.

advocate and purveyor of the old-fashioned slave theology.[98] Cleage's black nationalist theology, undergirded by an unorthodox interpretation of the Bible and the Christian faith, has made it impossible for him to fully discern the radical implications of King's theology and activism. Furthermore, Cleage fails to see King's connection with the revolutionary faith of pre–Civil War blacks. Even so, Cleage has expressed appreciation for how King's leadership and confrontations with white society enlightened black America and moved it closer to liberation. The confrontations King "created enabled us to see white people as they really are," Cleage declares. "A whole new black world has come into being, a Black Nation now exists," he continues. "And Dr. King had a large part in helping to shape it."[99] Cleage's point is well taken, but he remains one major black theologian who refuses to acknowledge the full meaning and significance of King's legacy for black theology, for the black liberation struggle, and for the movements of the poor and oppressed worldwide.

A similar critique can be made regarding the black theologian Joseph R. Washington, Jr. Writing at a time when King was still active and at the height of his popularity, Washington failed to grasp the theological underpinnings of King's nonviolent crusade and its full implications for human liberation. Washington concluded that the religion of the nonviolent mass movement led by King was not the Christian faith. "It is no surprise to find," he wrote, "that the protests of Denmark Vesey, Nat Turner, Adam Clayton Powell, Jr., and Martin Luther King, Jr., were rooted outside the teachings of American Protestantism."[100] Washington applied this analysis specifically to the Montgomery Bus Boycott, which in his view was motivated not by Christian love but by King's and King's followers' "will to dignity

98. Cleage, *Black Christian Nationalism*, 141, 150–51, and 224–25.
99. Cleage, *The Black Messiah*, 211; and Garber, "King Was a Black Theologian," 18–19.
100. Joseph R. Washington, Jr., *Black Religion: The Negro and Christianity in the United States* (Boston: Beacon Press, 1964), 240.

and justice."[101] For Washington, the nonviolence practiced in Montgomery and other southern towns under King's leadership was "a powerful technique," but it was "independent of Christian love." These claims stemmed primarily from Washington's inability to see King as a Christian theologian and to understand black religion as an authentic "Christian faith."[102]

Washington posited that King, "in his espousal of passive resistance" in Montgomery, "was thinking basically as a philosopher and not as a theologian." He referred to "the fuzziness of" King's "blend of philosophy with theology," and noted that "as a Baptist, King is not disciplined by a theology or a community of faith and thus is free to interpret the Bible as he feels led."[103] Washington believed that King's failure to bring a Christian theological dimension to his movement was clearly evident in the way he embraced and interpreted love and nonviolence. "King did not come to love or to Jesus through the eyes of the Christian faith," Washington declared. "King has come to understand love through the syncretistical religion of Gandhi." Washington accused King of naively attempting to blend two "apparent irreconcilables"—love as "passive" or "weak" and nonviolence as "resistance":

> But the reason they are irreconcilable is not apparent to King. Love and the strategy of nonviolence are two different forces. One is not more weak or passive than the other. They are both to be distinguished from sentiment and affection. They may both be best described as "passionate resistance," not "passive resistance." Love is the greater of the two, for love is not afraid of either physical or spiritual violence and, indeed, may use them creatively for its good end. But nonviolence fears violence; indeed, it is not nonviolence in violence, while love is love even in violence. Love and nonviolence may work together but they cannot be fused. The root of love is God, interpreted through

101. *Ibid.*, 11–12, 22, and 240.
102. *Ibid.*, 8–9 and 17.
103. *Ibid.*, 5–6 and 10.

theology. The root of nonviolence is in philosophy and it need not rely upon God.[104]

Washington's insistence on a dichotomy between love and nonviolence proves that he and King did not move from the same theological and ethical premises. King characterized both love and nonviolence as "active" rather than "passive" or "sentimental," and insisted that love found expression through nonviolent direct action. Moreover, King saw both love and nonviolence as rooted in God and supported by the life and teachings of Jesus Christ. Washington's refusal to understand this and to grasp the essential connection between love, power, and justice for King, led him to assert that

> insofar as the Martin Luther King, Jr. nonviolent technique dominates through calling men to bleed in social action for the purposes of a hamburger and calling them back from bloodshed in social intercourse, it is guided by faithlessness in God and distortion of the "suffering servant" mission.[105]

Washington's perspective on King after 1965 has appeared in works written since the death of the civil rights leader. In such works, he has devoted attention to King's method of nonviolence, to his perception of and relationship to black power, and to his connection with the contemporary black theology movement. Washington has been very critical of King's nonviolent ethic. He questions the civil rights activist's notion that the history of black slave rebellions proves the futility and impracticality of violence as a social ethic:

> The difficulty with Dr. King's thinking here is that he fails to make the important distinction between rebellion and revolution. The failures of Gabriel, Nat Turner, and Denmark Vesey lead Dr. King to hold that "violent rebellion is doomed from the start." He overlooks the fact that these were rebellions of slaves who

104. *Ibid.*, 8–9 and 11.
105. Joseph R. Washington, Jr., *The Politics of God: The Future of the Black Churches* (Boston: Beacon Press, 1967), 162.

had not gained support from the masses of their brethren. These insurrections were without real planning, organization, firepower, and strategic location. Such is not the case in total today; where it is in part, it need not be so in the future. The point is that although blacks are outnumbered ten to one, the ratio is less important in the consideration of a revolution than in a rebellion. A rebellion is an uprising for limited objectives. The revolution Black Power intends as violence is to bring the nation as a whole to a halt and turn it around.[106]

There is in Washington the same rejection of the spirit and efficacy of King's nonviolence that one finds in black theologians like James Cone and Albert Cleage. Washington rejects King's assertion that nonviolence, unlike violence, appeals to the conscience of the oppressor, thereby initiating the transforming process that leads to reconciliation and community. Of King, Washington states:

> He claims that violence is unable to appeal to conscience. Nonviolence alone can do so. Violence demands hatred because it presupposes an enemy to be destroyed. In the first place, the lesson should have been learned long ago that an appeal to the conscience of whites in the majority is unadulterated nonsense. Even if their consciences are twinged through nonviolence, no fundamental change is produced for the black masses. If an appeal to conscience means this, it is as foolish as trying to get by in this world by looking to the next one. But there can be no doubt that violence appeals to the consciences of those who engage in it. It unites consciences around a single goal. It not only appeals to consciences as the history of all wars attests, but violence creates the consciousness so necessary for a meaningful conscience. The enemy may not love the violent aggressor who is right in his demand for justice, but one thing is sure—he respects him. The nonviolent man is not respected; he is tolerated because he is manipulatable. More than that, violence

106. Joseph R. Washington, Jr., *Black and White Power Subreption* (Boston: Beacon Press, 1969), 199.

which is not rioting or revengeful can create community and brotherhood because it alone forces the oppressor to stop oppressing and join the once oppressed
in building a mutually healthy new society. Of course,
violence is chaotic, disruptive, contentious conflict.
But conflict, as Dr. King has taught, is the condition
for creativeness. The question is not one of violence or
nonviolence as Dr. King suggests. Rather, it is one
merely of quality.[107]

Washington attacks King for his failure to see that nonviolent resistance only becomes politically potent and significant in the face of widespread violence. According to
Washington, King's faith in nonviolence was not shared
by the young black power radicals, many of whom had
marched with the civil rights leader.[108] Furthermore,
King's campaign in Chicago in 1966, says Washington,
demonstrated "the non-adaptability of the nonviolent
technique to the urban, dynamic North." "Were there real
leadership his nonviolent approach would be seen as irrelevant in the North," Washington observes, "as in the
South, to the basic political power needs." Washington
believes that King avoided this problem late in his career
by shifting his direction from the northern ghettoes "to
demands for peace in Vietnam."[109]

Washington joins James Cone in viewing black power
as largely the product of King's work. Washington sees
King as one who, despite his critique of black power,
shared the objectives of black power advocates. "That is
why Dr. King worked so well with Black Power advocates
and they with him," Washington notes. Like Gayraud
Wilmore, Washington contends that King was irresistibly
drawn toward black power toward the end of his life, a
development essential to any estimation of his role in the
radicalization of black religion and theology.[110]

107. *Ibid.*, 202.
108. *Ibid.*, 199 and 202–03.
109. Washington, *The Politics of God*, 160–61 and 204.
110. Washington, *Black and White Power Subreption*, 203; and Seng-
Song and Wilmore, *Asians and Blacks*, 65.

Significantly, Washington is one of the few black theologians who have seriously considered King in relationship to *place* in a southern context. He describes King as "a remarkable product of the South; barely tainted by his academic exposure in the North."[111] Washington believes that the environment of the South profoundly shaped King's style and witness as a preacher. However, he largely ignores how King's vision transcended both the southern and national contexts to assume international implications. For Washington, King remained essentially a southern black preacher who helped raise to new heights the historical role of the black minister as the leader in civil rights.[112]

King's legacy for the contemporary black theology movement receives very little attention in Washington's writings. However, Washington is as mindful as Cone and Wilmore of how King's thought and activism inspired that new generation of black church activists and scholars who now loom large in the circles of black theology. Washington notes that "What black theologians have done to this point is call for rapid social change, by which they mean revolution. In this regard, they continue to be Martin Luther King's children."[113]

J. Deotis Roberts and Major J. Jones are considered moderate black theologians who are closer to King theologically and ethically than Washington, Cleage, Wilmore, and Cone.[114] James Cone describes Roberts and Jones as "major interpreters of black theology" who bridged "the gap between the Martin King era and the rise of black power in religion and in the churches."[115] Although they represent essentially one school of thought on King, Roberts' and Jones' differences in approach and emphases are such that their perspectives on King should be explored separately.

111. Washington, *Black Religion*, 3.
112. *Ibid.*, 3, 16, and 25.
113. Washington, *Black and White Power Subreption*, 121.
114. Garber, "Black Theology: The Latter Day Legacy," 104; and Garber, "Martin Luther King, Jr.: Theologian and Precursor of Black Theology," 405 and 408.
115. Cone, *For My People*, 75–76.

Roberts characterizes King as an "unsung theologian" who "spent many years reflecting upon a theological ethic for the movement he later was called upon to spearhead."[116] He reminds us that King's "theology was the foundation for his social activism."[117] More specifically, Roberts classifies King as a *black* theologian who did his "work out of the heritage lifted up by the latest group of so-called black theologians."[118] He calls on contemporary black theologians to give greater attention to King's role as a theologian "in their historical perspective in order to lay a solid historical foundation for their own work."[119]

The intellectual and experiential sources of King's theology and ethics are of primary importance for Roberts. He joins Cone, Wilmore, and Washington in highlighting the impact of black culture and the black religious experience on King's theological development. "Martin Luther King's program was centered in black religion and the black church," says Roberts. "The black church gave guidance, inspiration, and power to the movement."[120] Roberts insists, too, that "only those who take black religious history seriously are able to understand Dr. King's message and mission profoundly and to provide the necessary internal criticism upon its theory and praxis."[121] For Roberts, the influence of black religion on King is reflected in what he inherited from Atlanta's Ebenezer Baptist Church, from Montgomery's Dexter Avenue Baptist Church, and from black minister-scholars such as Benjamin Mays, George Kelsey, and Samuel Williams.[122]

---

116. J. Deotis Roberts, *Black Theology Today: Liberation and Contextualization* (Lewiston, N.Y.: The Edwin Mellen Press, 1983), 89 and 195.

117. J. Deotis Roberts, *Black Theology in Dialogue* (Philadelphia: The Westminster Press, 1987), 63.

118. *Ibid.*, 104–05.

119. Roberts, *Black Theology Today*, 89, 117, and 120–22.

120. J. Deotis Roberts, *A Black Political Theology* (Philadelphia: The Westminster Press, 1974), 153–54; and J. Deotis Roberts, *Roots of a Black Future: Family and Church* (Philadelphia: The Westminster Press, 1980), 70, 86–88, and 108.

121. Roberts, *Black Theology Today*, 89.

122. *Ibid.*, 121; and Roberts, *Roots of a Black Future*, 87.

Roberts pictures King as representing "the bridge between the older generation of black religious thinkers"—Mays, Kelsey, Williams, Mordecai Johnson, Howard Thurman, and others—and the new black theologians.[123] Roberts stresses the combined impact of family and church on King. He writes, "The making of King was the black family and church, both in Atlanta and Montgomery."[124]

At the same time, Roberts cautions us against denying "the refinement King received at Crozer and Boston." He notes that Reinhold Niebuhr was helpful to King as King struggled to find "an ethical perspective that would be useful in his attack upon the systemic evil of racism."[125] Roberts also points to the impact of the "radical empiricism" of the Boston Personalistic School on King. He explains how King's quest for a theology "to tackle racism on a massive scale" led "him outside of Christianity and to Gandhi."[126] But Roberts, unlike other current black theologians, has criticized King for going "outside the culture of blacks in dwelling on Gandhi":

> Few blacks feel any kinship or possess any real knowledge of Indian religion and ethics. Mass blacks have not heard of the *Gita*, but they have been nourished on the Bible. Furthermore, Indian religious nationalism is so different from black religious nationalism that any real parallel would be difficult to establish. Black theology will be wise to forge its ethic from the Bible with the Afro-American experience as the context for thought and action. As one who has spent several years studying and teaching Hinduism, I have a deep appreciation for the Indian religious heritage. What we are raising is the question of relevance. . . . Africa rather than India is the black man's cultural home. Christianity rather than Hinduism is the religion with which masses of blacks are most knowledgeable. While King,

123. Roberts, *Black Theology Today*, 121.
124. Roberts, *Roots of a Black Future*, 87.
125. *Ibid.*; Roberts, *Black Theology Today*, 121; and Roberts, *Black Theology in Dialogue*, 80.
126. Roberts, *A Black Political Theology*, 29 and 146.

by thought, example, and life, left a great ethical legacy, it is important that the black theologian work out a theological ethic informed by Biblical ethics and the black heritage using language and ideas familiar to the black masses.[127]

Roberts apparently ignores the points at which the theology and ethics of the black church tradition found affinity with Gandhian thought and methods in the case of King. Therefore, King's reliance on Gandhian principles amounted to an affirmation and not a rejection of Biblical ethics and the black religious heritage.[128] This makes the question of *relevance*, as raised by Roberts, a non-issue.

The importance of the Bible for King's theology and activism is seriously considered in Roberts' writings. He suggests that "one gets a feel for the holistic message of the Bible in the sermons of Martin Luther King, Jr." In other words, the Bible furnished the basic theological and ethical grounding for King's concern about all dimensions of life, and also for his efforts to bring together faith and action, and faith and moral development.[129] It is at this point that Roberts finds King's grasp of Biblical ethics to be sound.[130] He alludes specifically to how King prefigured contemporary black theologians in uncovering the power of the Old Testament prophetic tradition:

> Black theology has rediscovered the God of the Exodus—the God of Moses who led a whole people from bondage to freedom. But Dr. King had already

---

127. *Ibid.*, 146; Garber, "King Was a Black Theologian," 19–20; Garber, "Martin Luther King, Jr.: Theologian and Precursor of Black Theology," 411; and J. Deotis Roberts, *Liberation and Reconciliation: A Black Theology* (Philadelphia: The Westminster Press, 1971), 197.

128. Nathan I. Huggins, "Martin Luther King, Jr.: Charisma and Leadership," *The Journal of American History* 74, no. 2 (September 1987): 480–81; and Peter J. Paris, *The Social Teaching of the Black Churches* (Philadelphia: Fortress Press, 1985), 14–15, 24 n. 21, 50, and 111.

129. Garber, "Martin Luther King, Jr.: Theologian and Precursor of Black Theology," 412; Roberts, *Black Theology Today*, 10; and Roberts, *Black Theology in Dialogue*, 25 and 47.

130. Garber, "Martin Luther King, Jr.: Theologian and Precursor of Black Theology," 412.

uncovered the prophetic tradition. He clearly saw the biblical challenge for social justice in the Bible. For King the God of Amos was the God of Jesus.[131]

Roberts shows how this prophetic tradition found fulfillment in Jesus Christ for King. This helps explain the importance of the New Testament for King. Roberts states that King "gleaned ample insights from the New Testament to ground his program in the doctrine of love as *agape.*"[132]

Roberts has discovered several dominant themes in King's theology and ethics that he deems worthy of careful consideration. He focuses on King's Christian anthropology as the key concept around which King's entire perspective revolved. In Psalm 8:4 to 5, King found, according to Roberts, the Biblical basis for the dignity of all humans as reflections of the divine image. Roberts notes how King made special application of this *Imago Dei* concept—which embraced humans as spiritual and physical beings, as rational creatures, and as free beings—to racism. King "points to the fact that according to the Christian faith, life in the physical body is sacred and significant," says Roberts. "Man does not live by bread alone, but he cannot live without bread either."[133] While recognizing the soundness of King's insights into the limitations of certain philosophical explanations of human nature, Roberts, on the other hand, criticizes King for ignoring Sigmund Freud's and Karl Marx's contributions to our understanding of humanity:

> King points out the shortcomings of naturalistic and humanistic explanations of human nature that leave out Christian perspectives. He rejects the all too sentimental notions about man. Even his shortcomings are explained in terms of errors or lags of nature. The belief that human progress is inevitable and that man is gradually evolving into a higher state of perfection

131. Roberts, *Black Theology Today*, 183.
132. Roberts, *Roots of a Black Future*, 99.
133. Roberts, *Liberation and Reconciliation*, 104–05.

is rejected. Freudian terms are used to explain away
man's misdeeds. All bad deeds are said to be due to
phobias, inner conflicts—the conflict between the id
and the superego. King sees the real conflict as between man and God, man and himself and his brother
resulting from the estranged relation with God. This
is said to be a *realistic* understanding of man in the
light of the Christian faith. It is my view that King's
reflections upon the "misuse" of the Freudian explanation is sound, but that he might have said something about the constructive contribution of Freud to
Christian understanding as well. The same might be
said of Karl Marx's real contribution to our understanding of human collectivities. Since man is an individual and at the same time a person-in-community,
Freud and Marx cannot now be ignored by virtue
of their insights into individual man and social man,
respectively.[134]

King's conviction that humans are made to live in
community is fully shared by Roberts. Roberts recognizes the centrality of the Bible to King's idea of the
beloved community. He also concludes that "this theme
of the Beloved Community was at the center of King's
understanding of the church and the Kingdom. It
brought the Fatherhood of God and the brotherhood of
man together."[135] However, the manner in which King
applied this theme to black-white relationships poses
problems for Roberts. Roberts believes that King's idea
of integration, which is at the core of his beloved community ideal, does not allow for an equal exchange of
values and interests between the races. "King's dream
was for a promised land of integration"—he writes—
"one in which blacks would be admitted to the white
society with everything *to receive*, with little if anything
to give."[136] Contrary to Roberts' opinion, King did not
view integration as a continuation of a superordination-

---

134. *Ibid.*
135. Roberts, *Roots of a Black Future*, 87.
136. Roberts, *Liberation and Reconciliation*, 183.

subordination relationship between blacks and whites. As indicated previously, King, after 1965, clearly spoke of integration in terms of "mutual acceptance," "true inter-group and inter-personal living," and a sharing of values and institutions.[137]

Roberts also opposes King's notion that liberation and reconciliation must be achieved at the same time. Roberts speaks of liberation as a prerequisite for reconciliation, a position similar to that of James Cone and Gayraud Wilmore.[138] "Reconciliation between blacks and whites must henceforth be in 'deed and in truth'; it must be through humaneness and liberation and it must be between equals," Roberts declares.[139] Even so, Roberts does have "some affinity with King when he insists on bringing together the twin theological notions of liberation and reconciliation."[140] Roberts comments:

> While I do not hold the dream of Martin Luther King, Jr., I do see the need for interracial fellowship and cooperation in the pluralistic society in which we "live, move, and have our being." The goal for what King called "The Beloved Community" includes the humanizing in American society of all power for human liberation. That is to say, we all have a stake in better human relations. This is so in a pragmatic as well as a Christian sense.[141]

In a personal sense, Roberts has accepted King's view that nonviolence is the best means for achieving

137. Garber, "Martin Luther King, Jr.: Theologian and Precursor of Black Theology," 413–14; and Martin Luther King, Jr., "To Chart Our Course for the Future," an address delivered at an S.C.L.C. Retreat, Frogmore, S.C. (The King Center Archives, 29–31 May 1967), 4–5.
138. Garber, "King Was a Black Theologian," 19, 21, and 26–28; and Roberts, *Liberation and Reconciliation*, 24, 47, and 183. James Cone accuses Roberts of inconsistency on, and of distorting the Christian meaning of, reconciliation. See Cone, *God of the Oppressed*, 239–40.
139. Roberts, *Liberation and Reconciliation*, 24.
140. Garber, "King Was a Black Theologian," 19. Paul Garber's contention that J. Deotis Roberts "repudiates the notion of integration that King advocated from beginning to end" appears to be an overstatement. See Garber, "Martin Luther King, Jr.: Theologian and Precursor of Black Theology," 408.
141. Roberts, *Black Theology Today*, 174.

reconciliation and community.[142] Roberts holds that nonviolence, unlike violence, is consistent with the Christian ethic. In his estimation, the Gandhian method of nonviolence found classic expression in King's Christian love ethic.[143] Violence for Roberts, as for King, is not only anti-Christian, but also impractical for black people in their struggle:

> If reconciliation is a proper Christian goal, and I am convinced it is, then violence that destroys the one who is a party to reconciliation is not a good means. There can be no reconciliation between the dead—at least, not in this life. Violence begets violence rather than goodwill. The result of violence can only be a bloodbath which will be self-defeating as well as self-destructive for blacks. And even though such "black rage" could seriously disrupt the entire nation, it would not be productive of the ends that are being sought in the struggle.[144]

Roberts finds much positive value in King's assertion that unmerited suffering on the part of blacks can afford a means of healing and transforming the society. In language similar to King's, he concludes that undeserved suffering may be used as a creative and redemptive force by blacks in this white racist society, even while efforts are being made "to render it unnecessary as a way of life." "As we seek to *transmute* suffering into victory," Roberts declares, "we must strive to *transcend* suffering" so "that we as individuals and as a people may know the liberty of sons of God *here* as well as *hereafter*."[145] But Roberts does not go as far as King in emphasizing the need to make suffering a virtue. Even so, he is one major contemporary black theologian who

---

142. Roberts, *Liberation and Reconciliation,* 189–91; and Garber, "Black Theology: The Latter Day Legacy," 104.

143. Roberts, *Liberation and Reconciliation,* 190; and Roberts, *Black Theology in Dialogue,* 106.

144. Roberts, *Liberation and Reconciliation,* 191.

145. *Ibid.,* 59; and Garber, "Martin Luther King, Jr.: Theologian and Precursor of Black Theology," 419.

comes close to embodying King's idea of a suffering servant role for blacks.[146]

Roberts credits King with preparing the way for contemporary black theology by linking love inseparably with justice. King, he contends, "knew the meaning of love in the service of justice."[147] Roberts also points to King's skillfulness in relating love and justice to power:

> Power for King was the ability to achieve purpose. It is required to bring about social, political, and economic changes. Power is desireable and necessary to implement the demands of love and justice. Love and power are not polar opposites. Love is not the resignation of power and power is not the denial of love. In King's view, power without love is reckless and abusive and love without power is sentimental and anemic. Power, then, is love implementing the demands of justice. Justice, at its best, is love correcting everything that stands against love. With these understandings, King was prepared to assert that black power can be creative and positive. In this sense, the call for black power is a call to black people to assess the political and economic strength to achieve their legitimate goals. Power is essential for the struggle for justice. It is obvious that King was reaching out to the new black movement. He sought a means to absorb its

---

146. Roberts, *Liberation and Reconciliation*, 59–60; Washington, ed., *A Testament of Hope*, 41–42; Washington, *The Politics of God*, 160, 166, and 173–77; and William R. Jones, *Is God a White Racist: A Preamble to Black Theology* (New York: Doubleday and Company, Inc., 1973), 79–97.

147. J. Deotis Roberts, Sr. and James J. Gardiner, eds., *Quest for a Black Theology* (Philadelphia: Pilgrim Press, 1970), 72; and Roberts, *Black Theology in Dialogue*, 70 and 74. Roberts' point about King's blending of love and justice seems at odds with a statement he made in his second major work on black theology. He wrote: "Martin Luther King, Jr. was so captured by the agape motif in the theology of Nygren that he was not able to forge a theological relationship between love and justice, though he was deeply committed to both." See Roberts, *A Black Political Theology*, 103. In a book that appeared later, Roberts accused King of relying too much upon "the Lutheran version of agape" rather "than doing his own exegesis." See Roberts, *Black Theology Today*, 122.

best insights without abandoning the love ethic and the way of nonviolence.[148]

The image of King as "an unrealistic dreamer," which appears in the writings of Albert Cleage, is not accepted by Roberts. Roberts views King as essentially a realist who believed in Judeo-Christian values and American democratic principles, and who sacrificed his life in an effort to make America's social, economic, and political institutions more responsive to the needs of the poor and oppressed. This is why Roberts concludes that "any viable position in liberation ethics in this country must take seriously the legacy of Martin Luther King, Jr."[149]

The references of Major J. Jones to King are as varied in character as those of J. Deotis Roberts. However, Jones' treatment of King's ideas and methods is more positive and sympathetic than the treatments provided by Cone, Cleage, Washington, and Roberts. Paul R. Garber describes Jones as "the Black theologian who comes closest to saying what King was saying in the turbulent 50's and 60's." Garber has devoted considerable attention to what he calls "Major Jones' more King-like theology."[150]

Jones echoes Roberts' suggestion that King's social activism was rooted in his theology and ethics. "The sense of 'what ought to be' was the driving spirit of King's theological orientation and ethical action," says Jones. "In private

---

148. Roberts, *Black Theology in Dialogue*, 89–90. Roberts suggests that King's "understanding of the gospel of power was based upon his assertion of 'strength to love.'" This point is well taken, but Roberts is a bit confusing in his discussion of the wedding of love and power in King's thought. He contends that King, at one point in his career, "had not given proper theological and ethical attention to power. He considered power as being morally neutral, as did his Boston professors, but he did not give it adequate attention. He put all his confidence in *satyagraha*, 'truth force,' a type of moral power; but he equated it with *agape*, love, rather than with 'the pushing and shoving of justice.'" See Roberts, *A Black Political Theology*, 153 and 200–01. Roberts also charged King with failing "to reconcile justice and power in the theological grounding of his ethics." Roberts, *Black Theology Today*, 122.

149. Roberts, *Black Theology Today*, 120 and 171.

150. Garber, "Martin Luther King, Jr.: Theologian and Precursor of Black Theology," 412, 422, and 424.

and public this was his obsession."[151] Jones insists that King's theological and ethical idealism led him to act out of a sense of truth that was not defined by those in power:

> It was he who, perhaps more than many people who talk of revolution today, thought and acted out of a deep dimension of truth which was not dependent on political power and the rules of its games. Too many people could not accept this fact—that his frame of reference was theological, and he was, to a great extent, immune from anxiety and the seduction of political power. Precisely for that reason alone he became more and more in disfavor, and a greater threat to people in positions of great power than even the prophets of violence themselves.[152]

The way in which King "related God to the struggle" is significant for Jones. Jones believes that King had a vivid sense of divine involvement in human events, and of the need for humans to be co-workers with God in bringing God's Kingdom to earth. This is what Jones means when he says that "Martin Luther King, Jr. connected Holy Subjectivity with the human subjectivity of Black people."[153] For Jones, King's strong belief in the God who suffers with and delivers humanity stemmed primarily from the fact that he was "a child born in the Black religious tradition."[154]

Jones says very little about the theme of *hope* in King's theology. This is problematic in view of Jones' efforts to produce "a theology of hope" from a black perspective.[155]

---

151. Major J. Jones, *The Color of God: The Concept of God in Afro-American Thought* (Macon, Ga.: Mercer University Press, 1987), 54.

152. Major J. Jones, *Black Awareness: A Theology of Hope* (Nashville and New York: Abingdon Press, 1971), 98; and Major J. Jones, *Christian Ethics for Black Theology: The Politics of Liberation* (Nashville and New York: Abingdon Press, 1974), 159.

153. Jones, *Black Awareness*, 113–14; Major J. Jones, "Black Awareness: Theological Implications of the Concept," *Religion in Life* 37, no. 3 (Autumn 1969): 399–400; Jones, *The Color of God*, 103; and Garber, "Martin Luther King, Jr.: Theologian and Precursor of Black Theology," 425.

154. Jones, *The Color of God*, 54.

155. Jones, *Black Awareness*, 11–17.

He does suggest, however, that King's hope was utopian in several ways. First, utopian hope made it possible for King to reject injustice without ceasing to acclaim human nature and the beauty of this world. Second, it kept King sensitive to the reality of "the now of history." Finally, utopian hope allowed King to experience the joy of what he hoped for in the future. What Jones calls "a future-oriented, expectant stance" was clearly reflected in King's "I've Been to the Mountaintop" speech, which was delivered on the night before his assassination in Memphis.[156] Jones is sensitive to how this utopian hope theme related to King's black messianism—to the idea that blacks will not only be their own liberators in cooperation with the God of the future but also the liberators of white people.[157] Jones' failure to develop adequately the dimension of hope in King's thought, and to show how that dimension was the basis of King's cultural bond with his ancestry, results largely from his insistence on viewing hope in light of the theology of the German thinker Jurgen Moltmann.[158]

The similarity between Jones' and King's theologies and ethics is most evident in their conceptions of community. Like King, Jones envisions a future society in which "every person, race, or ethnic group shall take comfort in the fact of separateness and difference," while not allowing such realities to overshadow the need for human community:

> Identity will be no problem, for identity will have been achieved within a climate wherein it will be fully recognized, fully accepted, and fully respected. There will be a pluralism of ideologies, interests, aims and aspirations, and personhood; and no one will for any purpose be denied opportunity to achieve, or be excluded from community. . . . Such a climate, however, will not exclude the emergence of new concerns,

156. Jones, *Christian Ethics for Black Theology*, 197–98.
157. *Ibid.*, 42; Jones, *Black Awareness*, 107 and 137; and Garber, "Black Theology: The Latter Day Legacy," 110.
158. Jones, *Black Awareness*, 11–143.

new struggles, new aspirations, and a yearning for even newer levels of maturity.[159]

Jones essentially agrees with King's and Roberts' contention that nonviolence is *the* Christian method and is therefore the best way to achieve human community. Violence for Jones, as for King and Roberts, can never be sanctioned by the Christian faith.[160] Jones is very sensitive to the power of nonviolence as taught and practiced by King. He points to King as one who accepted nonviolence as "a way of life," as "a moral theological principle," and not as something demeaning to himself and his people:

> For him [King], nonviolence was not a capitulation to weakness and fear; rather, nonviolence demanded that difficult kind of steadfastness which can endure indignation with dignity. For King, nonviolence always attempted to reconcile and establish a relationship rather than humiliate the opponent. For him nonviolence was always directed against the evil rather than against the person responsible for the evil.[161]

Jones goes on to state that the basic principle of nonviolence based on love

> is its nonviolent way of insisting on one's just rights without violating the rights of anyone else. The whole strength of nonviolent action depends upon this absolute respect for the rights of the unjust oppressor, including his legal and moral rights as a person. It is only by insisting on this absolute ethical principle that the personhood of the adherent to the nonviolent way is preserved. In this way, nonviolent actions work not only for the good of those who are unjustly oppressed, but also for the good of the oppressor. Too few people

159. *Ibid.*, 142–43; Garber, "Black Theology: The Latter Day Legacy," 110; and Garber, "Martin Luther King, Jr.: Theologian and Precursor of Black Theology," 414.

160. Garber, "Black Theology: The Latter Day Legacy," 111; and Garber, "King Was a Black Theologian," 20.

161. Jones, *Christian Ethics for Black Theology*, 139 and 142; Jones, *Black Awareness*, 80–81; and Wilmore and Cone, eds., *Black Theology*, 405.

want to concede that one's own well-being is always related to the other.[162]

Jones suggests that it takes tremendous insight to realize that when persons like King "have committed themselves to the nonviolent way, they have committed themselves to a higher discipline and to a more radical self-control." Furthermore, they "have thought through their actions," have considered "a longer-range view of the results," and "are more objective in setting their goals beyond the struggle."[163] Nonviolent activists like King, according to Jones, direct their method at the heart of the adversary, and are determined to decrease the spiral of violence. In Jones' opinion, it was the moral power inherent in King's nonviolence that so confused the white oppressor:

> He [the oppressor] knew how to deal with violence. He has traditionally done so effectively on all sides, even to dealing ultimate death to many of the current Black Panthers. The oppressor has not yet learned how to deal with nonviolence. He still does not know how to deal with a man who has the moral initiative of love on his side.[164]

King's movement toward a more radical form of nonviolence toward the end of his life is discussed as a significant development by Jones. Jones believes that it was this move in the direction of a more bold and daring form of nonviolence, such as massive civil disobedience and nonviolent sabotage, that turned an increasing number of persons against King.[165] While recognizing the importance of this development, Jones, at the same time, is as mindful as J. Deotis Roberts and other black theologians, and certainly more conscious than King, of the limitations of nonviolence as a social ethic. The assassination of King was for Jones and other current black theologians

162. Jones, *Christian Ethics for Black Theology*, 141.
163. *Ibid.*, 143.
164. *Ibid.*, 144, 147, and 178.
165. *Ibid.*, 146–47.

an indication of the shortcomings of nonviolent strategy in a violently anti-black larger society. This tragedy contributed to the weakening of Jones' commitment to nonviolence, leading him to argue that while nonviolence is undoubtedly the Christian calling, there are times when such an ethical norm does not apply, especially in relationships between oppressors and the oppressed. In other words, situations sometime arise when humans must respond to provocation not as Christians, but as humans, accepting the necessity of counterviolence. This is not so much a matter of legitimizing violence, but, as Jones would say, a matter of doing what one must do for positive self-affirmation and freedom.[166]

Jones does not say much about the significance of King's fusion of love, power, and justice. However, he is aware of how "King's view was then and still is the central theme of Black theological ethics—the primordial identity of justice, power, and love."[167] Jones seems to suggest that this equation was not as clear in King's mind in 1956 as it was by 1963, when the civil rights leader declared that his people were moving beyond "tokenism," "gradualism," and "see-how-far-you've comeism" in a serious quest for *power*.[168] Jones states that King reached a point where the God of history was, for him, at one with justice, power, and love.[169]

A number of lesser known black theologians have emerged to reinforce and build on what has been said about King in the works of Jones, James Cone, Gayraud Wilmore, Albert Cleage, Joseph Washington, and J. Deotis Roberts. The writings of Henry J. Young, Cecil W. Cone, Noel Erskine, Josiah U. Young, James H.

---

166. Jones, *Black Awareness*, 102; Garber, "Black Theology: The Latter Day Legacy," 111; Garber, "King Was a Black Theologian," 20; and Garber, "Martin Luther King, Jr.: Theologian and Precursor of Black Theology," 409. Garber erroneously accuses Jones of finding "a way to legitimize violence." It is more correct to say that Jones leaves open the possibility of counterviolence on the part of blacks.
167. Jones, *The Color of God*, 54.
168. Jones, *Black Awareness*, 141–42.
169. Jones, *The Color of God*, 54.

Evans, Jr., Thomas Hoyt, Jr., and Carl H. Marbury immediately come to mind. These theologians have produced
brief but insightful treatments of King, and their names
should be considered in works that treat King in relationship to the contemporary black theology movement.[170]

Much of Henry Young's discussion of King appears in
a biographical and interpretive survey of selected black
leaders.[171] Young is concerned primarily with King as a
"minister, systematic theologian, and Nobel Peace Prize
Laureate."[172] He looks at King's early educational and
spiritual development within the southern context
and gives some attention to how King's studies at Morehouse College, Crozer Theological Seminary, and
Boston University shaped his theological outlook. Young
briefly discusses what he considers to be dominant
themes in King's theology—themes such as love, the nature of humanity, good and evil, nonviolence, and Christian hope. In his most recent work, he discusses King's
vision of the *beloved community* or the *world house* —
the idea that humans "must learn to live together as
a large family on an interdependent basis"—as "the
challenge facing cultural pluralism." King's vision, according to Young, lends support to a vital and healthy
social pluralism, a pluralism that is sensitive and relevant to the global, multicultural situation. Unfortunately, however, Young has said very little beyond this
about King's contribution as a creative theologian, focusing instead on his legacy as a social activist.[173]

Cecil Cone, the brother of James Cone, has made some
significant references to King in his book on black theology. He is among those black theologians who insist that

170. We are in serious need of a study that builds on Paul Garber's
important work on King and black theology. See Garber, "Martin Luther
King, Jr.: Theologian and Precursor of Black Theology," 10–442.
171. Henry J. Young, *Major Black Religious Leaders Since 1940*
(Nashville: Abingdon Press, 1979), 108–24.
172. *Ibid.*, 108.
173. *Ibid.*, 108–24; and Henry J. Young, *Hope in Process: A Theology of
Social Pluralism* (Minneapolis: Fortress Press, 1990), 72, 87, 103–04, 122–
23, and 140.

King's power, creativity, and successes as a minister and social activist stemmed from his religious conviction and his roots in the black Christian tradition.[174] Like Young, Cone does not emphasize King's role and contribution as a theologian, nor does he stress King's relationship to black theology.

Noel Erskine has studied King in relation to theological method. By putting King in conversation with Paul Tillich, Karl Barth, and James Cone, Erskine hopes to make a case for King as a theologian. Much of his focus is on King as a precursor of liberation theology—a focus similar to that of Paul Garber. In his published essays, Erskine recognizes King's connection with contemporary black theology. Furthermore, King represents for Erskine an important link with slave religion—a religion that combined an indomitable hope for the future with moral witness and political activism in the present:

> Martin Luther King, Jr. was the classic representation of this spirit which combined the most intense eschatological hopes for future blessedness with moral witness and political action in the present. King was in his life and ministry a true son and prophet of the Black Church whose dream for the future was informed not by starry-eyed idealism, but by the conviction that God is faithful to his promises. Concretely this meant for him that one day his children, and the children of all black people, would be judged not by the color of their skin but by the content of their character.[175]

Josiah Young and James Evans may be characterized as second-generation black theologians who have emerged with brief but perceptive examinations of King's thought and methods. For Young, King's importance lies primarily

174. Cecil W. Cone, *The Identity Crisis in Black Theology* (Nashville: The African Methodist Episcopal Church, 1975), 68–70.
175. A telephone interview with Dr. Noel L. Erskine, 14 August 1989; Noel L. Erskine, "Black Theology: Retrospect and Prospect," *Theology Today* 36, no. 2 (July 1979): 178–79; and Noel L. Erskine, "Christian Hope and the Black Experience," *The Journal of the Interdenominational Theological Center* 7, no. 1 (Fall 1979): 97.

in two areas. First, he articulated the goals and the ethic of the black freedom movement in the 1950s and 1960s. King's success in this effort, according to Young, was restricted by his inability to win lasting support from white Americans and young black radicals. Young writes: "White supremacy proved too formidable a foe for Dr. King's love ethic, and thus his talk of love-power appeared quixotic to younger blacks."[176] Second, Young, echoing the thoughts of James Cone and other first-generation black theologians, believes that King represented "an important watershed in the development of black theology." Young lists King among many African and African-American thinkers and activists who "helped impart the spirit that motivated black theologians to write of indigenization and liberation."[177]

Evans is equally concerned about King's importance for contemporary black theology. "The magnitude of Martin Luther King, Jr.'s contribution to the Afro-American theological enterprise is formidable," says Evans. Like James Cone and Gayraud Wilmore, Evans praises King for making the black church more active in the struggle for civil rights.[178] While recognizing the influence of liberal theology, Gandhi, and Henry David Thoreau on King's political and theological perspectives, Evans identifies "the Afro-American Baptist Church" as "the true source of King's theology" and as "the most important formative factor in his life."[179]

The prominence King gave to nonviolence as a method is highly appreciated by Evans. He views King as a part of a long tradition of nonviolent resistance in America—a tradition that includes the Quakers, Lewis and Arthur Tappan, and others. Evans assesses the efficacy of King's

176. Josiah U. Young, *Black and African Theologies: Siblings or Distant Cousins?* (Maryknoll, N.Y.: Orbis Books, 1986), 26–27.
177. *Ibid.*, 22 and 26.
178. James H. Evans, Jr., "Keepers of the Dream: The Black Church and Martin Luther King, Jr.," in David J. Garrow, ed., *Martin Luther King, Jr. and the Civil Rights Movement*, vol. 1 (New York: Carlson Publishing, Inc., 1989), 286.
179. *Ibid.*, 289–94.

nonviolent approach as a contemporary option for social change, noting that there are "five key themes in King's philosophy that are important for us today":

> First, King struggled with the contradiction between the spiritual values of his religious beliefs and the secular values of American society in general. Second, King claimed a kind of moral superiority for the victims of oppression. Third, King insisted that the target for his protests was the systems of injustice and not unjust persons. Fourth, King claimed that suffering for the sake of justice was redemptive. Fifth, absolute nonviolence as a way of life appears to be possible only for those few people like King himself who have reached a heightened level of religious and moral consciousness, while remaining a useful tactic or strategy for the masses of people. These themes form the basis for issues which arise when we consider whether or not nonviolent resistance can work today.[180]

Evans sees King's 1967 address against American involvement in Vietnam, delivered at the Riverside Church in New York, as evidence of "a profound change in his political vision and worldview."[181] It is more correct to say that this transition in King's vision and world view occurred as early as 1965. In any case, Evans is persuasive in setting forth those principles that today's black Americans can derive from King's theology, social vision, and political perspective. First, says Evans, King's legacy calls black people to "move *beyond* pessimism"— to reject the kind of "social quietism" that provides "fuel for the engines of injustice." Second, "we are called to move *beyond pragmatism*"—to avoid the style of politics that quenches idealism. Finally, Evans observes, "we are called to move *beyond materialism*"—to transcend the "crass materialism" that is currently attracting increasing numbers of black Americans. "The best hope for

180. James H. Evans, "'To Study War No More': Martin Luther King, Jr. and Nonviolent Resistance," *The A.M.E. Zion Quarterly Review* 97, no. 4 (January 1988): 3–4 and 7.
181. Evans, "Keepers of the Dream," 291–92.

America, and perhaps the world," Evans concludes, "may rest in our ability to let ourselves down into the stream of righteousness which nurtured the life, the dream, and the ministry, of this great spiritual genius [King]."[182]

Thomas Hoyt and Carl Marbury are Biblical theologians whose writings on King are of a special nature. Hoyt's writings focus on the theme of the poor in the Biblical tradition, "with the presupposition that this is one of the primary themes influencing King's thought."[183] Hoyt contends that the Old Testament tradition of the poor and its analogues provided the hermeneutical norms for King's more contemporary human concerns.[184] His reflections afford a point of departure for understanding King in relationship to the Hebrew prophets.

Marbury classifies King as "an eclectic" whose "daily faith" and "conceptualized theology" resulted from a conversation with "many disciplines and with many great minds." According to Marbury, King's rhetoric and preaching followed precisely the Biblical tradition and pattern. As a black preacher nurtured "within a southern and black 'fundamentalist' cultural tradition," says Marbury, King could not allow himself "to be 'non-Biblical.'"[185] Marbury is convinced that King spoke with "Biblical authority" and as one who "stood under the Scriptures" in spirit and in letter:

> He was not content to merely quote Scriptures, which all too often is out of context, but was concerned to interpret integrously. He was fully capable of moving around in the Bible with confidence and idiomatic ease. He was thoroughly familiar, on the other hand, with the "language" of the contemporary world so as

182. *Ibid.*, 294.
183. Thomas Hoyt, Jr., "The Biblical Tradition of the Poor and Martin Luther King, Jr.," *The Journal of the Interdenominational Theological Center* 4, no. 2 (Spring 1977): 12ff.
184. *Ibid.*
185. Carl H. Marbury, "An Excursus on the Biblical and Theological Rhetoric of Martin Luther King," in John H. Cartwright, ed., *Essays in Honor of Martin Luther King, Jr.* (Evanston, Ill.: Leiffer Bureau of Social and Religious Research, 1971), 14 and 16.

to have reached a similar degree of perception and genuine understanding.[186]

Marbury notes how King interpreted the Scriptures so that the past came alive and illumined the present "with new possibilities for personal and social transformation." In other words, King was able to make relevant the "good history" and the "good news" of the Bible, thereby establishing himself as something of a Biblical theologian.[187]

The foregoing discussion supports Paul Garber's conclusion that there is a definite line of development from King to contemporary black theologians. It is impossible to find a black theologian today who identifies unambiguously with King's philosophy and methods, but all black theologians view themselves as beneficiaries of the King legacy.[188]

KING AND CONTEMPORARY BLACK ETHICISTS

Black ethicists are currently exploring King's life and work from many different angles, and are making unique contributions to scholarship on King. This is clear from a reading of the writings of Preston N. Williams, John H. Cartwright, Peter J. Paris, Ervin Smith, Herbert O. Edwards, Sr., Enoch H. Oglesby, William D. Watley, Robert M. Franklin, Jr., Walter E. Fluker, Rufus Burrow, Jr., and Katie G. Cannon. The perspectives of these black ethicists on King are being developed around a variety of questions: How did King become a leader and symbol in the American society? How did he move from the *theoretical* to the *practical*? What was his vision of the goal of human society? What was the meaning of *community* for King? What led him to accept nonviolence as both a personal and social ethic? To what extent was King's ethics

---

186. *Ibid.,* 16–17.
187. *Ibid.,* 17–18.
188. Garber, "Martin Luther King, Jr.: Theologian and Precursor of Black Theology," 406–31.

grounded in the metaphysical context of Personalism? How did he contribute to our understandings of the "moral life" and of humans as "ethical agents?" Is it appropriate to characterize King as a *Christian social ethicist?* Are King's moral and conceptual resources relevant for "black womanist ethics"? What is his significance for black liberation ethics in general? These questions have led black ethicists to various conclusions concerning the meaning and significance of King's life and legacy, some of which are identical to conclusions made by professional black theologians.[189]

Preston Williams was among the first ethicists in black America to call for a serious consideration of King's theology and ethics in scholarly circles. Williams views King as one who symbolized the black experience, and who contributed substantially to a reawakening of protest among black Americans.[190] According to Williams, "at every stage in King's crusades, one was made increasingly aware of the peculiar history and tradition of the black man in America and the peculiar stamp that history made upon his character."[191] Williams concludes that King, in a broader sense, was a symbol of what is wrong with Americans and American culture, a conclusion similar

189. These questions were formed on the basis of a reading of the works of selected black ethicists concerning King. We still need a study that treats King as an ethicist and that examines how he is treated in the works of contemporary black ethicists. The most substantive and impressive discussion of King as an ethicist is provided in Smith, *The Ethics of Martin Luther King, Jr.,* 1–201.

190. Preston N. Williams, "The Ethical Aspects of the 'Black Church/Black Theology' Phenomenon," *The Journal of Religious Thought* 26, no. 2 (Summer Supplement 1969): 36; Preston N. Williams, "The Ethics of Black Power," in *Quest for a Black Theology,* eds. Roberts and Gardiner, 85; Preston N. Williams, "The Problem of a Black Ethic," in *The Black Experience in Religion,* ed. C. Eric Lincoln (New York: Anchor Press/Doubleday, 1974), 184; Preston N. Williams, "American Black Theology and the Development of Indigenous Theologies in India," *Indian Journal of Theology* 30 (April–June 1981): 55–61; Preston N. Williams, "The Public and Private Martin Luther King, Jr.," *The Christian Century* (February 25, 1987), 198; and Preston N. Williams, "A Review of Frederick L. Downing's *To See the Promised Land: The Faith Pilgrimage of Martin Luther King, Jr.* (1986)," *Theology Today* 45, no. 1 (April 1988), 128–29.

191. Williams, "The Ethical Aspects of the 'Black Church/Black Theology,'" 36; and Williams, "The Ethics of Black Power," 85.

to that made by the black sociologist of religion C. Eric Lincoln.[192]

For Williams, King was a theologian who "sought to lead humankind to fulfillment by the path of religion." Williams is mindful of the genius the civil rights leader displayed in applying the Christian ethic to American social, political, and economic dilemmas.[193] However, he stops short of classifying King as *a black theologian,* mainly because of the universal implications of King's theological perspective:

> Just as King's Civil Rights Revolution did not bear the label *black* even though it was chiefly oriented to improving the status and dignity of black persons in America, so too did his theology not bear an ethnic label. His theology was an attempt to proclaim and implement a Christian Faith understood as universal and embracing all sorts and conditions of persons regardless of their race, class, or national origin.[194]

Williams believes that King's reliance on a range of theological sources, black and white, prevented him from becoming strictly *a black theologian.* He appreciates the synthesis that existed in King's theology between his black church sources and his white theological

192. Williams, "The Ethics of Black Power," 85. Lincoln describes King as "a tragic hero" and "the magnificent intruder" who was "for white-oriented America the negation of negation; a contradiction in terms; a paradox *par excellence.* He could not be dismissed as a fool, or as a quack, or as a 'Negro cultist,' because his credentials in faith and learning were of the highest order, coming as they did from some of white America's most respected institutions." See C. Eric Lincoln, "Martin Luther King, The Magnificent Intruder," in *Martin Luther King, Jr. and the Civil Rights Movement,* ed. Garrow, vol. 3, 1–2; and C. Eric Lincoln, *Race, Race, Religion and the Continuing American Dilemma* (New York: Hill and Wang, 1984), 241–42.

193. Williams, "A Review of Frederick L. Downing's *To See the Promised Land (1986),*" 127; Williams, "The Problem of a Black Ethic," 184–85; and Williams, "American Black Theology," 57.

194. Williams, "American Black Theology," 55 and 58. Williams views contemporary black theologians such as J. Deotis Roberts, Major J. Jones, and Joseph R. Washington, Jr. as "writers of black awareness or black consciousness theology" who stood in the King tradition to a great extent. "Although their works are critical of King," writes Williams, "they are in the spirit of King and seek to be in continuity with a wholistic perspective on Afro-American religion."

sources, and seems to imply that both were equally important for King, a view not supported by the evidence. Williams criticizes King scholars for what he sees as their badly unbalanced interpretations of King—for their refusal to seriously examine how American theological liberalism and the black Christian tradition combined to form "the religious grounding" of the black freedom movement led by King:

> The thirteen year struggle of Martin Luther King, Jr. was supported by a Christian faith rooted in the American Social Gospel tradition of liberalism and stressing the motifs of love, justice, non-violence, and inclusive community. King's movement also relied upon the peculiar piety of the black American religious community, especially its worship setting of sermons, songs, and prayers.[195]

Considering "the contribution of the black churches to King's pilgrimage," Williams considers it unfortunate that contemporary black theologians are devoting so little attention to the black Christian roots of King's theology. "One of the most serious defects of most thought about Afro-American theologizing today," Williams declares, "is its failure to consider seriously King's theology and that of his many predecessors among black American religious thinkers."[196] Williams suggests that "the chief reason for that error is the change in mood and orientation of the freedom struggle by black Americans and consequently the change in the nature of doing theology and the labelling of theology."[197]

Williams says very little in his published writings about the ethical implications of King's fusion of love, power, and justice. Even so, he does recognize King's

195. Williams, "American Black Theology," 55; and Preston N. Williams, "The Black Experience and Black Religion," in *New Theology, No. 8,* eds. Martin E. Marty and Dean G. Peerman (New York: The Macmillan Company, 1971), 227.

196. Williams, "A Review of Frederick L. Downing's *To See the Promised Land (1986),*" 129; and Williams, "American Black Theology," 55.

197. Williams, "American Black Theology," 55 and 60–61.

importance in showing that "power should always be exercised with discipline" and love in order to affirm personal worth and dignity and to create "just institutions." Williams echoes King's belief that

> love is as crucial in situations of conflict and violence as it is in those of consensus and peace. It is the power that is capable of overcoming hatred and enmity and it is the power that creates and sustains mutuality and friendship. Without it there can be no justice or community. It makes possible union and reunion among persons and groups. It tempers every action and deed with an equal concern for the enemy and the friend.[198]

The degree to which the black power movement challenged King's notions of love, power, and justice is carefully appraised by Williams. He notes that by 1966 brutal white violence, less-than-vigorous enforcement of the new civil rights laws, and the rebellions by black youth led advocates of black power to question King's philosophy and methods. Williams further contends that King's "untimely death quickened the trend in favour of black power and, together with the increase of riots, rebellion and white resistance, weakened the persuasive force of some of his fundamental convictions."[199] Despite this development, Williams is convinced that King was far more successful than proponents of black power in securing material gains for his people:

> In spite of all the criticism made of Martin Luther King, Jr. by these groups, he achieved a greater measure of moral, economic, political, and social power for Afro-Americans than all of them combined. The concept of black power was and remains indefinite and imprecise and in those contexts where it acquired a specific meaning little real power was obtained for the masses. Possibly its most significant contribution was the increased recognition by some black Americans that they could not ultimately rely upon white

198. *Ibid.*, 67.
199. *Ibid.*, 55–57.

persons for their freedom, no matter how sensitive
their conscience or tender their heart.[200]

The significance of King's legacy for Williams is reflected not only in his achievement of a greater measure
of black power but also in how he influenced the racial
attitudes of white America and revolutionary movements
throughout the world.[201] Williams insists that the continuing interest in King's ideas and achievements in the
1980s by people across the globe proves that the King
legacy is still vital, despite the increasing shift toward
racial and religious conservatism:

> Martin Luther King, Jr., and his dream of a trans-
> formed America and world, is one legacy of the fifties
> and sixties that refuses to die in spite of the wide-
> spread growth of conservatism and the belief that
> tough-mindedness and tight-fistedness are needed in
> order to secure and preserve peace and justice. The
> persistence of interest in King's ideas and belief in the
> fundamental rightness of his cause stems perhaps
> from his teaching that love, not fear, makes peace and
> justice possible.[202]

The black ethicist John Cartwright's treatment of
King is somewhat different from that afforded by
Williams. Cartwright holds that the image of the "committed Christian minister" is the only image that truly
does justice to the whole of King's personhood.[203] He
further asserts that the decisively Christian character
of King's life and ministry determined his social philosophy as well as his vision of the transformed human
society:

> The point of departure of King's social philo-
> sophy and vision of the goal of human society was

200. *Ibid.,* 57.
201. Williams, "The Public and Private Burdens of Martin Luther
King, Jr.," 198; and Williams, "A Review of Frederick L. Downing's *To See
the Promised Land,*" 127.
202. Williams, "A Review of Frederick L. Downing's *To See the
Promised Land (1986),*" 127.
203. Cartwright, ed., *Essays in Honor of Martin Luther King, Jr.*, 1.

fundamentally religious, rooted in his faith in God and in the power of love to transform the hearts and minds of persons. And despite the degree of influence on him by non-Christian sources, it remained true that King's "intellectual" categories were drawn almost exclusively from Christian theology and morality. Hence, in addressing the problem of social eschatology, the primary question for King was (to borrow an ancient Greek philosophical form): From a Christian point of view, *what kind of society must human society be when human society truly becomes?*[204]

In contrast to Preston Williams, Cartwright is concerned primarily with King's "Christian social ideal," as embodied in the concept of the beloved community. According to Cartwright, King envisioned the beloved community, a fully integrated and inclusive society of love and justice, as "the ideal corporate expression of the Christian faith"—as the ethical equivalent of the Kingdom of God.[205] In other words, the beloved community for King was reflective of God's intention that *all* humanity should live together in community and share in the physical and spiritual necessities of life. Cartwright notes that King's strong devotion to this communitarian ideal led him to consistently highlight the moral superiority of integration over segregation.[206]

Cartwright identifies several qualities that King believed persons must acquire in order to ensure the creation and survival of the beloved community. "Cardinal among these is the adoption of nonviolence," writes Cartwright, "not merely as a policy or tactic, but as a moral imperative." King also "stressed the need for faithfulness and devotion in pursuit of community." Moreover, says Cartwright, King emphasized the importance of the New Testament concept of agapaic love. Cartwright

204. *Ibid.*, 1–2.
205. *Ibid.*, 2–6; and John H. Cartwright, "Foundations of the Beloved Community," *Debate and Understanding: A Semestral Review of Black Americans' Political, Economic and Social Development* 1, no. 3 (Semester 2 1977): 171–74.
206. Cartwright, ed., *Essays in Honor of Martin Luther King, Jr.*, 2–11.

takes an uncritical approach at this point, refusing to explore the ethical problems reflected in King's concept of love. While recognizing King's careful analysis of the communitarian ideal, Cartwright, on the other hand, alludes to King's failure to give serious attention to a specific plan for the actualization of the beloved community.[207] King's failure in this regard was inevitable because of the complexity and profundity of the problem of community when related to the American context, a fact largely ignored by Cartwright.

Cartwright does not question the depth of King's faith in the possibility of a *realized* beloved community. He claims that King was "a liberal-optimist," firmly convinced of the possibility of the actualization of the beloved community within history. "It is difficult to see how King would have come to any other conclusion," Cartwright observes, "given his interpretation of the Kingdom and firm conviction that the universe is on the side of justice and righteousness and that 'as we struggle to defeat the forces of evil, the God of the universe struggles with us.'"[208] Cartwright is essentially correct, but his observation is slightly undermined by his refusal to link King's Kingdom of God idea and his unshakable conviction concerning the ultimate triumph of God's justice and righteousness to the Christian optimism of the black religious heritage.

Surprisingly, Cartwright does not include the black Christian tradition among the several sources that informed King's idea of the beloved community. This constitutes a major weakness in his perspective on King. For Cartwright, King's concept brought together elements inherited from a variety of nonblack theological and philosophical sources:

> The idea of the Beloved Community is comprised of some primary elements taken from several sources. The Christian liberalism of the "Social Gospel" variety

207. *Ibid.*, 8–11; and Cartwright, "Foundations of the Beloved Community," 176.
208. Cartwright, ed., *Essays in Honor of Martin Luther King, Jr.*, 9–10.

provided the theological foundations; the personal idealism of Brightman, DeWolf, et al., contributed philosophical foundations; the philosophy of nonviolence of Henry David Thoreau and Mahatma Gandhi provided the means; and the "Christian realism" of Reinhold Niebuhr, with its emphasis on man's capacity for evil and its pessimism about human effort in attaining social ideals, qualified both King's optimism about its historical attainment and his attitude toward the kind of tactics needed for its fulfillment.[209]

Cartwright's de-emphasis on the black cultural roots of King's theological and ethical perspectives distinguishes him greatly from the black ethicist Peter Paris. Paris includes King in what he calls "the prophetic strand of the black Christian tradition."[210] In Paris's words, King was a prophet who "employed scriptural texts for the purpose of describing the nature of evil, the direction in which humanity should move in order to overcome the destructive forces, the way in which Jesus embodies the good, and the manner in which the civil rights struggle is commensurate with the life of Jesus." In Paris' understanding, much of the vitality of King's prophetic ministry was revealed in his capacity to combine tough-mindedness with tender-heartedness in his move toward the goal of freedom, justice, and community.[211]

Paris further declares that King spoke out of the black Christian tradition "when he asserted that nonviolent resistance was redemptive in itself, whether or not the desired goal was realized." This perspective sets Paris apart from most black ethicists and theologians, who view Gandhi as the dominant influence on King's nonviolent ethic. Paris insists that the power and efficacy of nonviolent resistance for blacks in the 1950s and 1960s resulted primarily from King's keen ability to relate Gandhian

209. Cartwright, "Foundations of the Beloved Community," 173.
210. Peter J. Paris, "The Bible and the Black Churches," in *The Bible and Social Reform*, ed. Ernest R. Sandeen (Philadelphia: Fortress Press, 1982), 140–44.
211. *Ibid.*

thought to practices already rooted deeply in the black churches:

> Thus the concept of nonviolence as promulgated by Martin Luther King, Jr., was not alien to the black churches. None resisted it. In fact, King was merely explicating and implementing the traditional means of protest long practiced by the black churches under the black Christian tradition. King's novelty was in his method of mass demonstrations and bringing Gandhi's thought about nonviolent resistance into positive relationship with the black Christian tradition.[212]

King's conflict with other profoundly political-religious perspectives in the black community—perspectives represented by Malcolm X, Adam Clayton Powell, Jr., and Joseph H. Jackson—is discussed at length in Paris' writings. Paris claims that King's prophetic posture placed him in opposition to the nationalism of Malcolm X, the political reformism of Powell, and the conservative pastoral approach of Jackson. Paris concludes nonetheless that effective opposition to racism necessarily "requires pluralistic appreciation of the problem and pluralistic forms of action, as advocated by these four leaders."[213] Here, he goes beyond the scholarly analyses of black religious thinkers like James Cone, Gayraud Wilmore, C. Eric Lincoln, William R. Jones, and Allan Boesak, all of whom stress the importance of the dialectic between King and Malcolm X.[214]

---

212. Paris, *The Social Teaching of the Black Churches*, 24 n. 21, 74, and 115.

213. Peter J. Paris, *Black Leaders in Conflict: Joseph H. Jackson, Martin Luther King, Jr., Malcolm X, Adam Clayton Powell, Jr.* (Philadelphia and New York: The Pilgrim Press, 1978), 13; and Paris, "The Bible and the Black Churches," 136–52.

214. See Cone, *Martin and Malcolm and America*, 1ff.; Seng-Song and Wilmore, *Asians and Blacks*, 64–74; C. Eric Lincoln, *The Black Muslims in America* (Boston: Beacon Press, 1973), 161–65; William R. Jones, "Liberation Strategies in Black Theology: Mao, Martin or Malcolm?," *Chicago Theological Seminary Register* 68, no. 1 (Winter 1983): 38–48; and Allan Boesak, *Coming in Out of the Wilderness: A Comparative Interpretation of the Ethics of Martin Luther King, Jr. and Malcolm X* (Kampen, Holland: J. H. Kok, 1976), 4–43.

Paris does not minimize the significance of King's dialogue with and indebtedness to sources outside the black community. He suggests that all of the key concepts pervading King's political and theological understanding—for example, God, love, nonviolence, justice, human dignity, reconciliation, freedom, power, and morality—were either directly or indirectly influenced by Evangelical Liberalism, Social Gospelism, Personalism, and the thought of philosophers such as Marx and Hegel.[215] In Paris' analysis, King emerges as a great synthesizer—as one who borrowed from many schools of theological and philosophical thought "without becoming a mere disciple of anyone." By "a certain dependence on Hegelian dialectical method," writes Paris, King was able to combine many differing forms of thought in arriving at "a synthesizing conclusion."[216] Paris' perspective at this point is consistent with that of other black theologians and ethicists.

For Paris, King's importance and uniqueness as a leader were most evident in three areas. First, King led "the first mass movement among blacks that succeeded in getting large numbers of whites (especially church people) existentially involved as participants for racial justice in the activities of direct nonviolent resistance." Second, Paris declares that King, through utilization of communal power in its full sense, provided the impetus for the black power movement, which was viewed by many "as the antithesis of communal power."[217] Finally, Paris alludes to King's unique ability to relate the problems of racism, poverty, and war. According to Paris, these constituted moral problems for King—problems that must be transcended through love and nonviolence in the interest of human community. Here Paris seems to accept uncritically King's notion that love and nonviolence are the most practical and moral means for

215. Paris, *Black Leaders in Conflict,* 71–72.
216. *Ibid.*
217. Paris, *The Social Teaching of the Black Churches,* 56 n. 29 and 118–19.

persons to overcome their alienation from each other and from God. The ethical difficulties inherent in King's conception of love and nonviolence, alluded to at various stages in this work, are not carefully considered nor critically examined by Paris. This lack of a critical focus suggests a close similarity between Paris' and John Cartwright's perspectives on King.[218]

Paris displays tremendous insight in his discussion of the implications of King's "God-centered ethic." He discusses how King constantly rebuked humanists who rejected God and relied only on human efforts to attain peace and harmony. "One important implication of King's God-centered ethic," Paris declares, "is that humanity's ultimate loyalty ought to be to God and not to any human-made construct."[219] Paris' suggestion that God is at the center of King's theology and ethics—that all of King's other important concepts "are either explicitly or implicitly related to his understanding of God"—is persuasive.[220] Paris has gone further than most black ethicists in establishing this claim, and in making it the point of departure for his reflections on King.

Like most black ethicists, Paris has two important concerns about King. First, he is concerned about the contribution that King's analysis of race and class can make to people's understanding of this socioethical dilemma. Second, he is concerned about the implications of King's thought and activism for a viable black liberation ethic. At the same time, Paris recognizes that the complexity and pervasiveness of America's social, political, and economic problems, particularly as related to race and poverty, warn against an over-reliance on King's analysis and style of ethical action.[221]

Ervin Smith's study of King's ethics is far more comprehensive and thorough than the studies of Peter Paris, John Cartwright, and Preston Williams. Smith analyzes

---

218. Paris, *Black Leaders in Conflict,* 9–13 and 70–108.
219. *Ibid.,* 71–86.
220. *Ibid.*
221. *Ibid.,* 9–13 and 197–224.

King's thought as Christian ethics, and points to several sources in explaining the background and development of King's ethical system. One such source, according to Smith, was the combined influence of King's family and the black church—sources that contributed to King's early recognition of "God, the religious idea, and the moral order."[222] Smith attaches special significance to the grounding of King's ethics in the metaphysical context of Personalism, noting, for example, that the civil rights leader's concept of the sacredness of human personality drew substantially on the ideas of Personalistic thinkers such as Edgar S. Brightman, Bodern P. Bowne, and Albert Knudson. In Smith's estimation, King's ethical perspective also borrowed considerably from Walter Rauschenbusch's Kingdom of God paradigm and Reinhold Niebuhr's Christian Realism. While recognizing King's indebtedness to numerous sources, Smith concludes that King was essentially a Personalist whose ethics amounted to an effort to create an integrated society in which racial antipathies would be transcended through love.[223]

Smith subjects several themes in King's ethical system to careful scrutiny. Of foremost importance for him are the ethical implications of King's doctrine of God. Smith claims that King followed the Personalists in making God, the Supreme Personality, "the personal ground" of his ethics:

> A central premise of personalism was the idea that the basic unity of the universe must be rooted in intelligence. Beneath the "harmonious system of selves," there must be a unitary being that binds the selves together. This unitary being must be more than a mere concept; such a being must be a person who orders the experiences of the universe according to his self-intelligence. This philosophical

222. Smith, *The Ethics of Martin Luther King, Jr.*, 1–2.
223. *Ibid.*, 1–92 and 151–60; and Gayraud S. Wilmore, "A Review of Ervin Smith's *The Ethics of Martin Luther King, Jr. (1981)*," in *Theology Today* 50, no. 2 (July 1983): 216.

explanation of personal experience was termed theistic monism. King gave intellectual assent to this
position and used the term "theistic monism" as a
philosophical expression for his religious idea of a
personal God.[224]

Smith has a keen sense of how King's involvement in
the black church and the black freedom movement took
him beyond intellectual ideas and assumptions about
God, to which he had been introduced in graduate
school, to a greater reliance on the "God of personal faith
and experience."[225] Smith comments:

> As King moved from his graduate studies into the cen-
> ter of the civil rights movement, the philosophical and
> hypothetical idea of a personal God became subordi-
> nate to the personal God of his religious experience
> who was ever near, ever present, and with whom he
> was in constant companionship. God became the per-
> sonal God to be consulted before every deed. . . .
> This fusion of the religious, philosophical, and experi-
> ential was peculiar to King for the remainder of his
> life. The hypothetical God of theistic personalism was
> fused with the absolute, infinite and immutable God
> of personal faith and experience. The God of human
> experience in liberal theology became the personal
> God who is the very ground of existence and value.
> The God of rationalism in student days became the
> personal God who shares the struggles of daily life.[226]

King's understanding of humans as ethical agents is
at the center of Smith's analysis. Smith notes that for
King, humans are created in "the image of God" and are
therefore "co-creative partners in the created order."
This necessarily means that humans—as moral, rational, and relatively autonomous social beings—are eminently capable of higher levels of development and
achievement toward individual fulfillment and the
common good. In setting forth this view, says Smith,

224. Smith, *The Ethics of Martin Luther King, Jr.*, 25.
225. *Ibid.*, 26–27.
226. *Ibid.*

King did not ignore the problem of sin and evil at the individual and social levels. Rather, King spoke of the freedom and moral capacity of persons to progressively improve human life and the social order despite the realities of sin and evil.[227]

Smith's reflections on King's concept of love as the norm of ethical action are most interesting and enlightening. He contends that "King's conception of the nature and power of love is probably his greatest singular contribution to Christian ethics and American social philosophy." "No other American," Smith continues, "has defined and applied the concept of love to ethics with such profundity as King did in the civil rights movement."[228] While recognizing King's fundamental interest in love as defined by Western philosophers and theologians, Smith insists that the foundations for King's "mature understanding" and practical application of the love ethic are traceable to his "own understanding of Christian faith and witness," and to "his experiences in the civil rights movement."[229]

Smith takes a somewhat critical approach in his discussion of King's view of love. He suggests that King probably overestimated the power and potentiality of "operational love"—that love that expresses itself in social action—in an evil and sinful world. Furthermore, Smith believes that King's interpretation of the perfect love of Christ was not as perceptive as that of Reinhold Niebuhr, who questioned the efficacy of agapaic love in complex social relations in which humans are required to meet power with power.[230]

The radical implications of King's fusion of love, power, and justice are as evident to Smith as to most other black ethicists and theologians. He underscores King's rejection of weak, sentimental, and accommodating love in

227. *Ibid.*, 47–57.
228. *Ibid.*, 61.
229. *Ibid.*
230. *Ibid.*, 61–90; and Wilmore, "A Review of Ervin Smith's *The Ethics of Martin Luther King, Jr. (1981),*" 216.

favor of a strong, unselfish, and demanding love that works through individual and social structures in the interest of justice, law, and power. Smith tells us that the love of God, as reflected in the Cross of Jesus Christ, became King's paradigm for this potent, self-sacrificing, active, and transforming love. Smith echoes King when he says that "justice, law and power which do not reflect" this kind of "love are at best tenuous." He further notes that for King, self-realization and the beloved community are more nearly achieved when love approaches full expression through justice, law, and power.[231]

One important dimension of Smith's work, which goes beyond treatments of King by other black ethicists, focuses on King's moral perspectives on selected social problems, such as marriage and family life, violence and nonviolence, racism and segregation, war and peace, poverty and economic injustice, and the relationship between church and society.[232] Smith reports that in many cases King took the traditional stance in Christian ethics with regard to these problems. However, King "appears to have broken new ground," Smith suggests, "in his interpretation of the radical applicability of love in social action as an alternative to segregation, violence and war."[233] Smith also believes that King challenged the institutional church in America with a new and more vital sense of social responsibility with respect to the problem of race relations:

> He also leveled the most challenging attack upon the institutional church since Reinhold Niebuhr in calling it to fulfill its social responsibility. As a result it is highly likely that he solicited from American churches as a whole their greatest contribution to American social progress in their support of civil rights activities

231. Smith, *The Ethics of Martin Luther King, Jr.*, 61–69.
232. *Ibid.*, chapter 7; and Wilmore, "A Review of Ervin Smith's *The Ethics of Martin Luther King, Jr. (1981)*," 216.
233. Smith, *The Ethics of Martin Luther King, Jr.*, 93.

and legislation which helped to change the whole climate of race relations in this country.[234]

In his reflections on "The Promise of Martin Luther King, Jr.," Smith speculates that King's contributions to Christian ethics will most likely influence America's response to social problems in the future. On this matter, Smith may be right, but he is wrong in assuming that racism, poverty, and war are near eradication mainly because King gave his life for that end.[235]

Smith's conclusions concerning King's contributions to a revitalized institutional church in America are not accepted uncritically by the black ethicist Herbert O. Edwards. Edwards maintains that it is erroneous to conclude that King's leadership inspired even black churches to become committed to and deeply involved in the civil rights struggle, to say nothing of white churches. Edwards appears more pessimistic than Smith about the capacity and potential of American churches to adapt Christianity to a radical black liberation agenda.[236]

Edwards regards King as essentially "a black Baptist preacher" whose work and writings, along with those of Malcolm X, "stand astride the entire black theological enterprise." "And as Black Theology is forced to come to grips with the socioethical implications of its explications of various doctrines," Edwards remarks, "King's legacy promises to grow in significance in terms of a demanding response."[237] In Edwards' view, it would be unwise for black Americans to ignore King's theology and ethics as they seek an "ethical analysis" and "a Black

234. *Ibid.*
235. *Ibid.*, 151–60; and Wilmore, "A Review of Ervin Smith's *The Ethics of Martin Luther King, Jr. (1981)*," 216 and 218.
236. Herbert O. Edwards, Sr., "Race Relations and Reformation-Oriented Theological Ethics," *The Journal of the Interdenominational Theological Center* 2, no. 2 (Spring 1975): 125 and 136; Herbert O. Edwards, Sr., "Toward a Black Social Ethic," *The Duke Divinity School Review* 40, no. 2 (Spring 1975): 97–99; and Herbert O. Edwards, Sr., "Black Theology: Retrospect and Prospect," *The Journal of Religious Thought* 32, no. 2 (Fall–Winter 1975): 57.
237. Edwards, "Black Theology," 57–58.

Christian social ethic" that is consistent with the quest for liberation.[238]

Enoch Oglesby's approach to the ethical and theological dimensions of King's thought is in some ways similar to Edwards' but is more in line with that of Ervin Smith. Like Smith, Oglesby treats King's thought as Christian ethics. "Although Martin Luther King was trained as a theologian," he writes, "he was primarily concerned with the business of Christian social ethics, particularly in light of his struggle to resolve one of the most perplexing moral problems to needle the American conscience: race."[239] Oglesby says further that King's ethics must be understood within the broad context of black Christian ethics:

> The point of departure for black Christian ethics is the community in which black people find themselves and what they believe about Jesus Christ in their struggle to make sense out of the American experience. Thus our reflection upon the ethics of King must necessarily begin with Christian beliefs and the appropriation of the ethical teachings of Jesus to the moral life in black.[240]

Oglesby declares that the social ethics of King, "viewed largely as an expression of liberation ethics *par excellence,* cannot be adequately understood apart from a Christian *context* and those forces which gave rise to the civil rights revolution."[241] Oglesby identifies four "primary moral considerations" in his discussion of King's social ethics. First, "the dilemma of powerless morality versus immoral power." Here Oglesby reflects

238. *Ibid.;* Edwards, "Toward a Black Christian Social Ethic," 97 and 105–08; and Edwards, "Race Relations," 125 and 136.

239. Enoch H. Oglesby, *Ethics and Theology from the Other Side: Sounds of Moral Struggle* (Lanham, Md.: University Press of America, Inc., 1979), 109–13; and Enoch H. Oglesby, "Martin Luther King, Jr., Liberation Ethics in a Christian Context," *The Journal of the Interdenominational Theological Center* 4, no. 2 (Spring 1977): 33–41.

240. Oglesby, *Ethics and Theology,* 109; and Oglesby, "Martin Luther King, Jr.," 33.

241. Oglesby, *Ethics and Theology,* 110; and Enoch H. Oglesby, *Born In the Fire: Case Studies in Christian Ethics and Globalization* (New York: The Pilgrim Press, 1990), 168.

on King's view of the moral implications of the unequal distribution of power along racial lines in the American society. He notes that for King, the collision of immoral white power with the powerless morality of black Americans constituted "the major crisis of our times." Moreover, says Oglesby, King's thoughts on this issue still raise serious questions for the "ethically sensitive person," some of which can only be answered within the context of the continuing struggle:

> Martin Luther King's cogently relevant perception of the crucial dilemma of our times, i.e., the dilemma of "powerless morality versus immoral power," raises for the ethically sensitive person many difficult questions. For example, what is the nature and role of power in human community? Can the oppressed black man in America achieve full manhood or a sense of "being somebody" without power? What is the ethical responsibility of those who hold power with respect to the powerless and dispossessed? What is the ethical relationship of love, power, and justice? In light of King's ethicotheological perspective, can one speak authentically of a "powerless morality," if love is in fact an integral part of the moral ethos of the black community as well as the controlling norm for social action? Can love *really* make a difference in the community of oppressed blacks? To be sure, there are some critical questions which may help to give greater shape and form to our discussion of the social ethics of Martin Luther King, Jr., especially in light of his apparent emphasis upon the ethical principle of love in human relations.[242]

A second moral consideration in Oglesby's examination of King's social ethics is "the principle of love-monism." According to Oglesby, the love ethic is at the center of King's social thought—"a basic principle for both his ethics and Christian theology." "The principle of love in Dr. King's social ethics," Oglesby continues, "is fairly consistent as the key integrative criterion for

242. Oglesby, *Ethics and Theology*, 111–12.

involvement in social action."[243] Oglesby claims that King's analysis of the concept of love poses theoretical difficulties at two levels, especially when viewed from "the contextualist's viewpoint." First, "King's ethics reflect an overcommitment to agapeistic love as the ultimate norm—without giving equal attention to other vital normative concepts of the Christian faith relative to the black man's quest for freedom and first-class citizenship in America."[244] Oglesby further observes:

> The second theoretical difficulty here in our analysis is in part derivative from the first. That is to say, Dr. King's stress upon agapeistic love as redemptive goodwill, at least sociologically considered, tends to be obscured when applied to the funky facts of life in a white-dominated society. On the one hand, the love-ethic places, perhaps, an unrealistic ethical burden upon oppressed blacks to "love your enemy"; while on the other hand, the oppressor is apparently left, if hindsight is any indicator of future socio-ethical patterns between blacks and whites, to interpret love as "sentimentality" as he continues to operate with racist attitudes—often disguised under the cloak of goodwill and universal brotherhood! In terms of black-white relations, there is a growing awareness among some people of the black community that the love ethic is, perhaps, too lopsided—a sort of burden the new black man is apparently no longer willing to bear. Many blacks feel today that they have already over-emptied themselves, have already gone the second mile of the way, have already been for too long the doormat and ashtray of white abuse and bigotry; that there must be a process of reciprocity in the areas of human and moral relations between blacks and whites, if we are to have a viable society.[245]

The relevance of justice, faith, and forgiveness is treated as a third moral consideration in Oglesby's

243. *Ibid.*, 114–15.
244. *Ibid.*, 113–15.
245. *Ibid.*, 115.

"assessment of King's ethics as reflective of a kind of 'agapeistic love-monism.'" Oglesby maintains that the principle of love in King's social ethics requires "justice, faith, and forgiveness as minimum preconditions for the moral life as well as for the construction of a new social order where each person can meaningfully participate and contribute based on his ability and interest."[246] Interestingly enough, Oglesby does not stress the importance of *power* for King at this point. He concludes that King, under the influence of Reinhold Niebuhr, focused primarily on justice as an "ethically relevant norm for the social order."[247]

The fourth primary moral consideration in Oglesby's analysis of King's social ethics is the concept of the beloved community as a formidable paradigm in the achievement of liberation in black-white relations.[248] Oglesby claims that the actualization of the beloved community is "perhaps the central eschatological, normative goal in King's ethics." He uses language such as "the new age," "the age of liberation for all oppressed people," and "a social vision of the new society" to describe King's beloved community ideal.[249] Oglesby further suggests that the essence of the moral life in the beloved community for King was primarily informed not by passive and submissive love, but by love that should be described as active and regenerative, transformative and creative, and liberating and reconciling. For Oglesby, the vision of the beloved community with love at its center highlights, perhaps more than anything else, the prominence of "universalism" as "an ever-present strand" in King's theology and ethics.[250]

Oglesby believes that King's importance and his uniqueness as a Christian social ethicist were reflected

246. *Ibid.*, 115–16.
247. *Ibid.*, 117–18.
248. *Ibid.*, 120–21; and Oglesby, "Martin Luther King, Jr.," 39–41.
249. Oglesby, *Ethics and Theology*, 120–21.
250. *Ibid.*

largely in the contribution he made to perceptions of "the moral life" in America. Oglesby remarks:

> From my own vantage point in ethics, the most signif-
> icant singular contribution of King to our understand-
> ing of the moral life, in a Christian context, is perhaps
> the growing awareness that he—more than any of his
> contemporaries, black or white—dared to believe the
> American dream of "freedom, equality, and justice for
> all" by deliberately internalizing those *same* values
> into his own personal life as the archsymbol of ethical
> conduct.[251]

Oglesby insists that King's ethics provide an important point of departure for contemporary activists
and thinkers who seek to define and embody the moral
life, concretely and contextually. This is why Oglesby—
along with a host of community leaders, educators,
theologians, and social ethicists—is calling for a reexamination of King's thought in light of present human
realities and future human possibilities. "It is never
easy to find one's way into another side or dimension of
a person's thought," Oglesby declares. "Yet as we attempt to discover more promising moral indicators for
the future, we are compelled by the sway of events to
investigate, critically and appreciatively, the ethical dimension of the thought of King."[252]

In some of his writings, Oglesby contrasts and compares King's theology with more contemporary expressions of black theology. He is particularly
concerned about differences and similarities between
King's "Engagement theology" and James Cone's
"Liberation theology."[253] "While Cone's primary concern is black liberation from white oppression," says
Oglesby, "the themes of 'confrontation,' 'engagement,'

251. Oglesby, "Martin Luther King, Jr.," 33.
252. Oglesby, *Ethics and Theology*, 109.
253. Enoch H. Oglesby, "Ethical and Educational Implications of
Black Theology in America," *Religious Education* 69, no. 4 (July–August
1974): 409.

and 'reconciliation' are major emphases in the ethical and theological thought of King." This difference in emphasis, particularly with regard to the reconciliation theme, leads Oglesby to the conclusion that King, unlike Cone, "is not a *black* theologian." At the same time, Oglesby acknowledges that King's contribution to the development of the contemporary black theology movement was essentially as significant as that of Cone. "The viewpoints of Cone and King," he claims, "represent two vital poles of ethical and theological reflection upon the black struggle in white America, and how the struggle must be waged in order for the black man to achieve authentic personhood in human community."[254]

The similarities between the theologies of King and Cone are carefully outlined by Oglesby. First, he asserts that both King and Cone emphasize the view "that God—in his righteousness and justice—takes sides with the oppressed." Second, Oglesby argues that the Exodus theme "is a compelling dynamic in King's Engagement theology as well as in Cone's Liberation theology." Finally, Oglesby admits that there is significant disagreement between King and Cone on methodology, especially on the question of liberation through nonviolent strategies versus "by any means necessary, although [both] believe that God wills for man to be 'engaged' in the world in order to ascertain authentic freedom—without which man cannot be a whole person." Oglesby believes that such similarities must be understood and appreciated if one is to grasp the full ethical and educational implications of King's and Cone's thought.[255]

Oglesby has been equally concerned about the ways in which the thought of King, Cone, Cleage, and other black religionists conform to the sociological theory of George E. Simpson and J. Milton Yinger. He applies the theoretical framework of Simpson and Yinger—which identifies

254. *Ibid.*, 404.
255. *Ibid.*, 408–09.

Avoidance, Acceptance, and *Aggression* as types of minority group responses to racism and discrimination—in his analysis of divergent themes in the thought of King, Cone, Cleage, and others. Oglesby considers King and Cone under the general category of *Aggression,* particularly "that mode of aggression which may be expressed in militant group leaders who champion religious or social causes, leading protest marches or organizing effective boycotts."[256] In Oglesby's understanding, King's and Cone's refusal to break contact completely with white people places them at odds with the *Avoidance* response—that response that is more typical of Albert Cleage, the Black Muslims, and other blacks who seek escape from racism and discrimination through separatism. Oglesby also disassociates King and Cone from the *Acceptance* response—a response characteristic of black people who accept, consciously or unconsciously, a status of inferiority in their relations with whites.[257] Oglesby's contention that the sociological theory of Simpson and Yinger can contribute to our understanding of how King's theology differs from that of other black religionists seems persuasive. However, Oglesby says very little about the limitations of white Western sociological theory as a guide for understanding black religious experience, thought, and action.[258] Consequently, his employment of the theoretical framework of Simpson and Yinger in analyzing the theology and ethics of King and other black religionists raises as many questions as it answers.

William D. Watley's approach to King's theology and ethics is not as complicated as Oglesby's. Watley develops two themes in relationship to King. One is his keen understanding of those sources that had a formative influence on King, namely, the black religious experience,

256. Enoch H. Oglesby, "Ethical Implications of the Works of Selected Black Theologians: A Critical Analysis" (Ph.D. diss., Boston University, 1974), 127–43.
257. *Ibid.*
258. *Ibid.* Oglesby carries his analysis of King and other black religionists, based on the sociological theory of Simpson and Yinger, much further than my study suggests.

Evangelical Liberalism, and Personalism.[259] Watley argues that King's basic theological and ethical perspective was formed within the context of the black church and black religion, and was shaped and refined by his formal introduction to Evangelical Liberalism and Personalism at Crozer Theological Seminary and Boston University. In Watley's opinion, King's receptivity to the dominant themes of Evangelical Liberalism and Personalism—themes such as God's involvement in human history, the existence of a moral order in the universe, the dignity and worth of human personality, and the essential social character of human life—was based to a great extent on the congruence between these themes and the ideas and beliefs King took with him to Crozer Theological Seminary and Boston University from his background in the black church.[260] Watley's argument is convincing, but it largely ignores the importance of family, of the larger black community of Atlanta, Georgia, and of the experience of oppression in the South as formative influences on King.

The development and application of King's nonviolent ethic is the second theme developed by Watley. Here, Watley displays insight and analysis that are not so evident in treatments of King by other black ethicists. He carefully outlines and discusses King's six principles of nonviolence under the following headings: (1) nonviolence is the weapon of the strong not the weak; (2) reconciliation is the goal of nonviolence; (3) nonviolence is directed against the structures of evil rather than the evildoers; (4) nonviolent direct action involves redemptive suffering; (5) the principle of love is at the center of nonviolence; (6) and nonviolence is based on the conviction that the moral order of the universe is on the side of justice.[261] According to Watley, "these six principles remained the

259. Watley, *Roots of Resistance*, 17–45; and William D. Watley, "King: A Black Hero for All People," *The Christian Century* (January 15, 1986): 39.
260. Watley, *Roots of Resistance*, 15 and 20.
261. *Ibid.*, 111–28.

central, integrating, constituent elements of his [King's] nonviolent ethic."[262]

Watley skillfully demonstrates how "King's nonviolent ethic developed along two concomitant lines"—from a method of social protest to a personal way of life.[263] This conclusion is borne out by King's own testimony in "Pilgrimage to Nonviolence."[264] In emphasizing nonviolence as a personal ethic for King, Watley goes beyond the analyses of those scholars who are primarily concerned about King's nonviolent ethic as a method for addressing racial issues.[265] Through a reading of Watley, one gets a clear sense of the intensity of King's commitment to nonviolence even as he considered other avenues to human liberation and community.

Watley is essentially correct in claiming that King's nonviolent ethic developed and matured over time as he struggled with the problems of racism, economic justice, and international peace. He writes: "King's nonviolent ethic was an 'ethic of exigencies' in that it was honed in the midst of those crisis situations and developed through the conflict engendered by black protest against the institutional and personal racism of white America."[266] For Watley, King's struggle "in the midst of conflict and action" did more to clarify his thinking on nonviolence than all of the philosophical and theological principles he had studied at Morehouse College, Crozer Theological Seminary, and Boston University.[267] This view is consistent with King's own account of his pilgrimage. In his discussion of civil rights campaigns led by King in Montgomery, Albany, Birmingham, Selma, and Chicago, Watley shows how King struggled with the limitations of nonviolent strategies even as he marveled at their power and successes.[268]

262. *Ibid.*, 111.
263. *Ibid.*, 15 and 47.
264. King, *Strength to Love*, 151–52.
265. Watley, *Roots of Resistance*, 15.
266. *Ibid.*
267. *Ibid.*, 15ff.
268. *Ibid.*, 63–100; and King, *Strength to Love*, 151–52.

The extent to which King employed nonviolence as a "coercive" and "manipulative" tactic is carefully assessed by Watley. Watley suggests that King achieved his greatest victories when his tactics provoked his enemies to violence. King believed, says Watley, that love and justice demanded the kind of healthy conflict that his nonviolent direct action campaigns generated. While recognizing King's effective use of nonviolence as a "constructive coercive power"—as that power that creates tension that ultimately leads to reconciliation—Watley, at the same time, remains sensitive to King's vulnerabilities as a strategist and tactician.[269] Those vulnerabilities, according to Watley, were painfully evident during the Albany and Chicago campaigns, when King showed a rare tendency for ill preparation, bad timing, and poor decision-making.[270]

Watley discusses in some detail King's view that nonviolence should become a method for serious experimentation in international relations. In Watley's view, King's suggestion on this subject is indicative of how his nonviolent ethic matured during the pilgrimage from Montgomery to Memphis. For Watley, King's attack on the Vietnam War grew largely out of his conviction that war between nations could no longer be defended on rational terms—that it presented ominous possibilities for human destruction.[271] Interestingly enough, Watley does not refer to King's thoughts on the violence caused by South African apartheid and by white Western imperialism throughout the so-called Third World. By confining his attention to Vietnam, Watley overlooks information in King's writings and speeches that further clarifies King's thoughts on the applicability of nonviolence in international relations.

In Watley's opinion, the central question that dominated King's life was: How should the Christian respond to principalities and powers and evil in high places?

269. Watley, *Roots of Resistance*, 8, 65–70, and 94–100.
270. *Ibid.*
271. *Ibid.*, 100–10.

Watley believes that King answered this question in a profound way through his Christian prophetic witness and through his great capacity to live in accordance with higher human values. For Watley, this was King's most precious gift to his people, to the American society, and to the world.[272]

Watley's claim that King was, above all, a black Christian pastor who translated ethical principles into ethical activity is supported by the black ethicist Robert M. Franklin.[273] Franklin maintains that "King was a Christian pastor who was profoundly sensitive to the moral dimensions of human interaction." Convinced that "King's entire ethical system is a species of theological ethics," Franklin advances the view that "the major categories and claims of King's ethical thought" cannot be apprehended apart from a serious consideration of his role as "a pastoral social ethicist." Concerning King's contributions as a pastoral social ethicist, a constructive ethical thinker, and a religious leader and thinker, Franklin comments:

> As a pastoral social ethicist he analyzed and condemned the unjust behavior of social institutions. He frequently told his staff that his message to America was, "Repent, it is not too late, you can come back home." And as a constructive ethical thinker, he advanced proposals and claims for reparations and redistributive justice. To his credit as a religious leader and thinker King always went beyond employing general phrases such as a "fair share of resources," etc. and elaborated the programmatic measures which would satisfy the demands of fairness and mercy.[274]

---

272. *Ibid.*, 14–15; and Watley, "King: A Black Hero for All People," 39.
273. Watley, *Roots of Resistance*, 17–18; and Robert M. Franklin, "Martin Luther King, Jr. as Pastor," *The Iliff Review* 42, no. 2 (Spring 1985): 4–20.
274. Robert M. Franklin, "An Ethic of Hope: The Moral Thought of Martin Luther King, Jr.," *Union Seminary Quarterly Review* 40, no. 4 (January 1986): 42–43 and 45; and Robert M. Franklin, *Justice and Human Fulfillment: Images of the Moral Life and the Just Society in African-American Moral Thought* (unpublished manuscript), 9.

Franklin contends that King's method of practical theology as a pastor emphasized the image of the complete
life as an ethical norm. Franklin remarks:

> King's image of the complete life functioned as an ethi-
> cal norm which consistently informed his ministerial
> decisions and public actions. Unlike other pastors who
> worked carefully with parishioners but often without a
> clear sense of the kind of person they were seeking to
> nurture, King never lost sight of the *telos* of Christian
> maturity on the personal level, and was thus able to be
> very intentional in his sermons, pastoral counseling,
> religious education, and public ministry.[275]

Franklin insists that the Bible, and especially the
apocalyptic symbolism of John in the Book of Revelation, provided the foundational text for King's understanding and description of the complete life or of
human fulfillment. "Inspired by the geometric perfec-
tion of the new city of God described in the Apoca-
lypse," says Franklin, King "suggested that the complete
life had three dimensions, each representing a major
agenda for the individual's life. . . . The length,
breadth, and height of one's life corresponded to, first,
an inner concern for one's own welfare, second, the
welfare of others, and third, one's upward reach for
God."[276] At the same time, Franklin is mindful of other
sources, aside from the Bible, that contributed to King's
vision of human fulfillment—sources such as the social
sciences, philosophy, black cultural values, and King's
own personal faith pilgrimage.[277]

Several themes are emphasized in Franklin's discussion of King's vision of the complete life. One is the
sacredness of human personality. In Franklin's understanding, this was "the most central norm of King's reflections on morality and social justice":

> This norm operated as the criterion by which King se-
> lected and appropriated insights from a variety of

275. Franklin, "Martin Luther King, Jr. as Pastor," 5.
276. *Ibid.*
277. *Ibid.*, 4–6.

sources and by which he assessed the adequacy of alternative conceptions of human nature and fulfillment. As he examined the thoughts and social strategies of others his fundamental concern was with their effects on the development of the whole person. Repeatedly, he argued that "Any law that degrades human personality is unjust. Any law that uplifts human personality is just."[278]

Franklin uses the term *magnanimity* in reference to a second theme in King's image of the complete life. According to Franklin, *magnanimity* refers to "the capacity to bear trouble calmly, to disdain revenge against one's enemies, and to make sacrifices for worthy ends." For Franklin, the power of King's sense of mission was most evident in the ways he displayed *magnanimity*, and how he encouraged this character virtue in others. Because of this virtue of *magnanimity*, Franklin concludes, "King's vision of fulfillment unfolded beyond self-love to reveal an equal concern with neighbor-love"—that love that is enriched by altruism, civic spiritedness or responsibility, and friendliness.[279]

Community is another theme Franklin associates with King's image of the complete life. He notes that, for King, healthy communal life involved not only the building of wholesome, one-on-one relationships between individuals but also strengthening marital and familial harmony, establishing amicable relationships between different racial and ethnic groups, and creating peace and harmony between nations. Here Franklin's treatment of King's communitarian ideal is similar to that of Ervin Smith.[280] Franklin suggests that King saw harmony between individuals and in marital and familial relationships as a precondition for any experience of community across racial, ethnic, class, religious,

278. *Ibid.*
279. *Ibid.*, 6–8 and 14.
280. *Ibid.*, 5–20; and Smith, *The Ethics of Martin Luther King, Jr.*, 93–149.

political, and national boundaries.[281] Furthermore, Franklin concludes that King had two major concerns regarding the whole question of how community should be actualized at the national and international levels. First, King envisioned a *just* American society—"a society in which democratic socialist ideals were established to secure equal justice for all." Second, King was concerned about each person's achievement of "the integrative life"—that life that leads one to a realization of one's fundamental identity as a member "of an interconnected, global human family."[282]

Franklin tells us that King's idea of the complete life also embraced the need for a personal relationship with God—a relationship that "entailed a demanding moral agenda in which the person was energized by God to challenge all forms of evil and to work for the creation of the beloved community."[283] King's idea of the personal relationship with God, in Franklin's understanding, entailed three positive functions of religion. First, it entailed the integration of religious and scientific knowledge, a process that, in King's logic, helped to refine naive faith and to provide evidence for the existence of the God confessed by the moral person. Second, it required the integration of the spiritual and the material, the body and soul. "King believed," says Franklin, "that his warrants for a religious faith which integrated concern for the welfare of the body along with the soul were biblically and rationally grounded." Finally, King held that the personal relationship with God, when examined from the standpoint of the Christian faith, encouraged religious tolerance and a respect for religious pluralism. Franklin believes that King's idea of the divine-human relationship, coupled with other ingredients that formed his vision of the moral

---

281. Franklin, "Martin Luther King, Jr. as Pastor," 5–20.
282. Franklin, *Justice and Human Fulfillment*, 13 and 15; and Robert M. Franklin, *Liberating Visions: Human Fulfillment and Social Justice in African-American Thought* (Minneapolis: Fortress Press, 1990), 103–58.
283. Franklin, "Martin Luther King, Jr. as Pastor," 15.

or complete life, commends itself to us as we seek to overcome the many obstacles to human community.[284]

Franklin goes much further than Enoch Oglesby in examining the evolution of King's Christian social ethics during the last three years of his life. Franklin contends that "After the Selma crusade of 1965 King began to articulate more radical analyses of oppression and bolder strategies for transforming the nation he loved." Franklin characterizes "this moral dimension" of King's "later public discourse" as an "ethic of hope"—an ethic nurtured by the values and traditions of black America:

> This ethic was not peculiar to King. . . . Rather, it was a fundamental element of common Afro-American Christian morality. King was the product of a black theology of hope. The hopefulness of his own personality was nurtured in the rich black family and black church traditions of music, preaching and social action. King's achievement was to embody the tradition so fully that he made it a compelling attractive possibility to other oppressed persons.[285]

For Franklin, a careful reconsideration of King's ethics suggests three shifts in his "evolving moral and strategic thought":

> First, his analysis of America's problems expanded from a mono-causal focus on racism to include the increasing significance of economic dimensions of oppression. Second, he revised his vision of the just society from a mere participatory political democracy to a democratic socialist society in which America's highest values could be realized. Third, in the light of this revised analysis and social vision, he realized that moral agents were obligated to engage in action far more militant than he had advocated earlier. In short, King realized that in order to eradicate racism, economic exploitation and militarism, a revolutionary transformation of American society and values was required. In order to achieve that ideal of

284. *Ibid.*, 15–20.
285. Franklin, "An Ethic of Hope," 41 and 49.

an authentic America, persons would have to engage in civil disobedience and actively work to change the present order.[286]

In Franklin's opinion, King's evolving ethical position clearly reflected his changing perception of himself as a leader. "As King's analysis of racism in America expanded to consider the interaction of economic interests and of military power," writes Franklin, "he began to think of himself, no longer as the leader of a small black movement in the southern United States, but as a world leader, compelled to speak out on threatening international issues such as Vietnam and nuclear proliferation."[287] Franklin's assessment of the emergence of King's vision beyond southern particularism to internationalism is one of the best offered by a black ethicist. He agrees with other black ethicists and theologians in suggesting that King's evolving awareness and analysis of world problems, and of his place in the ranks of world leadership, "merit a new appraisal of his contributions to American life and thought."[288]

Franklin suggests that King's expanded awareness and vision were influenced, directly and indirectly, by his critics. First, there were those critics, black and white, who urged King to limit his focus to civil rights concerns. Such critics, Franklin observes, forced King to think deeply and critically about the connection between civil rights issues and world problems, and to clarify his own role in relation to both. Franklin goes on to suggest, at another level, that Malcolm X "won a symbolic victory by influencing King to redefine the scope and semantics of the Civil Rights Movement." More specifically, Malcolm helped move King "from a civil rights to a human rights orientation," thereby placing the black freedom struggle "in a global rather than a national context."[289] For Franklin, this point is essential

286. *Ibid.*, 43–44.
287. *Ibid.*, 45.
288. *Ibid.*, 43.
289. *Ibid.*, 44–46.

to any careful consideration of the links between Malcolm's "redemptive nationalism" and King's "prophetic radicalism."[290] Here Franklin's analysis is very similar to James Cone's and Gayraud Wilmore's.

Like other black ethicists and theologians, Franklin is primarily concerned about King's legacy and its meaning for America. He declares that King's impact on America must be measured in terms of the social, the political, and the religious:

> While his public ministry lasted a mere twelve years, during that time he placed his unique stamp on this nation's public life, especially the future shape of its relations, mass politics, and social Christianity. Despite her persistent, blatantly sinful actions, he never gave up on America. As he continued to demand repentance, his pastoral love for the prodigal nation increased, as did his priest-like willingness to effect reconciliation among America's many ethnic and economic "tribes."[291]

Although King's faith in and love for America remained strong, says Franklin, he realized that the ideal society he envisioned might never be realized in this society and in this life. Franklin declares that despite this awareness, King was driven on by "an ethic of hope." In Franklin's view, this "ethic of hope" undergirded King's sense of personal responsibility as well as his understanding of the black messianic vocation. Indeed, it was the primary motivating force behind King's and his people's effort to "complete a process of democratization" in America. More importantly, King's "ethic of hope," in Franklin's words, "continues to inspire struggling masses throughout the world to intensify their pursuit of justice and human fulfillment."[292]

290. *Ibid.;* Robert M. Franklin, "Religious Belief and Political Activism in Black America: An Essay," *The Journal of Religious Thought* 43, no. 2 (Fall–Winter 1987): 63 ff.; and Franklin, *Justice and Human Fulfillment,* 9 and 13–15.
291. Franklin, "An Ethic of Hope," 41.
292. *Ibid.,* 41, 43, and 47–49.

The nature and importance of King's legacy are measured at a somewhat different level by the black ethicist Walter Fluker. Fluker focuses largely on King's contribution to "religious and moral formulations of human community." For Fluker, King was a pastor and a social prophet who made the search for community "the defining motif" of his life and thought.[293] Concerning King's lifelong quest for community, Fluker writes: "From his early childhood until his death, there is a progression in his personal and intellectual understanding of the nature and goal of human existence which he refers to as 'the beloved community.'"[294]

Fluker contends that King's communitarian ideal was shaped and informed by many experiential and intellectual sources. Of foremost importance for Fluker are King's background and his experiences as an African-American. "King's search for community," he observes, "was characterized by an insatiable thirst for truth and a deep-seated religious faith that began in his early years in the intimate contexts of his family, the black church, and the larger black community of Atlanta, Georgia."[295] Fluker argues that King's conception of community was affected by his experiences with noncommunity in the segregated South. In Fluker's opinion, these various experiential or social sources led King to struggle very early with the nature and meaning of community.[296]

The intellectual sources of King's communitarian ideal are discussed at great length by Fluker. Fluker asserts that "the development of the ideal in King is discernible in his educational pursuits at Morehouse College, Crozer Theological Seminary, and later Boston University." In Fluker's view, the Morehouse College experience exposed King to racial dialogue and exchange

293. Fluker, *They Looked for a City*, xi (Introduction), 81, and 188; and Walter E. Fluker, "They Sought a City: A Comparison of the Ideal of Community in the Thought of Howard Thurman and Martin Luther King, Jr." (Ph.D. diss., Boston University, 1988), 1–18.
294. Fluker, *They Looked for a City*, 81.
295. *Ibid.*, 81–82.
296. *Ibid.*, xi (Introduction); and Fluker, "They Sought a City," 3–5.

that helped him to conquer an "anti-white feeling" and that increased his belief in "the potential for wholesome relations with white people." This exposure resulted from King's work with the Atlanta Intercollegiate Council, an interracial student group that attracted a considerable number of Morehouse College students. Fluker notes that King's idea of community also benefited from frank discussions with Benjamin Mays, George Kelsey, Walter Chivers, and other Morehouse College professors—professors who constantly talked about racism and the need to alleviate the tensions and divisions between blacks and whites.[297] Fluker thinks that the experiences at Crozer Theological Seminary and Boston University—which exposed King to George Davis, Walter Rauschenbusch, Mohandas K. Gandhi, Reinhold Niebuhr, Edgar S. Brightman, L. Harold DeWolf, and other major religious, theological, and philosophical thinkers—helped King to refine and articulate his vision of community in intellectual terms and categories.[298]

Fluker suggests at other points in his writings that King's involvement in the civil rights struggle contributed more to his communitarian ideal than all of the books he read at Crozer Theological Seminary and Boston University. "After his formal education and training," Fluker explains, "his [King's] experiences as pastor and spokesman for the black community in Montgomery served as a 'proving ground' for his embryonic, theoretical formulation of community that would be refined in the praxis of the Civil Rights Movement."[299] This conclusion is supported by most black ethicists and theologians, especially those who emphasize community as the central theme in King's thought and activity.

Fluker claims that the beloved community for King "was synonymous with the Kingdom of God"—"the Christian social eschatological ideal which served as

297. Fluker, *They Looked for a City,* 82 and 87–88.
298. *Ibid.,* 102–05.
299. *Ibid.,* 82 and 89–90.

the ground and the norm for ethical judgment." This view of the nature of King's communitarian ideal is shared by James Cone and John Cartwright.[300] But Fluker goes beyond Cone, Cartwright, and others in emphasizing the "triadic relationship between persons, God, and the world" as central to King's understanding of the nature of community. Here, Fluker underscores King's conviction that persons are social beings who experience wholeness only through a harmonious relationship with other persons, God, and the world (i.e., the cosmos, nature, human history, human society, and the state).[301]

Fluker examines two very important themes in King's articulation of the beloved community vision. One is "The American Dream," a theme that King developed and articulated from 1957 to the historic March on Washington in 1963. "Here one sees an intense focus," according to Fluker, "on the role of the federal government and the place of the Declaration of Independence, the Emancipation Proclamation, and the Constitution in his articulation of the beloved community." Fluker concludes that the March on Washington signaled a turning point in King's conceptualization and articulation of the beloved community:

> The early development of the ideal of community in King reaches its zenith in the March on Washington in 1963, but the following four and a half years proved to be a period in which his vision of community received its severest criticisms and challenges. These final years of his life and ministry, although beleaguered with controversy and sabotage, are the most crucial in understanding the maturation of his personal and intellectual growth in respect to community. It is in this period that one sees most clearly King's wrestling with nonviolence as a means of achieving human

300. *Ibid.*, 110; a letter from James H. Cone to Lewis V. Baldwin, 23 June 1982; and Cartwright, "Foundations of the Beloved Community," 171–74.
301. Fluker, *They Looked for a City*, 114–28.

community, his increased realization of the international implications of his vision of community, and his understanding of the nature and role of conflict in the realization of human community.[302]

"The World House" is a second important theme in King's articulation of the beloved community ideal. Fluker develops this theme to a much greater extent than most black ethicists. For Fluker, King's use of the metaphor of the "world house" after 1963 suggests that his vision of community "had become international in scope." In other words, King increasingly began to speak of a universal human community that transcends the categories of race, class, sex, creed, and nationality.[303] Fluker's contention is strongly reinforced by King's own testimony as well as by the findings of other King scholars.

Fluker devotes considerable attention to King's idea of evil and sin as barriers to community. According to Fluker, King identified evil with "disorder, disruptiveness, intrusion, recalcitrance, and destruction," and noted that "'there is a tension at the heart of the universe between good and evil.'" Fluker further contends that sin for King was "distinguished from evil in that it involves human volition, freedom, and responsibility. Sin is related to evil in that egoism, selfishness, and ignorance lead one to cooperate with the enterprises of malevolence."[304] Fluker states, in more specific terms, that King placed special emphasis on racism, economic injustice, and war as forms of collective sin and evil, and as barriers to community. Although King emphasized these social manifestations of sin and evil, he, as Fluker points out, did not ignore the importance of individual or personal sin as a barrier to community. Fluker claims that King clearly recognized personal sin and evil as internal barriers "that the moral agent must overcome

302. *Ibid.*, 82 and 93.
303. *Ibid.*, 99.
304. *Ibid.*, 129 and 131–32.

in order to realize inner harmony and to struggle for creative change in the world. At various places, he identifies these internal barriers as ignorance, fear, and hatred."[305]

Fluker echoes other black ethicists and theologians in arguing that nonviolence was, for King, the most moral and practical means of overcoming the barriers to community. In other words, nonviolent action, which involves redemptive suffering, represented for King the burden of every moral agent who struggled for peace and harmony among persons. In Fluker's understanding, King's idea of nonviolent direct action related closely to two other themes in his thought. First, it related to King's idea "that spirituality is the basis of social transformation." Second, it was connected with King's emphasis on love, power, and justice as necessary ingredients for overcoming the internal and external forces that conspire against personal wholeness and human community.[306]

Fluker's perspective is penetrating and refreshing at those points where he compares and contrasts King's communitarian ideal with that of the black theologian Howard Thurman. Fluker suggests that the continuities between King and Thurman exist at several levels. First, the two thinkers agreed on the nature of community. "For both thinkers," Fluker declares, "the nature of community is rooted in the interrelatedness of all life, which is teleological." Second, "For Thurman and King there is a triadic relationship between God, persons (individuals), and the world." "These three principles are integrally related," says Fluker, "and form the basis for the dynamic character of community." Third, Fluker argues that Thurman and King took similar approaches to the whole question of the actualization of human community:

> Common themes in Thurman's and King's treatments
> of the actualization of community include: evil and sin

305. *Ibid.*, 133.
306. *Ibid.*, 137–48 and 177–78; and Walter E. Fluker, "Transformed Nonconformist: Reflections on Spiritual and Social Transformation in Martin Luther King, Jr." (Unpublished paper), 1–35.

as barriers to community, community as the norm and goal of the moral life, love as the means of actualization for community, and the nature and role of the moral agent in the creation of community. While their views of evil differed, both recognized that sin is both a personal and social phenomenon which erects internal and external barriers that must be overcome in the creation of community. For each, the internal barriers of sin find greater manifestation in social evils such as racism, classism, and religious exclusiveness.[307]

Finally, Fluker concludes that Thurman's and King's understandings of community "arose initially from their common experience of oppression and segregation as black Americans in the Deep South."[308] Here Fluker stresses the importance of *place* in a southern context for both men. He asserts that out of the particularity of Thurman's and King's "experiences of community and non-community in the segregated South, there emerged a universal vision of human community which transcended race, class, religion, and other forms of sectarianism." Fluker further declares that Thurman's and King's early childhood experiences in the contexts of family, the black church, and the black community in the South "provided them with a sense of personal worth and an awareness of the interrelatedness of life which became central elements in their respective views of community."[309]

The discontinuities between Thurman's and King's conceptions of community are equally important for Fluker. First, "Thurman's treatment of community is more clearly developed and systematic than King's." Fluker explains that "this is due primarily to their respective lifestyles, careers, and lengths of life."[310] In other words, Thurman lived eighty years as a thinker and writer, with limited social involvement, whereas King

307. Fluker, *They Looked for a City*, 158–60.
308. *Ibid.*, 156.
309. *Ibid.*
310. *Ibid.*, 161.

died at thirty-nine as the active leader of an expanding civil rights struggle. Second, Fluker notes that Thurman and King moved from different points of departure in their conceptions of community. "The individual serves as the point of departure for Thurman's understanding of community," says Fluker, but "King's conception begins with the social existence of persons." Third, Fluker maintains that while Thurman stressed the human encounter with the living God (theocentric vision) as creating "the grounds for authentic community," King emphasized "both the historical Jesus and the cosmic Christ (Christocentric vision) as the normative character for community." Finally, Fluker observes that Thurman saw evil as a "constituent part of life"—as a "positive and destructive principle that works against harmony, wholeness, and integration," whereas King viewed evil as an unwelcomed "intruder" that impedes "the actualization of community in the world."[311]

Fluker takes largely an uncritical approach in his discussion of Thurman's and King's conceptions of community. He admits that "the problem of community does not receive a definitive answer from Thurman and King," which he regards as a measure of "the profundity of the problem," but he does not pinpoint areas in which the two thinkers are vulnerable in their views. Fluker is more interested in showing how Thurman's and King's approaches to community "can serve as resources for the explication of the principal elements involved in the creation of community."[312]

Fluker's conclusions regarding the impact of racism on King's life and thought are supported and reinforced to some extent by the observations of Rufus Burrow. Burrow has written very little on King's life and thought, but his approach to the subject is no less important than the approaches taken by other black ethicists. Burrow is most concerned about the patience and courage King

311. *Ibid.*, 162 and 167–72.
312. *Ibid.*, xiv (Introduction) and 188.

demonstrated in pursuing a vision of racial harmony through struggle even as he expressed disappointment with the silence and indifference of white moderates and liberals. Burrow suggests that King still provides inspiration and a noble example for black and white Americans who choose to be prophetic on the issue of race relations.[313]

The black ethicist Katie Cannon offers a unique perspective on King—one not found in the writings of Fluker, Burrow, or other black ethicists. Cannon is primarily interested in "black womanist ethics" as revealed in the faith, the practical wisdom, and the literary tradition of black women like Zora Neale Hurston. She concludes that the novels, essays, and folklore of Hurston reflect the moral dilemma of black women, and also the values and virtues ("invisible dignity," "quiet grace," and "unshouted courage") that can guide and enhance the black female struggle for liberation and survival.[314] The distinctiveness of Cannon's approach is suggested in her contention that the moral resources in the writings of Hurston and in the theologies of Howard Thurman and Martin Luther King, Jr., when combined or synthesized, "provide conceptual elements for enhancing the moral agency of Black women." Cannon's use of Thurman and King in this regard is surprising, especially since the two "pre-liberation theologians" never experienced the unique moral situation imposed on black women by sexism. Cannon presses her claim further, arguing that the works of Thurman and King provide "the most relevant theological resources for deepening the moral wisdom in the Black community."[315]

Cannon points to several ethical themes in Thurman and King that she feels can contribute to the development of an ethic for black women's lives. One is the *imago dei* concept, which holds that every individual

---

313. Rufus Burrow, Jr., "Martin Luther King, Jr., Racism, the White Moderate and Liberal" (Unpublished paper), 1–20.
314. Cannon, *Black Womanist Ethics*, 99–123.
315. *Ibid.*, 9 and 160.

reflects the divine image and is therefore sacred and endowed with inherent worth. Cannon states that Thurman's ethics center on "the experiential-mystical element of religion," which "calls on each person to act and to reflect the divine in her actions." Cannon further observes: "It is important to note that for King, unlike Thurman, the dignity and worth of all human personality are the inalienable rights of human beingness. These rights are unchangeable and universal."[316] Some Thurman and King scholars would probably disagree with this distinction. Even so, Cannon seems on solid ground in contending that Thurman's and King's principle of *imago dei* has important implications and relevance for black women in their struggle against the twin evils of racism and sexism.

A second theme in Thurman's and King's thought that can inform "Black womanist ethics," according to Cannon, is *love as grounded in justice and social change.* Cannon views both Thurman and King as leading protagonists of this principle. The theological ethics of the two theologians, Cannon insists, "was love centered. However, King's theology required him to give much greater significance in his ethics to the *relationship* of love and justice than Thurman's more concentrated love motif."[317] The distinction Cannon draws here between Thurman and King is not entirely clear and is open to debate. However, she is right in claiming that Thurman's and King's love ethic, which encourages justice and social change, calls black women forth to challenge all barriers to liberation.[318]

The need for community is another theme in Thurman's and King's works that, in Cannon's view, is useful for the shaping of a liberation ethic for black women. Here, Cannon does not provide the depth of discussion that one finds in Walter Fluker's treatment of community in Thurman and King. However, Cannon argues as strongly as

316. *Ibid.*, 160–63.
317. *Ibid.*, 164–65.
318. *Ibid.*, 164–67.

Fluker for the centrality of *community* in the writings
of the two thinkers. Yet, Fluker seems to differ with
Cannon's suggestion that "Martin Luther King, Jr.'s theological ethics emphasized even more strongly than Thurman's a commitment to the actualization of an inclusive
human community." Despite this point of difference,
Cannon and Fluker are one in suggesting that Thurman's
and King's thought affords moral and conceptual resources for enhancing the liberation and wholeness of the
black community.[319]

The foregoing discussion reveals that black ethicists
have inherited as much from King's life and thought as
black theologians. It is difficult to find a trained black
ethicist who has not written about King's legacy for
black ethics or liberation ethics in general. This is another indication of how King still lives in the consciousness of black America.

KING AND THE FUTURE OF BLACK
THEOLOGY AND ETHICS

The importance of King's life and thought for the future of black theology and ethics is a subject of serious
debate among black religious thinkers. Scholars like
William R. Jones, the black philosopher of religion, suggest that black theologians and ethicists should move beyond King in search of other more relevant and effective
ideologies and strategies for liberation.[320] On the other
side of this argument, scholars like the black theologian
J. Deotis Roberts, argue that any viable position in liberation ethics in America in the future must focus extensively on King's life and legacy. "As we reflect upon
King's program and seek to update his unusual contribution to ethical thought and action," Roberts declares,

319. *Ibid.*, 168–74.
320. Jones, "Liberation Strategies in Black Theology," 42–47; and
William R. Jones, "Martin Luther King: Black Messiah or White
Guardian?," a paper presented before the First Unitarian Society of Minneapolis, Minneapolis, Minn. (6 April 1986), 1–10.

"we must find a way to modify the norm and the goal as we confront a new type of racism initiated by 'benign neglect'." Roberts is essentially right in claiming that black America is now confronted with a racism that "is subtle, respectable, highly intellectual and nationwide." Roberts continues: "The white conscience no longer exists, or if it does, it does so in a callous, self-righteous and antagonistic form. The white liberals are tired, and many are now avowed racists."[321] With this disturbing trend toward racial conservatism, questions about the relevance of King's philosophy and methods for the future become all the more pressing for black theologians and ethicists.

With the recent appearance of Katie Cannon's book, many black womanist theologians and ethicists will be compelled to reexamine King's ethical principles and activity in light of their struggle.[322] Cannon's contention that King's moral and conceptual resources are relevant for a black womanist ethic of liberation will undoubtedly generate much debate and discussion. Some black womanist theologians and ethicists—among whom are Kelly Brown, Jacquelyn Grant, Pauli Murray, Delores Williams, Cheryl Gilkes, and Marcia Riggs—may be critical of such an argument, especially since King sometimes exhibited sexism in his thought and actions. It will take a broad perspective and much open-mindedness on the part of black womanist thinkers to look beyond King's sexism to determine his usefulness for their community's struggle against racism, classism, and sexism.

King will undoubtedly remain an important source and inspiration for those black theologians and ethicists who see coalitions between the oppressed, at both the national and international levels, as a viable approach to total human liberation. James Cone has

---

321. Roberts, *Black Theology Today*, 120–22.
322. Cannon, *Black Womanist Ethics*, 1ff. Up to this point, black female ethicists and theologians have said very little in their published writings about Cannon's treatment of King in relation to black womanist ethics.

written extensively on this concern, and he seems convinced that King's beloved community ideal has something to offer in the quest for coalitions among the poor and oppressed.[323] Although King's vision of community shows some promise in this regard, black theologians and ethicists, especially those who are concerned about moving beyond theory to praxis, are still confronted with the challenge of finding ways to transcend the ethnic, political, philosophical, religious, and national barriers that keep the poor and oppressed divided. This is the pressing concern that undergirds James Cone's and Cornel West's call for greater dialogue between the black church and Marxist thinkers around the world regarding their respective projects for liberation.[324] King's thought and legacy have something to contribute to such a dialogue, especially since he appreciated Karl Marx's love for the poor and his passion for social justice.[325]

In their future search for a liberation ethic, black theologians and ethicists should do more comparative studies of King and other important activists in black history. James Cone's extensive work on King and Malcolm X, and Walter Fluker's and Katie G. Cannon's writings on King and Howard Thurman, are important examples of such studies. Peter Paris' study of King, Malcolm X, Adam Clayton Powell, Jr., and Joseph H. Jackson is equally important, and so are treatments of the Black Womanist tradition by Katie Cannon, Jacquelyn Grant, and Delores S. Williams.[326] Studies of this

323. Cone, *For My People*, 140–207.

324. *Ibid.*, chapter 9; and Cornel West, *Prophesy Deliverance!: An Afro-American Revolutionary Christianity* (Philadelphia: The Westminster Press, 1982), 95–127.

325. King, *Strength to Love*, 100–01.

326. Cone, *Martin and Malcolm and America*, 1ff.; Fluker, *They Looked for a City*, 1ff.; Cannon, *Black Womanist Ethics*, 1 ff.; Jacquelyn Grant, *White Women's Christ and Black Women's Jesus: Feminist Christology and Womanist Response* (Atlanta: Scholar's Press, 1989), 9–61 and 195–230; Delores S. Williams, "Womanist Theology: Black Women's Voices," *Christianity and Crisis* 47, no. 3 (March 2, 1987): 66–70; and Paris, *Black Leaders in Conflict*, 1ff.

nature will help black theologians and ethicists to understand more fully the complexity of the problems of racism, sexism, classism, and violence on a national and international scale. Furthermore, such studies will offer a broad political and theological foundation for the formulation of a viable liberation ethic in the black American community.

Those who formulate theology and ethics in the black community in the years ahead must realize that King spoke out of a black tradition of thought that embodies its own argument and critique of society and culture. The black philosopher Cornel West recognizes this when he places King in the "exceptionalist tradition" of black thought—that stream of thought that holds that blacks, because of a "unique proclivity" for virtues such as meekness and nonviolence, are part of a divine plan to save themselves and their oppressors. West goes on to speak of three other traditions in black thought—the "assimilationist tradition," which "posits Afro-American inferiority" to "white Americans"; the "marginalist tradition," which "promotes a self-image of both confinement and creativity, restriction and revolt"; and the "humanist tradition," in which black culture is not romanticized, but, rather, seen as "the expression of an oppressed human community imposing its distinctive form of order on an existential chaos."[327] Here, West provides a theoretical model that is useful for doing theology and ethics from the perspective of King and other black thinkers and activists throughout history. Thus, there is

---

327. West, *Prophesy Deliverance!* 72, 75, 78, 80, and 85. West advances his analysis of these thought traditions in the black community far beyond what these references suggest. Another important source that should be read in conjunction with West's book is Franklin, *Liberating Visions*, 1ff. Both West and Franklin have set forth some of the major paradigms that have shaped and informed the political views, theologies, and moral thought of African-American leaders and thinkers. Their works should not be ignored by political scientists, theologians, historians, Christian social ethicists, moral-development theorists, and others who are interested in interdisciplinary dialogue around the issues of black oppression and black liberation and uplift.

no need for black theologians and ethicists to overlook figures like King while quoting freely from white theologians and ethicists. Because their main task is to provide some perspective in liberation ethics, the works of King and others in the tradition of black thought are far more important.[328]

---

328. Roberts, *Black Theology Today,* 121. Important insights into the shaping of liberation ethics are afforded in Mark Ridley-Thomas, "Toward an Ethics of Liberation: Sources, Norms, and Praxis," *The Journal of Religious Thought* 47, no. 2 (Winter– Spring, 1990–91): 30–41.

ETHIOPIA SHALL STRETCH FORTH HER HANDS:

THE AFRICAN AND AFRICAN-AMERICAN STRUGGLES

3

I look for the day when black men in this country, roused to a sense of their duty in Africa, will rush to those shores to bless that benighted continent. "Ethiopia shall soon stretch forth her hands unto God."

Edward W. Blyden, 1862[1]

The Negro struggle is universal and to us indivisible.

Tom Mboya, 1962[2]

I have no doubt that the question of the relationship of the American Negro to Africa is one of great importance. I am convinced that we have a moral as well as a practical responsibility to keep the civil rights movement in America close to our African brothers.

Martin Luther King, Jr., 1963[3]

What you [black Americans] have done during the years has had very crucial repercussions for those of us in South Africa. . . . A part of the whole of your mission has been helping us to recover the sense that we, too, have a share in this wonderful heritage which St. Paul calls "the glorious liberty of the children of God."

Desmond Tutu, 1984[4]

1. Quoted in Hollis R. Lynch, ed., *Black Spokesman: Selected Published Writings of Edward W. Blyden* (London: Frank Cass and Company Limited, 1971), 20 and 35–37. Gayraud Wilmore has written: "The great prophecy of Psalm 68:31 became a forecast of the ultimate fulfillment of the people's spiritual yearning. It is impossible to say how many sermons were preached from this text during the nineteenth century, but we know that Richard Allen, Lott Carey, Henry Highland Garnet, Alexander Crummell, Edward W. Blyden, James T. Holly, and Bishop Henry M. Turner were all eloquent expositors of Psalm 68:31. They made it the cornerstone of missionary emigrationism both in the United States and Africa." See Gayraud S. Wilmore, *Black Religion and Black Radicalism: An Interpretation of the Religious History of Afro-American People* (Maryknoll, N.Y.: Orbis Books, 1983), 121.

2. A telegram from Tom Mboya to Martin Luther King, Jr., care of A. G. Gaston Auditorium, Birmingham, Ala., 24 September 1962, The King Papers, Mugar Memorial Library, Boston University, Boston, Mass., 1.

3. A letter from Martin Luther King, Jr., to Theodore E. Brown, 1 April 1963, The Archives of the Martin Luther King, Jr. Center for Nonviolent Social Change, Inc., Atlanta, Ga.

4. Desmond Tutu, "The South African Struggle," a speech delivered at the Partners in Ecumenism Conference of the National Council of Churches, Washington, D. C. (26 September 1984), 1.

King's thought on Africa and the black world as a whole is an important aspect of any study of how his vision transcended the American South and nation to assume international implications. Unfortunately, his attitude toward Africans and blacks in the diaspora has not been seriously studied. The same can be said of King's experiences in various parts of the black world and of his activities on behalf of universal black liberation.[5] Such experiences and activities affected King's vision of racial conditions in America in profound ways, and they suggest some relationship between King and the widespread interest in Africa and things *African* among black people in the late 1960s and beyond.[6]

King's attitude toward and influence on Africans and blacks in the diaspora is the central theme of this chapter. Major attention is devoted to King's recognition of bonds and obligations between people of African ancestry everywhere, and to his contributions to the struggle for universal black liberation and independence. The discussion develops in this manner: (1) establishing ties with Africa and the black diaspora; (2) King's work with the American Committee on Africa (A.C.O.A.) and the American Negro Leadership Conference on Africa (A.N.L.C.A.); (3) the impact of King's assassination on the black world; and (4) African-Americans and Africa since King.

5. Lewis V. Baldwin, ed., *Toward the Beloved Community: Martin Luther King, Jr. and South African Apartheid* (manuscript in progress), Introduction and Concluding Essay. For reasons not always clear, scholars have either ignored or minimized the importance of King's ties with Africa and the black world generally. An investigation of King's views on and experiences in Africa, and of his work on behalf of African independence, would contribute to our knowledge of how important members of the black intelligentsia have traditionally regarded Africa. Sterling Stuckey called for a study of the views of the black intelligentsia on Africa in 1969—a study that would include John E. Bruce, Bishop Alexander Walters, Benjamin Brawley, William H. Ferris, and James Weldon Johnson. Interestingly enough, Stuckey did not mention King in this regard. See Sterling Stuckey, "Contours of Black Studies: The Dimension of African and Afro-American Relationships," *The Massachusetts Review* 10, no. 4 (Autumn 1969): 753.

6. Baldwin, ed., *Toward the Beloved Community*, Introduction and Concluding Essay.

ESTABLISHING TIES WITH AFRICA
AND THE BLACK DIASPORA

The nationalist elements in King's thought were clearly reflected in those parts of his writings and speeches in which he focused on specific problems faced by peoples of African ancestry throughout the world. His attention to the condition of his people in the United States has already been established and documented. As early as the Montgomery Bus Boycott, King expressed a deep interest in Africa's struggle against European racism and colonial domination. "We could turn our eyes to Africa," he declared in 1956, "and notice there two hundred million black men and women under the pressing yoke of the British, the Dutch and the French. For years all of these people were dominated politically, exploited economically, segregated and humiliated."[7] King said a year later that "you also know that for years and for centuries Africa has been one of the most exploited continents in the history of the world"—"the continent that has suffered all of the pain and affliction that could be mustered up by other nations."[8] For King, the oppression and exploitation inflicted upon Africa over time were most evident in the slave trade, which raped the Gold Coast in West Africa and extended into the British West Indies and North America. He also noted that the white Western world's exploitation of the continent continued well into the twentieth century, stunting not only the growth and development of West Africa, but also the Union of South Africa and other parts of southern Africa, eastern African countries like Uganda and Kenya, and North African areas such as Egypt, Ethiopia,

7. Martin Luther King, Jr., "An Address at the First Annual Institute on Nonviolence and Social Change under the Auspices of the Montgomery Improvement Association," delivered at the Holt Street Baptist Church, Montgomery, Ala. (The King Center Archives, 3 December 1956), 5.
8. Martin Luther King, Jr., "The Birth of a New Nation: Ghana and Other African Countries," transcript of a taped speech (The King Center Archives, April 1957), 1–21.

Morocco, and Libya.[9] King's perspective on the African condition as a whole led him to conclude in 1959 that "It is impossible for Angola to stand in Africa and not be affected by what is happening in Nigeria and Kenya and Rhodesia."[10]

King's interest in Africa and in the black world generally found expression in other ways in March, 1957, when he and his wife accepted a personal invitation from Prime Minister Kwame Nkrumah to witness "the attainment of independence by the Gold Coast within the British Commonwealth under the name of Ghana."[11] Coretta Scott King described Nkrumah's invitation as "one of the most exciting things that happened to us," and noted that the African leader "knew America well and had invited a number of outstanding American Negroes to share Ghana's great day." Concerning Dr. King's excitement over the trip, she wrote:

> Martin always saw a close relationship between the black struggle in America and the struggle for independence in Africa. In his early speeches and sermons he had often compared European colonialism with Negro oppression in America. Now he eagerly anticipated the experience of going to Africa and being a

9. *Ibid.*, 1–3.
10. A letter from Martin Luther King, Jr., to Miss Deolinda Rodrigues, 21 July 1959, The King Papers, Boston University.
11. A letter from Kwame Nkrumah to Martin Luther King, Jr., 22 January 1957, The King Papers, Boston University; and a letter from Martin Luther King, Jr., to the Secretary for External Affairs, Accra, Gold Coast, 12 February 1957, The King Papers, Boston University; and "King Accepts Bid to Visit India, Africa," *The Montgomery Advertiser,* Montgomery, Ala. (February 16, 1957): 1ff. The money for the Kings' Ghana trip was donated by Montgomery's Dexter Avenue Baptist Church and the Montgomery Improvement Association. Coretta Scott King writes: "The church people were excited because it would be the first time that Martin would travel outside the country, and since a number of them had been abroad, they wanted their pastor to have this experience. They realized how enriching it would be for him and that it could mean that he would contribute even more to the life of the church and the community." See Coretta Scott King, *My Life with Martin Luther King, Jr.* (New York: Avon Books, 1969), 163–64; and *A List of the Names of the Reception Committee for Dr. King on His Trip from Ghana,* The Montgomery Improvement Association, 7 March 1957, The King Papers, Boston University, 1.

part of the independence celebration of a new black nation.[12]

King himself spoke at length concerning the importance of the Nkrumah invitation, suggesting that it was a positive affirmation of the Montgomery struggle and of the ties that existed between black Americans and the Gold Coast:

> When I received from Prime Minister Nkrumah the invitation to the Independence Ceremonies in Ghana, I felt that I held in my hand a fraternal greeting to the Negro people of Montgomery whose tenacious struggle and sacrifices had won the admiration of all freedom-loving people. There is necessarily a close bond between the American Negro and the Negroes of the Gold Coast, since a very large number of us trace our ancestry to that part of Africa which is now Ghana.
>
> The achievement of a free and independent Negro Nation in Ghana highlights the fact that in our nation elementary rights of citizenship and equality are still unrealized for millions, and in particular, for the Southern Negro. This condition explains the intense interest and pride we have in this historic event.
>
> Ghana represents a victorious sector in the worldwide movement of colonial peoples toward the dawn of freedom. Our own struggle in the United States is a part of this great democratic upsurge, and the knowledge that Ghana has won liberation inspires us with the confidence that our fight for justice will be won not in a distant tomorrow, but in a day closer at hand than we have heretofore realized.[13]

The trip to Ghana, "King's first sojourn on the continent of his fathers," contributed immensely to the civil rights leader's perception of the black condition

12. King, *My Life with Martin Luther King, Jr.*, 163–64.
13. Martin Luther King, Jr., "A Statement Regarding the Invitation from Prime Minister Kwame Nkrumah" (Unpublished document from The King Papers, Boston University, March, 1957), 1.

worldwide. He and his wife were accompanied on the trip by Prime Minister Norman W. Manley of Jamaica, and by black American leaders such as Ralph Bunche, Lester Granger, Adam Clayton Powell, Jr., A. Philip Randolph, and Roy Wilkins—an entourage that, when considered in conjunction with the Nkrumah invitation, was a metaphor for what King's relationship with the entire black world would eventually become.[14] In Ghana, the Kings and their fellow travelers were amazed by the handsome streets and the magnificent government-owned Hotel Ambassador, "more modern and luxurious than many hotels in America." "We realized that we ourselves had been the victims of the propaganda that all Africa was primitive and dirty," Coretta Scott King recalled. But there was another side to Ghanaian life that reflected the tragic impact of European colonialism—a side that deeply disturbed Dr. King. Coretta Scott King later recounted:

> Almost everyone we saw in Accra had servants. We were told that they were paid only twenty-eight cents a day, the result of colonialism. Seeing how that system had demoralized them bothered us and marred our trip. Martin was extremely upset by the servile attitude to which their suffering had brought them. They had been trained to bow, almost to cringe; their stature was decreased. It was heartbreaking.[15]

On March 9, 1957, the Kings were among the thousands of people of African descent from various parts of the world who heard Nkrumah shout: "At long last the battle has ended. Ghana, our beloved country, is free forever." Fifty thousand African voices responded in unison with a mighty roar, "Ghana is free." "It was an immensely thrilling moment for Martin and me," Coretta

14. "Conversation in Ghana: Editorial Correspondence," *The Christian Century* (April 10, 1957): 446–47; King, *My Life with Martin Luther King, Jr.*, 164; and Walter E. Fluker, *They Looked for a City: A Comparative Analysis of the Ideal of Community in the Thought of Howard Thurman and Martin Luther King, Jr.* (Lanham, Md.: University Press of America, Inc., 1989), 93.
15. King, *My Life with Martin Luther King, Jr.*, 164.

Scott King remembered. "We felt a strong sense of identity and kinship with those African people shouting 'Freedom!' in their different tribal tongues. We were so proud of our African heritage, and saw in Ghana a symbol of the hopes and aspirations of all our people."[16] This sense of a close relationship to Africa was enhanced by the Kings' lengthy conversation with Nkrumah—a conversation that centered largely on the problems of blacks in America, and on the vitality of nonviolence as a method for social change.[17]

Following the independence celebration in Accra, Ghana, the Kings flew to Lagos, Nigeria, and eventually to Kano in central Nigeria. Coretta Scott King recalled that the high level of poverty in Nigeria caused King to lash out angrily at the exploitation of Africa by England:

> There, the appalling poverty of the people burst upon us. I think that in Ghana there may have been a certain amount of "dressing up" for the occasion; perhaps we saw not much more than we were meant to see. In Kano we saw people living under conditions of filth and squalor that exceeded even the worst state of Negroes in America. Martin talked angrily about the exploitation of Africans by the British, and later, when we got to London, he compared the grandeur of England and the Empire to conditions in Nigeria. But he took comfort from the thought of our people throwing off their oppressors in modern times. He pointed out that there was once a time when the sun never set on the British Empire; now it hardly rises on it.[18]

When King returned to Montgomery in April, 1957, he preached an inspiring sermon at Dexter Avenue Baptist Church entitled, "The Birth of a New Nation." Here he drew on the Exodus story to highlight Africa's struggle against colonialism—to show how the struggles

16. *Ibid.*, 165. Walter Fluker is essentially correct in suggesting that the Ghana experience "made a momentous impact upon King's understanding of the liberation struggles of colonized nations and their role in the creation of world community." See Fluker, *They Looked for a City*, 93.

17. King, *My Life with Martin Luther King, Jr.*, 166.

18. *Ibid.*, 166–67.

of Moses and his followers to get out of Egypt closely
paralleled Africa's struggle against white Western domination. King focused specifically on Ghana and its
movement against colonialism and imperialism.[19]
He later spoke of the Ghanaian struggle as an illustration of the power of nonviolence, and predicted that
Ghana, under capable leadership, would eventually
take her rightful place among the great nations of the
world:

> Ghana is a beautiful example of the fact that freedom
> can be achieved through nonviolence. I predict a great
> future for the new nation. It has marvelous possibili-
> ties. Of course it will have problems like any new na-
> tion. It will be necessary to industrialize the new
> nation in order to lift the economic standards. It will
> be necessary to extend free education in order to lift
> the cultural standards, for ninety percent of the peo-
> ple are still illiterate. But in spite of these difficulties
> I am sure that with competent leadership Ghana will
> move to the top.[20]

The Ghana experience created in King a desire to
learn more about Africa. He read Nkrumah's autobiography and many news accounts of the Ghanaian independence celebration from *The Daily Graphic* in Accra, *The
Los Angeles Herald-Dispatch,* and other newspapers.
By the early 1960s, King had accumulated many books
on Africa and was collecting news on the subject from
*The Pittsburgh Courier, The New York Age, The New York
Herald Tribune,* and several African newspapers and
journals.[21] He also kept in touch with developments
in Africa through friends and acquaintances on the

19. King, "The Birth of a New Nation," 1–21.
20. If there was a serious weakness in King's perspective on Africa,
it was his underestimation of the depths of African cultures and of the
sophistication of African peoples even under colonialism. This is reflected in this remark concerning Ghana. See a letter from Martin
Luther King, Jr., to the Rev. Galal Kernahanof, 29 April 1957, The King
Papers, Boston University.
21. King, "The Birth of a New Nation," 14.

continent.[22] In April, 1960, King was invited by an African friend to return to Ghana for the adoption of the new Republic Constitution there, but he was unable to accept the invitation because of a commitment in Rio de Janeiro, Brazil.[23] In December, 1960, King returned to Africa, and was amazed at the number of countries that had followed Ghana in throwing off the yoke of colonialism:

> In 1957 when Mrs. King and I went to Africa to attend the independence celebration of the new nation of Ghana, there were only seven independent nations in the whole of Africa. Just last month I went back to Africa. I went to Nigeria to attend the inauguration of the new Governor-General. As I got off the plane in Africa, I thought of the fact that there are 27 independent countries in Africa. Within less than three years, more than 18 countries have received their independence in Africa. They are looking over here. The wind of change is blowing all about, all throughout the age. They want to know what we are doing about democracy and they are making it clear that racism and colonialism must go.[24]

King consistently spoke of the bonds and obligations that existed between black Americans and Africans. He recognized that blacks in America and Africa were not only connected by blood and condition but also shared ideas, ambitions, and values. "It is always a very happy privilege to hear from my friends and brothers in Africa," he said in a letter to the Reverend Amin Msowoya of Nyasaland in 1958. "While we are separated by many,

22. A letter from Cephas Munanairi to Martin Luther King, Jr., 7 September 1960, The King Papers, Boston University.

23. A letter from K. A. Gbedemah to Martin Luther King, Jr., 23 April 1960, The King Papers, Boston University; and a letter from Martin Luther King, Jr., to Mr. A. Q. Smart-Abbey, 6 June 1960, The King Papers, Boston University.

24. Martin Luther King, Jr., "Speech at a Rally," Savannah, Ga. (The King Papers, Boston University, 1 January 1961), 6. Also see Martin Luther King, Jr., "The Rising Tide," a speech to the National Urban League (The King Papers, Boston University, 6 September 1960), 1 ff.

many miles, we are united in a common struggle for freedom and human dignity, and also in the bonds of Christian love."[25] King made this point even more emphatically
in another letter to an African friend in April, 1960:

> I am deeply sympathetic with what is happening in
> Central Africa and indeed all over Africa. I have had a
> long interest in the problems of Africa and consider
> them a part of our problems because we in a real sense
> are a part of Africa, and our struggle in the United
> States is not an isolated struggle, but a part of the
> worldwide struggle for freedom and human dignity.[26]

In 1962, King alluded to "a direct correlation between
the U. S. Negro integration struggle and the anti-colonial
fight of African nations." He continued:

> Colonialism and segregation are nearly synonymous;
> they are legitimate first cousins because their com-
> mon end is economic exploitation, political domina-
> tion, and the debasing of human personality. In many
> ways the future of the emergent African nations (par-
> ticularly those below the Sahara) and the American
> Negro are intertwined. As long as segregation and
> discrimination exist in our nation, the longer the
> chances of survival are for colonialism and vice versa,
> for the very same set of complex politico-economic
> forces are operative in both instances.[27]

This sense of a shared experience and struggle with
Africans led King to call for more black American diplomats to serve in Africa. "One of the means by which we
could demonstrate sincerity of purpose," he noted in a
statement aimed at the federal government in 1962, "is
a broader use of Negro Americans in our diplomatic

25. A letter from Martin Luther King, Jr., to the Rev. Amin Msowoya,
22 August 1958, The King Papers, Boston University.

26. A letter from Martin Luther King, Jr., to Mr. Cephas Munanairi,
7 April 1960, The King Papers, Boston University; and King, "The Rising
Tide," 1 ff.

27. Martin Luther King, Jr., "Press Statement regarding 'Stand-ins,'"
Atlanta, Ga. (The King Center Archives, 19 February 1962), 1; and Martin
Luther King, Jr., "The Negro Looks at Africa," *The New York Amsterdam
News* (December 8, 1962): 1 ff.

corps that serve the independent and emergent nations of Africa." King expressed regret that "In a diplomatic corps of more than a hundred ambassadors, . . . there are only two Negroes." In his view, this explained the insensitivity of the American government toward African problems.[28]

King's relationships with various African heads of state grew out of his recognition of obligations between Africans and black Americans—out of his conviction that they must work together to overcome the forces that oppressed them. His conversations and correspondences with Kwame Nkrumah always centered around this concern. Nkrumah promised King on several occasions that he and his people in Ghana would make it clear to the United States and her allies "through the United Nations and other diplomatic channels that beautiful words and extensive handouts cannot be substitutes for the simple responsibility of treating our colored brothers in America as first-class human beings."[29] Nkrumah's knowledge of the black American condition resulted largely from his earlier training at the predominantly black Lincoln University in Pennsylvania, from his exposure to black communities in Pennsylvania, and from his reading of King's *Stride Toward Freedom: The Montgomery Story* (1958). His interest in King's leadership and in the plight and struggle of black Americans remained strong even after 1966, when he was ousted by the Ghanaian military. Nkrumah died in 1972, four years after King was assassinated.[30]

King also developed a close friendship with Tom Mboya, who led the independence movement in Kenya in the 1950s and early 1960s. Mboya shared King's and

28. King, "The Negro Looks at Africa," 1 ff.
29. Martin Luther King, Jr., "A View of the Dawn," *Interracial Review* 30, no. 5 (May 1957): 84; and a letter from Martin Luther King, Jr., to Prime Minister Kwame Nkrumah, 17 April 1959, The King Papers, Boston University.
30. King, *My Life with Martin Luther King, Jr.*, 166; and a letter from Martin Luther King, Jr., to Prime Minister Kwame Nkrumah, 17 April 1959.

Nkrumah's perspective on the relationship between the African and Afro-American struggles. The Southern Christian Leadership Conference (S.C.L.C.) invited Mboya to Atlanta in the spring of 1959, at which time King and a distinguished committee of some 250 persons honored the African leader with an African Freedom Dinner.[31] On that occasion, King told Mboya: "I am absolutely convinced that there is no basic difference between colonialism and segregation. They are both based on a contempt for life, and a tragic doctrine of white supremacy. So our struggles are not only similar; they are in a real sense one."[32] Mboya later expressed deep gratitude for the dinner, and admitted that he had been significantly influenced by King's civil rights leadership and by his ideas as set forth in *Stride Toward Freedom*:

> It was a pleasure to meet you and all of the leaders of the Southern Christian Leadership Council. I have always been impressed and inspired by your devoted and dedicated leadership in the struggle for equality and the dignity of man. I have no doubt that victory will be yours in the near future. I have since read your book and want you to know that I have never found myself so completely captured by a book and ideas. It is particularly significant that you succeed in putting forth your ideas and championing our coloured people's cause without emotion, hate, or fear. Your leadership will inspire many of us.[33]

In a letter to King in 1962, Mboya linked the oppression of Africans to that of New World blacks. Referring to the

31. *The Crusader: S.C.L.C., Inc.* 1, no. 2 (November 1959), The King Center Archives, 4; *Report of the Director to the Executive Board of S.C.L.C.* (The King Center Archives, 15 May 1959), 1; and a letter from Martin Luther King, Jr., to Tom Mboya, 8 July 1959, The King Center Archives.
32. Quoted in David J. Garrow, *Bearing the Cross: Martin Luther King, Jr., and the Southern Christian Leadership Conference* (New York: William Morrow and Company, Inc., 1986), 118.
33. A letter from Martin Luther King, Jr., to Tom Mboya, 8 July 1959; and a letter from Tom Mboya to Martin Luther King, Jr., 16 June 1959, The King Papers, Boston University.

black struggle as "indivisible" and "universal," Mboya said to King:

> I send greetings and support for the cause you fight for. . . . I say to the United States that so long as there is no full respect for all human beings in America, so much there is time remaining hypercritical in the eyes of the world. You do not only have the right to equality, but have a duty to free yourselves. History and justice is on our side, so let us fight on till victory is achieved.[34]

In another letter, Mboya congratulated King "for the hard campaign you have been carrying out in the south," and declared, "You have our entire support and I am sure that your efforts are beginning to bear fruit." Because of his friendship with Mboya, King was invited to Kenya's independence celebration in December, 1963, but was unable to appear because of other commitments.[35] King always regarded Mboya as one who symbolized the black struggle worldwide. "Your dedication to the ideals of freedom, and your wise leadership," said King to Mboya, "has endeared you to the hearts of millions." It is noteworthy that both men died at age thirty-nine at the hands of persons they tried to liberate. Mboya was assassinated on July 5, 1969, at a time when King's death still rested heavy on his heart.[36]

---

34. A telegram from Tom Mboya to Martin Luther King, Jr., 24 September 1962.

35. A letter from Tom Mboya to Martin Luther King, Jr., 22 October 1962, The King Papers, Boston University; and a letter from Martin Luther King, Jr., to Tom Mboya, 12 October 1962, The King Papers, Boston University. King developed friendships with other Kenyan leaders aside from Tom Mboya. Dr. Julius G. Kiano, a member of Kenya's Parliament, referred to King as "my good friend" in 1959. See a letter from Dr. Julius Gikonyo Kiano to the President of Alabama State College, 17 July 1959, The King Papers, Boston University. King referred to Dr. Kiano as "my dear friend." See a letter from Martin Luther King, Jr., to Dr. Julius G. Kiano, 19 August 1959, The King Papers, Boston University.

36. A letter from Martin Luther King, Jr., to Tom Mboya, 2 August 1960, The King Papers, Boston University; and George M. Houser, *No One Can Stop the Rain: Glimpses of Africa's Liberation Struggle* (New York: The Pilgrim Press, 1989), 90.

King's relationship with Premier Ben Bella of the New Algerian Republic was of a similar nature. In October, 1962, the two leaders met for almost two hours and "discussed issues ranging from the efficacy of nonviolence to the Cuban crisis." "However, it was on the question of racial injustice that we spent most of our time," King recalled:

> As I sat talking with Mr. Ben Bella he displayed again and again an intimate knowledge of the Negro struggle here in America. The details of the Montgomery bus protest were immediately at his finger tips. He understood clearly what the issues were. The "Sit-ins" of 1960 were discussed animatedly and he expressed regret at the violence that accompanied the Freedom Rides. . . . He knew all about Albany, Georgia, too, and Oxford, Mississippi was currently in the headlines. The significance of our conversation was Ben Bella's complete familiarity with the progression of events in the Negro struggle for full citizenship.[37]

The exchange of information and ideas between King and Ben Bella gave them a sense of oneness in the crusade for universal black liberation. "All through our talks," King recounted, "he [Ben Bella] repeated or inferred, 'We are brothers.'" It was out of this sense of solidarity that King acknowledged that "the battle of the Algerians against colonialism and the battle of the Negro against segregation is a common struggle."[38]

King saw the emergence of African freedom fighters and leaders like Nkrumah, Mboya, and Ben Bella as a major influence and inspiration for black students involved in the civil rights movement. In May, 1962, he commented:

> The liberation struggle in Africa has been the greatest single international influence on American Negro students. Frequently I hear them say that if their African

37. Martin Luther King, Jr., "My Talk with Ben Bella," *New York Amsterdam News* (October 27, 1962): 12.
38. *Ibid.*

brothers can break the bonds of colonialism, surely the American Negro can break Jim Crow. African leaders such as President Kwame Nkrumah of Ghana, Governor-General Nnamdi Azikiwe of Nigeria, Dr. Tom Mboya of Kenya, and Dr. Hastings Banda of Nyasaland are popular heroes on most Negro college campuses. Many groups demonstrated or otherwise protested when the Congo leader, Patrice Lumumba, was assassinated. The newspapers were mistaken when they interpreted these outbursts of indignation as "Communist-inspired."[39]

King was equally mindful of the impact of leaders from the Caribbean on the civil rights movement and on the black struggle worldwide. For him, Marcus Garvey had represented to the fullest the bonds and obligations that existed between Africans, West Indian blacks, black Americans, and others in the black diaspora. Harry Belafonte, Stokely Carmichael, Sidney Poitier, and other black artists of Caribbean background, who donated their time, talents, and resources to the civil rights movement, symbolized for King the relationship between the liberation struggles of West Indians and blacks in the United States. African-Caribbean leaders such as Prime Minister Norman W. Manley of Jamaica and Dr. Francois Duvalier (Papa Doc) of Haiti were held in high esteem by King, mainly because they, too, shared the vision of universal black freedom and independence. Manley and Duvalier also had a high regard for King, viewing him as a voice for oppressed blacks everywhere. This explains why Duvalier referred to King as a leader of "Negro-African peoples," and noted that King "shall remain for us Negroes the Mahatma of the Western Hemisphere."[40]

39. Martin Luther King, Jr., "A Speech Regarding the Influence of African Movements on U. S. Students" (The King Center Archives, May, 1962), 3; King, "The Rising Tide," 1 ff.; and Martin Luther King, Jr., *Why We Can't Wait* (New York: The New American Library, 1964), 21–22.
40. King, *Why We Can't Wait*, 21–22, 33, 35, and 38; and Dr. Francois Duvalier, *A Tribute to the Martyred Leader of Nonviolence, Reverend Dr. Martin Luther King, Jr.*, trans. John E. Pickering (Port-au-Prince, Haiti: Presses Nationales, 1968), 20 ff.

King held that the fact that black men like Manley, Duvalier, and Nkrumah ruled their countries in the West Indies and Africa, and were strong voices in the United Nations and in other international arenas, inspired black Americans in their quest for power and political progress:

> The Negro saw black statesmen voting on vital issues in the United Nations—and knew that in many cities of his own land he was not permitted to take that significant walk to the ballot box. He saw black kings and potentates ruling from palaces—and knew he had been condemned to move from small ghettoes to larger ones. Witnessing the drama of Negro progress elsewhere in the world, witnessing a level of conspicuous consumption at home exceeding anything in our history, it was natural that by 1963 Negroes would rise with resolution and demand a share of governing power.[41]

King frequently described black Americans as a people who were, consciously or unconsciously, caught up in the *Zeitgeist* with their brothers in Africa, South America, and the Caribbean.[42] This perception led him, while en route to Oslo, Norway, to receive the Nobel Peace Prize in December, 1964, to participate in the organization of "a movement to bring together colored people in the London area." Here, King joined with Africans, West Indians, and other people of color in calling upon England to address "a growing color or race problem"—a problem resulting from "the large number of persons that migrated to England from various points of the British Commonwealth."[43]

King's relationships with black students provide yet another angle from which to view his ties to the black world. The civil rights movement, and his efforts on

    41. King, *Why We Can't Wait*, 22.
    42. Martin Luther King, Jr., "Dreams of Brighter Tomorrows," a speech (The King Center Archives, March, 1965), 1–2.
    43. *Ibid.*; and Martin Luther King, Jr., "Transcript of an Interview Regarding Nobel Peace Prize," Oslo, Norway (The King Center Archives, 9 November 1964), 1–2.

behalf of the oppressed worldwide, brought him in contact with black students in the United States, Africa, and the West Indies. The commitment of black high school and college students to the African-American struggle in the United States always impressed King, leading him to assert in 1962:

> The striking quality in Negro students I have met is the intensity and depth of their commitment. I am no longer surprised to meet physically attractive, stylishly dressed young girls whose charm and personality would grace a junior prom and to hear them declare in unmistakably sincere terms, 'Dr. King, I am ready to die if I must.'"[44]

African students impressed King in a similar manner, especially since they represented the brightest hope for full African independence. This explains why King, as early as the Montgomery Bus Boycott, called upon the Dexter Avenue Baptist Church to assist in educating African students in the United States. While at Dexter, he supported African students who matriculated at Tuskegee Institute and Alabama State College.[45] In a letter to John C. Miyengi of Kenya in 1959, King remarked:

> Since I have received so many letters from African friends who are interested in pursuing further studies in the United States, I have decided to talk personally with some college presidents and some governmental officials and see if scholarship aid cannot be offered to make these studies possible. Please know that I am deeply interested in African students studying in the United States. I hope one day our dream will come true.[46]

44. King, "A Speech Regarding the Influence of African Movements," 3.
45. See a letter from Tom Mboya to Martin Luther King, Jr., 16 June 1959; and a letter from Tom Mboya to Martin Luther King, Jr., 7 September 1959, The King Papers, Boston University.
46. A letter from Martin Luther King, Jr., to Mr. John Cleopas Miyengi, 1 June 1959, The King Papers, Boston University. Most of the letters King exchanged with African students are stored at the Mugar Memorial Library at Boston University. For example, see a letter from

In the fall of 1959, King recommended that the
S.C.L.C. give a scholarship each year to an African student. In making this recommendation, he noted:

> In order to express our deep sympathy with our
> African brothers in the struggle for freedom and hu-
> man dignity, and in order to reveal our awareness of
> the oneness of our struggle, I recommend that we give
> a scholarship of at least $500.00 per year to assist in
> the education of some African student. This will do a
> great deal to develop a sense of self respect within
> African students, and contribute in some little way
> toward the developing of persons to take over leader-
> ship responsibilities in that great continent.[47]

The recommendation was accepted and approved by the
S.C.L.C., and King made the education of African students an official part of his quest for black liberation. In
the early 1960s, he worked with Tom Mboya and Dr.
Gikonyo Kiano of Kenya in placing and supporting

Justus M. Kitonga to Martin Luther King, Jr., 15 February 1960; a letter
from Martin Luther King, Jr., to Mr. Justus M. Kitonga, 6 April 1960; a
letter from Martin Luther King, Jr., to Mr. E. Nathan Ogeto, 12 April 1960;
a letter from Martin Luther King, Jr., to Mr. Simon Gray, 13 April 1960; a
letter from Martin Luther King, Jr., to Mr. John C. Miyengi, 13 April 1960;
a letter from Amin Msowoya to Martin Luther King, Jr., 27 May 1960; a
letter from Christopher Elirehema to Martin Luther King, Jr., 30 May
1960; a letter from Martin Luther King, Jr., to Christopher Elirehema, 16
June 1960; a letter from Martin Luther King, Jr., to Mr. Gideon G. Okello
Dolla, 17 June 1960; a letter from Martin Luther King, Jr., to Mr. Jopelle
Dzimba, 18 June 1960; a letter from Otini Kambona to Martin Luther
King, Jr., 17 August 1960; a letter from Joshua Kazzungu to Martin Luther
King, Jr., 11 September 1960; a letter from Eliud G. W. Karuga to Martin
Luther King, Jr., 29 September 1960; a letter from Amos Kiringin to Mar-
tin Luther King, Jr., 30 September 1960; a letter from Justus M. Kitonga to
Martin Luther King, Jr., 3 October 1960; a letter from Augustine K. In-
gutia, Jr., to Martin Luther King, Jr., 19 August 1961; a letter from Martin
Luther King, Jr., to Mr. Augustine K. Ingutia, Jr., 10 October 1961; and a
letter from Rev. Amin Msowoya to Martin Luther King, Jr., 14 August
1961.

47. Martin Luther King, Jr., "Recommendations to the Board of the
S.C.L.C.," The Southern Christian Leadership Conference Meeting, Columbia, South Carolina (The King Center Archives, 29 September–1 October 1959), 3; *The Crusader: S.C.L.C., Inc.* (November, 1959), 4; and a letter
from Martin Luther King, Jr., to Amin Msowoya, 19 September 1960, The
King Papers, Boston University.

African students in American colleges and universities.[48] King was often frustrated because his resources were insufficient to meet the needs of students from various parts of the African continent who wrote him for assistance. "I am confronted with real limitations in offering financial assistance to African students," he once complained. "My limited resources only makes it possible for me to assist one or two students per year."[49] In many instances, King referred African students to the American Committee on Africa in New York, an organization with which he was affiliated. He viewed this organization as "an agency in our country which has more knowledge of Africa and the possibilities for African students than any other."[50]

King's efforts on behalf of African students, and for black freedom worldwide, earned him the respect and admiration of Africans everywhere—a level of respect and admiration enjoyed by very few black American leaders in our history. King's interest in and support for African students were frequently mentioned in African newspapers.[51] He often received expressions of gratitude from Tom Mboya and other African leaders, and from African students as well. "I have heard so much about your endless kindness which you have been giving to some of our fellow Africans yearly as to enable them to come to America for their farther education," said one African student in a letter to King.[52] Another called King

48. A letter from Martin Luther King, Jr., to Mr. Edward Obedi Lichenga, 7 April 1960, The King Papers, Boston University; a letter from Martin Luther King, Jr., to Mr. Lawrence L. Makotsi, 14 April 1960, The King Papers, Boston University; and a letter from Eliud G. W. Karuga to Martin Luther King, Jr., 8 May 1961, The King Papers, Boston University.

49. A letter from Martin Luther King, Jr., to Mr. John C. Miyengi, 13 April 1960; and a letter from Martin Luther King, Jr., to Mr. Christopher Elirehema, 16 June 1960.

50. A letter from Martin Luther King, Jr., to Mr. George S. Obong, 12 April 1960, The King Papers, Boston University.

51. A letter from Mr. George P. Nohungu to Martin Luther King, Jr., 2 February 1960, The King Papers, Boston University.

52. A letter from Tom Mboya to Martin Luther King, Jr., 7 September 1959, The King Papers, Boston University; and a letter from Christopher Elirehema to Martin Luther King, Jr., 30 May 1960.

"a great man," and declared, "I always hoped to see a day when I could be amongst the audience or congregation to which you could be delivering a speech or sermon." "I hope that you will keep on struggling until you will attain a favorable destination," the student continued. "We—all that believe in equal human dignity, will unite behind you, whether we be in the troubled Africa, Europe, Asia or in the segregated South."[53] Ouma Namwambe, a Ugandan educator and trade union leader, requested King's permission to start a technical school in his name in 1962, a request to which King responded affirmatively and with humility. In a letter to King, Namwambe observed:

> What you have done to Africans who come for education in America is very important, and as one of the Africans who like the extension of our children's education, I am hereby forced to open up a school in your name. The name I propose to write on the list is *Dr. Martin Luther King Memorial College*, or *Dr. King Memorial Technical College*.[54]

During the 1960s, many student leaders and organizations from Africa either visited King in Atlanta or invited him to visit Africa. In the summer of 1964, Operation Crossroads Africa brought a number of African youth leaders to the United States for six weeks, and in their final reports, they indicated that their visit with King and the S.C.L.C. in Atlanta "was the high point of the whole trip." In the summer of 1965, twenty-six youth leaders from twelve countries in East, West, and Central Africa came to America to meet with King and to learn more about the African-American struggle. James H. Robinson, the Director of Operation Crossroads Africa, said of the students in a letter to King: "Of all the people they wanted to see, you were first; and of all things they

53. A letter from Augustine K. Ingutia, Jr., to Martin Luther King, Jr., 19 August 1961.
54. A letter from Ouma Namwambe to Martin Luther King, Jr., 10 June 1961, The King Papers, Boston University.

wanted to know about, civil rights was highest on their list."[55] Also in the summer of 1965, Pan-African Students' Organization in the Americas, Inc. (P.A.S.O.A.) invited King and the S.C.L.C. to "an all-African students conference" in New York. In extending the invitation, the group wrote:

> Your efforts to eradicate social injustice in your own country have aroused the conscience of all people of good will and common sense. In the continent of Africa we are equally determined to wipe out once and for all the human indignities, indecencies and abuses that have been experienced by us since time immemorial. For this reason we feel that our target is identical to yours. . . . It is therefore only natural that we would like to share our views with your group during our conference.[56]

The students wanted King, at the opening session of the conference, to address the topic, "The Relationship between Africans and Their Descendants in the World Today."[57] King declined the invitation owing to a long-standing engagement in Puerto Rico.[58] He received a similar invitation from P.A.S.O.A. in July, 1967, but again had to decline because of other obligations.[59]

King's ties and correspondence with black students from the West Indies occurred on a much smaller scale. Even so, West Indian students were as interested as African students in the meaning and implications of King's leadership and mission for all people of African

55. A letter from James H. Robinson to Martin Luther King, Jr., 22 June 1965, The King Center Archives.

56. A letter from Sylvester A. Okereke to Martin Luther King, Jr., 10 June 1965, The King Center Archives.

57. A letter from Sylvester A. Okereke to Martin Luther King, Jr., 27 July 1965, The King Center Archives.

58. A letter from Miss Dora McDonald, Secretary to Martin Luther King, Jr., to Mr. Sylvester Okereke, 21 July 1965, The King Center Archives; and a telegram from Martin Luther King, Jr., to Mr. Sylvester A. Okereke, 6 August 1965, The King Center Archives.

59. A letter from the Pan-African Students' Organization in the Americas, Inc., to Martin Luther King, Jr., 10 July 1967, The King Center Archives.

ancestry. This helps explain why King, in June, 1965, was invited to deliver an address at the valedictory service at the University of the West Indies in Mona, Jamaica. In his address, King thanked the students, the university officials, and the officials of the Jamaican government "for the support that you have given in terms of your prayers and your concern for the work that I am trying to do in the United States of America." King went on to talk about the "magnificent drama of independence" taking place on the stage of African history and in the Caribbean area.[60] The address was clearly representative of his view that people of African descent everywhere shared a common condition and struggle. This view became the foundation stone of King's activities on behalf of black people.

KING'S WORK WITH THE A.C.O.A. AND THE A.N.L.C.A.

Much of King's activities for African liberation and independence occurred under the auspices of the A.C.O.A. and the A.N.L.C.A., both of which were headquartered in New York. He worked with both agencies, and the S.C.L.C. became one of their sponsoring organizations. The A.C.O.A. was an interracial organization established in May, 1953.[61] King became involved with this organization in 1957. The A.N.L.C.A. was organized in New York in November, 1962, by King and other civil rights leaders, among whom were Roy Wilkins, the Executive Secretary of the NAACP; A. Philip Randolph, President of the Brotherhood of Sleeping Car Porters and Vice President of the American Federation of Labor and Congress of Industrial Organizations; Dorothy Height, President of the National Council of Negro Women; James Farmer, the Executive Director of the Congress of Racial Equality;

---

60. Martin Luther King, Jr., "Facing the Challenge of a New Age," a Valedictory Address at the University of the West Indies, Mona, Jamaica (The King Center Archives, 20 June 1965), 1–12.
61. Houser, *No One Can Stop the Rain*, 63.

and Whitney M. Young, Jr., the Executive Director of the National Urban League.[62] Both the A.C.O.A. and the A.N.L.C.A. were concerned about United States policy toward Africa, and specifically about economic development, racial equality, and political freedom in the emerging nations of Africa. The A.N.L.C.A. was different in that it was also founded with the recognition of bonds and obligations between black Americans and Africans. In one of its first resolutions, the A.N.L.C.A. stated:

> The American Negro community in the United States has a special responsibility to urge a dynamic African policy upon our government. Although we have a serious civil rights problem which exhausts much of our energy, we cannot separate this struggle at home from that abroad. If the United States cannot take vigorous action to help win freedom in Africa, we cannot expect to maintain the trust and friendship of the newly independent and soon-to-be independent peoples of Africa and Asia. . . . Further, the American Negro community has a responsibility in simple terms of historical continuity. Since the turn of the century Negro leaders and scholars have expressed the concern of Negro Americans for the elimination of colonialism and its evils. While our conference will not initiate a new interest on the part of American Negroes, it will launch a

62. "A Call to the American Negro Leadership Conference on Africa" (Unpublished document, The King Papers, Boston University, June 1962), 1; *The American Negro Leadership Conference on Africa: Resolutions,* presented at Arden House, Campus of Columbia University, Harriman, New York (The King Center Archives, 23–25 November 1962), 1–6; a letter from Miss Dora McDonald, Secretary to Martin Luther King, Jr., to Mr. George M. Houser, 18 June 1962, The King Papers, Boston University; a letter from George M. Houser to Clarence Jones, 26 June 1962, The King Papers, Boston University; a letter from Martin Luther King, Jr., to Mr. George M. Houser, 2 July 1962, The King Papers, Boston University; "U. S. Negroes Urge More African Aid," *The New York Times* (November 24, 1962): 1 ff.; "U. S. Negroes Link Aid to Sub-Sahara African Nations with Rights Struggle," *The New York Times* (November 25, 1962): 1 ff.; "Leading Negroes Agree on Goals," *The New York Times* (November 26, 1962): 1 ff.; a letter from Martin Luther King, Jr., to Mr. Theodore E. Brown, 1 April 1963, The King Center Archives; "U. S. Negroes Plan Active Link with Peoples of African Nations," *The New York Times* (April 4, 1963): 1 ff.; and "Negroes Ask Role in Foreign Policy," *The New York Times* (July 9, 1964): 1 ff.

more aggressive determination to make our influence felt on the policies of our government in these critical areas of that vast continent.[63]

The A.C.O.A. and the A.N.L.C.A. gave impetus and continuity to King's idea that black Americans, in particular, and Americans, in general, had a contribution to make to the awakening and uplift of Africa. King contributed to the work of these organizations in many ways. Under his direction, the Southern Christian Leadership Conference made numerous financial contributions to the A.C.O.A.'s Africa Defense and Aid Fund, which was created in 1958 to help address emergency situations in South Africa and Central Africa.[64] King frequently allowed George M. Houser, the white Methodist minister who served as Director of the A.C.O.A. in the 1950s and 1960s, to use his name and influence in support of the organization's appeals, petitions, declarations, and conferences. Although King was not always present at the A.C.O.A.'s Human Rights Day ceremonies, which were held each year on December 10, and its Africa Freedom Day events, which were observed annually in April, he occasionally got involved as a speaker and an honorary chairman.[65] Largely because of King's support and influence, the A.C.O.A. was successful in bringing to the United States a number of African leaders in the 1950s

63. *The American Negro Leadership Conference on Africa: Resolutions (1962)*, 1–2; and *The American Negro Leadership Conference on Africa: Resolutions*, presented at the Shoreham Hotel, Washington, D. C. (The King Center Archives, 24–27 September 1964), 3.
64. A letter from Martin Luther King, Jr., to Potential Contributors to The Africa Defense and Aid Fund, 12 November 1959, The King Papers, Boston University; a letter from George M. Houser to Potential Contributors to The Africa Defense and Aid Fund, 10 February 1960, The King Papers, Boston University; and Houser, *No One Can Stop the Rain*, 85 and 127.
65. A letter from George M. Houser to Potential Contributors of The Africa Defense and Aid Fund, 10 February 1960, The King Center Archives; a letter from Donald Harrington to Martin Luther King, Jr., 16 February 1960, The King Center Archives; and a letter from Mary Louise Hooper to Miss Dora McDonald, 29 November 1965, The King Center Archives.

and 1960s, among whom were Tom Mboya of Kenya and Kanyama Chiume and Joshua Nkomo of Central Africa. King's activities in this and other ways help explain why he, on March 14, 1960, was invited to a conference in Accra, Ghana "to consider nonviolent positive action for peace and security in Africa in light of the Atom tests in the Sahara."[66]

From 1962 until his death, King worked with both the Call Committee and the Policy Committee of the A.N.L.C.A. When black leaders met to establish the organization, King emphatically stated that "the problems of Africa are so great that there is a need for a sort of Marshall Plan for Africa."[67] Additionally, he called for the recruiting of black Americans "for official and unofficial American jobs of all categories in Africa," and for "an intensive effort to cultivate African diplomats and their families in this country." King's suggestions were promptly endorsed by other organizers of the A.N.L.C.A.[68] His idea of a Marshall Plan for Africa was put before President John F. Kennedy in December, 1962, and before President Lyndon B. Johnson in January, 1965. King and other Call Committee members also sent other joint statements to Presidents Kennedy and Johnson, informing them of the purpose of the A.N.L.C.A. and

66. A letter from George M. Houser to Potential Contributors to the Africa Defense and Aid Fund, 10 February 1960, The King Center Archives; and a telegram from C. D. of Accra, Ghana, to Martin Luther King, Jr., 14 March 1960, The King Papers, Boston University. King was also asked to join a number of African organizations, such as The Africa League. See a letter from Angier B. Duke to Martin Luther King, Jr., 20 January 1961, The King Papers, Boston University; and a letter from Martin Luther King, Jr., to Mr. Angier B. Duke, 9 March 1961, The King Papers, Boston University.

67. "U. S. Negroes Link Aid to Sub-Sahara African," 1ff.; "Africa 'Marshall Plan' Asked by Negro Leaders," *The Washington Post* (December 18, 1962): 1 ff.; and "U. S. Negroes 'Goal: To Set Africa Policy,'" *U. S. News and World Report* (January 11, 1965): 60–61.

68. "U. S. Negroes Link Aid to Sub-Sahara African," 1ff. A year earlier, in April, 1961, King recommended Dr. I. J. K. Wells "to serve America and Africa" as "an Ambassador to Africa." See a letter from Martin Luther King, Jr., to the Honorable Chester Bowles, Undersecretary of State, 26 April 1961, The King Papers, Boston University.

urging them "to recognize the United States' moral responsibility to Sub-Sahara Africa as a whole."[69]

In keeping with his promise to become more active in the A.N.L.C.A., King took several other steps. On July 20, 1965, he persuaded the Administrative Committee of the S.C.L.C. to pledge at least $1,000.00 annually to the organization, a contribution that was generous in view of the budgetary problems the S.C.L.C. was experiencing at the time. King also joined other A.N.L.C.A. members in urging foundations to support the organization.[70] Because of his efforts, the Alpha Phi Alpha Fraternity, Inc., of which he was a member, became a sponsor of the A.N.L.C.A., and so did other fraternal, church, cultural, educational, civil rights, and trade union groups.[71] In 1966, King joined Theodore E. Brown, the Director of the A.N.L.C.A., and others in seeking to expand the organization's political, economic, and educational

69. A letter from the membership of The American Negro Leadership Conference on Africa to President John F. Kennedy, 17 December 1962, The King Papers, Boston University; "U. S. Negroes' Goal: To Set Africa Policy," 61; and a letter from the Call Committee of The American Negro Leadership Conference on Africa to President Lyndon B. Johnson, 25 January 1964, The King Papers, Boston University.

70. A letter from Martin Luther King, Jr., to Mr. Roy Wilkins, 20 July 1965, The King Center Archives; and a letter from Miss Dora McDonald to Mr. Theodore E. Brown, 30 July 1964, The King Center Archives.

71. A letter from Martin Luther King, Jr., to Mr. Theodore E. Brown, 1 April 1963, The King Papers, Boston University. The following groups became sponsors of the A.N.L.C.A.: Alpha Kappa Alpha Sorority, Inc.; Alpha Phi Alpha Fraternity, Inc.; The American Committee on Africa; The American Society of African Culture; Bible Way Church of Our Lord Jesus Christ World-Wide; Brotherhood of Sleeping Car Porters, AFL-CIO; The California Negro Leadership Conference; *The Chicago Daily Defender*; The Congress of Racial Equality; Delta Sigma Theta Sorority, Inc.; The Gandhi Society for Human Rights, Inc.; Improved Benevolent Protective Order of Elks of the World; The Links, Inc.; The NAACP; the National Association of Fashion and Accessory Designers, Inc.; The National Council of Negro Women; The National Newspaper Publishers Association; The National Urban League; The Negro American Labor Council; Operation Crossroads Africa, Inc.; Phelps-Stokes Fund; The S.C.L.C.; The Student Nonviolent Coordinating Committee; The Trade Union Leadership Council; The United Automobile Workers of America, AFL-CIO; The United Packinghouse Workers of America, AFL-CIO; The United Steel Workers of America, AFL-CIO; and The Western Christian Leadership Conference. For references to a partial list of sponsors, see *The American Negro Leadership Conference on Africa: Resolutions (1964)*, 12.

functions.[72] All of these activities were consistent with King's idea of "the need for some type of continued organizational setup to relate the American Negro with Africa and its many problems."[73]

In conjunction with others in the A.C.O.A. and the A.N.L.C.A., King turned his attention to a number of specific areas in Africa where anticolonial struggles reached a critical stage in the 1950s and 1960s. One such area was North Africa, where the Algerian revolution against French domination was in full swing.[74] The war in Algeria had begun in 1954, and it directly involved France, some 850,000 Europeans living in Algeria, more than nine million Algerians, and all of the countries bordering Algeria (Tunisia, Morocco, Libya, Mauritania, Mali, and Niger). In 1959, King, George Houser, Homer Jack, and other A.C.O.A. members signed a statement calling for peace in Algeria. They were motivated by two pressing concerns. The first was the level of violence associated with the struggle. Thousands had died by that time, resources beyond measure had been expended, and hundreds of thousands had been imprisoned, exiled, and left homeless. The second was that King and others in the A.C.O.A. believed that the United States Government, by refusing to encourage peaceful negotiations between the French and the Algerian nationalists, was ruining its reputation among Africans as a nation that stood for freedom throughout the world. "We urge our government," they declared, "to support any resolution in the present session of the United Nations General Assembly which stimulates such negotiations and works to guarantee a free referendum in which the Algerian

72. See Theodore E. Brown, "A Memorandum: To the Call Committee of The American Negro Leadership Conference on Africa" (The King Center Archives, 29 June 1966), 1–5.

73. A letter from Martin Luther King, Jr., to Mr. Theodore E. Brown, 1 April 1963.

74. Houser, *No One Can Stop the Rain*, 91–98; and "A Call for Peace in Algeria," a statement released by members of the A.C.O.A. and others (The King Papers, Boston University, 4 December 1959), 1 ff.

people will decide their own future status."[75] When Algerian independence became official in 1962, King was among those in the A.C.O.A. and the newly formed A.N.L.C.A. who celebrated the occasion by calling upon the United States Government to build bridgeheads of goodwill and rapport by demonstrating its concern for an Algeria governed by Algerians.

King's statements on behalf of Algerian independence undoubtedly enhanced his popularity among people throughout North Africa. He was held in high esteem by the Algerians, the Libyans, the Moroccans, and the Tunisians. A Sudanese citizen expressed the sentiments of many in North Africa when he, in a letter to King in 1960, recognized the civil rights leader's substantial influence, spiritually and materially, on black America and Africa:

> All your efforts are regarded by us with admiration, sympathy, and hope. We prayed that Almighty God is to bless your struggle into successful achievement. We also prayed day and night that you—yourself and Afro-Americans would succeed one day to return back to your Motherland Africa, and develop to the best of your knowledge, Sciences, and Arts. . . . She is waiting for you. . . . It is your education, your culture, your sense, your tactics, and your self-absorption into the struggle [which have] rendered it successful, and well known, not only to your citizens in America, but also to us here in Africa.[76]

The anticolonial conflict in parts of Central Africa was also addressed by King under the auspices of the A.C.O.A. and the A.N.L.C.A. In November, 1959, King, in a letter to supporters of the A.C.O.A., described the oppression of Africans in Nyasaland (Malawi), a British colony, in these terms:

> In Central Africa at this moment there are 500 Africans imprisoned, their families deprived of income. Their

75. "A Call for Peace in Algeria," 1 ff.
76. A letter from M. O. Idris to Martin Luther King, Jr., 8 July 1960, The King Papers, Boston University.

"crime" is that they are members of African organizations—legal at the time of their arrest—which seek
greater political rights for the African majority, and
an end to the color bar. The Nyasaland government
(part of the Central African Federation), alleging a
"massacre plot," rounded up some 2,000 Africans early
this year and declared a state of emergency. The British
government sent in an investigating commission which
reported that not only was there no evidence of such a
plot, but that under present conditions Nyasaland is
a police state.[77]

King went on to suggest that the A.C.O.A.'s Africa Defense
and Aid fund afforded "a responsible channel" for aiding
"the families of these Africans who are being held indefi-
nitely and without specific charges." He urged supporters to contribute at least $10.00 to the effort on behalf of
Africans in Nyasaland, noting that "Your support will
help serve justice in Africa today, and build our friendship with Africans in the crucial period ahead." Considering the nature of the emergencies in Central Africa,
King found it disturbing that "the American Committee
on Africa is the only organization in this country today
which is actively trying to channel American aid in support of Africa's struggle for greater democracy."[78] This
situation changed in 1962 with the formation of the
A.N.L.C.A. In one of its first resolutions, this organization
denounced the Central African Federation (Nyasaland,
Northern Rhodesia, Southern Rhodesia) as a tool for the
maintenance of European colonial domination. Interestingly enough, in 1964, two years after resolution was
made, Nyasaland achieved independence as Malawi, and
Northern Rhodesia became Zambia, an independent
African-ruled nation. Southern Rhodesia emerged a year
later as "an independent white-ruled settler colony."[79]

77. A letter from Martin Luther King, Jr., to Supporters of The American Committee on Africa, 12 November 1959, The King Papers, Boston
University.
78. *Ibid.*
79. *The American Negro Leadership Conference on Africa: Resolutions (1962)*, 3–4; and Margaret C. Lee, *SADCC: The Political Economy of*

The Belgian Congo was another part of Central or Middle Africa that attracted King's attention during this period. Although the Congo (Zaire) achieved independence from Belgium in June, 1960, becoming one of seventeen African countries to become independent in that year, the tragic events that followed worried King, George Houser, and other A.C.O.A. members. The Congolese became seriously divided along tribal and political lines. The newly chosen Prime Minister Patrice Lumumba and the newly elected President Joseph Kasabubu competed for power and dominance in the political realm of the Congo, while political organizations such as the National Congolese Movement (N.C.M.), the Confederation of Ktanga Tribal Associations (C.O.N.A.K.A.T.), and the Balubakat Party in Northern Katanga were hopelessly divided. Such divisions led to internal warfare, the secession of Katanga from the Congo, and the murder of Lumumba by elements of Moise Tshombe's C.O.N.A.K.A.T. in January, 1961. King and others in the A.C.O.A. greeted this internal turmoil with expressions of regret, but also regarded it as natural for a new nation trying to establish itself. They were particularly disturbed with the murder of Lumumba, who was supported by the A.C.O.A.[80] Even more disturbing for them was the involvement of the superpowers, the United States and the Soviet Union, who fought for control in the Congo. Because the United States supported President Kasabubu and regarded Lumumba as a potential Fidel Castro, King and other A.C.O.A. members suspected the involvement of the United States Government in Lumumba's assassination. Compounding the problem for them was the determination of the Belgians to maintain economic control over the mineral-rich Congo, an approach typical of European powers in their dealings with former colonies.[81]

Development in Southern Africa (Nashville: Winston-Derek Publishers, Inc., 1989), 44.

80. Houser, *No One Can Stop the Rain*, 134–49.
81. *Ibid.*

The Congo crisis was still capturing the headlines worldwide when King and other A.N.L.C.A. members gathered for the first time in November, 1962. In the early stages of this three-day meeting, the group, deeply concerned about unity among the Congolese, resolved to

> regard the restoration of the territorial unity, integrity and unification of the Congo with Katanga as an integrated part of the country as an immediate necessity and to that end we support the use of sanctions and force, if necessary, to bring Katanga into a unified Congo. We call upon our government to exert its full power to achieve this objective. We endorse the continued United States financial support of the United Nations operation in the Congo.[82]

By 1964, King and others in the A.N.L.C.A. and the A.C.O.A. were demanding that all external forces, including those of the United States, disengage themselves from all military involvements in the Congo. At its meeting in September, 1964, the A.N.L.C.A. declared that it was incumbent on the United States to achieve a cessation of hostilities in the Congo, to assist the Organization of African Unity in its attempts to solve the Congolese problem, and "to initiate administrative steps and foster social and political forces to reduce the major sources of tension and weakness in the Congolese nation."[83] Furthermore, the A.N.L.C.A. chided the United States Government for its "failure to consider the Congo as primarily an African problem rather than in its European context," and for "the failure to consider the Congo as a question of an evolving society."[84] In November, 1964, the A.C.O.A., in a

---

82. *The American Negro Leadership Conference on Africa: Resolutions (1962)*, 3–4.
83. *The American Negro Leadership Conference on Africa (1964)*, 5–6.
84. *Ibid.* Although King supported Lumumba as the rightful Prime Minister of the Congo, he did not agree with Lumumba on the question of violence and revolution. In a statement following Malcolm X's assassination in February, 1965, King wrote: "Like the murder of Lumumba, the murder of Malcolm X deprives the world of a potentially great leader. I could not agree with either of these men, but I could see in them a

communication with Secretary of State Dean Rusk, urged the United States Government "to take the initiative in calling for an international pact of noninterference in the Congo."[85] King echoed these concerns in an interview in Oslo, Norway, in December, 1964, noting:

> I've been very much concerned about the problem in the Congo, and it is my conviction that we must see the Congo situation for what it is and deal with it in that light. What we have in the Congo is several wars, essentially civil strife, and I don't think that the problem will be solved until there is a withdrawal of all foreign troops and mercenaries. And I think this needs to be done immediately and that the Congo situation be dealt with by the Organization of African States under the auspices of the United Nations. I believe firmly that this will be a better way to get at the problem, and it will bring about the only meaningful and permanent solution; so that there is a need at this time for a withdrawal of all foreign troops and all mercenaries that are presently there.[86]

King went on to describe the problems in the Congo as "the harvest, a violent harvest, that came into being as a result of seeds of injustice, seeds of neglect, and seeds of man's inhumanity to man planted across the years." "We must seek to get rid of all the conditions that made that situation as it presently stands," he continued, "and I think one of the best ways to do it is to move through the realm of negotiation. I don't see a military solution to

---

capacity for leadership which I could respect, and which was only beginning to mature in judgment and statesmanship." King went on to say that black America could not afford to destroy Malcolm X any more than the Congo could Lumumba. See Martin Luther King, Jr., "The Nightmare of Violence: A Statement Regarding the Death of Malcolm X" (Unpublished document, The King Papers, Boston University, 25 February 1965), 2–3.

85. "International Pact on Congo Proposed," a statement released by The American Committee on Africa. (The King Center Archives, 29 November 1964), 1–2.

86. "A Radio Interview with Martin Luther King, Jr. Regarding the Nobel Peace Prize," Oslo, Norway (The King Center Archives, 9 December 1964), 3–4.

the problem in the Congo."[87] King, James Farmer, Whitney Young, Roy Wilkins, and Theodore Brown, speaking for the A.N.L.C.A., reiterated this point early in 1965.[88] After 1965, the Congo moved progressively toward a stable central government, and the A.N.L.C.A. and the A.C.O.A. became less vocal with regard to the Congolese situation.

King was not a member of the A.C.O.A. when it first expressed support for anticolonial movements in East Africa in 1953. When the A.C.O.A. demonstrated that support by inviting the Kenyan statesman Tom Mboya to the United States in August, 1956, King was still heavily involved in the Montgomery Bus Boycott.[89] However, when the A.C.O.A. invited Mboya to make another speaking tour in the United States in 1959, to coincide with its observance of the first Africa Freedom Day on April 15, King was among several national leaders who met privately with the Kenyan leader.[90] Because of Mboya's tremendous popularity and ties with the A.C.O.A., Kenya became one major focal point of the A.C.O.A.'s involvement in the independence struggles of East Africa. King's personal interest in Kenya was fueled by his admiration for Mboya and by his growing concern for Africa as a whole. Although he, George Houser, and other A.C.O.A. members had serious reservations about the violent Mau Mau rebellions against British colonial domination, which occurred on a high level from 1952 to 1959, they nevertheless gave financial and moral support to the Kenyans' nationalist struggle at the request of

87. *Ibid.* The fact that King spoke out against violence in the Congo in Norway in 1964, and because he attached his name to several A.N.L.C.A. statements challenging the invasion of the Congo by foreign governments, it is difficult to accept uncritically James Cone's contention that King "was strangely silent about the U. S. invasion of the Congo." Cone believes that King's alleged silence on this issue illustrated the limitations of his "view of Africa and the Third World when compared with Malcolm X's." A letter from James H. Cone to Lewis V. Baldwin, 18 February 1987.
88. "U. S. Negroes' Goal: To Set Africa Policy," 61.
89. Houser, *No One Can Stop the Rain*, 81–86.
90. *Ibid.*, 86–87.

Mboya.[91] In November, 1962, the A.C.O.A. and the
A.N.L.C.A., in anticipation of Kenyan independence, supported a resolution that read:

> As the independence of Kenya approaches we look with
> hope and pride toward its future development. It is in
> the interest of the Kenya people and the United States
> Government to have a free and stable Kenya Nation.
> Therefore, we urge the United States Government to
> consider seriously, in consultation with Kenya Na-
> tionalists, affording financial aid and assistance to
> help Kenya develop a viable political entity.
>
> We urge the British Government in the pending consti-
> tutional negotiations and elections to adopt a hands-off
> policy in regard to the internal affairs of Kenya.
>
> We further urge Great Britain to continue to give aid
> and technical assistance to Kenya after it attains
> independence.
>
> We urge our government to grant the 15 million dol-
> lar aid requested of it by a joint mission representative
> of the Kenya African National Union and the Kenya
> African Democratic Union.[92]

As the A.C.O.A. and A.N.L.C.A. had anticipated, independence within the Commonwealth of Nations came on December 12, 1963, when the Kenya African National Union
Party formed a government headed by Jomo Kenyatta.

King's interest in the anticolonial struggles in West
Africa became a matter of public knowledge in 1957,
when he attended Ghana's independence celebration and
became a member of the A.C.O.A. The visit to Ghana, formerly the British Gold Coast colony, heightened King's

91. When Tom Mboya was saddled with legal fees and other financial needs and obligations in his struggle against the British, he wrote
George Houser in April, 1958: "I cannot refrain from approaching
A.C.O.A. and other friends for help since on our own we are completely
helpless." The A.C.O.A. immediately responded to the appeal by sending
$2,000 to Mboya. See Houser, *No One Can Stop the Rain*, 85.

92. *The American Negro Leadership Conference on Africa (1962)*,
4–5.

knowledge of the whole of West Africa, from whence many of his slave forebears had come many centuries earlier. After 1957, he was kept informed of events and developments in Ghana and other West African countries largely through the A.C.O.A. In 1960, King was invited to the independence celebration of Nigeria, another West African country formerly under British control. There, he witnessed the ceremonies marking Nigeria's full independence as a federation under a parliamentary form of government.[93] In subsequent years, King studied developments in Nigeria closely and was apparently pleased when the country declared itself a federal republic in 1963.

In the late 1960s, King and others in the A.C.O.A. and the A.N.L.C.A. observed a Nigeria increasingly under the menace of internal political crises. Tribal and racial tensions evoked a successful revolt early in 1966 by army units led by Major General J. T. U. Aguiyi-Ironsi. Aguiyi-Ironsi was killed in a second coup later in the year, and Lieutenant Colonel Yakubu Gowon emerged as head of the Federal Military Government (F.M.G.). Internal tribal unrest continued, and in 1967, the Ibos in the East announced secession from Nigeria and the formation of the Republic of Biafra. This development, and the prospect of a bloody civil war between Nigeria and Biafra, registered heavily on the minds of A.N.L.C.A. members. "It is generally agreed that a very serious crisis is imminent regarding the future of the nationhood of Nigeria," said Theodore Brown in a letter to the Call Committee of the A.N.L.C.A. "The situation presents a unique but extremely vital opportunity for Negro American leaders to aid in a troubled situation."[94] In March, 1967, King, Roy Wilkins,

93. King, "Speech at a Rally," Savannah, Ga., 6; a letter from Clarence Akpuaka to Martin Luther King, Jr., 7 February 1960, The King Papers, Boston University; and a letter from Martin Luther King, Jr., to Mr. Clarence Akpuaka, 16 June 1960, The King Papers, Boston University.

94. A letter from Theodore E. Brown to Dorothy Height, Martin Luther King, Jr., A. Philip Randolph, Roy Wilkins, and Whitney Young, 21 March 1967, The King Center Archives.

Dorothy Height, and others in the A.N.L.C.A. responded
to Brown's challenge by signing the following statement:

> American Negroes viewed with pride the emergence
> of the independent nation of Nigeria in 1960. Our rela-
> tions with Nigerian students and leaders in the United
> States over two generations developed a community
> of interest and fast friends. The world recognition of
> Nigerian art as well as other Nigerian achievements
> past and present have given self-respect to our chil-
> dren in their studies and to our people in their daily
> lives.
>
> In the past two years we have watched with great
> anxiety the political problems in Nigeria, in some re-
> spects not too different from those of our own coun-
> try in the first nine decades of its existence. Now
> events cause us to fear the breakup of Nigeria and the
> prospect of bloody civil war.
>
> We ask our brothers in Nigeria to mediate their differ-
> ences for the sake of us all, to make new starts at
> resolving their conflicts. We offer our services in such
> an enterprise in the hope that this largest, richest, and
> in many respects most promising nation in Black
> Africa may fulfill the destiny it so richly deserves, to
> the benefit of Africa, the world, and ourselves.[95]

In behalf of the A.N.L.C.A., and in an effort to avert
civil war in Nigeria, Martin Luther King, Jr., Roy
Wilkins, A. Philip Randolph, and Whitney Young, Jr.,
offered their services to the government and the four
regions of Nigeria.[96] This gesture was welcomed by several African leaders. Simon Obi Anekwe, deeply concerned about his native land, sent a warm letter to King
and other A.N.L.C.A. members, expressing appreciation
"for your efforts to aid in the resolution of the Nigerian
crisis, and in particular for sponsoring Mr. [Theodore]

95. "Negro Leaders Offer to Mediate Nigerian Civil Crisis: A Release
to all News Media and Wire Services" (The King Center Archives, 27
March 1967), 1–3.
96. *Ibid.*

Brown's two trips to Nigeria." Anekwe went on to inform the A.N.L.C.A. of efforts to end the crisis through an appeal to other potential negotiating parties, such as the Organization of African Unity (O.A.U.) and the United Nations Secretary General U Thant. His letter continued:

> I am calling these two points to your attention in the hope that you will bring the moral strength of the 22 million black Americans whom you represent to support both moves—through action with the United States Government, direct encouragement of African governments, and by involving a wider segment of the American population in the grave crisis in Nigeria— to the end that Africans there may stop killing each other and, with outside help, resolve their differences over a conference table.[97]

Lieutenant Colonel C. Odumegwu Ojukwu, head of the State Republic of Biafra, also expressed his gratitude to the A.N.L.C.A. for "your concern in the Nigerian-Biafran war." Ojukwu and his personal representative, Charles Nwabueze Lemeh, invited Martin Luther King, Jr., Roy Wilkins, A. Philip Randolph, Whitney Young, and Theodore Brown to Biafra for "a personal conference" regarding the crisis in January, 1968.[98] During the same time, President William Tubman of Liberia expressed the hope that these black American leaders "will journey together to Africa as soon as possible on a peace mission regarding Nigeria."[99] In mid-March, 1968, such a mission was seriously considered and planned for mid-April

97. A letter from Simon Obi Anekwe to the Members of The American Negro Leadership Conference on Africa, 18 August 1967, The King Center Archives.

98. A telegram from Charles Nwabueze Lemeh, Personal Representative of His Excellency Lieutenant Colonel C. Odumegwe Ojukwu, to The American Negro Leadership Conference on Africa, 9 January 1968, The King Center Archives.

99. "The Emissary Trip to Africa in November, 1967 Regarding the Nigerian Civil War: A Statement" from Theodore E. Brown to Roy Wilkins, Whitney Young, A. Philip Randolph, and Martin Luther King (The King Center Archives, 10 January 1968), 1–6.

of that year, but the assassination of King kept this A.N.L.C.A. venture from materializing.[100]

Southern Africa's bout with racism and colonialism was addressed on many levels by King in connection with the A.C.O.A. and the A.N.L.C.A. In March, 1957, while attending the independence celebrations of Ghana, he expressed admiration for the bus boycott outside Johannesburg, South Africa, "with thousands of Africans actually walking ten to fifteen miles a day" in protest against apartheid. King regarded this nonviolent action as reminiscent of Gandhi's struggle in India and of his own movement in Montgomery, Alabama. "Nonviolence in India and in Alabama did something to the oppressors, " he noted, "so it will even in South Africa. The willingness to suffer will eventually make the oppressor ashamed of his method, and the forces of both history and providence are on the side of freedom."[101]

From 1957 until his death, King communicated with several black South African leaders about the apartheid problem, among whom were Albert J. Luthuli, Oliver R. and Adelaide Tambo, and Dennis Brutus. King's contact with these leaders was made possible largely through the A.C.O.A. and the A.N.L.C.A. His correspondence with Luthuli is especially noteworthy. Luthuli—a chief by Zulu tradition, the President General of the African National Congress (A.N.C.), and a proponent of nonviolent direct action—was held in high esteem by King. King was aware of Luthuli's intimate involvement in the defiance campaigns that swept South Africa in 1952. During those campaigns, Luthuli had taken the lead in organizing sit-in demonstrations against segregation in libraries, on railway seats, and in other facilities. In 1956, he was among the 156 men and women of all races accused of and

100. "Martin Luther King and A. Philip Randolph Clarify Nigerian Mission: For Immediate Release to All News Media" (The King Center Archives, 13 March 1968), 1–2; and George W. Shepherd, Jr., "Who Killed Martin Luther King's Dream?: An Afro-American Tragedy," *Africa Today* 15, no. 2 (April–May 1968): 2.
101. See "Conversation in Ghana," 447.

arrested for treason by the South African government.[102] Luthuli's amazing courage and calm in the face of such persecution, coupled with his nonviolent philosophy and methods, led King to believe that the A.N.C. leader represented the brightest hope for peaceful change and coexistence between the races in South Africa. In December, 1959, King said to Luthuli in a letter:

> May I say that I too have admired you tremendously from a distance. I only regret that circumstances and spacial divisions have made it impossible for us to meet. But I admire your great witness and your dedication to the cause of freedom and human dignity. You have stood amid persecution, abuse, and oppression with a dignity and calmness of spirit seldom paralleled in human history. One day all of Africa will be proud of your achievements.[103]

In April, 1964, King called Luthuli "one of the truly great men of our age." "I have written him on several occasions," King continued, "but because of this censoring of his mail, it is possible that my letters fail to get through."[104] In December, 1964, King made special mention of Luthuli in his Nobel Prize Acceptance Speech in Oslo, Norway, noting, "You honor, once again, Chief Luthuli of South Africa, whose struggles with and for his people, are still met with the most brutal expression of man's inhumanity to man."[105] King's comment was significant, especially since Luthuli had received the Nobel Peace Prize for his own nonviolent activism in 1960.[106]

102. "Foe of Apartheid: Albert John Luthuli," *The New York Times* (October 24, 1961): 1 ff.
103. A letter from Martin Luther King, Jr., to Chief Albert Luthuli, 8 December 1959, The King Papers, Boston University.
104. A letter from Martin Luther King, Jr., to the Rev. James W. King, 6 April 1964, The King Papers, Boston University.
105. Quoted in Flip Schulke, ed., *Martin Luther King, Jr.: A Documentary—Montgomery to Memphis* (New York: W. W. Norton and Company, Inc., 1967), 219.
106. "Foe of Apartheid: Albert John Luthuli," 1 ff.; and "A Gesture of Honor," *Sojourner's* (December, 1984): 4–5. For an interesting essay comparing and contrasting King, Gandhi, and Luthuli, with a special focus on their nonviolent philosophies and methods, see William R.

Early in 1968, almost a year after Luthuli's death, King compared the A.N.C. leader's practical civil disobedience with that of Socrates and Shadrach, Meshach, and Abednego, and declared:

> I'm convinced that if I had lived in South Africa, I would have joined Chief Luthuli, the late Chief Luthuli, as he had his campaigns, openly to disobey those [apartheid] laws, and to refuse to comply with the pass system, where people had to have passes and all that stuff to walk the streets.[107]

Equally important were Luthuli's admiration and respect for King. When G. McLeod Bryan, a friend of King in East Nigeria, visited Luthuli in September, 1959, the South African activist informed him of his great indebtedness to King. Bryan later wrote King concerning what Luthuli had said about him:

> [Luthuli] told me that the greatest inspiration to him was your *Stride Toward Freedom* [that Bishop Reeves had put into his hands]. Luthuli had been reading it in his cane fields the very day I visited him. He wished for copies to be put into the hands of his African National Congress leaders. I told him I would put the request to you, believing that you would contribute this much and more to South African freedom. His eyes were the brightest when I referred to him as the "King" of South Africa. His odds are so much greater, but he is a profound Christian sharing your views.[108]

While visiting South Africa in January, 1964, James W. King, a clergyman from Dayton, Ohio, "asked Chief Luthuli what he would want Americans to know." Luthuli

---

Duggan, "Three Men of Peace," *The Crisis* 81, no. 10 (December 1974), 331–37.

107. Martin Luther King, Jr., "Why We Must Go to Washington," a speech at the S.C.L.C. Staff Retreat, Ebenezer Baptist Church, Atlanta, Ga. (The King Center Archives, 15 January 1968), 14–15; and James M. Washington, ed., *A Testament of Hope: The Essential Writings of Martin Luther King, Jr.* (San Francisco: Harper and Row, Publishers, 1986), 50.

108. A letter from G. McLeod Bryan to Martin Luther King, Jr., 10 October, 1959, The King Papers, Boston University.

replied: "Give my highest regards to Martin Luther. It is not often that we see clergymen taking a stand on social issues. It means a lot to us here. Martin Luther King is my hero."[109] Although circumstances prevented King and Luthuli from meeting, the impelling spiritual, moral, and intellectual power they drew from each other must have reinforced their convictions about the need for Africans and African-Americans to join forces in the struggle against racism and colonialism. It was out of this sense of a common vision and a common struggle that King wrote: "I have done a considerable amount of reading on the whole of Africa and have taken a particular interest in the problems in South Africa because of the similarities between the situation there and our own situation in the United States."[110] More specifically, King believed that apartheid in South Africa and Jim Crow in the American South led, in some cases, to the same tragic social, economic, and political conditions.[111]

King also recognized that South African apartheid was, on the whole, much more intense and destructive than Jim Crowism in the southern United States. Echoing the thoughts of W. E. B. Du Bois, Paul Robeson, and other black leaders before him, King insisted that the nonwhites in South Africa were engaged in "a far more deadly struggle for freedom," and concluded that "there

109. A letter from James W. King to Martin Luther King, Jr., 25 March 1964, The King Papers, Boston University.
110. Baldwin, ed., *Toward the Beloved Community*, 277–80 (Concluding Essay); and a letter from Martin Luther King, Jr., to Mr. Enoch Dumas, 11 January 1960, The King Papers, Boston University. For an interesting exchange between King and the white novelist and folklorist Harold Courlander concerning similarities between South African apartheid and southern Jim Crowism, see a letter from Harold Courlander to Martin Luther King, Jr., 30 August 1961, The King Papers, Boston University; and a letter from Martin Luther King, Jr., to Harold Courlander, 30 October 1961, The King Papers, Boston University.
111. See Baldwin, ed., *Toward the Beloved Community*, 6–11 (Introduction); and George M Houser, "Freedom's Struggle Crosses Oceans and Mountains: Martin Luther King, Jr., and the Liberation Struggles in Africa and America" in Peter J. Albert and Ronald Hoffman, eds., *We Shall Overcome: Martin Luther King, Jr. and the Black Freedom Struggle* (New York: Pantheon Books, 1990), 169–96.

can be no doubt of the fact that South Africa is the most
stubborn and rugged place in the world in the area of
race relations."[112] "We read of tortures in jails with elec-
tric devices, suicides among prisoners, forced confes-
sions," he continued, "while in the outside community
ruthless persecution of editors, religious leaders, and
political opponents suppresses free speech and a free
press."[113] King argued further:

> Even in Mississippi we can organize to register Negro
> voters, we can speak to the press, we can in short
> organize the people in nonviolent action. But in South
> Africa even the mildest form of nonviolent resistance
> meets with years of imprisonment, and leaders over
> many years have been restricted and silenced and im-
> prisoned.[114]

In King's view, the harshness of the oppression in
South Africa resulted in large measure from the lack of a
natural rights tradition, and from the fears and insecuri-
ties created by the numerical superiority of blacks and
other peoples of color over whites. These realities, according to King, clearly distinguished South Africa from
the United States, and they encouraged an apartheid system in South Africa similar to "the nightmarish ideology
and practices of Nazism."[115]

The fundamental issue of how to overcome apartheid
and create community in South Africa was confronted
forthrightly by King. He considered active coalitions between various racial, ethnic, and religious groups, inside
and outside South Africa, essential to the achievement of
this goal. He believed that the pressure applied through
the concerted efforts of people of color and their white
allies in South Africa could be much more effective
when supplemented by the antiapartheid activities of

112. *Ibid.*; and a letter from Martin Luther King, Jr., to Mr. Enoch
Dumas, 11 January 1960.
113. Baldwin, ed., *Toward the Beloved Community*, 10–11 (Introduction).
114. *Ibid.*
115. *Ibid.*

coalitions in other parts of the world. This is why King joined George Houser and other whites and blacks in the A.C.O.A. in making speeches against South African apartheid, and in drafting and signing appeals, declarations, letters, and other statements calling for nonviolent action against apartheid.[116] In July, 1957, King, Eleanor Roosevelt, and Bishop James A. Pike, under the auspices of the A.C.O.A., sponsored a "Declaration of Conscience" that designated December 10, 1957, "Human Rights Day," and called for an international protest against South African apartheid. This document—signed by more than 130 world leaders of different racial, ethnic, religious, and national backgrounds— read in part:

> The South African government has relentlessly over the past few years extended its policy of organized racism—*apartheid*. 156 leaders who have peacefully sought a just society for all, black and white, are now charged with treason and involved in court action. Laws have just been passed making it a crime for white and non-white to pray in the same church or to study in the same school. Outstanding intellectuals are under court charge for addressing a racially mixed meeting. Africans are being forced from homes they have occupied for many years so that whites can take over their land. The right to vote is being taken away from colored people in the same manner in which Africans were disenfranchised twenty-one years ago. The Bantu Education Act is being vigorously implemented to educate the African for a role no higher than that of servant in the white man's world. . . . People everywhere who care about freedom can no longer remain silent while justice and reason are being sacrificed by a Government still enjoying friendly relations with democratic nations of the world. . . . We call upon free men and women throughout the world to appeal on this day to the Government of the Union of South Africa to observe its moral and legal obligations as a signatory to the United

---

116. *Ibid.*, Introduction, Parts I and V, and Concluding Essay.

Nations Charter. We call upon men and women everywhere to concentrate their moral and spiritual forces
in an universal effort—through prayer, public meet-
ings, and all other peaceful means—on December 10,
1957. We call upon all members of free associations
including churches, trade unions, fraternal societies,
business, professional, veterans, and other groups to
petition their governments and their organizations to
mobilize their influence in bringing about a peaceful,
democratic and just solution in South Africa.[117]

This "Declaration of Conscience," drafted and signed
only nine years after the Afrikaaner-backed Nationalist
Party swept to power and espoused an explicit policy of
apartheid, contributed to King's amazing popularity
among the oppressed in South Africa and their white
allies. In a letter to King in November, 1957, Oliver R.
Tambo, the Secretary General of the A.N.C., declared,
"We, the oppressed people of South Africa, highly appreciate this step and we now appeal to you to give your
full support."[118] A similar statement of approval was
sent to King by Albert Luthuli. Michael Scott—an Anglican clergyman, Honorable Director of The Africa Bureau in London, and signatory of the "Declaration of
Conscience"—sent a warm letter to King in January,
1958, requesting "any practical suggestions you may
have to make whereby the Declaration of Conscience,
echoed we feel sure in the minds of many people
throughout the world, can be brought to bear in practical forms of action."[119]

King believed that financial contributions represented
one means by which coalitions outside of South Africa
could have an impact on the antiapartheid struggle
within that country. This is why he agreed to serve as a
sponsor of the new Africa Defense and Aid Fund of the

117. *Ibid.*, 214–26.
118. A letter from Oliver R. Tambo to Martin Luther King, Jr., 18
November 1957, The King Papers, Boston University.
119. A letter from Michael Scott to Martin Luther King, Jr., 23 January 1958, The King Papers, Boston University.

A.C.O.A. in December, 1959.[120] A month earlier, King had written a lengthy letter requesting each supporter of the A.C.O.A. to donate ten dollars to the Africa Defense and Aid Fund's effort to address emergencies in South Africa. He reminded supporters that the Africa Defense and Aid Fund, an extension of the A.C.O.A.'s South Africa Defense Fund, represented hope for political prisoners and their families in South Africa. "Through the South Africa Defense Fund, set up by the Committee three years ago when 156 opponents of *apartheid* were arrested," he wrote, "the American Committee on Africa sent $50,000 for aid in the extensive legal costs and family hardships of the accused."[121] By duplicating this effort through the Africa Defense and Aid Fund, King believed that the A.C.O.A. could reaffirm its support for South Africa's freedom fighters while sending a clear message of defiance to the intransigent South African government.

In 1960, the A.C.O.A. sent $19,050 to South Africa "to support and sustain the families of the victims of the Sharpeville Massacre," "to defend those arrested in the aftermath of the massacre," and "to provide legal aid for those on trial for treason." Deeply disturbed about the 69 peaceful protesters against pass laws who had been killed during this massacre on March 21, 1960, and about the 200,000 who had been detained under the Unlawful Organizations Act, King and others in the S.C.L.C. gave freely to this effort.[122] King openly attacked the

120. A letter from Martin Luther King, Jr., to Miss Ann Morrissett, 23 December 1959, The King Papers, Boston University.
121. A letter from Martin Luther King, Jr., to Supporters of the American Committee on Africa, 12 November 1959.
122. A letter from George Houser to the Friends of The American Committee on Africa, 1 March 1961, The King Papers, Boston University; a letter from Martin Luther King, Jr., to Mr. George Houser, 21 December 1961, The King Papers, Boston University; a letter from George Houser to the Members of The American Committee on Africa, 23 April 1960, The King Papers, Boston University; a letter from George Houser to the Members of The American Committee on Africa, 3 May 1960, The King Papers, Boston University; a letter from Donald Harrington to the Members of the American Committee on Africa, 23 September 1960, The King Papers, Boston University; and Baldwin, ed., *Toward the Beloved Community*, 11.

actions of the South African government at Sharpeville, and along with George Houser and others in the A.C.O.A., gave support to the formation of a South Africa Emergency Committee by twenty-five key organizational people in New York on April 21, 1960.[123] Such actions led Albert Luthuli to insist in December, 1961, that his Nobel Peace Prize was not merely a personal tribute, but a tribute to the gallant antiapartheid efforts of the A.C.O.A. and "all men everywhere who have *sacrificed* for the Brotherhood of Man." Luthuli went on to insist, in a letter to King and other A.C.O.A. members, that "the Committee has been a source of inspiration. As Alan Paton has said: 'To us in South Africa, the American Committee on Africa represents the conscience of America. I do not know what we would do without it.'"[124] King's many contributions to the A.C.O.A.'s various South African emergency funds help explain why Dennis Brutus, the Director of the International Defense and Aid Fund in London, asked the civil rights leader to associate his name with the world campaign for the release of South African political prisoners in October, 1967.[125]

In the early 1960s, King repeatedly called on the nations of the world to apply strong diplomatic and economic pressure against the South African government. Outraged by the slaughter of 69 peaceful protestors against Pass Laws at Sharpeville by South African police on March 21, 1960, King joined other Americans for Democratic Action (A.D.A.) three weeks later in urging "that the U.S. Ambassador to South Africa be recalled to Washington for consultation, and that American purchases of

123. Baldwin, ed., *Toward the Beloved Community,* 11 and 279.

124. A letter from Albert J. Luthuli to the Members of The American Committee on Africa, 10 December 1961, The King Papers, Boston University.

125. A letter from Dennis Brutus to Dr. Martin Luther King, Jr., 20 October 1967, The King Center Archives. King's range of contributions to the struggle against South African apartheid undermines James Cone's claim: "And even in relation to his strong opposition to South Africa, he [King] seems to have limited that opposition primarily to a few speeches about it, and only brief references to it in most of his other speeches." A letter from James H. Cone to Lewis V. Baldwin, 18 February 1987.

gold from South Africa be suspended during his time of consultation." The "Appeal for Action Against Apartheid," initially sponsored by King and Albert Luthuli under the auspices of the A.C.O.A. in 1962, urged the United States government and other governments to take dynamic action, including economic sanctions, "to press South Africa toward interracial justice without which wholesale bloodshed and a war between the races seems inevitable."[126] King, Roy Wilkins, Whitney Young, and others in the A.N.L.C.A. made a similar appeal in a statement to *The New York Times* in November, 1962.[127] Around the same time, King suggested that the United States support the United Nations' economic sanctions against South Africa.[128] In a speech in London in December, 1964, King insisted that substantial economic pressure from the United Kingdom and the United States alone could strangle the apartheid system:

> If the U. K. and the U. S. decided tomorrow morning not to buy South African goods, not to buy South African gold, to put an embargo on oil; if our investors and capitalists would withdraw their support for that racial tyranny, then apartheid would be brought to an end. Then the majority of South Africans of all races could at last build the shared society they desire.[129]

126. "Appeal for Action Against Apartheid," sponsored by Martin Luther King and Albert J. Luthuli (The King Center Archives, Fall 1962). This appeal was signed by heads of state, clergymen, writers, playwrights, physicians, and other professionals from around the world. Also see "Liberals Urge Ambassador to South Africa Be Recalled for Consultation—Suspension of Gold Purchases," a statement by Americans for Democratic Action, Washington, D. C. (17 April 1960), 1–3. This statement was signed by King, Eleanor Roosevelt, Senator Hubert Humphrey of Minnesota, Roy Wilkins of the NAACP, the social ethicist Reinhold Niebuhr, and 65 other liberal national leaders.
127. "Leading Negroes Agree on Goals," 1 ff.
128. King, "The Negro Looks at Africa," 1 ff.
129. Martin Luther King, Jr., "A Speech Regarding South African Independence," London, England (The King Center Archives, 7 December 1964), 1–2; and *Four Decades of Concern: Martin Luther King, Jr.* (Atlanta: printed by the Martin Luther King, Jr. Center for Nonviolent Social Change, Inc., August 1, 1986), 18–19. Adam Clayton Powell, Jr., the black clergyman and congressman in New York, also consistently called for international sanctions against South Africa during the same time. See "Powell Seeks Boycott of S. African Goods," *New York Amsterdam News* (April 16, 1960): 20.

In December, 1965, a year later, King made his most extensive statement on the need for sanctions against South Africa at Hunter College in New York. He chided the United States Government for giving "massive support" to South Africa "through American investments in motor and rubber industries," for extending its government "some forty million dollars in loans through our most distinguished banking and financial institutions," for "purchasing its gold and other minerals mined by black slave labour," for giving South Africa "a sugar quota," for "maintaining three tracking stations there," and for "providing them with the prestige of a nuclear reactor built with our technical cooperation and fueled with refined uranium supplied by us." King continued:

> When it is realized that Great Britain, France and other democratic powers also prop up the economy of South Africa—and when to all of this is added the fact that the U.S.S.R. has indicated its willingness to participate in a boycott—it is proper to wonder how South Africa can so confidently defy the civilized world. The conclusion is inescapable that it is less sure of its own power, but more sure that the great nations will not sacrifice trade and profit to oppose them effectively. The shame of our nation is that it is objectively an ally of this monstrous Government in its grim war with its own black people.[130]

King went on to challenge all nations with the possibility of "a massive international movement for nonviolent economic sanctions against South Africa":

> Have we the power to be more than peevish with South Africa, but yet refrain from acts of war? To list the extensive economic relations of the great powers with South Africa is to suggest a potent nonviolent

---

130. Martin Luther King, Jr., "South Africa Benefit Speech," Hunter College, New York City (The King Center Archives, 10 December 1965), 3–4; and *Four Decades of Concern,* 19–22. Also see "U. S. Negroes' Goal: To Set Africa Policy," 61; and a letter from Theodore E. Brown to the members of The American Negro Leadership Conference on Africa, 29 June 1966, The King Center Archives.

path. The international potential of nonviolence has never been employed. Nonviolence has been practiced within national borders in India, the U. S. and in regions of Africa with spectacular success. The time has come fully to utilize nonviolence through a massive international boycott which would involve the U.S.S.R., Great Britain, France, the U. S., Germany and Japan. Millions of people can personally give expression to their abhorrence of the world's worst racism through such a far-flung boycott. No nation professing a concern for man's dignity could avoid assuming its obligations if people of all states and races adopted a firm stand.[131]

King's antiapartheid activities drew considerable recognition and praise from many South Africans. Adelaide Tambo and others in the A.N.C. warmly received him at the Africa Unity House in London in the early 1960s.[132] In 1966, King received invitations to serve as the annual Thomas B. Davie's Memorial Lecturer by the Students' Visiting Lecturers Organization at the University of Capetown, to open the 41st Annual Congress of the National Union of South African Students, and to address the Anglican Students' Federation in South Africa.[133] King graciously accepted the invitations but was denied a visa to enter South Africa, for obvious reasons.[134] Unable to fulfill lecture engagements in South Africa, King accepted with humility and gratitude the decision of the National Union of South African Students to publish his views on segregation, violence, and other subjects.[135]

131. King, "South Africa Benefit Speech," 4–5.
132. See a letter from Adelaide Tambo to Martin Luther King, Jr., 17 May 1962, The King Papers, Boston University.
133. King correspondence with South African students and professors from 1965 to 1966 are included in Baldwin, ed., *Toward the Beloved Community*, Part III.
134. A letter from Martin Luther King, Jr., to the South African Embassy, New Orleans, Louisiana, 9 February 1966, The King Center Archives; and a letter from N. M. Nel to Martin Luther King, Jr., 17 March 1966.
135. See "Martin Luther King: A Statement on His Views" (Capetown, South Africa: The National Union of South African Students, circa 1965), The King Center Archives, 1–35.

Also in 1966, King was contacted by Claudie Erleigh of the University of the Witwatersrand in Johannesburg about writing an article for the school's journal.[136] During that same year, Bode Wegerif, an executive in a Johannesburg publishing company, and Dale White, Anglican priest and Director of the Wilgespruit Christian Fellowship and Conference Center near Johannesburg, distributed more than a thousand long-playing records of a speech by King. When questioned about their actions, Wegerif and White commented:

> We have undertaken the sponsorship of this record in our individual capacities because we believe that Dr. Martin Luther King's address has direct relevance to the churches and to all men of goodwill in South Africa. We consider it of utmost importance that this statement of conviction by King, whose words and actions encourage and inspire millions of people throughout the world, should be heard in this country.[137]

These sentiments were not shared by most whites in South Africa. The Dutch Reformed Church in South Africa joined the white-ruled government in labeling King "a Communist" and "a troublemaker," and objected to the awarding of an honorary degree to him by the University of Amsterdam.[138] Prime Minister John Vorster repeatedly reminded South African clergymen who sought to "do the kind of thing here that Martin Luther King did in America" to "cut it out, cut it out immediately for the cloak you carry will not protect you if you try to do this in South Africa."[139] J. D. Vorster, Registrar of the

136. A letter from Miss Claudie Erleigh to Martin Luther King, Jr., 28 October 1966, The King Center Archives.
137. "The Racial Scene," *The Christian Century* (July 20, 1966): 930. The topic of the speech distributed by Wegerif and White was not specifically mentioned in this source, but there is reason to believe that it was King's "I Have a Dream" speech. In 1971, the white-ruled government in Pretoria, South Africa banned recordings of King's "I Have a Dream" speech. See *New York Amsterdam News* (January 2, 1971): 1 ff.
138. "Same Dreary Old Distortions: Dr. Luther King is No Communist," *The Cape Times*, Cape Town, South Africa (November 15, 1965): 1 ff.; and Baldwin, ed., *Toward the Beloved Community*, Part VI.
139. Quoted in John W. de Gruchy, *The Church Struggle in South Africa* (Grand Rapids, Mich.: William B. Eerdmans Publishing Company, 1986), 118.

Nederduitse Gereformeerde Kerk and a brother of the South African Prime Minister, denounced King's human rights activities as counterproductive.[140] Even so, King's influence on the antiapartheid struggle would remain evident in South Africa throughout the 1960s, 1970s, and 1980s.

King's interest in the freedom movements of Southern Africa extended to the Rhodesian crisis in the 1950s and 1960s. In June, 1959, in a letter to the Editorial Committee of *Dissent* magazine in Salisbury, Rhodesia, King wrote: "Although we are separated by many miles, we are close together in a mutual struggle for freedom and human brotherhood." "We can well understand what you are going through," he continued, "because your struggle there is so similar to our struggle here in the American South."[141] In King's estimation, the struggle of the African nationalists against British domination in Southern Rhodesia was also essentially the same as that of people of color against South African apartheid. The fact that South Africa, Portugal, and the United States gave open aid to Rhodesia as a whole greatly disturbed King. In November, 1962, he joined others in the A.N.L.C.A. in condemning

> the present government of Southern Rhodesia as being both politically bankrupt and callous. Its primary function has been to keep Africans in a depressed and subservient political, economic and social status through legal and extra-legal means, including discriminatory and repressive laws and the denial of freedom of speech, assembly and free movement of Africans. . . . We deplore the fact that the United States abstained on a resolution in the United Nations on Southern Rhodesia in the 17th Assembly which, among other things, called for lifting of the ban against the nationalist party, Z.A.P.U. [Zimbabwe

140. "Roundup: Foreign Tributes to Dr. King," *The Christian Century* 85, no. 19 (May 8, 1968): 630.
141. A letter from Martin Luther King, Jr., to the Editorial Committee of *Dissent*, Salisbury, Rhodesia (The King Papers, Boston University, 1 June 1959).

African People's Union], release of political prisoners, and for discussions between the British Government and representatives of African nationalist
organizations leading to a new constitution giving
full voting rights to Africans. . . . We seek full dis-
closure of all facts which will detail the manner and
extent of American economic influence, both public
and private, in this part of Africa.[142]

In November, 1964, two years later, King and other
A.N.L.C.A. members produced another carefully worded
statement on Southern Rhodesia, which had previously
been a part of the white-controlled Central African Federation. This statement condemned the white government of Prime Minister Ian Smith, and called upon the
United States to affirm, through its votes at the United
Nations, "its opposition to the independence of Southern
Rhodesia until the African majority of that country en-
joys full participation in government based on the principle of 'one man, one vote,' and until such representative
government has given its consent to independence." It
stated further:

> The grave danger in Southern Rhodesia is that the
> colony will gain independence while still under the
> dominance of a minority, reactionary white govern-
> ment headed by Ian Smith. Should this happen, a his-
> tory of racial oppression not too different from that of
> the Republic of South Africa would follow.[143]

In October, 1965, King made several statements on
Southern Rhodesia in Paris. He warned that international sanctions against the white-ruled government were
necessary to avoid widespread bloodshed:

> We have Southern Rhodesia seeking to turn back the
> clock of history and have the audacity to suppose that
> 250,000 white persons can govern and make decisions

142. *The American Negro Leadership Conference on Africa: Resolutions (1962)*, 3–4.
143. *The American Negro Leadership Conference on Africa: Resolutions (1964)*, 5.

for 4 million black men. . . . Nothing seems a more deliberate invitation to strife and violence, than the threat of Ian Smith to unilaterally declare independence. This is 1965. Times are far different than the period in which South Africa developed its apartheid policies. Great Britain and the world have a critical decision to make. Either they will apply the nonviolent sanctions which may bring Southern Rhodesia to her senses, or they will face a potential bloodbath in the not too distant future when Zambia, Tanzania and internal forces within Southern Rhodesia coalesce to form the military or terrorist operation to throw off this final yoke of oppression. Segregation and colonialism are dead in every shape and form. The sooner we get about the business of cooperative inter-racial nation building, the sooner we can rid the world of war and the causes of war.[144]

King went on to argue, in another statement, that

the world cannot stand another South Africa. Another one only augments the problem, and I think it is very urgent that a positive stand be taken against Southern Rhodesia, and that they not be allowed to engage in this kind of dastardly act, blocking representation on the part of the African people themselves. . . . I think the U. N. should be the force that will stand behind the British Government in not granting independence to Southern Rhodesia as it is presently seeking it. I'm all for independence, but it must be an independence with a one-man, one-vote idea behind it.[145]

The A.N.L.C.A. and the A.C.O.A. issued many statements consistent with King's position on Southern Rhodesia in 1965 to 1966.[146] Little did King know that it

144. Martin Luther King, Jr., "A Lecture to the Federation Protestante de France Mutualite," Paris, France (The King Center Archives, 24 October 1965), 18.
145. Martin Luther King, Jr., "On the World Taking a Stand on Rhodesia: An Interview," Paris, France (The King Center Archives, 25 October 1965), 1.
146. For examples, see "A Statement Concerning United States Policy in the Rhodesian Crisis," prepared by The American Committee on

would be another fourteen years, in 1980, before Southern Rhodesia would become the independent African-
ruled nation known as Zimbabwe.

King did witness with pride the events that transformed Northern Rhodesia into Zambia, an independent
African-ruled nation, in 1964. Northern Rhodesia had
also been under British rule, and a part of the Central
African Federation as well.[147] When President Kenneth
Kaunda of the Republic of Zambia came to the United
States at the invitation of the A.N.L.C.A. in 1966, King
was among those who warmly greeted and met with
him.[148] King never envisioned that Zambia, like Southern
Rhodesia, would become one part of Southern Africa
over which South Africa would maintain some hege-
mony in the 1970s and 1980s.

Much of King's attention in the 1960s was directed at
the independence movements in Portuguese territories
in Africa. In November, 1962, King was among those in
the A.N.L.C.A. who urged the United States government
"to use its influence to persuade other Western powers to
urge Portugal to grant Angola, Mozambique, and Portuguese Guinea their independence."[149] Two years later,
the A.N.L.C.A. resolved:

1. That the United States free itself from dependence
   on Portugal by exploring and developing alternative sites for its military bases in the Azores.
2. That restrictions and controls on arms sales and
   transfers to Portugal be tightened to insure that
   neither N.A.T.O. weapons nor American counter-
   insurgency equipment reinforce Portuguese military power.

Africa, New York, New York (The King Center Archives, October, 1965),
1–3; "A Statement on American Policy Towards Rhodesia," prepared by
George M. Houser, Executive Director of The American Committee on
Africa (The King Center Archives, 18 November 1965), 1–3; and *The
American Negro Leadership Conference on Africa: Resolutions (1964),* 5.
  147. *The American Negro Leadership Conference on Africa: Resolutions (1962),* 3.
  148. Houser, *No One Can Stop the Rain,* 108 ff.
  149. *The American Negro Leadership Conference on Africa: Resolutions (1962),* 3–4.

3. That refugee students from Angola, Mozambique and Portuguese Guinea, namely the hundreds in Leopoldville, Lusaka and Dakar, be aided by a crash program to provide them with higher education.
4. That the United States seriously urge Portugal to promote massive educational and economic development in Portuguese Africa, or to join with other nations, such as Brazil, or act through the United Nations to that end.[150]

King continued to speak out against Portugal's colonial policies in Africa in the late 1960s.[151] However, his vision of an Africa independent of Portuguese control was not realized until 1975, when both Angola and Mozambique became independent nations.

Two points should be strongly reemphasized if King's vision for Africa and the black world generally is to be fully understood. First, King's attitude toward black people in Africa and in the diaspora placed him squarely in a tradition that stretched back to the earliest African-American thinkers and leaders. In his call for a united struggle against oppression on the part of people of African descent everywhere, he was echoing the sentiments of Richard Allen, Paul Cuffee, David Walker, Henry Highland Garnet, Henry McNeil Turner, W. E. B. Du Bois, Paul Robeson, and countless others before him. Indeed, King was a part of this long line of American blacks who stressed the need for "more advanced" African-Americans to play a vanguard role in the liberation of blacks throughout the world.[152]

Second, King's vision of an independent black world and his efforts to translate that vision into reality must

150. *The American Negro Leadership Conference on Africa: Resolutions (1964)*, 5.
151. "U. S. Negroes' Goal: To Set Africa Policy," 61.
152. This contention is borne out by a reading of Wilmore, *Black Religion and Black Radicalism*, 74–134; and Sterling Stuckey, *Slave Culture: Nationalist Theory and the Foundations of Black America* (New York: Oxford University Press, 1987), 98–358. Although Wilmore and Stuckey fail to link King directly with this tradition of thought, their discussions of that tradition are useful for locating King within it.

be understood within the contexts of the civil rights and black power movements in the 1950s and 1960s. It was during this time that Malcolm X and the Black Muslims captured the imagination of black America with their stirring call for racial pride and black unity and uplift, and with their persistent claims that Africa was the ancestral home and spiritual cradle of all black people. It was in this period that Maulana Ron Karenga, the principal black cultural nationalist, founded Kwanzaa as a tribute to the rich cultural roots of Americans of African descent. It was also during this time that young radicals like Stokely Carmichael and Willie Ricks began to deemphasize integration and to raise the banner of "black power." Furthermore, this was the time when black leaders with profoundly different political-religious perspectives released the African-American struggle from its domestic context and related it to the struggles of people of color all over the world. It was largely in response to these developments and challenges that King's perspective on the bonds and obligations between black people everywhere found shape and maturity.[153]

THE IMPACT OF KING'S DEATH
ON THE BLACK WORLD

The assassination of Martin Luther King, Jr., by the forces of racism on April 4, 1968 created a storm of anger and grief throughout the black world. That anger and grief reached fever pitch minutes after King's death as thousands of black Americans engaged in window-breaking, rock-throwing, and looting, causing property damage that was incalculable. "From Washington to Oakland, Tallahassee to Denver," reported *Newsweek* a week or so later, "the murder of Martin Luther King, Jr. in Memphis last week touched off a black rampage

---

153. We need a serious study of how King's perspective was shaped and refined within the contexts of these developments. Fleeting attention is devoted to this in Baldwin, ed., *Toward the Beloved Community*, Introduction and Concluding Essay.

that subjected the U. S. to the most widespread spasm of racial disorder in its violent history."[154] One of the culprits spoke for all black Americans when he cried, in the streets of Washington, D. C., that "they killed my brother; they killed my Luther King." Another, watching with solemn satisfaction as whole blocks burned in Chicago, insisted that "this is the only answer." Yet another added: "It feels good. I never felt so good before. When they bury King, we gonna bury Chicago." "I thought I was dead until they killed the King," intoned a young gang leader. "They killed the King and I came to life. We gonna die fighting. We all gonna die fighting." One black man offered a fitting footnote to these volatile expressions of anger and grief when he said: "I'm a hard man and I want some revenge. King's dead and he ain't ever gonna get what he wanted. But we're alive, man, and we're getting what we want."[155]

For one of the few times during the 1960s, black leaders on both the militant and moderate ends of the spectrum agreed in their assessments of the furies brooding in the shadows of America's sullen ghettoes. Stokely Carmichael, the militant young leader of the S.N.C.C., asserted that King's assassination proved that the only way blacks could survive was "to get some guns." "When white America killed Dr. King," he maintained, "she declared war on us":

> I think white America made its biggest mistake when she killed Dr. King, because when she killed Dr. King she killed all reasonable hope. When she killed Dr. King she killed the one man of our race that this country's older generations, the militants and the revolutionaries and the masses of black people would still listen to. Even though sometimes he did not agree with them, they would still listen to him. . . . When white America killed Dr. King, she opened the eyes of every black man in this country. When white America

154. Quoted in *Newsweek* (April 15, 1968): 31.
155. *Ibid.*, 32–33.

got rid of Marcus Garvey [Jamaican Negro leader deported in 1927], she did it and said he was an extremist—he was crazy. When they got rid of Brother Malcolm X, they said he was preaching hate—he deserved what he got. When they got rid of Brother Martin Luther King, they had absolutely no reason to do so. He was the one man in our race who was trying to teach our people to have love, compassion and mercy for what white people had done.[156]

Carmichael went on to note that "the rebellions that have been occurring around these cities and this country is just light stuff compared to what is about to happen. We have to retaliate for the deaths of our leaders."[157] Floyd McKissick, the Director of the Congress of Racial Equality, echoed Carmichael's sentiments, insisting that "the philosophy of nonviolence died with Dr. King. . . . Black Americans no longer will tolerate this killing of its males. . . . White people are going to suffer as much as black people."[158] Many "Negroes feel that, somehow, white America is responsible for the death of Martin Luther King," declared Dr. Daniel C. Thompson, Professor of Sociology at New Orleans' Dillard University. "The Negro in the city has been angry—very angry," Thompson continued. "But he had hope. And I think that the assassination of Martin Luther King just said to many of these people: 'there is no hope.'"[159] Whitney Young of the Urban League described the riots in America's cities as the normal "reaction of a Negro community after their hero, Martin Luther King, had been assassinated by a white man." Young went on to capture the impact of the King assassination on black America in these terms: "There are no moderates today. Everybody is a militant. The difference is there are builders and there are burners."[160]

156. *Ibid.*, 31; and "Negro Leaders—More Militant Now," *U. S. News and World Report* 64, no. 17 (April 22, 1968): 19 and 49–50.
157. "Negro Leaders—More Militant Now," 50.
158. *Ibid.*, 19.
159. *Ibid.*, 47.
160. *Ibid.*, 19 and 46.

The murder of King was for some moderate civil rights leaders a time to reaffirm the power of nonviolence as an alternative to violence and human destruction. The tragedy was, according to Roy Wilkins of the NAACP, further evidence of the need for America to follow "a peaceful course." Ralph D. Abernathy, King's closest friend and co-worker in the S.C.L.C., agreed, declaring that "We thank God for a leader who was willing to die and not to kill." Whitney Young said that if the killing of King failed to turn white America from its obsession with violence and oppression, then he had no choice but to give up on his country. "Either I get out of it and go to Africa," he explained, "or I just conclude that America has no capability of responding in a moral tone to anything but violence."[161]

As black America reeled with shocked anger and dismay in the days immediately following King's death, tributes poured in from black people in Canada, South America, the West Indies, and other parts of the world. One of the most glowing tributes came from President Francois Duvalier of the Republic of Haiti. In his *A Tribute to the Martyred Leader of Nonviolence, Reverend Martin Luther King, Jr. (1968)*, Duvalier called King "a brother" who had "fallen for the dignity of the Race." At Duvalier's request and urging, memorial services for King were held in churches throughout Haiti, and the Port-au-Prince City Council passed a decree naming an avenue after King. For Duvalier, these tributes were an affirmation of "the ethnic and cultural bonds of the First Free Negro Republic in the world, Haiti, with Africa and her solidarity with the Black World."[162]

Africans reacted to the King assassination in a similar manner. "Perhaps nowhere was the impact of the assassination of Dr. King greater than in Africa," wrote J. Lowrie Anderson, a white American who served as a fraternal worker under the United Presbyterian

161. *Ibid.*, 19–20 and 45–46.
162. Duvalier, *A Tribute to the Martyred Leader*, 18–23.

Commission on Ecumenical Mission and Relations in Nairobi, Kenya. "Africans identified themselves with the civil rights movement in America, and with Dr. King. They felt that in his fight for equality for the disinherited in America, he was fighting for black men everywhere." Anderson also related this account of an exchange he and a co-worker had with an African friend soon after King was killed:

> As a colleague and I sat down to tea with an African friend he said bitterly, "We hate you Americans. You killed our Martin Luther King." My colleague replied "Yes, I was ashamed of being an American—until I remembered that Martin Luther King was an American also. Then I was proud."[163]

George W. Shepherd, Jr., in a commentary on King's death in the April–May, 1968, issue of *Africa Today*, reported that "the loss to Africa of Martin Luther King is second only to the loss to America." He added:

> Not only was this Black American a representative of the finest blending of African and American culture, but also he was an inspirational leader to many Africans as well as Americans. It was a genuine two-way relationship. King himself frequently acknowledged the debt he had for the development of his nonviolent methods to the freedom movement of the South Africans who back in the early 1950's began their first passive resistance campaigns. The quick successes of King in Montgomery and the civil rights movement in this country in turn inspired the African leaders to move more rapidly toward freedom. This Nkrumah and others acknowledged when they returned to their Alma Mater, Lincoln University, to receive degrees and to renew their contacts with Afro-Americans. . . . Moreover, King was one of those Afro-American leaders who was continuously conscious of the ties and responsibilities of Americans for African developments. He was a prime mover in the

---

163. "Roundup: Foreign Tributes to Dr. King," 629.

formation of the Negro Leadership Conference on Africa. And he repeatedly sought out American officials on behalf of African freedom.[164]

Shepherd observed that the tragedy of King's death for Africa was compounded by the fact that it occurred while the civil rights leader was involved in efforts to end the Nigerian crisis:

> Perhaps one of the greatest losses of all to Africa was the end of his role in the mission to Nigeria that King and a number of other Afro-American leaders were to undertake in mid-April. They had gained the acceptance of both sides in the tragic struggle in Nigeria to attempt to assess the possibilities for a negotiated settlement. Some hope existed that a man with King's universal respect might be able to persuade the antagonists that an end to the killing was possible. At this point the future of this mission is in doubt.[165]

Shepherd concluded that King's death, like that of Chief Albert Luthuli in the summer of 1967, marked the end of an era of efforts to achieve peaceful reform through nonviolence. "The lives of these two men joined together in their faith and common African heritage," wrote Shepherd, "symbolize the fate of the dream of human brotherhood in our age of violence."[166] This perspective coincided with that of millions of black South Africans, many of whom assigned King a special place in the palace of martyrs. Joseph Louw, a young black South African photographer who was working with King on a documentary film when the tragedy occurred in Memphis, spoke the minds of many of his oppressed brothers and sisters when he suggested that King's death should disturb the complacency of a world caught in the web of hatred and violence.[167]

---

164. Shepherd, "Who Killed Martin Luther King's Dream?," 2.
165. *Ibid.*
166. *Ibid.*
167. "Roundup: Foreign Tributes to Dr. King," 630; and George P. Hunt, "I Knew I Must Record it for the World," *Life* 64, no. 16 (April 19, 1968): 1 ff.

The memorial services held for King in parts of Africa were as well attended and touching as many of those among blacks in the United States and the West Indies. In Nairobi, several Kenyans led a simple service that brought together Americans, Europeans, and Asians as well as Africans. Unable to attend himself, President Jomo Kenyatta sent personal representatives to express his condolences. Three cabinet ministers who had associated with King "spoke of the impact his humility and dedication had had upon them." Tom Mboya, the Minister of Planning, read the speech King gave shortly before his death, and added: "Martin Luther King is dead. His soul goes marching on. We Kenyans join that march." Similar expressions of respect and admiration were offered in memorial services by Ethiopians, Ghanaians, and South Africans.[168] Such expressions afforded additional proof that King's influence on Africans and their struggles was far more substantial, materially and spiritually, than we have been led to believe.

AFRICAN-AMERICANS AND AFRICA SINCE KING

The question of the relationship between African-Americans and Africa has remained a critical one since the death of Martin Luther King, Jr. King died at a time when many black Americans, inspired by the black power thrust and imbued with a deepening sense of how their struggle related to that of other peoples of color, were developing a strong African consciousness. This emerging consciousness led to an emphasis on the need for black Americans to ground themselves in African traditions and values, and to create self-propelled movements reflective of their African heritage.[169] Millions of blacks

168. "Roundup: Foreign Tributes to·Dr. King," 629–30.
169. For evidence of this development in black consciousness, see "Pan-African Congress Adopts Black Unity as First Priority," *Jet* 42, no. 26 (September 21, 1972): 46; Lerone Bennett, Jr., "Pan-Africanism at the Crossroads," *Ebony* 29, no. 11 (September 1974): 148–54; Anthony

adopted Afro hair styles, studied African history and languages, and clothed themselves in dashikis and other African modes of dress. The Republic of New Africa, described as "an independent and sovereign black nation" within a nation, was founded in Detroit in March, 1968 by Milton and Richard Henry, two brothers who believed that an embracement of African-based values would enhance their people's creative faculties and, consequently, their quest for liberation. This perspective was carried to new heights of clarity and power in the writings and activities of Pan-Africanists such as Malauna Karenga and Imamu Amiri Baraka, and was reinforced with the publication of Alex Haley's *Roots: The Saga of an American Family* in 1976. Martin Luther King, Jr., would not have endorsed all of these developments, but his life, work, and legacy—coupled with that of Malcolm X, W. E. B. Du Bois, Paul Robeson, and others—inspired them.[170]

Many African-American leaders emerged in the 1970s and 1980s to further advance King's conviction that the United States, and particularly black Americans, must become more involved in the political and economic empowerment of Africa. In the early 1970s, Dr. Samuel C. Adams, Jr., a pioneer in the diplomatic field and an assistant administrator for the United States Government's Agency for International Development, dispensed millions of dollars to African countries. Determined to use the influence of the United States to

Monteiro, "The Sixth Pan-African Congress: Agenda for African-Afro-American Solidarity," in *Freedomways Reader: Afro-America in the Seventies*, ed. Ernest Kaiser (New York: International Publishers, 1977), 396–405; and "Interview with Dr. Malauna Karenga," *African Commentary* 1, no. 1 (October 1989): 61–64.

170. Lewis H. Wilson, "The Hawkish Doves: A History of the Republic of New Africa" (M.A. thesis, Mississippi College, Clinton, Miss., December, 1986), 11–16; Bennett, "Pan-Africanism at the Crossroads," 148–54; "Pan-African Congress Adopts Black Unity," 46; "Afrikan-American Nation Notes 'Human Rights Day,'" *Jet* 45, no. 17 (January 17, 1974): 26; "Haley Gets Warm Welcome in Return to Juffure," *Jet* 57, no. 8 (May 12, 1977): 14–16; Monteiro, "The Sixth Pan-African Congress," 396–405; and "Interview with Dr. Malauna Karenga," 61–64.

improve relationships between black Americans and Africa, Adams commented in 1973: "We have made a rather heroic effort to employ minority firms as contractors for programs in Africa."[171] In the late 1970s, United Nations Ambassador Andrew Young also used his diplomatic influence to encourage an African/African-American coalition, and to press for more United States aid to African countries. The work of these men was complemented by that of civil rights activist A. Philip Randolph, Randall Robinson of TransAfrica, Roy Innis of the Congress of Racial Equality (CORE), Representative Charles C. Diggs, Jr. of Michigan, Leon Sullivan of the Opportunities Industrialization Centers (O.I.C.), Jesse Jackson of People United to Save Humanity (P.U.S.H.), and other black Americans who devoted their resources to the African struggle and to the solidarity of all components of the black world.[172] Some of these men had worked closely with Martin Luther King, Jr., and all had been influenced by the ways in which he articulated and strove for the realization of the hopes, dreams, and aspirations of black people everywhere.

The 1980s witnessed continued efforts on the part of black leaders to establish the mutuality of the goals of black Africa and black America, and to lift Africa from the social, political, and economic chaos caused by racism and Euro-American imperialism. TransAfrica, founded in 1977, became one of the preeminent Washington-based lobbies for African and Caribbean causes under Randall Robinson, its Executive Director.[173] Congressmen Ronald Dellums of California, Walter Fauntroy

171. "Africans Feel They Lead U. S. Blacks, Diplomat Says," *Jet* 44, no. 2 (April 5, 1973): 12.
172. *Ibid.*; D. Michael Cheers, "TransAfrica: The Black World's Voice on Capitol Hill," *Ebony* 42, no. 9 (July 1987): 108, 110, 112, and 114; "CORE Director Roy Innis Set for Visit to Uganda," *Jet* 43, no. 24 (March 8, 1973): 46; "Diggs Says Ex-Child Star's Appointment to Ghana O.K.," *Jet* 46, no. 25 (September 12, 1974): 33; and "Jesse Jackson Urges U. S. to Step Up African Relief," *Jet* 44, no. 22 (August 23, 1973): 50.
173. Cheers, "TransAfrica: The Black World's Voice," 108.

of the District of Columbia, William Gray of Pennsylvania, George M. "Mickey" Leland of Texas, and others in the Congressional Black Caucus pushed for increased aid from the United States to Africa, and sought to forge a solid constituency for Africa in 138 congressional districts where African-Americans had major voting power.[174] In July, 1989, Mayor Andrew Young of Atlanta and Mayor Johnny Ford of Tuskegee, Alabama were selected for "a major Pan-African honor" by *African World News* "for their distinctive roles in fostering the cause of African freedom and development." Young focused consistently on issues affecting Atlanta's relations with parts of Africa, and Ford urged Africans and black Americans "to develop the strategy to increase trade" between themselves.[175] Jesse Jackson and his entourage of experts and technicians visited Gabon, Nigeria, Zambia, Zimbabwe, and many other African countries in the 1980s, and called for a rebuilding of "the spiritual bridges between Africans and the millions of African-Americans whose ancestors were torn away from the continent in the infamous slave trade."[176] Jackson spoke the heart-felt sentiments of untold numbers of black Americans in 1986 when he said, "To the extent that Black Africa is strong, so, too, is Black America."[177] Jackson reiterated this point while in Africa in 1989, reminding his people in America, "We're the largest ethnic group in our multi-ethnic society, and as a matter of cultural integrity and historical accuracy, we are the

174. "O.A.U. Leader Meets with Black Politicos in D.C. to Cement U. S.–African Ties," *Jet* 72, no. 10 (June 1, 1987): 14; and "What Black Americans and Africans Can Do for Each Other," *Ebony* 41, no. 6 (April, 1986), 155–56.

175. A. B. Assensoh, "A Salute to Africa's Goodwill Ambassadors: Mayor Johnny Ford and Mayor Andrew Young," *African World News* (July–September, 1989): 6–8.

176. D. Michael Cheers, "Jesse Jackson: Rebuilding Bridges to Africa—P.U.S.H. Founder Renews Spiritual Bond between U. S. Blacks and Africans," *Ebony* 42, no. 2 (December, 1986): 132–33, 136, and 138; and Roger D. Hatch, *Beyond Opportunity: Jesse Jackson's Vision for America* (Philadelphia: Fortress Press, 1988), 50–93.

177. "What Black Americans and Africans Can Do," 155.

link between Africa and America. The blood of two continents flows through our bodies."[178]

African-American leaders devoted special attention to
two problems that stunted Africa's growth and development in the 1970s and 1980s. One was the horrible
drought conditions, famine, and starvation that struck
Mali, Mauritania, Niger, Senegal, Chad, the Sudan,
Ethiopia, and other parts of Africa. In the summer of 1973,
Jesse Jackson openly criticized the United States Government's handling of the famine in West Africa during testimony before a House Africa Subcommittee hearing on the
world food crisis in Washington, D. C., and encouraged
"the government to use idle military machinery and man-
power to transport and deliver the food to six West African
nations where millions may starve because of severe
drought."[179] During the same time, the African-American
columnist Carl T. Rowan wrote at length concerning the
desolation caused by drought and famine in six countries
south of the Sahara Desert, insisting, "Unless millions of
black Americans give generously themselves, and inspire
the rich nations to give more than token help, even after
the end of the drought, hunger and misery and sickness
will still be chronic features of life in these countries that
lie at the mercy of nature at the foot of the cruel Sahara."[180] Similar statements were issued in 1974 by Representative Walter Fauntroy and other black members of
Congress, who challenged the leaders of African-American fraternities, sororities, churches, and civil rights organizations to join the effort to save Africa.[181] For the most
part, black Americans responded positively to these challenges, as evidenced by the fact that nearly $25,000 were
collected from the black community of Boston alone, to

178. D. Michael Cheers, "After Visit to African Nations, Jesse Jackson
Urges Joint Partnership," *Jet* 75, no. 17 (January 30, 1989): 12–16.
179. "Jesse Jackson Urges U. S. to Step Up African Relief," 50.
180. Carl T. Rowan, "Death Stalks West Africa," *Ebony* 29, no 1
(November 1973): 35–40.
181. "Representative Fauntroy Planning New Drought Relief Conference," *Jet* 45, no. 17 (January 17, 1974): 27; and "Scott Sees Despair in
Drought-Stricken African Countries," *Jet* 46, no. 8 (May 16, 1974): 28–29.

say nothing of the thousands contributed by blacks in other major United States cities.[182]

The effort to free Africa from the terrible specter of starvation and death found its greatest intensity in the late 1980s in the famine-relief mission of George M. "Mickey" Leland. Leland not only became personally involved in the shipping of grain and other food products to the Horn of Africa, but also took several famine-relief trips to Ethiopia before being killed in a plane crash in that country in the summer of 1989. At a memorial service for Leland, Andrew Young likened the Texas Congressman's legacy to King's.[183] The famine relief efforts of Leland, like those of King and others, belabors the point that a healthy Africa means a healthy black America. The contributions of these leaders still stand as a challenge to black America, especially since some 30 of the 43 poorest countries in the world today are in Africa, and given that African countries are still last among those receiving economic aid from the United States.

Racism was the other major African problem addressed by African-American leaders in the 1970s and 1980s. Much of their assault on this problem in the 1970s was directed at the racist regime in Rhodesia. Congressman Andrew Diggs consistently attacked Rhodesia and applauded the International Olympic Committee (I.O.C.) for expelling that white-ruled nation from the 1972 Olympic games.[184] In 1978, TransAfrica's Randall Robinson, Mayor Maynard Jackson of Atlanta, the S.C.L.C.'s President Joseph E. Lowery, the Georgia State Representative Hosea Williams, and Martin Luther King, Sr., protested Rhodesian Prime Minister Ian Smith's visit to the United States and challenged

182. "Massachusetts Blacks Raise Funds for Drought-Ravaged Africa," *Jet* 47, no. 21 (February 13, 1975): 17.

183. "What Black Americans and Africans Can Do," 156; D. Michael Cheers, "Leland's Legacy: 'He Died Trying to Feed Starving Blacks,'" *Jet* 76, no. 22 (September 4, 1989): 6–11; and "Africa Loses An Advocate," *Africa News* 32, nos. 1 and 2 (August 1989): 1 ff.

184. "Olympic Boycott Wins; Congressman Diggs Applauds Rhodesia's Expulsion," *Jet* 42, no. 24 (September 7, 1972): 45.

black Americans to lock arms with the oppressed in
Rhodesia. The elderly King declared that "blacks in the
U. S. must support their brothers and sisters in southern
Africa who are striving for their rights and freedom."
"And if brother Ian Smith won't give them their rights,"
King proclaimed, "we be damned if we won't go out and
take them."[185] In the spring of 1979, a flurry of tele-
grams and letters from Andrew Young, Randall
Robinson, and other black leaders cascaded on President Jimmy Carter, demanding that he use his influence
to stop conservatives in Congress from resuming aid to
Rhodesia. Convinced that the election of Bishop Abel
Muzorewa as Rhodesia's first black head of state was
designed to pacify black Rhodesians rather than to
allow them a fair share of power, these black Americans
urged Carter "to make an early determination in
favor of continued sanctions enforcement against
Rhodesia."[186] In 1980, a year later, Rhodesia bowed to
the pressure exerted by antiracism forces and achieved
independence as Zimbabwe.

The system of racial exploitation and oppression in
South Africa was subjected to intense criticism in the
1970s by black Americans in many fields, ranging from
the tennis professional Arthur Ashe to the civil rights activist Bayard Rustin. Rustin, whose interest in South
Africa dated at least as far back as the 1950s, advocated a
nonviolent solution to the problem of apartheid, a position consistent with that proposed by Martin Luther
King, Jr., in the 1960s.[187] Jesse Jackson shared this stance
as well. The greatest opposition to South African
apartheid came in the 1970s from Charles Diggs and
Leon Sullivan, both of whom took giant steps in influencing United States policy toward South Africa. Diggs,

185. "Thousands Protest Ian Smith's U. S. Visit," *Jet* 55, no. 8 (November 9, 1978): 14–15.
186. "Carter Urged to Halt Move by Congress to Lift Sanctions
Against Rhodesia," *Jet* 56, no. 10 (May 24, 1979): 40.
187. See "Ashe Advises Blacks Following Visit to South African Cities,"
Jet 45, no. 16 (January 10, 1974): 12–16; and Joseph Beam, "The Elder of
the Village: an Interview with Bayard Rustin," *B/Out* (1987): 17.

Chairman of the House African Sub-Committee, pushed for United States sanctions against South Africa in 1974, after being denied a visa to visit that country.[188] In 1977, Sullivan, a member of the Board of General Motors, introduced "The Sullivan Principles," a voluntary code of conduct for United States companies with affiliates in South Africa. This document called for nondiscrimination in employment practices, in eating, comfort, and work facilities, and in employment benefits. "The Sullivan Principles," a compromise solution, were eventually adopted by churches, universities, and other organizations as a minimal standard of conduct for South Africa–related United States companies in which they owned stock.[189]

Organizations that made a special claim to the legacy of Martin Luther King, Jr., also felt compelled to challenge the morality and legitimacy of South African apartheid in the 1970s. The S.C.L.C. and the Martin Luther King, Jr., Center for Nonviolent Social Change, Inc., headquartered in Atlanta, Georgia, became notable examples. In September, 1976, Bernard Lee, the Executive Vice President of the S.C.L.C., sent a strongly worded letter to United Nations Secretary General Kurt Waldheim, protesting the disregard for black life in South Africa. Lee insisted that the indiscriminate killing of blacks in that country made it impossible for them "to continue the nonviolent tactics they learned from the late Dr. Martin Luther King, Jr." Lee suggested that the United Nations dispatch a peace-keeping force to South Africa, a recommendation that never materialized.[190] Coretta Scott King, President of the King Center, essentially agreed with Lee's advocacy of a nonviolent

188. "Diggs Renews Drive Against South Africa," *Jet* 45, no. 26 (March 21, 1974): 29; "South Africa Seeks to Silence Black Leaders," *Jet* 46, no. 1 (March 28, 1974): 14; and "Representative Diggs Halted in South Africa Airport," *Jet* 47, no. 22 (February 20, 1975): 12.
189. Ranganath Murthy, "Good Intentions Aren't Enough: A Critique of the Sullivan Principles" (Unpublished paper, 24 April 1986), 1–2; and Theodore Cross, *The Black Power Imperative: Racial Inequality and the Politics of Nonviolence* (New York: Faulkner Books, 1986), 32–33.
190. "S.C.L.C. V.P. Demands U.N. Peace Force in South Africa," *Jet* 50, no. 26 (September 16, 1976): 18.

solution to the apartheid problem. In December, 1975, after returning from South Africa, she proudly recalled the "serious efforts to resolve problems nonviolently" in spite of "the danger of greater warfare." Two years later, in a speech in Washington, D. C., Coretta Scott King urged President Jimmy Carter "to find nonviolent answers to this growing and disturbing situation" in South Africa.[191]

The extent to which black American churches addressed issues related to southern Africa in the 1970s is open to debate. The black church in its national institutional form was preoccupied with survival issues in the United States, and was more of a spectator than a participant in the events associated with Rhodesia and South Africa. However, there were exceptions. In 1975, the Bishops' Council of the African Methodist Episcopal Church, representing two million constituents, pledged its support for black majority rule in both Rhodesia and South Africa. The council was led by Bishop H. H. Brookins, who had previously been expelled from Rhodesia and South Africa because of his attacks on their racial policies, and because of his support for Rhodesia's African National Council, a black nationalist group.[192] In 1978, the A.M.E. Church, the African Methodist Episcopal Zion Church (A.M.E.Z.), the National Baptist Convention of America, the National Baptist Convention, U.S.A., and the Progressive National Baptist Convention united under the auspices of the National Council of Churches and asked major banks in the United States to "establish a policy that no new loans will be made nor existing loans renewed to the Pretoria, South Africa government."[193] These developments were in line with the black church's

---

191. *Four Decades of Concern*, 27–28.
192. "A.M.E. Bishops' Council to Seek Kissinger Meeting," *Jet* 49, no. 1 (September 25, 1975): 31.
193. "Black Churches Tell Banks to Halt South African Loans," *Jet* 54, no. 2 (March 30, 1978): 31.

long-standing interest in strengthening ties with Africa as a whole.[194]

The election of Ronald Reagan to the Presidency of the United States in 1980 created many new problems for African-Americans who struggled for the immediate demise of South African apartheid. Reagan's "Constructive Engagement" policy, implemented during his two terms in office, held that the interests of the oppressed in South Africa could be better served by developing stronger economic and cultural links between that country and the United States.[195] This invariably meant more United States investments in South Africa, an approach frowned upon by broad sectors of the African-American community. Faced with the Reagan administration's unqualified support for South Africa, black leaders in America turned to more radical forms of protest in the 1980s. In November, 1984, Randall Robinson, Walter Fauntroy, and United States Civil Rights commissioner Mary Frances Berry staged "a 1960s-style sit-in" outside the South African Embassy in Washington. This led to "daily protests lasting 53 consecutive weeks in Washington and at South African consulates in 26 cities across the U. S."[196] More than 4,000 persons were arrested, among whom were 23 members of the United States Congress, and a number of mayors, civil rights activists, celebrities, and presidents of fraternities, sororities, and other black organizations. TransAfrica and its spin-off organization, The Free South Africa Movement, secured a national stage on which to make their case against South Africa's racial policies. Through protest and their persistent lobbying for global

---

194. Wilmore, *Black Religion and Black Radicalism*, 99–134; "Black Episcopalians Visit Africa 'To Strengthen Ties,'" *Jet* 55, no. 1 (September 21, 1978): 57; and "A.M.E. Bishops Vexed Following Meeting with Carter Says Bishop Morris," *Jet* 56, no. 9 (May 17, 1979): 16.

195. One of the most brilliant discussions of Reagan's "Constructive Engagement" policy is offered by Robert Fatton, "The Reagan Foreign Policy Toward South Africa: The Ideology of the New Cold War," *The African Studies Review* 27, no. 1 (March, 1984): 57–82.

196. Cheers, "TransAfrica: The Black World's Voice," 108 and 110.

economic sanctions against that country, TransAfrica and other lobby groups succeeded in applying sufficient pressure to force Congress to override Reagan's veto and to impose sanctions on South Africa in 1986.[197]

Several black Americans who worked closely with Martin Luther King, Jr., emerged as major prophetic voices against apartheid in the 1980s. They included Walter Fauntroy, Joseph Lowery, Jesse Jackson, and Coretta Scott King. Fauntroy, a clergyman as well as a Congressman, used both the pulpit and the halls of Congress as forums for discussing and shaping public opinion around the problem. He, along with Congressmen George M. "Mickey" Leland of Texas, Ronald Dellums of California, and William H. Gray III of Pennsylvania, led the way in making Congress more sensitive and responsive to issues surrounding apartheid, thus creating the kind of mood that made sanctions against the racist South African Government possible.[198]

Joseph Lowery of the S.C.L.C. constantly encouraged Americans of all races and ethnic backgrounds to include apartheid within the scope of their active moral concern. In a speech delivered on December 10, 1983, "Human Rights Day," he remarked:

> I am painfully aware of the failure of my own nation to act with courage and moral sensitivity in efforts to eliminate apartheid and express moral outrage through sanctions and other diplomatic means. It is indeed as ironic, as it is sad, that a nation born out of the hunger for liberty and self-determination would defend or cooperate in any manner with such a tyrannical regime as the government of South Africa. We must urge support and cooperation of the artists and athletes ban. Churches must refuse to do business with South Africa. And we must organize nationally to address the issue of doing business with

197. *Ibid.;* and "What Black Americans and Africans Can Do," 155.
198. Cheers, "TransAfrica: The Black World's Voice," 108 and 110; Cheers, "Leland's Legacy," 9; and "What Black Americans and Africans Can Do," 155.

corporations that do business with South Africa, individually as well as institutionally."[199]

In 1988 Lowery launched a strong attack against conservative white Republicans who persisted in downplaying the moral ramifications of apartheid. He called upon Ronald Reagan to "show the same concern for human rights in South Africa that he showed for human rights in the Soviet Union," noting that "We don't want to see Mr. Reagan segregate his concern for human rights."[200] Lowery also attacked Pat Robertson, the ultraconservative Republican presidential candidate, who suggested that black Americans were wrong in linking the struggle against apartheid with civil rights. In words that call to mind Martin Luther King, Jr., his former associate and leader in the S.C.L.C., Lowery commented:

> Robertson doesn't understand that Blacks have an affinity to their brothers and sisters in Africa just as others in this country have an affinity to people in Poland, Italy, or England. And we don't apologize for that.[201]

Lowery's position on the need for black Americans to assume a special role in the antiapartheid movement is essentially the same as that of Jesse Jackson. Jackson, another associate and follower of King, carried his prophetic witness against apartheid to various parts of the world in the 1980s. Back in September, 1979,

199. Joseph E. Lowery, "An Appeal to Eliminate Apartheid on Human Rights Day," a speech (10 December 1983), 1 ff. The S.C.L.C. has prepared a small pamphlet in which Lowery's comments are included along with a statement from King's and Albert Luthuli's "Appeal for Action Against Apartheid" (10 December 1962), and along with King's call for an international boycott against South Africa at New York's Hunter College (10 December 1965).

200. "Lowery Suggests Reagan Show Concern for South Africa," *Jet* 74, no. 13 (June 27, 1988): 38.

201. "Lowery Chides Robertson on South Africa Comments and on Killing Libya's Gadhafi," *Jet* 73, no. 22 (February 29, 1988): 54. For other references to Lowery in relation to South Africa, see "South Africa to Be Focus of Coming King Lectures," *Vanderbilt Register* (January 10, 1986): 1 and 3; and "South Africa Discussed This Week," *Vanderbilt Register* (January 24, 1986): 1–3.

following a seventeen-day visit to South Africa, he had testified before the United States House of Representatives Subcommittee on Africa, Committee on International Relations, expressing views that would later become a vital part of his campaign rhetoric as a presidential candidate. Echoing views King expressed in the 1960s, Jackson warned, "We have reached the countdown stage in the long struggle between the forces of freedom and institutionalized racism." "It would be unwise, to say the least," he continued, "for our country to be on the side of supporting moral bankruptcy and institutionalized racism." Also in terms strikingly suggestive of King, Jackson recommended "world economic sanctions" against South Africa, declaring that "the human community cannot coexist with apartheid. It is a moral illegitimacy that we must fight."[202]

Early in 1985, Jackson toured Europe and joined many demonstrations against apartheid South Africa. In Bonn, West Germany, he locked arms with 100 protestors representing the Christian Initiative to Free South Africa and Namibia Movement outside the South African Embassy there. In words similar to those spoken by King two decades earlier, Jackson reminded the protestors that apartheid was essentially a continuation of the Nazism that sent six million Jews to their deaths during World War II:

> Forty years ago, we declared the end to a reign of terror that tore at the soul and seam of the human family with such devastation that we still tremble. Forty years ago this continent lay in waste and blood and ashes. Forty years later the Phoenix has emerged from rubble with a new lease on life. The stench of

202. Hatch, *Beyond Opportunity*, 70–71; and Roger D. Hatch and Frank E. Watkins, eds., *Reverend Jesse L. Jackson: Straight from the Heart* (Philadelphia: Fortress Press, 1979), 232–45. Jackson's statement on "American Options on Apartheid," included in this source, compares favorably with King's South Africa benefit speech of 1965. For a trenchant critique of South Africa, and of the Israeli government's complicity with that regime, see "A Dialogue with Jesse Jackson," *Tikkun* 2, no. 5 (1987), 40–41.

blood has given way to the fragrance of life. . . .
Though the Nazi troops surrendered officially forty
years ago, Nazism has not yet surrendered. It has simply shifted. The same ethical grounds (that were used)
for rejecting the Third Reich in Germany must be employed to stop the Fourth Reich in South Africa. So
many of the SS troops went from Germany to South
Africa. Thus, in some measure, the germ of genocide
was not buried in Bitburg, it was transferred to
Johannesburg. Shifting the site of the cancer is inadequate. We must root the death germ out of our body
politics. If it simply shifts or remains dormant in the
right climate or temperature it will rise again.[203]

At Plotzensee, Jackson laid a wreath at the point where
twenty-five hundred Jewish men, women, and children
had been either hanged or beheaded, and he explained
that the salvation of the human soul demanded that
apartheid be eliminated. "With all of our passion and
with all of our pain we cannot resurrect the dead," he
proclaimed. "But if we learn from their deaths, and be-
have differently, we can rob death of its sting and add
immeasurably to the worth of their lives.[204]

Also in 1985, Jackson engaged in an interesting and
provocative debate around the apartheid problem with
the fundamentalist leader Jerry Falwell. After a five-
day fact-finding trip to South Africa, during which he
met with President P. W. Botha, Falwell concluded that
reinvestment in the South African economy was the
best route to the elimination of apartheid, an approach
he claimed was supported by most black South
Africans.[205] In opposition to Falwell, Jackson insisted
that "To reinvest in a system that is economically col-
lapsing is not feasible. The use of economic sanctions to

203. D. Michael Cheers, "Jackson Tours Europe and Joins Marches
Against South Africa," *Jet* 68, no. 12 (June 3, 1985): 30–33.
204. *Ibid.*
205. "Falwell Raises a Stir by Opposing Sanctions Against South
Africa," *Christianity Today* (October 4, 1985): 52–54; D. Michael Cheers,
"Rev. Jackson Travels to Lynchburg to Take Issue with Rev. Jerry Falwell," *Jet* 69, no. 2 (September 23, 1985): 6–9.

get the attention of the government is where you can get the cancer out of apartheid and reserve an industrial democracy which is appealing." Jackson reasoned that it was illogical for Falwell to oppose apartheid while advocating investments in South Africa. He stated further: "That's like being against prostitution but investing in a whore house, like being against liquor and investing in a distillery, like being against smoking and investing in a tobacco company."[206] Jackson called Falwell's friendly meeting with Botha "a disservice," and his reference to the South African Bishop Desmond Tutu as "a phony" "unfortunate." "Anyone who would choose Botha over Tutu," Jackson asserted, "would choose Bull Connor over Martin Luther King; would choose Hitler over the Jews; would choose Herod over Jesus; and would choose Pharaoh over Moses." The S.C.L.C.'s Joseph Lowery concurred, adding that Falwell was "like a reincarnation of the old George Wallace."[207]

The Falwell-Jackson debate occurred on ABC-TV's "Night Line" and at the Thomas Road Baptist Church in Lynchburg, Virginia, a congregation pastored by Falwell.[208] The tone of the debate called to mind King's exchange with conservative white clergymen in Birmingham in 1963. In a real sense, the debate that took place between Jackson and Falwell in 1985, and the exchanges between Lowery and Pat Robertson three years later, provide a model for the kind of discussions that should take place today between black and white churches with regard to apartheid in particular and racism in general.

Jesse Jackson continued his assault on apartheid in the late 1980s. In 1986, he spent seventeen days in southern Africa's front-line states, attempting "to seize the moral offensive against apartheid" and to rebuild the spiritual bridges between blacks there and black Ameri-

---

206. Cheers, "Rev. Jesse Jackson Travels to Lynchburg," 6–9.
207. *Ibid.;* and "Falwell Lambasted for His Remarks about Tutu," *Jet* 68, no. 26 (September 9, 1985): 16.
208. Cheers, "Rev. Jesse Jackson Travels to Lynchburg," 6–9.

cans. In conversations with the leaders of Angola, Botswana, Mozambique, Tanzania, Zambia, and Zimbabwe, Jackson emphasized the need for black unity in ending South Africa's racist system and her aggression toward surrounding African states.[209] He promised these leaders that he would recommend that the United States "impose tougher economic sanctions against South Africa," and that "a Marshall Plan" be implemented "for respect, aid, trade, development, and defense for the southern region of Africa."[210] Interestingly enough, these same concerns had been expressed by Martin Luther King, Jr., in the 1960s.

Coretta Scott King's antiapartheid activities in the 1980s, like those of Jesse Jackson, covered a broad spectrum of events. In a statement at the King Center in December, 1981, she noted that her efforts against apartheid should be regarded as an extension of her husband's work: "As further testament to the growing international recognition of my husband's work and of our efforts here (at the King Center) to fulfill his dream, it is our intention for the King Center to become the forum for which new advances can be made in (the) long campaign to eliminate the indignities and inhumanities of apartheid."[211] Between 1981 and 1987, Coretta Scott King made several strong statements against apartheid at the King Center, at a meeting of the United Nations in New York, at protest rallies in Washington, D. C., and at women's conferences in this country and abroad. During the same period, symposia, seminars, and workshops took place under her leadership at the King Center, featuring Joseph Lowery, Randall Robinson, Congressmen Charles Diggs and William Gray, A. W. Clausen of the World Bank, Dr. Allan Boesak and Bishop Desmond Tutu

209. Cheers, "Jesse Jackson: Rebuilding Bridges," 132–33, 136, and 138; and Cheers, "After Visit to African Nations, Jesse Jackson," 12–14 and 16.
210. Cheers, "Jesse Jackson: Rebuilding Bridges," 136 and 138; and "What Black Americans and Africans Can Do," 156.
211. *Four Decades of Concern*, 28.

of South Africa, United Nations Secretary General Kurt Waldheim, and many other dignitaries from around the world.[212] In addition to these involvements, Coretta Scott King worked with the Free South Africa Movement, and was once arrested along with other immediate family members for protesting outside the South African Embassy in Washington. In 1986, Mrs. King visited South Africa and discussed the prospects for peaceful change and nonracial democratic rule with Winnie Mandela and other leaders of the struggle there. In many ways, Coretta Scott King's relationship to Winnie Mandela, Allan Boesak, and Desmond Tutu resembled her husband's relationship to African leaders such as Tom Mboya and Albert Luthuli in the 1950s and 1960s.[213]

The role women should assume in the antiapartheid movement and in the development of Africa generally was addressed throughout the 1980s by Coretta Scott King. "Let us make no mistake about it," she explained in Nairobi, Kenya in 1985. "Apartheid, like starvation in Africa, is very much a women's issue. . . . Freedom, self-determination and world peace are nothing if not women's issues, and they cannot be achieved without the active involvement of women."[214] On another occasion, Coretta Scott King commented on specific roles women could play in overcoming racism:

> The women of every nation, particularly the United States and Great Britain, should begin to organize selective patronage campaigns in support of freedom and justice in Namibia and South Africa. Another (form of support) is to deepen our involvement in politics, especially in this election year and to make the endorsement of strong anti-apartheid legislation a precondition for our support of all political candidates.[215]

---

212. *Ibid.*, 27–36 and 43–56.
213. *Ibid.*, 31; "What Black Americans and Africans Can Do," 155; and Baldwin, ed., *Toward the Beloved Community*, concluding essay.
214. *Four Decades of Concern*, 31.
215. *Ibid.*, 30.

Concerning the contributions American women could make to the general uplift of Africa, she said:

> One of the things American women could do in support of their brothers and sisters in Africa is to organize their consumer power in service to the cause of African development. Wouldn't it be wonderful if we could organize a national selective patronage council composed of representatives from every major American women's organization? I believe such an institution could have a great impact on African development. For one thing, we could strive to increase the volume of trade with African nations. For another, we could influence corporate policies toward investment in Africa. A national selective patronage council could encourage companies who are responsible investors and bring pressure to bear on those who are not.[216]

Coretta Scott King asserted in 1984 that South African apartheid is a world problem and that it could only be resolved through an international alliance against racism. Martin Luther King, Jr., made that same point in 1965.[217] Coretta Scott King went a step further in urging the peoples of the world to support the Southwest Africa Peoples Organization and the African National Congress in their courageous efforts for freedom and human dignity for people of color in Namibia and South Africa. In her view, such involvement at the international level offered the only hope for ending apartheid through nonviolent means:

> Each day the international community refuses to take action, the South African government feels victorious. The successful use of nonviolent tactics in South Africa remains our last chance to prevent a bloodbath of unprecedented proportions. . . . Every day Nelson Mandela remains incarcerated, it threatens the use of nonviolence; each day trade unionists are tortured and arrested, each day church leaders are

216. *Ibid.*, 29.
217. *Ibid.*, 19–22 and 30.

banned and detained, each day innocent people are
murdered in the streets of South Africa, nonviolence
is threatened.[218]

Black churches took a number of positions on
apartheid in the 1980s that reflected the spirit of Martin
Luther King, Jr. In 1985, Prime Minister P. W. Botha and
South Africa's separatist government came under heavy
criticism from the National Baptist Convention, U.S.A.,
Inc., a body of seven million that once claimed King as a
member. Theodore J. Jemison, its president, committed
the body's resources to the struggle for a more peaceful
and just South Africa.[219] Other black Baptist groups made
similar commitments, and so did the A.M.E. Church, the
A.M.E.Z. Church, and the Christian Methodist Episcopal
(C.M.E.) Church.

Black churches also came together across denomina-
tional and organizational lines to deal with the apartheid
problem. In 1986, the Governing Board of the National
Council of the Churches of Christ in the U.S.A., of which
the A.M.E. Bishop Philip R. Cousin served as president,
set forth an agenda for churches concerned about
apartheid. Several black churches and denominations
were involved. The group condemned South Africa for its
racism and its destabilization of its neighboring African
states, and encouraged the Christian community to push
for economic sanctions against that country. This statement was an addendum to the 1977 policy statement of
the National Council of the Churches of Christ on Southern Africa.[220] In 1989, "The Final Statement of the Black
Church Summit on Southern Africa" was published,
bringing together the antiapartheid sentiments of the
A.M.E. Church, the A.M.E.Z. Church, the C.M.E. Church,
the Church of God in Christ, the National Baptist

218. *Ibid.*, 29 and 32–33.
219. "National Baptist Confab Raps South African Racism; Gears for
Economic Growth," *Jet* 69, no. 3 (September 30, 1985): 24–25; and *National Baptist Union-Review* 89, no. 20 (October 1985): 2.
220. "A Resolution of The National Council of the Churches of Christ
in the U.S.A.: Current Developments in Southern Africa," Chicago, Illinois (November 5–7, 1986), 1–2.

Convention of America, the National Baptist Convention, U.S.A., and the Progressive National Baptist Convention. This statement expressed the group's intention to "work for total, comprehensive new U. S. sanctions," to "keep the Southern African struggle before the U. S. public," to "pray without ceasing for all the peoples of the region of Southern Africa," and to take other steps consistent with the Christian faith.[221]

The attitude of President George Bush and his administration toward Southern Africa and Africa as a whole will present a new challenge for African-Americans. Elected in 1988, Bush has continued to follow the Reagan policy toward Africa, though he has made greater use of diplomatic channels in dealing with South Africa. He has repeatedly opposed tougher economic sanctions against South Africa, arguing that "any further measures to weaken the South African economy threaten the strategic importance of having a stable, pro-Western government in Pretoria."[222] Bush's position on sanctions has softened even more since the South African government released the black activist Nelson Mandela in February, 1990. Mandela's release, and the increasing openness of President F. W. de Klerk's government to negotiation with black South Africans, are viewed as major positive steps by Bush. It is doubtful that Mandela's tour of America in June, 1990, during which he met with Bush, will alter significantly the United States president's perception. Bush seems terribly insensitive to the fact that the apartheid system remains essentially intact despite the recent changes. The fact that South Africa's military budget has grown more than 860% since 1971, and that she continues to destabilize and terrorize other parts of Africa, is not being met with a sense of urgency. In the face of this tragic moral laxity, the crucial question for black leaders and

221. "Final Statement of Black Church Summit on Southern Africa," *The A.M.E. Church Review* 104, no. 333 (1989): 53–54.
222. Andrew Meldrum, "The Bush Agenda in Southern Africa," *Africa Report* (January–February 1989): 16–17.

ordinary people determined to build on King's legacy continues to be: What steps can we take to help save our African brothers and sisters from the destructive forces of racism and neocolonialism? The answer provided to that question will help determine the future course of relations between black Americans, Africans, and other people of African descent across the globe.

Undoubtedly, black Americans will continue to identify with Africa and the struggles of African people in the post-King era. The recent shift from "black American" and "Afro-American" to "African-American" as a way of describing blacks in this country—supported by Jesse Jackson, John E. Jacob, Walter Fauntroy, and others—indicates this continuing identification.[223] This wave of rediscovery of self in the black American community agrees essentially with King's view, expressed boldly in the last three years of his life, that we are both *African* and *American*.[224] These and other considerations serve to impress on one the seeming timelessness of certain of King's concerns with regard to Africa.

Black America's concern for Africa today cannot be separated from that expressed by King in the 1950s and 1960s. In both cases, the central message is the same, namely, that the liberation of African-Americans cannot occur apart from the liberation of Africa. Furthermore, this message suggests that an independent and strong Africa is vital to a peaceful and harmonious world.[225]

---

223. James Strong, "Black or African-American: What's the Difference?," *African Commentary* 1, no. 2 (November 1989): 6–7. The label "African-American" is pushed by many today who believe that black Americans—spiritually, aesthetically, and philosophically—are still closer to Africa than to Euro-America. See Patricia A. Ackerman, "'African-American': A New Opportunity for Teaching," *Education Week: N.A.B.S.E. Newsletter* (February 22, 1989): 1 ff.; and Clarence E. Glover, Jr., "On Being African American," *N.S.B.E. Journal* (February 1988): 35.

224. Martin Luther King, Jr., *Where Do We Go from Here: Chaos or Community?* (Boston: Beacon Press, 1967), 53.

225. Lewis V. Baldwin, "The Deferred Dream of Martin Luther King, Jr.: The Unfinished Agenda of the United States and South Africa," Parts I and II, *National Baptist Union Review* 91, nos. 9 and 12 (August and October 1987): 4–6.

CAUGHT IN AN INESCAPABLE NETWORK:

4

A VISION OF WORLD COMMUNITY

"My People, My People!" This very minute, nations of people are moaning it and shaking their heads with a sigh. Thousands and millions of people are uttering it in different parts of the globe. Differences of geography and language make differences in sound, that's all. The sentiment is the same.

Zora Neale Hurston, 1937[1]

I speak for my race and my people—the human race and just people.

Pauli Murray, 1943[2]

We are caught in an inescapable network of mutuality, tied in a single garment of destiny. Whatever affects one directly, affects all indirectly.

Martin Luther King, Jr., 1963[3]

When we build fences to keep others out, erect barriers to keep others down, deny to them the freedom that we ourselves enjoy and cherish most, we keep ourselves in and hold ourselves down; and the barriers we erect against others become prison bars to our own souls.

Benjamin E. Mays, 1983[4]

King's experiences of community and noncommunity in the segregated South had a profound influence on his vision of and quest for world community. As stated previously, his earliest understanding of and search for community began in Atlanta, Georgia, within the contexts of

1. Zora Neale Hurston, *Dust Tracks On a Road: An Autobiography*, ed. and with an Introduction by Robert Hemenway (Urbana and Chicago: The University of Illinois Press, 1984), 291.

2. Pauli Murray, *The Autobiography of a Black Activist, Feminist, Lawyer, Priest, and Poet* (Knoxville: The University of Tennessee Press, 1989), 437.

3. Martin Luther King, Jr., *Why We Can't Wait* (New York: The New American Library, 1964), 77.

4. Benjamin E. Mays, *Quotable Quotes of Benjamin E. Mays* (New York: Vantage Press, Inc., 1983), 13.

his family environment, the fellowship of the black church, and the larger black community. In time, King's vision of community and the sense of mission that accompanied that vision, matured to embrace the entire South, the nation, and the world.[5] This view is clearly suggested in William R. Miller's "The Broadening Horizons: Montgomery, America, the World," and also by William D. Watley's discussion of King's "maturing ethic" in *Roots of Resistance: The Nonviolent Ethic of Martin Luther King, Jr.*[6]

This chapter offers a probing analysis of the international implications of King's communitarian ideal, a subject largely ignored in most of the scholarship on King.[7] Major attention is given to King's articulation and pursuit of the ideal of world community, and to his meaning and significance for the continuing quest for world community. The discussion develops along these lines: (1) the search for world community; (2) the major barriers to world community; (3) King as an international symbol of community; and (4) King and the continuing quest for world community.

5. Walter E. Fluker, *They Looked for a City: A Comparative Analysis of the Ideal of Community in the Thought of Howard Thurman and Martin Luther King, Jr.* (Lanham, Md.: University Press of America, 1989), 82–86 and 99–102; James H. Cone, "Martin Luther King, Jr. and the Third World," *The Journal of American History* 74, no. 2 (September 1987): 455–56; and Coleman B. Brown, "Grounds for American Loyalty in a Prophetic Christian Social Ethic—with Special Attention to Martin Luther King, Jr." (Ph.D. diss., Union Theological Seminary in New York City, April, 1979), 48–55.

6. William Robert Miller, "The Broadening Horizons: Montgomery, America, the World," in *Martin Luther King, Jr.: A Profile*, ed. C. Eric Lincoln (New York: Hill and Wang, 1984), 40–71; and William D. Watley, *Roots of Resistance: The Nonviolent Ethic of Martin Luther King, Jr.* (Valley Forge, Pa.: Judson Press, 1985), 87–110.

7. For an important discussion of the need for King scholars to treat Dr. King in relation to global issues of justice and peace, see Lewis V. Baldwin, ed., *Toward the Beloved Community: Martin Luther King, Jr. and South African Apartheid* (manuscript in progress), Introduction and Concluding Essay.

THE SEARCH FOR WORLD COMMUNITY

It is difficult to determine the precise point at which King's vision transcended southern particularism to assume a special meaning and significance for the nation and the world. William D. Watley claims that such a shift in King's vision occurred after the Selma campaign of 1965, which led to the Voting Rights Act and the guaranteed right to vote for black southerners:

> After Selma, then, King expanded his vision to include more than those concerns that could be isolated and characterized as "Southern" or "black" problems. His ethic went beyond region and race and became national in its thrust and international in its scope. . . . Selma, then, was a turning point for Martin Luther King, Jr., and the civil rights movement.[8]

It is better to say that King's vision had national and international implications as early as the Montgomery Bus Boycott in 1956, and that that vision expanded and found its fullest maturity and expression between 1963 and the time of King's death in 1968. During the Montgomery Bus Boycott, King often referred to the South as the proving ground for the flowering of democracy throughout America, and he insisted that the struggle of black southerners was related to that of the oppressed worldwide. "The people of the Third world are now rising up," King declared in May, 1956, "and at many points I feel that this movement in Montgomery is a part of this overall movement in the world in which oppressed people are revolting against the imperialism and colonialism that have too long existed."[9] Here King's testimony seems to support C. Eric Lincoln's conclusion that the Montgomery Bus Boycott gave King a sense of a larger calling or a broader vision of his responsibility,

8. Watley, *Roots of Resistance*, 89.
9. Martin Luther King, Jr., "Statement Regarding the Legitimacy of the Struggle in Montgomery, Alabama" (The King Papers, Mugar Memorial Library, Boston University, Boston, Massachusetts, 4 May 1956), 1.

which in time matured and found focus in relationship to national and global concerns.[10]

King came to see the connection between the American South, the nation, and the world from another important angle. For him, the successes achieved by southern blacks during and after the Montgomery protest, through the employment of nonviolent direct action, resulted substantially from national censure and world pressure. Whenever the southern racists "reached for clubs, dogs, and guns" to destroy the confidence, courage, and defiance of blacks, King asserted in 1967, "they found the world was watching, and then the power of nonviolent protest became manifest. It dramatized the essential meaning of the conflict and in magnified strokes made clear who was the evildoer and who was the undeserving victim." King went on to explain that "The nation and the world were sickened" by the South's brutal treatment of its black citizens, and that partly because of this view from the outside, national legislation had been enacted to wipe out "a thousand Southern laws, ripping gaping holes in the edifice of segregation."[11] This significant interplay between South, nation, and world remained deeply etched in King's consciousness, shaping his understanding of the human struggle and reinforcing his sense of purpose and mission.

King's trips to Africa in 1957 and to India and the Middle East in 1959 contributed significantly to his international perspective. In Africa, his perspective on world problems was heightened through conversations with the leaders of Ghana and Nigeria. After completing trips to India, Israel, and Cairo, King wrote, in "My Trip to the

10. Lincoln, ed., *Martin Luther King, Jr.*, xiii.
11. Martin Luther King, Jr., *The Trumpet of Conscience* (San Francisco: Harper and Row, 1967), 5. The influence of the nation and the world as principal forces behind improved racial harmony in the South is underscored in David R. Goldfield, *Black, White, and Southern: Race Relations and Southern Culture, 1940 to the Present* (Baton Rouge: Louisiana State University Press, 1990), 118–278. At the same time, Goldfield contends that internal forces were as important in transforming the South as external forces and outside intervention.

Land of Gandhi": "We were looked upon as brothers with the color of our skins as something of an asset. But the strongest bond of fraternity was the common cause of minority and colonial peoples in America, Africa and Asia struggling to throw off racialism and imperialism." By 1963, after more trips abroad, King was advocating bonds and obligations between the oppressed everywhere in even stronger terms, asserting that "I must be concerned about Africa, Asia, South America, and Europe because we are all tied together."[12] This world perspective was expressed with telling insight in King's 1963 "Letter from the Birmingham City Jail."[13]

Walter E. Fluker contends that "the early development of the ideal of community in King reaches its zenith in the March on Washington" in August, 1963, and that "the following four and a half years proved to be a period in which his vision of community received its severest criticisms and challenges."[14] Here Fluker has in mind King's communitarian ideal as it related to the American context. Although his "I Have a Dream" speech at the March on Washington focused mostly on the ideal of national community, it also had significant implications for human liberation and reconciliation on a global scale.

King's view of his own role in the search for world community was enhanced when he received the Nobel Peace Prize in December, 1964. Frederick L. Downing insists that "the Nobel Prize left King with a commission to increase his efforts and to develop a world perspective."[15] James H. Cone concurs, noting that "for King, the

12. Martin Luther King, Jr., "My Trip to the Land of Gandhi," in *A Testament of Hope: The Essential Writings of Martin Luther King, Jr.*, ed. James M. Washington (San Francisco: Harper and Row, 1986), 24; and Martin Luther King, Jr., "What a Mother Should Tell Her Child," a sermon delivered at Ebenezer Baptist Church, Atlanta, Ga. (The Archives of the Martin Luther King, Jr. Center for Nonviolent Social Change, Inc., 12 May 1963), 4.

13. King, *Why We Can't Wait*, 77.

14. Fluker, *They Looked for a City*, 82.

15. See Frederick L. Downing, "A Review of David J. Garrow's *Bearing the Cross: Martin Luther King, Jr., and the Southern Christian Leadership Conference (1986)*," in *Theology Today* 44, no. 3 (October 1987): 391.

Nobel Prize was an 'unutterable fulfillment,' given in recognition of those fighting for freedom all over the world."[16] Coretta Scott King has written concerning her husband: "I remember saying to him so many times, especially after he received the Nobel Peace Prize, 'I think there is a role you must play in achieving world peace, and I will be so glad when the time comes when you can assume that role.'"[17] King himself accepted this challenge without hesitation, declaring in 1965, a few months after receiving the Nobel Prize, "Though I will continue to give primary attention to the problems of the South, I realize that I must more and more extend my work beyond the boundaries of the South."[18] Subsequently, King increasingly advocated extending the movement beyond a quest for basic constitutional rights for southern blacks to embrace: (1) the ideal of a truly democratic nation for all Americans; and (2) the ideal of a world devoid of racism, economic exploitation, and wars of aggression. In March, 1965, King expressed satisfaction with the fact that:

> All over the world, like a fever, the freedom movement is spreading in the widest liberation struggle in history. The great masses of people everywhere are determined to end the exploitation of their races and lands. And consciously or unconsciously, the Negro of America has been caught up in the *Zeitgeist*, and with his black brothers of Africa and his brown and yellow brothers of Asia, South America and the Caribbean, he, too, is on the move.[19]

16. Cone, "Martin Luther King, Jr. and the Third World," 460.
17. Coretta Scott King, *My Life with Martin Luther King, Jr.* (New York: Avon Books, 1969), 294.
18. Martin Luther King, Jr., "Dreams of Brighter Tomorrows," *Ebony* 20 (March 1965), 34–35.
19. Herbert W. Richardson, "Martin Luther King—Unsung Theologian," in *New Theology*, no. 6, eds. Martin E. Marty and Dean G. Peerman (New York: The Macmillan Company, 1969), 181; King, "Dreams of Brighter Tomorrows," 34–35; and Martin Luther King, Jr., *Where Do We Go from Here: Chaos or Community?* (Boston: Beacon Press, 1967), 169.

King's internationalism, especially his sense of global responsibility, was reinforced as he continued to travel to various parts of the world in the late 1960s.

King used the metaphor of the "great world house" to explain his world perspective in intellectual and theoretical terms. This metaphor captured for him the ideal of a totally integrated world based on love, justice, and equality of opportunity—a world in which loyalties to race, class, sex, tribe, religion, philosophical orientations, political differences, ethnicity, and nationality would be transcended in the interest of total human community. In 1967 King wrote:

> We have inherited a large house, a great "world house" in which we have to live together—black and white, Easterner and Westerner, Gentile and Jew, Catholic and Protestant, Moslem and Hindu—a family unduly separated in ideas, culture and interest, who, because we can never again live apart, must learn somehow to live with each other in peace.[20]

King went on to declare that a truly democratic America for blacks and whites would be possible only within the confines of a truly democratic and peaceful world, a view that further substantiated the significant interplay between South, nation, and world in his thinking:

> However deeply American Negroes are caught in the struggle to be at last at home in our homeland of the United States, we cannot ignore the larger world house in which we are also dwellers. Equality with whites will not solve the problems of either whites or Negroes if it means equality in a world society stricken by poverty and in a universe doomed to extinction by war.[21]

This and other statements concerning the "world house" corroborates Benjamin E. Mays' assertion that King

---

20. King, *Where Do We Go from Here?*, 167.
21. *Ibid.*

"was suprarace, supranation, supradenomination, supra-
class, and supraculture."[22]

This sense of a "world house" or "world-wide neighborhood"—a situation in which "all inhabitants of the
globe are now neighbors"—was rooted in a communitarian or solidaristic conception of society and the world,
which holds that each person is a distinct ontological
entity that finds growth, fulfillment, and purpose
through personal and social relationships based on the
agape love ethic.[23] In other words, King held that humans
are not *individuals* who are completely self-sufficient but
social beings who find authentic existence through social
contact and social relations under the guidance of a personal God who works for universal wholeness. Regarding
the interrelatedness and interdependence of human beings, King remarked:

> We are made to live together because of the interre-
> lated structure of reality. Did you ever stop to think
> that you can't leave for your job in the morning with-
> out being dependent on most of the world? You get up
> in the morning and go to the bathroom and reach over
> for the sponge, and that's handed to you by a Pacific
> Islander. You reach for a bar of soap, and that's given
> to you at the hands of a Frenchman. And then you go
> into the kitchen to drink your coffee for the morning,
> and that's poured into your cup by a South American.
> And maybe you want tea; that's poured into your cup
> by a Chinese. Or maybe you're desirous of having co-
> coa for breakfast, and that's poured into your cup by a
> West African. And then you reach over for your toast,
> and that's given to you at the hands of an English-
> speaking farmer, not to mention the baker. And before
> you finish eating breakfast in the morning, you've de-
> pended on more than half of the world. This is the way
> our universe is structured, this is its interrelated qual-
> ity. We aren't going to have peace on earth until we

22. Quoted in King, *My Life with Martin Luther King, Jr.*, 348.
23. *Ibid.;* and Fluker, *They Looked for a City*, 120–21.

recognize this basic fact of the interrelated structure of all reality.[24]

King also believed that "this world-wide neighborhood has been brought into being largely as a result of the modern scientific and technological revolutions."[25] He pointed specifically to the invention of the radio, the television, motion pictures, the telephone, airplanes, and other amazing developments that increased significantly the means and levels of communication between humans worldwide, thus making the world much smaller than it was in the eighteenth and nineteenth centuries. King went on to predict that:

> The years ahead will see a continuation of the same dramatic developments. Physical science will carve new highways through the stratosphere. In a few years astronauts and cosmonauts will probably walk comfortably across the uncertain pathways of the moon. In two or three years it will be possible, because of the new supersonic jets, to fly from New York to London in two and one-half hours. In the years ahead medical science will greatly prolong the lives of men by finding a cure for cancer and deadly heart ailments. Automation and cybernation will make it possible for working people to have undreamed-of amounts of leisure time. All this is a dazzling picture of the furniture, the workshop, the spacious rooms, the new decorations and the architectural pattern of the large world house in which we are living.[26]

This view of the world led King to insist that "the first thing that parents should instill within their children is the world perspective." Convinced that many parents, especially in the white American community, were giving their children an isolated perspective that rendered

---

24. Martin Luther King, Jr., *The Trumpet of Conscience*, 69–70; and King, *Where Do We Go from Here?* 181.
25. King, *Where Do We Go from Here?* 167–69.
26. *Ibid.*

them incapable of relating properly and effectively with persons unlike themselves, King commented:

> Every parent should seek to get over to their children that the world in which we live is one world; it is certainly geographically one, and now we are challenged to make it spiritually one. So urge your child to rise above the narrow confines of his or her individualistic concerns to the broader concerns of all humanity. Teach your child early that other people live in the world, and he who lives alone has already defeated himself before he gets started. Always we must add other concerns to self-concern. . . . And so get over to your child that he or she is involved in humanity, and for some strange reason I can never be what I ought to be until you are what you ought to be, and you can never be what you ought to be until I am what I ought to be. . . . I must be concerned about what happens to men and women in Asia. I must be concerned about what happens to men and women in Africa. I must be concerned about what happens to men and women in South America or Europe or anywhere else in the world because we are all involved. That is what John Donne meant when he said: "No man is an island entire to himself. Every man is a piece of the continent, a part of the main." And then he goes on towards the end to say: "Any man's death diminishes me, because I am involved in mankind; therefore it must be known for whom the bell tolls. It tolls for thee."[27]

King's world perspective included the concepts of *civil egalitarianism, economic egalitarianism, international egalitarianism,* and *spiritual egalitarianism. Civil egalitarianism* refers to the civil rights movement in America, which, in King's view, could not be separated from the call and quest for human rights on a global scale. *Economic egalitarianism* characterized King's struggle for economic improvement for the poor, a struggle that led him to accept democratic socialism. In other

27. King, "What a Mother Should Tell Her Child," 4–5.

words, this concept of economic egalitarianism under-girded King's efforts on behalf of the Memphis sanita-tion workers, the Poor People's Campaign, and the world war against poverty. *International egalitarianism* de-scribes King's role as an advocate of world peace, and as one who inspired the peace movement in the late 1960s. King's *spiritual egalitarianism* affirmed all humans as creatures made in the divine image (Imago Dei), and also Christ's love for all.[28]

King's ideal of world community was essentially *Christian* in that it upheld: (1) the impartiality of God in creating and dealing with human beings; (2) a sacra-mentalistic conception of the cosmos as echoed by the Psalmist, "the earth is the Lord's, and the fullness thereof; the world, and they that dwell therein"; (3) a belief in the dignity and worth of all human personality; and (4) the idea of the social nature of human life and existence.[29] King discovered theological support for those concepts in the black Christian tradition and in Personalism and Social Gospelism.

In more specific terms, King's goal of community was Christocentric but not Christomonistic, because the "world house" metaphor embraced Jews, Buddhists, and other non-Christian groups as well. King was con-cerned essentially about the universal importance and implications of Christ's person and message for the lib-eration of the whole human community. Here, he reached for a wholeness in which neither the oppressor nor the oppressed could be redeemed without each other. In short, King's life, thought, and work were a testimony to the fact that all thought of liberation and activism are irrelevant and futile if they fail to go

28. Baldwin, ed., *Toward the Beloved Community*, 1–20; and Fluker, *They Looked for a City*, 120–28. Kenneth L. Smith persuasively argues that in time, democratic socialism became synonymous with King's vi-sion of the beloved community or the Kingdom of God on earth. See Kenneth L. Smith, "The Radicalization of Martin Luther King, Jr.: The Last Three Years," *Journal of Ecumenical Studies* 26, no. 2 (Spring, 1989): 270–88.
    29. Baldwin, ed., *Toward the Beloved Community*, 1–20.

beyond a narrow, sectarian model of the oppressor and the oppressed.[30]

Although King found the language and concepts to articulate his vision of world community in Western philosophical sources, Personalism, and the Social Gospel, his actual search for world community was inspired and influenced mostly by his contact with black life and culture. Here again the connection between the American South, the nation, and the world in his consciousness became evident. He lived and struggled among people who had long expressed the realization, especially in their religion, that their being, welfare, and value as individuals were linked to that of all humans. "The Negro's religion revealed to him," said King, "that God loves all of his children, and that every man, from a bass black to a treble white, is significant on God's keyboard."[31] Within this principle alone King discovered sensibilities and values that, if understood, could significantly enlarge humanity's capacity for creative, universal human fellowship grounded in love and justice. This view correlated with King's conviction, held since the Montgomery Bus Boycott in 1955, that the black American "may be the vanguard in a prolonged struggle that may change the shape of the world, as billions of deprived shake and transform the earth in their quest for life, freedom, and justice."[32]

King also found this vision of world community brilliantly formed throughout the writings and speeches of Benjamin E. Mays and Howard Thurman—black intellectual giants who had long been supporters of liberation causes around the world. Mays' association with the

30. Fluker, *They Looked for a City*, 120–28.
31. Martin Luther King, Jr., "An Address at the 47th Annual NAACP Convention," San Francisco, California (The King Papers, Boston University, 27 June 1956), 2–3; and Martin Luther King, Jr., "Address at the First Annual Institute on Nonviolence and Social Change under the Auspices of the Montgomery Improvement Association," Holt Street Baptist Church, Montgomery, Ala. (The King Center Archives, 3 December 1956), 7.
32. King, *The Trumpet of Conscience*, 17.

American chapter of the Fellowship of Reconciliation and Thurman's bold efforts in establishing the Church for the Fellowship of All Peoples in San Francisco in 1944 were but a measure of the commitment they shared to world community. It is not surprising, therefore, that King, considering his deep sense of identification with and obligation to the oppressed people of the world, constantly turned to the wise counsel and works of these men for guidance and inspiration. King's vision of world community was parallel to, and largely derived from, the vision of Mays and Thurman.[33]

Displeased with the chasm that existed between the ideal and the reality of human community, King wanted to unify and to meld those realms. His vision of world community and his willingness to pursue that vision with every fiber of his being made conflict between him and the oppressors of the world inevitable. To this day, King remains a tremendous challenge for the Pharaohs of the world, not only because he articulated the beloved community ideal with disturbing clarity, but also because of his passionate commitment to translating that ideal into practical reality.

THE MAJOR BARRIERS TO WORLD COMMUNITY

In 1967, Martin Luther King, Jr., referred to racism, poverty, and war as the greatest impediments to the actualization of world community. He variously described

33. Important works that affirm Mays' and Thurman's communal ethic as it related to global concerns are Mays, *Quotable Quotes*, 12 ff.; Benjamin E. Mays, *Born to Rebel: An Autobiography* (New York: Charles Scribner's Sons, 1971), chapters 11 and 18; Howard Thurman, *Footprints of a Dream: The Story of the Church for the Fellowship of All Peoples* (New York: Harper and Row, 1959), 1ff.; Howard Thurman, *The Search for Common Ground: An Inquiry into the Basis of Man's Experience of Community* (Richmond, Ind.: Friends United Press, 1986), 1–104; Howard Thurman, "Desegregation, Integration, and the Beloved Community" (Unpublished essay, The Thurman Papers, Mugar Memorial Library, Boston University, n.d.), 1–19; and Fluker, *They Looked for a City*, 81–190.

these fundamental problems as "the three major evils," "the giant triplets," and "the evil triumvirate."[34] At the same time, King refused to view racism, poverty, and war as three different problems. Instead, they were, for him, manifestations of the same evil system that tormented the poor and oppressed worldwide—that system that had to be dismantled before world peace and community could be realized:

> These problems are tied together in a very real way and in a sense inextricably bound together. I cannot conceive of the possibility of peace on an international scale as long as we don't have justice in every nation. Racial injustice is a constant threat to the peace and to the harmony of the world, and I would say in that sense that it is just as great a threat to the human race as the atomic bomb, so to speak, because you can't have any real harmony in the world until these problems are solved which exist in the nations of the world. When men learn how to live together as brothers, then we will not have to worry about a day emerging when atomic bombs will be dropped and nuclear weapons will be used to destroy nations of men. I think the peace of the world is dependent on the justice that is established in the world, and I think that the justice that we establish in the world will determine also the kind of peace that we are going to have.[35]

The considerable attention King gave to the global impact of racial injustice toward the end of his life should not have been surprising, especially considering

34. King, *Where Do We Go from Here?* 173–86; King, "What a Mother Should Tell Her Child," 6; Fluker, *They Looked for a City*, 99–100; Lewis V. Baldwin, "King's 'Triple Evils' Start with Racism," *The Sunday Tennessean*, Nashville, Tennessee (February 1, 1987): 1H and 3H; Lewis V. Baldwin, "King's War Against Poverty Continues," *The Sunday Tennessean* (February 8, 1987): 1H and 3H; Lewis V. Baldwin, "Martin Luther King: A 'Drum Major' for Peace," *The Sunday Tennessean* (February 15, 1987): 1H and 2H; and Lewis V. Baldwin, "Woes of the 'World House' were Dr. King's Concerns," *The Tennessean* (January 18, 1989): 7A.

35. "A Transcript of a Radio Interview with Martin Luther King, Jr.," Oslo, Norway (The King Center Archives, 9 December 1964), 4.

his background and experiences as a black southerner. He had come to see clearly that racism was not merely a southern problem or a national problem but a problem for humanity as a whole. "Racism is no mere American phenomenon," he wrote. "Its vicious grasp knows no geographical boundaries. In fact, racism and its perennial ally—economic exploitation—provide the key to understanding most of the international complications of this generation."[36] King placed the responsibility for the problem squarely on the shoulders of white people:

> I think we have to honestly admit that the problems in the world today, as they relate to the question of race, must be blamed on the whole doctrine of white supremacy, the whole doctrine of racism, and these doctrines came into being through the white race and the exploitation of the colored peoples of the world.[37]

Noting that "In country after country we see white men building empires on the sweat and suffering of colored people," King pointed specifically to racist practices that were employed against Africans in various parts of the world:

> Portugal continues its practices of slave labor and subjugation in Angola; the Ian Smith government in Rhodesia continues to enjoy the support of British-based industry and private capital, despite the stated opposition of British Government policy. Even in the case of the little country of South West Africa we find the powerful nations of the world incapable of taking a moral position against South Africa, though the smaller country is under the trusteeship of the United Nations. Its policies are controlled by South Africa and its manpower is lured into the mines under slave-labor conditions.[38]

36. King, *Where Do We Go from Here?* 173.
37. "Doubts and Certainties: A Transcript of an Interview with Martin Luther King, Jr.," London, England (The King Center Archives, Winter, 1968), 1.
38. King, *Where Do We Go from Here?* 173–74.

King explained that in many parts of Africa, Asia, and Latin America, racism assumed a "more sophisticated form" called *neocolonialism*. He declared that the racism of the United States and other Western nations had created much anger and resentment among peoples of color, and he held that when Africans, Asians, and Latin Americans

> look around and see that the only people who do not share in the abundance of Western technology are colored people, it is an almost inescapable conclusion that their condition and their exploitation are somehow related to their color and the racism of the white Western world.[39]

For King, the United States and South Africa represented classic examples of organized and institutionalized racism. He saw the two countries as willing partners in the preservation of racist structures and institutions. He attacked both American and South African government officials for remaining insensitive to and notoriously silent about the racist exploitation within their own nations, and he insisted that nothing provided the Communists "with a better climate for expansion and infiltration than the continued alliance" of the United States with South Africa and "with racism and exploitation throughout the world."[40]

In King's opinion, the prevalence of racism as a world phenomenon in the 1960s proved the validity and profundity of W. E. B. Du Bois' prophetic utterance, offered in 1903, that "the problem of the twentieth century will be the problem of the color line." Reflecting further on the timelessness of Du Bois' remark, King commented: "Now as we stand two-thirds into this exciting period of history we know full well that racism is still that hound of hell which dogs the tracks of our civilization."[41]

39. *Ibid.*, 174–76.
40. *Ibid.*, 173–74.
41. *Ibid.*, 173.

King's diagnosis went beyond merely describing the global effects and implications of racism to exploring ways of eliminating that problem. He called on all people of goodwill to recognize that the struggle against racial injustice "is among the moral imperatives of our time," and "to work all over the world with unshakeable determination to wipe out the last vestiges of racism."[42] King saw the black movement in the United States as "a part of a world-wide thrust into the future" to abolish racism: "to replace institutionalized handicaps with free opportunity."[43] Beyond this, he pointed to the need for powerful interracial coalitions or alliances to challenge racism. "There must be a grand alliance of Negro and white," he said on one occasion. "This alliance must consist of the vast majorities of each group. It must have the objective of eradicating social evils which oppress both white and Negro." King continued:

> The powerful unity of Negro with Negro and white with Negro is stronger than the most potent and entrenched racism. The whole human race will benefit when it ends the abomination that has diminished the stature of man for too long. This is the task to which we are called . . . , and our response should be swift and unstinting. Out of this struggle will come the glorious reality of the family of man.[44]

King concluded that racial injustice would never end as long as whites throughout the world minimized or ignored the problem. Their failure to act in positive ways to abolish white world domination and notions of white supremacy could, in King's view, lead ultimately to a global race war:

> I think ultimately this is going to depend to a large extent on the white peoples of the world. The fact

42. *Ibid.*
43. Martin Luther King, Jr., "After Desegregation—What?," a speech (The King Papers, Boston University, n.d.), 2.
44. Martin Luther King, Jr., "South Africa Benefit Speech," Hunter College, New York, N.Y. (The King Center Archives, 10 December 1965), 5–7.

is that the colored races have been terribly exploited, and trampled over with the iron feet of oppression, and this exploitation is not going to exist
any longer. The cup of endurance has run over, and
there is a deep determination on the part of people
of color to be freed from all of the shackles that
they faced in the past. Now if the white world does
not recognize this and does not adjust to what has to
be, then we can end up in the world with a kind of
race war. So it depends on the spirit and the read-
justing qualities of the white peoples of the world,
and this will avoid the kind of violent confrontation
between the races if it is done properly by the white
peoples.[45]

Overcoming racism as a world problem, King thought,
involved removing both internal prejudices as well as
external systems and symbols of white domination and
privilege. He maintained that it

is very important for every white person to search his
own soul and seek to remove all of the vestiges of
racism and white supremacy. But along with this must
be concrete justice, that the white person and the
white power structure will go out to establish. It's not
enough, as you say, to invite a Negro to dinner, but it
means establishing within this society [and world] all
the patterns of justice necessary to make colored people free. As long as there is discrimination on any level
the Negro is not free. Colored people generally in
other countries are not free, so there must be concrete justice.[46]

For King, the very survival of Western civilization was
in jeopardy as long as racism remained. Noting that

---

45. "Doubts and Certainties," 1–2.
46. *Ibid.* Aside from discussing racism, poverty, and war as "external
barriers," Fluker also treats ignorance, fear, and hate as "internal barriers" to world community. According to Fluker, both the "external barriers" and the "internal barriers" fall under King's general idea of sin and
evil. See Fluker, *They Looked for a City*, 129–52.

racism "is a treacherous foundation for a world house," King, in a moment of stern prophecy, remarked:

> Racism can well be that corrosive evil that will bring down the curtain on Western civilization. Arnold Toynbee has said that some twenty-six civilizations have risen upon the face of the earth. Almost all of them have descended into the junk heaps of destruction. The decline and fall of these civilizations, according to Toynbee, was not caused by external invasions but by internal decay. They failed to respond creatively to the challenges impinging upon them. If Western civilization does not now respond constructively to the challenge to banish racism, some future historian will have to say that a great civilization died because it lacked the soul and commitment to make justice a reality for all men.[47]

One of King's most critical commentaries on world problems centered on poverty and economic injustice. He suggested, "Another grave problem that must be solved if we are to live creatively in our world house is that of poverty on an international scale."[48] In his analysis of the problem, King began with his own country, where high levels of poverty and economic exploitation existed despite vast wealth and resources. The fact that in America "we have an underclass—an underclass that is not a working class"—disturbed him greatly. Equally disturbing to him was the fact that millions of blacks and other poor Americans were working on full-time jobs with part-time income, a situation that required them to work on two and three jobs to make ends meet.[49] In King's view, such a situation was inexcusable in light of the millions spent by the American government on weapons that could only bring mass destruction. "A

---

47. King, *Where Do We Go from Here?* 176.
48. *Ibid.*, 176–77.
49. Martin Luther King, Jr., "Why We Must Go to Washington," a speech delivered at the S.C.L.C. Retreat, Ebenezer Baptist Church, Atlanta, Ga. (The King Center Archives, 15 January 1968), 6–7.

nation that continues year after year to spend more on
military defense than on programs of social uplift is approaching spiritual death," he warned. King further
noted that it was "folly to talk about nonviolence" without creating the climate of economic justice "which allows nonviolence to operate." "This means that we must
go all out to impress upon the mayors of cities, the gover-
nors of states, as well as the federal government," he
said, "to get rid of the conditions of poverty, social isolation , and the conditions of despair that cause some people to turn to violence."[50]

When King looked beyond the shores of the United
States, he saw poverty and economic injustice in their
most glaring forms. He wrote in 1967:

> Two-thirds of the peoples of the world go to bed hun-
> gry at night. They are undernourished, ill-housed and
> shabbily clad. Many of them have no houses or beds to
> sleep in. Their only beds are the sidewalks of the cities
> and the dusty roads of the villages. Most of these
> poverty-stricken children of God have never seen a
> physician or a dentist.[51]

King observed that the problems of hunger, malnutri-
tion, disease, and death were most abundantly evident
in the so-called Third World—in Africa, Asia, the
Caribbean, and Latin America.[52] Such problems were,
in his understanding, a part of a natural process of moving from oppression and dependency to liberation and
autonomy:

> Every new nation confronts overwhelming prob-
> lems. During the days when they were struggling to
> remove the yoke of colonialism, there was a kind of

50. Martin Luther King, Jr., "A Statement Regarding Riots
in Rochester and New York City" (The King Center Archives, 27
July 1964), 2; and Martin Luther King, Jr., "On Pre-Election Day Moratorium: Youngsters and Jobs," a speech delivered in New York (The King
Center Archives, 6 November 1964), 1; and King, *Where Do We Go from
Here?* 188.
51. King, *Where Do We Go from Here?* 177.
52. *Ibid.*, 177–81; King, *The Trumpet of Conscience*, 69; and Cone,
"Martin Luther King, Jr. and the Third World," 455–67.

pre-existent unity of purpose that kept things moving in one solid direction. But as soon as independence emerges, all the grim problems of life confront them with stark realism: the lack of capital, the strangulating poverty, the uncontrollable birth rates and, above all, the high aspirational level of their own people. The postcolonial period is more difficult and precarious than the colonial struggle itself.[53]

King continued:

The West must also understand that its economic growth took place under rather propitious circumstances. Most of the Western nations were relatively underpopulated when they surged forward economically, and they were greatly endowed with the iron ore and coal that were needed for launching industry. Most of the young governments of the world today have come into being without these advantages, and, above all, they confront staggering problems of overpopulation. There is no possible way for them to make it without aid and assistance.[54]

King contended that those concerned about economic injustice and inequity in the United States and abroad had to be prepared to examine critically their own lifestyles and values, and to raise the question: "Why should there be hunger and privation in any land, in any city, at any table, when man has the resources and the scientific know-how to provide all mankind with the basic necessities of life?"[55] The essential problem for King was rooted in the greed and indifference of those who were more concerned about personal power and profit than about devoting their resources to the general uplift of humankind as a whole:

Even deserts can be irrigated and topsoil can be replaced. We cannot complain of a lack of land, for there are 25 million square miles of tillable land on earth,

53. King, *Where Do We Go from Here?* 179.
54. *Ibid.*
55. *Ibid.*, 177.

of which we are using less than seven million. We have amazing knowledge of vitamins, nutrition, the chemistry of food and the versatility of atoms. There is no deficit in human resources; the deficit is in human will.[56]

Although King did not claim expertise in the areas of economic policy and development, he did elaborate the means by which economic injustice and poverty could be eliminated. One approach for him involved organizing coalitions of the poor to dramatize economic injustice and poverty. This idea found practical application in his efforts on behalf of the Poor People's Campaign and the Memphis sanitation workers from 1967 to 1968. Bringing poor blacks, Appalachian whites, Puerto Ricans, Mexican-Americans, Hispanic-Americans, Native Americans, and other racial and ethnic communities together to challenge economic injustice and inequity was consistent with King's belief in the power of economic self-help.[57] He wished for an extension of this kind of coalition-building on a global scale.

King believed that much of the moral responsibility for "the world-wide war against poverty" rested with the wealthy, so-called developed nations, many of which had solidified their wealth and power by exploiting Third World countries. Convinced that there had to be a sharing and a "stabilization of economic resources" before genuine world peace and community could exist, King suggested that "the rich nations must use their vast resources of wealth to develop the underdeveloped,

56. *Ibid.*
57. "America's Racial Crisis: Dr. King's Plan to End Poverty," *Current* (May 1968): 6–18; and Frank L. Morris, "A Dream Fulfilled: The Economic and Political Policies of Martin Luther King, Jr.," a paper presented at the Annual Celebration Commemorating the Birth of Martin Luther King, Jr., Garrett-Evangelical Theological Seminary, Evanston, Ill. (13 January 1977), 1–20.

to school the unschooled and to feed the unfed."[58] In more precise terms, he stated:

> All the wealthy nations—America, Britain, Russia, Canada, Australia, and those of Western Europe— must see it as a moral obligation to provide capital and technical assistance to the underdeveloped areas. These rich nations have only scratched the surface in their commitment. There is need now for a general strategy of support. There must be a sustained effort extending through many years. The wealthy nations of the world must promptly initiate a massive, sustained Marshall Plan for Asia, Africa, and South America. If they would allocate just 2 percent of their gross national product annually for a period of ten to twenty years for the development of the underdeveloped nations, mankind would go a long way toward conquering the ancient enemy, poverty.[59]

At the same time, King cautioned that it would be immoral and unethical for rich nations to use economic aid as a means to control and dominate Africa, Asia, the Middle East, and Latin America. He insisted that foreign aid be motivated not by political considerations or expediency but by a spirit of goodwill and compassion:

> The aid program that I am suggesting must not be used by the wealthy nations as a surreptitious means to control the poor nations. Such an approach would lead to a new form of paternalism and neo-colonialism which no self-respecting nation could accept. Ultimately, foreign aid programs must be motivated by a compassionate and committed effort to wipe out poverty, ignorance and disease from the face of the earth. Money devoid of genuine empathy is like salt devoid of savor, good for nothing except to be trodden under foot of men.[60]

58. King, *Where Do We Go from Here?* 178.
59. *Ibid.*
60. *Ibid.*, 178–79.

According to King, addressing global poverty involved not only meeting the material needs of people but also affirming that which was rational, spiritual, and moral. Thus, he said:

> But the real reason that we must use our resources to outlaw poverty goes beyond material concerns to the quality of our mind and spirit. Deeply woven into the fiber of our religious tradition is the conviction that men are made in the image of God, and that they are souls of infinite metaphysical value. If we accept this as a profound moral fact, we cannot be content to see men hungry, to see men victimized with ill-health, when we have the means to help them.[61]

Indeed, he pushed his analysis further, arguing that efforts to uplift the poor and weak amounted to an affirmation of higher communal values—to a rejection of the principle that "self-preservation is the first law of life" to an unqualified acceptance of the view that "other-preservation is the first law of life." "In the final analysis," he declared, "the rich must not ignore the poor because both rich and poor are tied together. They entered the same mysterious gateway of human birth, into the same adventure of mortal life." King continued: "The agony of the poor impoverishes the rich; the betterment of the poor enriches the rich. We are inevitably our brother's keeper because we are our brother's brother."[62] At this point, the profundity of King's ethical perspective became unmistakably clear. His essential belief was that the future prosperity of the world community as a whole depended on the degree to which prosperity was made available to the "have-nots":

> A genuine program on the part of the wealthy nations to make prosperity a reality for the poor nations will in the final analysis enlarge the prosperity of all. One of the best proofs that reality hinges on moral foundations is the fact that when men and governments work

61. *Ibid.*, 180.
62. *Ibid.*, 180–81.

devotedly for the good of others, they achieve their own enrichment in the process.[63]

The prospect of global warfare was as frightening to King as the reality of global poverty. This was to be expected from one who understood the potential destructive power of nuclear weapons, and who was predisposed to nonviolence as a result of his upbringing, formal training, and experiences as a civil rights leader. King said in 1967 that "a final problem that mankind must solve in order to survive in the world house that we have inherited is finding an alternative to war and human destruction." He further explained:

> Recent events have vividly reminded us that nations are not reducing but rather increasing their arsenals of weapons of mass destruction. The best brains in the highly developed nations of the world are devoted to military technology. The proliferation of nuclear weapons has not been halted, in spite of the limited-test-ban treaty.[64]

King took an ethical position on war long before he emerged as a national and international figure. Prior to the Montgomery Bus Boycott, he actually concluded that there could be some redemptive qualities in war, especially when it is employed to halt the encroachment of evil nations and their leaders on other nations:

> Now, on the question of whether war is justifiable, I have gone through a kind of intellectual pilgrimage on the whole question of war and the pacifist position. There was a time when I felt that war could serve a negative good—by that I mean I went through the feeling that war could at least serve as a force to block the surge of an evil force in history like Hitler, a misguided individual who is leading a nation and who can cause the destruction of many individuals. I never felt that war could be a positive good, but I did

63. *Ibid.*
64. *Ibid.*

think it could prevent the flowering of a negative force in history.[65]

This perspective on war as "a negative good" changed as King's nonviolent ethic evolved and matured from a strategy to a philosophy and way of life. By the late 1950s, after the successful outcome of the Montgomery protest, King was calling for the total eradication of war in his speeches and writings. This helps explain why he was so displeased with the charge, made in 1959 by the black militant Robert F. Williams of Monroe, North Carolina, that he was inconsistent and evasive on the whole question of war. King's response to Williams' charge, offered one year after he had called for the cessation of nuclear tests, was swift and candid:

> I am reluctant to inject a personal defense against charges by Mr. Williams that I am inconsistent in my struggle against war and too weak-kneed to protest nuclear war. Merely to set the record straight, may I state that repeatedly, in public addresses and in my writings, I have unequivocally declared my hatred for this most colossal of all evils, and I have condemned any organizer of war, regardless of his rank or nationality. I have signed numerous statements with other Americans condemning nuclear testing and have authorized publication of my name in advertisements appearing in the largest circulation newspapers in the country, without concern that it was then "unpopular" to so speak out.[66]

Throughout the 1960s, King maintained that "wisdom born of experience should tell us that war is obsolete"— that "the destructive power of modern weapons eliminates even the possibility that war may serve any good at all."[67] The Cuban missile crisis, which brought the United

65. Martin Luther King, Jr., "Interview on World Peace," *Red Book Magazine* (November 1964), 3–7.

66. Martin Luther King, Jr., "The Social Organization of Nonviolence," *Liberation Magazine* (October 1959), 5–6; and Watley, *Roots of Resistance*, 101.

67. King, *Where Do We Go from Here?* 183.

States and the Soviet Union to the brink of nuclear war in October, 1962, reinforced King's conviction. Although he was pleased with President John Kennedy's decision to blockade Cuba to prevent the delivery of jet aircraft and military supplies by the Soviets, a move that brought the crisis to a successful end, King believed nevertheless that the confrontation between the super powers proved the need for a greater affirmation of world peace. "Everyone of us knows full well that we came dreadfully close to the precipice of nuclear war in 1962," he recalled later. "There is grave danger, however, that our 'success' in handling the Cuban crisis could be misused. We must not allow the delicate balance that has been established in matters of foreign policy to be destroyed by our arrogance."[68] King reiterated this point in 1964, suggesting that

> if man assumes that he has a right to survive, then he must find some substitute for war; and the sooner we come to see that war is obsolete and must be cast into unending limbo, the sooner we will develop the kind of world where we can survive and live together as brothers.[69]

In time, King wrote about the dangers of even "limited war." To his dissatisfaction, the principle of "limited war," viewed by some as a more modern version of the traditional *just war* theory, found considerable support from ethicists and government officials in the 1960s. Convinced that any "limited war" could escalate to the point of global conflict, King declared in 1967:

> A so-called limited war will leave little more than a calamitous legacy of human suffering, political turmoil and spiritual disillusionment. A world war will leave only smoldering ashes as mute testimony of a

68. Martin Luther King, Jr., "New Year Hopes," *New York Amsterdam News* (January 5, 1963): 1 ff.
69. King, "Interview on World Peace," 3–7. A similar comment can be found in King, *Where Do We Go from Here?* 183–84.

human race whose folly led inexorably to ultimate death. If modern man continues to flirt unhesitatingly with war, he will transform his earthly habitat into an inferno such as even the mind of Dante could not imagine.[70]

King's expanding ethic and enlarged global perspective were prominently revealed in his strong opposition to the United States' involvement in the Vietnam war. Contrary to commonly held views, his position on this issue did not represent a shift in his thinking and activism. King was consistent in that he was simply advocating that nonviolence be lifted from the domestic context and applied to America's foreign policy. He was convinced that "our role in the Vietnam war demanded closer scrutiny and stronger resistance" on the part of those who wished to bring America more in line with her democratic and Judeo-Christian values.[71]

King began to publicly express his views on Vietnam in 1965, soon after receiving the Nobel Peace Prize. In 1967, he gave three major speeches on the subject. In "A Time to Break Silence," delivered at a meeting of Clergy and Laity Concerned at the Riverside Church in New York City on April 4, 1967, he moved beyond a mere denunciation of the Vietnam war to a direct attack on the Johnson administration's military policy as a whole. On April 11, 1967, a week later, King gave a similar speech at the Ebenezer Baptist Church in Atlanta. In November and December, 1967, as a part of the Massey Lectures, sponsored by the Canadian Broadcasting Corporation, he spoke on "Conscience and the Vietnam War."[72]

70. King, *Where Do We Go from Here?* 184.

71. King, *A Trumpet of Conscience,* xi.

72. See "Transcript of an Interview with Martin Luther King, Jr. by Local Newscasters," KNXT-TV, Los Angeles, California (The King Center Archives, 10 July 1965), 2; "Transcript of an Interview with Martin Luther King, Jr.," on "Face the Nation," a Broadcast of the CBS Television Network (The King Center Archives, 29 August 1965), 3. "A Time to Break Silence" can be found in Washington, ed., *A Testament of Hope,* 231–44. Excerpts of the speech given at Ebenezer are included in the only major film about King produced by black people, called "Dr. Martin Luther

In these and other statements on Vietnam, King claimed that he was speaking "as an American to the leaders of my own nation," "as a child of God and brother to the suffering poor of Vietnam," and "as a citizen of the world."[73] Several concerns accounted for King's decision to bring the Vietnam war into the sphere of his moral vision. One had to do with the tremendous loss of life suffered by both the Vietnamese and the American soldiers. Concerning the violence visited daily on the Vietnamese, he noted in 1967: "They wander into the hospitals, with at least twenty casualties from American firepower for one 'Viet–Cong'-inflicted injury. So far we have killed a million of them—mostly children."[74] Furthermore, he complained about the thousands of young men who returned to America "from dark and bloody battlefields physically handicapped and psychologically deranged."[75] Such a wanton disregard for human life and welfare was unacceptable to King, especially given his strong belief in nonviolence and in the dignity and worth of *all* human personality.[76]

King also opposed the war because he believed that it was morally inconsistent to denounce violence in America while condoning the violence of the American government in Vietnam. After all, he was unalterably convinced that love expressed through nonviolence afforded the best avenue to world peace and harmony. The need to be morally consistent on this issue of violence versus nonviolence became even more pressing as King sought to counsel young black ghetto militants against inciting

King, Jr.: An Amazing Grace," Del Mar, Calif.: McGraw Hill Films, 1978 (62 min). "Conscience and the Vietnam War" appears in its entirety in King, *The Trumpet of Conscience*, 18–34. All three of these speeches overlapped to a great extent in terms of their content.

73. King, *The Trumpet of Conscience*, 31.
74. Quoted in Washington, ed., *A Testament of Hope*, 236.
75. Quoted in John J. Ansbro, *Martin Luther King, Jr.: The Making of a Mind* (Maryknoll, N.Y.: Orbis Books, 1982), 256.
76. *Ibid.*, 256–57.

riots and inflicting physical injury on white racists and oppressors:

> As I have walked among the desperate, rejected, angry young men, I have told them that Molotov cocktails and rifles would not solve their problems. I have tried to offer them my deepest compassion, while maintaining my conviction that social change comes most meaningfully through nonviolent action. But, they asked, and rightly so, what about Vietnam? They asked if our own nation wasn't using massive doses of violence to solve its problems, to bring about the changes it wanted. Their questions hit home, and I knew that I could never again raise my voice against the violence of the oppressed in the ghettoes without having first spoken clearly to the greatest purveyor of violence in the world today: my own government.[77]

King's desire to be faithful to his calling as a Christian minister also figured into his opposition to the Vietnam war. He believed that he had a prophetic responsibility to proclaim "thus saith the Lord" to individuals as well as nations—"to constantly speak to the moral issues of our day far beyond civil rights."[78] This conviction grew largely out of King's exposure to the prophetic tradition of the black church, a tradition that had long insisted on challenging social evils through nonviolent means.[79] The New Testament and the ancient church tradition also influenced King's perspective at this level. For him, the Sermon on the Mount and the Parable of the Good Samaritan testified to Jesus Christ's prophetic challenge to the use of violence in human relations.[80] As he studied the character of the ancient church, he found that "the

77. King, *The Trumpet of Conscience*, 23–24.
78. "Transcript of an Interview with King by Local Newscasters," 2.
79. See Peter J. Paris, *The Social Teaching of the Black Churches* (Philadelphia: Fortress Press, 1985), 14–15, 24 n. 21, 50, 74, and 111. Paris affords one of the best treatments of the black church's historic opposition to violence and war on moral grounds. Also see Martin Luther King, Sr., *Daddy King: An Autobiography*, written with Clayton Riley (New York: William Morrow and Company, Inc., 1980), 82 ff.
80. Martin Luther King, Jr., *Strength to Love* (Philadelphia: Fortress Press, 1981), 151.

early Christians would not go to war." "They were thrown into the lion's den and placed on the chopping blocks," King said, "but they went there with the songs of Zion on their lips, and in their souls, because they had discovered that there was something so true, and so precious, that they had to follow it."[81] Obviously, King was standing in a tradition that extended back two thousand years when he observed that a commitment to the Christian ministry necessarily required a devotion to peace.

The Nobel Peace Prize was yet another motivating factor in King's decision to oppose the Vietnam war. Speaking of the meaning of this award, he explained that "it should also challenge us to work passionately and unrelentingly to discover the international implications of nonviolence."[82] Significantly, the Nobel Peace Prize provided King with the kind of global recognition, support, and reinforcement needed to address international conflicts such as the war in Vietnam.[83]

Nothing disturbed King more than what he regarded as "the damaging effects" of Vietnam "on civil rights programs." This, too, helps explain his disapproval of the war. He noted that prior to the United States' intervention in Vietnam, "It seemed as if there was a real promise of hope for the poor—both black and white—through the poverty program. There were experiments, hopes, new beginnings." He continued:

> Then came the buildup in Vietnam and I watched the program broken and eviscerated as if it were some idle political plaything of a society gone mad on war, and I knew that America would never invest the necessary funds or energies in rehabilitation of its poor so long as adventures like Vietnam continued to draw men and skills and money like some demonic destructive suction tube. So I was increasingly compelled to

81. King, "Why We Must Go to Washington," 14–15.
82. A letter from Martin Luther King, Jr. to A. Philip Randolph, 2 November 1964, The A. Philip Randolph Papers, The Library of Congress, Washington, D. C.
83. Ansbro, *Martin Luther King, Jr.*, 260–61.

see the war as an enemy of the poor and to attack it as such.[84]

King suggested further that there was "a very obvious and almost facile connection" between the war in Vietnam and the struggle he and others were waging in America.[85] In his thinking, the relationship between the despair and cynicism of young blacks drawn to violence in the slums and the climate of confused purposes and violence engendered by an indefensible war was unmistakable. King was convinced that the masses of his people, especially those who suffered most from poverty, shared his analysis of the problem:

> There is deep and widespread disenchantment among Negroes with the war in Vietnam—first, because they are against war itself, and secondly, because they feel that it has caused a significant and alarming diminishing of concern and attention to civil rights progress. I have held these views myself for a long time, but I have spoken more frequently in the recent period because Negroes in so many circles have explicitly urged me to articulate their concern and frustration.[86]

King's refusal to separate Vietnam from his efforts to promote freedom and social justice in the United States disturbed a few well-known civil rights leaders and other prominent blacks. Senator Edward Brooke of Massachusetts charged that King was "doing irreparable harm to the civil rights movement—losing thousands and thousands of allies—in tying the Vietnam war to the civil rights movement."[87] Similar sentiments were expressed by Ralph Bunche, the United Nations Undersecretary; Martin Luther King, Sr., the senior pastor of

84. Quoted in Washington, ed., *A Testament of Hope*, 232–33.
85. *Ibid.;* and King, *The Trumpet of Conscience*, 22–23.
86. Martin Luther King, Jr., "The Effects of the Vietnam War on the Black Community," a statement given at the Biltmore Hotel, Los Angeles, Cal. (The King Center Archives, 12 April 1967), 1–2.
87. Edward Brooke, "A Statement Regarding M.L.K.'s Anti-Vietnam Stand," given in Washington, D. C. (The King Center Archives, 22 May 1967), 1.

Atlanta's Ebenezer Baptist Church; Roy Wilkins of the NAACP; Whitney Young of the National Urban League; Carl T. Rowan, newspaper columnist; Jackie Robinson, then Special Assistant on Community Affairs to Governor Rockefeller of New York; Representative Jonathan B. Bingham of New York; George Weaver, Assistant Secretary of Labor in the Johnson administration; and several members of the S.C.L.C.'s staff.[88] Bunche later retracted his position after looking carefully at King's. Daddy King did likewise after listening to his son's speech at Riverside Church. The elderly King later remarked:

> I could not speak out against M. L. on the peace statement, though, at the time, I thought he was wrong. But when he finished his great speech, I knew—the whole audience knew—the man was right. He was a genius. I'm not talking about my son when I say that, I'm talking about a world citizen. He moved beyond us early. He did not belong to us, he belonged to all the world.[89]

In his outstanding essay, "When 'Civil Rights' and 'Peace' Join Forces," David Halberstam elaborated on the many reasons why major civil rights leaders opposed King's public denunciation of the Vietnam war:

> On the peace issue none of King's associates really questioned how he felt; rather they questioned the wisdom of taking a stand. Would it hurt the civil rights movement? Would it deprive the Negroes of King's desperately needed time and resources? And some of these peace people, were they really the kind of people King wanted to play with?[90]

---

88. Henry E. Darby and Margaret N. Rowley, "King on Vietnam and Beyond," in *Martin Luther King, Jr. and the Civil Rights Movement*, vol. 2, ed. David J. Garrow (New York: Carlson Publishing, Inc., 1989), 255–56.
89. Quoted in King, *My Life with Martin Luther King, Jr.*, 295.
90. David Halberstam, "When 'Civil Rights' and 'Peace' Join Forces," in *Martin Luther King, Jr.*, ed. Lincoln, 188.

King's response to such questions was always swift, forthright, and emotional, especially considering his closeness to those who criticized him. "And when I hear such questions," he commented, "I have been greatly saddened, for they mean that the inquirers have never really known me, my commitment, or my calling. Indeed, that question suggests that they do not know the world in which they live."[91] In April, 1967, slightly more than a week after the Riverside speech, King issued a statement to moderate civil rights leaders, noting that "I challenge the NAACP and other critics of my position to take a forthright stand on the rightness or wrongness of this war, rather than going off creating a non-existent issue."[92]

The Vietnam issue was the one point at which King broke with moderate civil rights leaders and joined militants like the late Malcolm X and Stokely Carmichael of the S.N.C.C. This was a significant development in light of the sharp tensions that previously existed between King's S.C.L.C. and more militant groups like the black nationalist followers of Malcolm and S.N.C.C. Black militants like Carmichael genuinely appreciated King's growing radicalization in the late sixties, particularly as expressed in his position on Vietnam and economic injustice, and they openly supported and embraced him. However, King found his greatest support from his family as he sought to weather the storm of criticism created by his public statements on Vietnam. His wife Coretta, who had been active in the Women's Strike for Peace and the Women's International League for Peace and Freedom, made many speeches on Vietnam for him.[93] In

91. King, *The Trumpet of Conscience*, 21.
92. King, "The Effects of the Vietnam War on the Black Community," 3. Herbert Richardson persuasively contends that by the very fact that King refused to separate Vietnam from civil rights, "he showed the profundity of his theological insight into the nature of evil today. And who, today, would deny that what he first affirmed as a lone prophetic voice has now come to pass and been acknowledged by all among us as a basic social fact?" See Richardson, "Martin Luther King," 181–84.
93. Watley, *Roots of Resistance*, 102.

time, King's parents also accepted his views on Vietnam and publicly supported him.[94]

King had other important reasons, aside from those already discussed, for attacking the Vietnam war and for linking that conflict with civil rights. He, as one who loved his country, was deeply concerned about the image the United States projected throughout the world through her involvement in Vietnam.[95] That image, as he saw it, was one of violence and militarism, not freedom, justice, and democracy. King held that the United States' image as the "moral leader of the free world" had been seriously damaged for essentially two reasons. First, because most of the soldiers she was sending to fight for liberty and justice in Southeast Asia were poor whites and poor and oppressed blacks—young men who had not even enjoyed the fruits of democracy at home:

> Perhaps the more tragic recognition of reality took place when it became clear to me that the war was doing far more than devastating the hopes of the poor at home. It was sending their sons and their brothers and their husbands to fight and to die in extraordinarily high proportions relative to the rest of the population. We were taking the black young men who had been crippled by our society and sending them eight thousand miles away to guarantee liberties in Southeast Asia which they had not found in southwest Georgia and East Harlem. So we have been repeatedly faced with the cruel irony of watching Negro and white boys on TV screens as they kill and die together for a nation that has been unable to seat them together in the same schools. So we watch them in brutal solidarity burning the huts of a poor village, but we realize that they would never live on the same block in Detroit. I could not be silent in the face of such cruel manipulation of the poor.[96]

94. King, *My Life with Martin Luther King, Jr.*, 295.
95. Ansbro, *Martin Luther King, Jr.*, 259.
96. Quoted in Washington, ed., *A Testament of Hope*, 233.

This manipulation of the poor and oppressed was absolutely unacceptable to King, especially since wealthy whites used their money and influence with local draft boards to shield their sons from the draft by getting them into the National Guard or Reserves. The disproportionate numbers of blacks and other poor groups in Vietnam help explain why King emphasized conscientious objection as a moral imperative and as an alternative to military involvement. In counseling young black men not to fight for an America that denied them equality of opportunity, King was standing in a tradition of black thought that stretched from David Walker in 1829 to Paul Robeson, Malcolm X, Elijah Muhammad, and Muhammad Ali in this century.[97]

Second, King insisted that the United States denied the Vietnamese the right of self-determination. This was for him morally unacceptable in view of his country's long tradition of participatory democracy, a tradition that upheld the right of persons to determine their own vocation and destiny. He believed that the United States' refusal to recognize the independence of the Vietnamese was symptomatic of a "malady within the American spirit." Indeed, it was indicative of the same "deadly Western arrogance that has poisoned the international atmosphere for so long." Furthermore, King believed that his country's claim that "the Vietnamese people were not 'ready' for independence" amounted to a perpetuation of the same kind of racism that victimized black America.[98] The

97. King raised the issue of conscientious objection in a version of his sermon, "A Time to Break Silence," delivered at Ebenezer Baptist Church, Atlanta, Georgia (The King Center Archives, 11 April 1967), 1ff. For a serious study of this tradition in black thought, one would have to go back at least as far as David Walker. See Charles M. Wiltse, ed., *David Walker's Appeal to the Coloured Citizens of the World* (New York: Hill and Wang, 1965; originally published in 1829), 66.

98. Washington, ed., *A Testament of Hope*, 235–40. David Halberstam's claim that King "does not particularly think of the war in Vietnam as a racial one (although the phrase 'killing little brown children in Vietnam' slips in)" is questionable, especially given King's sensitivity to and reflections on the international implications and impact of white racism. See Halberstam, "When 'Civil Rights' and 'Peace' Join Forces," 207; King, *Where Do We Go from Here?* 173–76; Washington, ed., *A*

United States, he charged, had done more to destroy Vietnam than to liberate her:

> We have destroyed their two most cherished institutions: the family and the village. We have destroyed their land and their crops. We have cooperated in the crushing of the nation's only non-Communist revolutionary political force—the unified Buddhist church. We have supported the enemies of the peasants of Saigon. We have corrupted their women and children and killed their men. What liberators![99]

The possibility that the Vietnam conflict would lead to a war with China and ultimately to a world war also affected King. This was inescapable in view of his sense of mission on a global scale, a mission that involved striving to make human brotherhood and sisterhood a reality across geographical boundaries. War anywhere was for him a threat to human life, community, and peace everywhere. Thus, he accepted and constantly mentioned President John Kennedy's warning that "mankind must put an end to war or war will put an end to mankind." In a similar vein, he warned: "We still have a choice today: nonviolent coexistence or violent coannihilation. This may well be mankind's last chance to choose between chaos and community."[100]

In 1967, King suggested five concrete steps that the United States had to take immediately "to begin the long and difficult process of extricating ourselves from this nightmarish conflict" in Vietnam. He listed them in this order:

1. End all bombing in North and South Vietnam.
2. Declare a unilateral cease fire in the hope that such action will create the atmosphere for negotiation.

Testament of Hope, 235; and Martin Luther King, Jr., "Who are We?," a sermon delivered at Ebenezer Baptist Church, Atlanta, Ga. (The King Center Archives, 5 February 1966), 9.

99. Quoted in Washington, ed., *A Testament of Hope*, 236.

100. King, *Where Do We Go from Here?* 183 and 191; and Ansbro, *Martin Luther King, Jr.*, 257.

3. Take immediate steps to prevent other battle-grounds in Southeast Asia by curtailing our military buildup in Thailand and our interference in Laos.
4. Realistically accept the fact that the National Liberation Front has substantial support in South Vietnam and must thereby play a role in any meaningful negotiations and in any future Vietnam government.
5. Set a date that we will remove all foreign troops from Vietnam in accordance with the 1954 Geneva agreement.[101]

King went on to recommend that the United States, as a part of her ongoing commitment to international peace and community, "make what reparations we can for the damage we have done" in Vietnam, and that we "offer to grant asylum to any Vietnamese who fears for his life under a new regime which included the Liberation Front." King also concluded that the Christian churches and Jewish synagogues in America had a moral responsibility to assist in ridding their country of a tragic intervention in Vietnam:

> Meanwhile, we in the churches and synagogues have a continuing task while we urge our government to disengage itself from a disgraceful commitment. We must continue to raise our voices if our nation persists in its perverse ways in Vietnam. We must be prepared to match actions with words by seeking out every creative means of protest possible. . . . As we counsel young men concerning military service we must clarify for them our nation's role in Vietnam and challenge them with the alternative of conscientious objection . . . . Moreover, I would encourage all ministers of draft age to give up their ministerial exemptions and seek status as conscientious objectors. These are the times for real choices and not false ones. We are at the moment when our lives must be placed on the line if our nation is to

101. Quoted in Washington, ed., *A Testament of Hope*, 239. Representative Jonathan B. Bingham of New York believed that King's five-point plan was unrealistic and that his perspective on the situation in Vietnam was misinformed and one-sided. See Darby and Rowley, "King on Vietnam and Beyond," 255.

survive its own folly. Every man of humane convictions must decide on the protest that best suits his convictions, but we must all protest.[102]

King's recommendations evoked criticism from many circles in the United States and abroad. Many liberal whites withdrew their financial support from the S.C.L.C.[103] Conservative whites rebuked King for taking a stand on Vietnam, and some suggested that his stand proved his communist sympathies and ties.[104] Forces in the United States Government distanced themselves from King and sought to discredit him. What greatly angered the Johnson administration was the civil rights leader's fearlessness in addressing foreign policy issues— issues that did not relate to "black issues" as narrowly defined by the government. Instead of viewing King as a much-needed voice of moderation on the issue of Vietnam, most Americans questioned his patriotism. Such actions were difficult for King to understand at a time when increasing numbers of Americans were questioning the wisdom of their country's interference in Vietnam.[105] He described his position not as unpatriotic but as a moving "beyond the prophesying of smooth patriotism to the

102. Quoted in Washington, ed., *A Testament of Hope*, 239–40.
103. Darby and Rowley, "King on Vietnam and Beyond," 255–56; and Halberstam, "When 'Civil Rights' and 'Peace' Join Forces," 187–211.
104. Constant efforts to associate King with Communism help explain his reluctance to associate with the *left* at home and abroad. His position on Vietnam made the charge of Communist sympathies more believable for conservative whites. Small wonder that at the time of his assassination, James Earl Ray, his accused killer, received numerous letters of congratulation from white conservatives and racists who believed King was a Communist. See William B. Huie, *He Slew the Dreamer: My Search, with James Earl Ray, for the Truth About the Murder of Martin Luther King* (New York: Delacorte Press, 1970), 207–12. King often referred to his ties with the black Christian tradition in offering what was perhaps his strongest rebuttal to the view that he was Communist. In one letter he wrote: "You must realize that a very great part of Negro life is church-centered, and thusly, his native religious appetite would not be prone to a godless system such as Communism." See a letter from Martin Luther King, Jr., to Mr. David C. Dautzer, 9 May 1961, The King Papers, Boston University.
105. Darby and Rowley, "King on Vietnam and Beyond," 256.

high grounds of a firm dissent based upon the mandates of conscience and the reading of history."[106]

The ultimate strength of King's position rested in his call for a world free of violence. "I would suggest that modern man really go all out to study the meaning of nonviolence, its philosophy and its strategy," he counseled.[107] In his writings, King urged the peoples of the world to move beyond an intellectual analysis of nonviolence to a practical application of that method— to engage in a "serious experimentation" with nonviolence "in every field of human conflict, by no means excluding the relations between nations."[108] He continued: "We live each day on the verge of nuclear co-annihilation; in this world, nonviolence is no longer an option for intellectual analysis, it is an imperative for action."[109] Interestingly enough, King's effort "to make nonviolence into a force for international peace" occurred at a time when violence against his own people in America had reached a horrid intensity, and also during a period when the prophets of doom were predicting the decline of nonviolence as a force in human relations.[110]

Establishing nonviolence as a force in relations between nations was for King a matter of means and ends coming together. He explained that "if we are to have peace in the world, men and nations must embrace the nonviolent affirmation that ends and means must cohere."[111] From his point of view, it was essentially impossible for one to successfully pursue peaceful ends on the

106. Quoted in Washington, ed., *A Testament of Hope,* 231. Coleman Brown is correct in contending that King's "Loyalty to America" was "a provisional loyalty to be sure—critical, prophetic, indeed grief-stricken." See Brown, "Grounds for American Loyalty," 18–19.

107. King, *The Trumpet of Conscience,* 68.

108. King, *Where Do We Go from Here?* 184.

109. King, *The Trumpet of Conscience,* 64.

110. Richard Lentz, *Symbols, The News Magazines, and Martin Luther King* (Baton Rouge: Louisiana State University Press, 1990), 168.

111. King, *The Trumpet of Conscience,* 70.

world stage through violent means, a fact more than adequately supported by history itself:

> The stages of history are replete with the chants and choruses of the conquerors of old who came killing in pursuit of peace. Alexander, Genghis Khan, Julius Caesar, Charlemagne and Napoleon were akin in seeking a peaceful world order, a world fashioned after their selfish conceptions of an ideal existence. Each sought a world at peace which would personify his egotistic dreams. Even within the life span of most of us, another megalomaniac strode across the world stage. He sent his blitzkrieg—bent legions blazing across Europe, bringing havoc and holocaust in his wake. There is grave irony in the fact that Hitler could come forth, following nakedly aggressive expansionist theories, and do it all in the name of peace.[112]

It was to America's best interest, King thought, to keep this history in mind. He also warned that "before it is too late," Americans "must narrow the gaping chasm between our proclamations of peace and our lowly deeds which precipitate and perpetuate war."[113] Only in this way could America assume a central role in the struggle for world peace and community.

King actually had in mind the creation of a new human perspective and agenda that would lead people beyond a mere concern for their own liberation to an interest in ending racism, poverty, and war everywhere. More specifically, his recommendation for creative change that would result in world community was a call for nations to move beyond a preoccupation with "things" to a deeper appreciation for "persons," and from loyalties that are sectional to loyalties that are ecumenical in character. King referred to such a maturation process as a "shift from a 'thing'-oriented society to a 'person'-oriented society."[114] He reminded America that

---

112. King, *Where Do We Go from Here?* 182.
113. *Ibid.*, 183.
114. Fluker, *They Looked for a City*, 99; and King, *Where Do We Go from Here?* 186 and 190.

she, because of her unique democratic tradition and her enormous resources of wealth and technology, should be the leader in this revolution.[115] He was equally clear in stating that America would be incapable of forming the vanguard of such a revolution—of leading in the shaping of "a new kind of man"—as long as she gave materialism, power, and supremacy over other nations primacy over the emotional, the spiritual, and the moral dimensions of life. Only through "a revolution of values" would America be prepared to lead the world on a new and more noble course—a course that would ultimately involve a mingling of the highest human values of peoples from every part of the globe.[116]

KING AS AN INTERNATIONAL SYMBOL OF COMMUNITY

In the spring of 1957, Martin Luther King, Jr., received the first of his many honorary degrees during Morehouse College's commencement exercises in Atlanta. He was both pleased and honored that his alma mater recognized him in this manner. On awarding the degree, Dr. Benjamin E. Mays, president of the college, said of King: "Your name has become a symbol of courage and hope for suppressed peoples everywhere."[117] This characterization of King would become increasingly true over the course of the next eleven years as the civil rights leader assumed a more active role in world affairs.

World recognition of King as a vital symbol of community found dramatic expression in 1964, when he was named *Time* magazine's "Man of the Year" and the Nobel Peace Prize winner.[118] Dr. Gunnar Jahn, who presented

115. Fluker, *They Looked for a City*, 99; and Washington, ed., *A Testament of Hope*, 241.
116. King, *Where Do We Go from Here?* 186–91; and "Doubts and Certainties," 5.
117. Quoted in King, *My Life with Martin Luther King, Jr.*, 168.
118. Lentz, *Symbols, The News Magazines, and Martin Luther King*, 113. Chapter 4 of Lentz's book, entitled "Honors for the Prophet," affords a good discussion of King's symbolic significance in the American

King with the Nobel Prize in Oslo, Norway, spoke of the international implications of the civil rights leader's work in the most glowing terms:

> Though Martin Luther King has not personally committed himself to the international conflict, his own struggle is a clarion call to all who work for peace. He is the first person in the western world to have shown us that a struggle can be waged without violence. He is the first to make the message of brotherly love a reality in the course of his struggle, and he has proclaimed a message to all men, to all nations and races.[119]

Also in 1964, King had a personal audience with Pope Paul VI in Rome and a meeting with Mayor Willy Brandt in Berlin.[120] From 1964 to the time of his death, King met with South Vietnam's Foreign Minister Fran Van Do, Premier Ben Bella of the New Algerian Republic, President Kenneth Kaunda of the Republic of Zambia, and other so-called Third World leaders.[121] Such associations did essentially as much to enhance King's role as a world citizen and a world symbol as did the hundreds of awards and honors he received during his lifetime.[122]

The assassination of King in April, 1968, brought tributes and condolences as well as expressions of grief, contrition, and rage from every corner of the globe. Such reactions provided another angle from which to assess King's symbolic significance on the world stage. Dr. Eugene Carson Blake and other leaders in the World

---

context. However, the work offers very little on King's meaning and significance as an international symbol.

119. Quoted in Ansbro, *Martin Luther King, Jr.*, 260–61; and King, *My Life with Martin Luther King, Jr.*, 25–26.

120. John H. Johnson, et al., compilers, *Martin Luther King, Jr., 1929–1968: An Ebony Picture Biography* (Chicago: Johnson Publishing Company, Inc., 1968), 48–49.

121. *Ibid.*, 72; and Lewis V. Baldwin, "Martin Luther King, Jr.'s Vision of an Independent Africa," *African Commentary* 2, no. 3 (March, 1990): 6–8.

122. *Martin Luther King, Jr., 1929–1968: An Ebony Picture*, 8. King estimated that he received some four hundred awards alone during his thirteen years as a public figure, to say nothing of the many other honors bestowed on him.

Council of Churches, the World Alliance of Reformed Churches, and the Lutheran World Federation mourned the civil rights leader as "a brilliant, valiant, beloved man," and asserted, "By international consensus Dr. King was a first citizen of the world."[123] *The London Times* called King's assassination "a great loss to all Negroes, to the United States and to a world that had come to love and respect him."[124] U Thant, the Secretary General of the United Nations, declared that the tragedy was especially heart-breaking given that King had "worked so unceasingly and by nonviolent means for the cause of peace, international understanding and human rights." Prime Minister Indira Gandhi of India described the tragedy as "a setback to mankind's search for light," and noted that "violence has removed one of the great men of the world."[125] Pastor Frank Wood of Union Church in Mexico shared this view, insisting that "this great man made within himself and before God and man a solemn and irrevocable decision to give his life and his death to change the face of human history." "The ugly and wanton act of the assassin," Wood continued, "robbed all mankind of a wise friend and plundered the world of one of its greatest treasures."[126] J. Lowrie Anderson, a white Presbyterian missionary stationed in Africa, said that "In the life and death of Martin Luther King America gave a message to the world. It is a message she dare not herself disregard."[127] A fitting climax to all of these tributes was offered by Pope Paul VI, who vowed to pray that "the virtues of justice and international love, for which Dr. King stood, can come to be respected everywhere."[128]

---

123. "Roundup: Foreign Tributes to Dr. King," *The Christian Century* 85, no. 19 (May 8, 1968): 630; and Quoted in Lerone Bennett, Jr., *What Manner of Man: A Biography of Martin Luther King, Jr.* (Chicago: Johnson Publishing Company, Inc., 1968), 145.

124. Quoted in Bennett, *What Manner of Man*, 146; and Stephen B. Oates, *Let the Trumpet Sound: The Life of Martin Luther King, Jr.* (New York: Harper and Row, 1982), 494.

125. Quoted in Bennett, *What Manner of Man*, 146.

126. "Roundup: Foreign Tributes to Dr. King," 629.

127. *Ibid.*

128. Quoted in Bennett, *What Manner of Man*, 145.

Memorial services were held for King throughout the world. His funeral in the United States had "the trappings of an affair of state," with flags hanging at half-staff, messages of sympathy dispatched, and national and international dignitaries attending the services. In Mexico, hundreds of citizens and American residents met on Chapultepec Heights and sang, prayed, and gave eulogies. In Rome, Turin, and other Italian cities, Catholics, Protestants, and Jews joined memorial prayers for King. Pope Paul VI alluded to "the warning in the murder which stirred the whole world," and appealed for peace in Vietnam and "for replacement of racism, nationalism and class hatred by love."[129] In Oxford, England, approximately four hundred mourners honored King by marching some distance to a church, where a memorial service occurred. Eulogies, tributes, and prayers were offered by thousands in France, Germany, and various parts of Asia, Africa, the Caribbean, and Latin America. The memorial services held for King in Madrid and other parts of Spain were so well attended and emotional that one observer reported, "The outpouring of sympathy and concern for the King family and for America, not only here in Madrid but all over Spain, has staggered the imagination of all observers." Such memorial services were matched by the many spontaneous gifts of money put into special funds in various parts of the world to support continuing efforts toward the actualization of King's ideal of global peace and community.[130]

World recognition of King has taken many other forms since his death more than two decades ago. King's birthplace has become a landmark, drawing millions of admirers and curious spectators from various parts of the United States and abroad.[131] Atlanta's Ebenezer Baptist Church, located approximately two blocks from King's

129. "Roundup: Foreign Tributes to Dr. King," 629–30; and Lentz, *Symbols, The News Magazines, and Martin Luther King*, 302.
130. *Ibid.*
131. Renee D. Turner, "Birthplace of a National Hero: Sixty Years After His Birth, King's Birth Home is Restored to Original State," *Ebony* 44, no. 3 (January, 1989): 40–42.

birth home, is probably one of the fifty most well-known local churches in the world. The fact that King grew up in Ebenezer, and served as an associate pastor there with his father and brother, helps explain why millions from around the world have visited the church since 1968. The King birthplace and Ebenezer Church are a part of a much larger landmark called the Martin Luther King, Jr. Historic Site. Located here also is the Martin Luther King, Jr. Center for Nonviolent Social Change, Inc., which holds the largest existing collection of civil rights materials in the world and which is devoted to preserving King's symbolic importance and to promoting his philosophy and methods as the key to the elimination of racism, poverty, war, and other global problems.[132] The King Center's contribution in these areas justifies J. Lowell Ware's description of Atlanta as "the Mecca" for admirers of King everywhere.[133]

Other memorials dedicated in King's honor "range from the impressive to the controversial" and are as representative of his spirit as the eternal flame that burns at his crypt on the grounds of the King Center. Throughout the world, there are streets, bridges, parks, churches, hospitals, schools, libraries, college and university dormitories, community centers, public housing developments, social service centers, and works of art that bear King's name. Among the most notable of these memorials are the Martin Luther King Memorial Library in Washington, D. C., the Martin Luther King General Hospital in Los Angeles, the Dr. Martin Luther King, Jr. Expressway in Memphis, the massive portrait of King that hangs in the Georgia capital, the huge statue of King on the Morehouse College campus in Atlanta, and the forest in Israel and churches in

132. *Ibid.*; Clayborne Carson, et al., eds., *The Papers of Martin Luther King, Jr.: A Preview* (Berkeley: University of California Press, 1987), 7; and "The Woman Behind the King Anniversary Featured in January *Ebony* Magazine," *Jet* 77, no. 14 (January 15, 1990): 10.
133. J. Lowell Ware, "A Birthday Celebration Befitting Dr. King," *The Tuskegee Voice* 10, no. 41 (January 15, 1977): 1.

Hungary which carry King's name.[134] A National Civil Rights Museum has been erected on the site in Memphis where King was assassinated in 1968. Commemorative stamps in the civil rights leader's honor "are of many varieties and colors," and have been issued by the United States, Ghana, Grenada, Haiti, India, Liberia, Mali, Mexico, Panama, the Virgin Islands, and other countries. It has been reported that King's "likeness appears on more stamps around the world than that of any other black American."[135] His picture can be found, almost as an icon, in the studies, bedrooms, living rooms, and churches of millions. It is no exaggeration to say that no other American, black or white, has received such recognition from the world community.

The symbolic force of King and what he stood for led the United States Senate, on October 19, 1983, to vote overwhelmingly to designate the third Monday in January, beginning in 1986, as a federal holiday in honor of the civil rights leader. This successful achievement was spearheaded by former Indiana Congresswoman Katie Hall, Coretta Scott King, the noted singer Stevie Wonder, and others who cherish King's symbolic meaning and significance for humanity.[136] By officializing the King holiday, the United States joined more than a hundred other countries throughout the world that celebrate King's birthday in January of each year.[137] Musical

134. "In Memory of Martin Luther King, Jr.: Streets, Buildings, Works of Art Honor Him Around the World," *Ebony* 41, no. 3 (January 1986): 64, 66, 68, and 72.

135. "The World Honors Dr. Martin Luther King, Jr. with Stamps: A Colorful Commemorative Collection from Various Countries," *Ebony* 41, no. 3 (January 1986): 82–84; and Lewis V. Baldwin, "Martin Luther King, Jr. as a National and International Symbol of Community," *The A.M.E. Zion Quarterly Review* 101, no. 1 (April 1989): 2–4.

136. The effort to make King's birthday a national holiday began at the time of his death. See "Anniversaries: King Day," *Newsweek* (January 26, 1970): 24–25; "Katie Hall Leaves House But Claims Victory in King Bill and Vows to Return," *Jet* 67, no. 13 (December 3, 1984): 38–40; and "The Continuing Struggle for a National King Holiday," *Ebony* 43, no. 3 (January 1988): 27–28, 30, and 32.

137. "The Continuing Struggle for a National King Holiday," 27; and "Observances Nationwide Honor Martin Luther King," *Jet* 73, no. 16 (January 18, 1988): 22.

tributes, worship services, parades, nonviolent demonstrations, seminars, and special lectureships are among
the events that mark this celebration, and state em-
ployees and federal and postal workers get the day off
with pay.[138] The King holiday is perhaps the best example of how King has become bigger than life—of how the
symbol has become larger than the man himself.

The symbolism of the King holiday goes beyond what
Kenneth L. Smith calls "ritualistic hoopla."[139] The occasion makes several points. First, it says to whites and people of color all over the world that there is a black man,
one from an oppressed community, who deserves the
highest measure of recognition and respect. Second, the
holiday is proof of the prevailing definition of King as a
symbol of American values and ideas.[140] This is another
reason why the occasion is so important in terms of symbolism and American mythology. Kenneth Smith has said
that King represented "the brightest and best" in "the
American tradition of dissent in the struggle for social
justice and peace"—something that has not been explained "except in the vaguest of terms."[141] Finally, the
holiday means that King's dream must become for all humanity a sustaining vision—"an opportunity to consider
the unfinished agenda of his holy crusade." "We must use
the King holiday to promote nonviolent responses to the
world's problems," says Andrea Young. "We must use the
holiday to teach nonviolent action as a better way to be in
the world. To do less is to fail to honor the life of Martin
Luther King, Jr."[142] If there is no real commitment on the

138. "Memphis Plans Parade, Musical Tribute to King on 20th
Anniversary of Death," *The Tennessean* (January 28, 1988): 3B; *Bulletin
from the Hill*, Colgate-Rochester Divinity School/Bexley Hall/Crozer
Theological Seminaries, Rochester, New York, 43, no. 2 (March 1986):
1; and "Observances Nationwide Honor Martin Luther King," 22, 24,
and 26.
139. Kenneth L. Smith, "Equality and Justice: A Dream or Vision of
Reality," *Report from the Capital* 39, no. 1 (January 1984): 5.
140. *Ibid.*; and Lentz, *Symbols, The News Magazines, and Martin
Luther King*, 119.
141. Smith, "Equality and Justice," 5.
142. Andrea Young, "Martin Luther King, Jr.: The Legacy Lives,"
Christianity and Crisis 45, no. 22 (January 13, 1986): 532.

part of humans to King's dream, the holiday will lose its symbolic meaning in the midst of the commercialism and celebration that center around it.[143] It will then become simply another example of what Max Weber once called "the routinization of charisma."[144]

King's symbolic meaning and significance has also become evident in the persons and movements that continue to bear his influence. Dr. Joseph Lowery, Hosea Williams, Jesse Jackson, and others who worked with the S.C.L.C. still advocate nonviolence as a moral and practical method in the human struggle for full liberation.[145] Peace activists like Daniel and Philip Berrigan still reflect King's influence, and so do nonviolent theorists like Gene Sharp.[146] In a real sense, the world followed King's work and learned from his ideas and activities. The illustrious group of men and women who met in Dubrovnik, Yugoslavia, from June 26 to July 8, 1983 to study meanings, forms, and uses of nonviolence were heavily touched by the spirit and example of activists like King and Gandhi. They included Narayan Desai, a leader of the International Peace Brigade from India; Danilo Dolci, who had used ingenious nonviolent methods for thirty years in rural Sicily to improve the lives of citizens amid poverty, indifference, and the terrorism of the Mafia; Jim Forest, an editor of the *Catholic Worker* and an antiwar activist; A. Paul Hare, who had taught, written about, and participated in nonviolence in

143. Smith, "Equality and Justice," 5; Lewis V. Baldwin, "King: Celebrating the Legacy, Renewing the Dream," *The Sunday Tennessean* (February 22, 1987): 2H; and Jerry Gentry, "How to Celebrate King's Birthday," *The Christian Century* (January 16, 1985): 36–37.

144. Smith, "Equality and Justice," 5.

145. "His Truth is Marching On: Dr. King's Key Aides Continue His Crusade," *Ebony* 44, no. 3 (January 1989): 44–48.

146. King's influence is clearly evident in Philip Berrigan's "Letter from a Baltimore Jail," a precious document that emerged out of the peace movement in America. See Philip Berrigan, *Prison Journals of a Priest Revolutionary* (New York: Ballantine Books, 1971): 15–22. King is also mentioned many times in Gene Sharp's three-volume work on nonviolent action. See, for example, Gene Sharp, *The Politics of Nonviolent Action: The Dynamics of Nonviolent Action*, Part III (Boston: Porter Sargent Publishers, 1973), 95 ff.

many parts of the world for approximately thirty years; June Hare, who had worked for many years in Cape Town as a social worker; Bernard Lafayette, a former associate of King in the S.C.L.C.; and Gene Sharp, one of the world's leading students of civilian nonviolent resistance.[147]

The symbolism of King must also be measured in terms of his impact on other movements against oppression. King and the civil rights movement contributed to the direction and momentum of numerous organized causes in the late 1960s, the 1970s, and the 1980s, among which were the Feminist Movement, the peace movement, the gay rights movement, movements against abortion and capital punishment, the Religious and Political Right Phenomenon, efforts to secure rights for the elderly and the handicapped, the consumer movement, and environment protection. "We Shall Overcome," a song popularized by King and others in the civil rights movement, has been adopted by many of these movements. The pivotal role served by King and the civil rights movement in helping to spawn a succession of organized causes will become clearer as that subject finds fuller exploration in the literature.[148]

In some cases, efforts to limit and even destroy King's image as a national and international symbol have been as intense as those geared toward preserving that image. Richard Lentz documents the extent to which major news magazines like *Time, Newsweek,* and *U.S. News and World Report* may have contributed, consciously or unconsciously, to such efforts.[149] In the early 1980s, Senator Jesse Helms of North Carolina and his small

147. Danilo Dolci, "On Building a Humane Society," a lecture scheduled for presentation (February 23, 1983), 1 ff.; and *Program Booklet: A Course on Nonviolence—Meanings, Forms and Uses,* Inter-University Centre of Postgraduate Studies, Dubrovnik, Yugoslavia (June 26–July 8, 1983), 1–9.

148. Ansbro, *Martin Luther King, Jr.,* xiv–xv (Preface); and Andrew Young, "The Rich Legacy of Martin Luther King," *Chicago Sun-Times,* Chicago, Illinois (January 12, 1981): 22.

149. Lentz, *Symbols, The News Magazines, and Martin Luther King,* 1–342.

band of conservative allies fought desperately to block the passage of the King holiday bill, thus uniting their voices with many other Americans who viewed King as an advocate of subversive means and policies rather than as a symbol of Americanism and of the struggle for human liberation and community.[150] Full recognition of King's symbolic meaning and significance was challenged throughout the late 1980s as eight of the fifty states in the United States, under the leadership of figures like Governor Evan Mecham of Arizona, resisted "the rising tide of popular support" for the King holiday.[151] The mood for such resistance had been set to a great extent by President Ronald Reagan, who begrudgingly signed the King holiday bill in November, 1983, but who never wholly disassociated himself from King's detractors.[152]

One of the greatest challenges to King's symbolism in the 1980s has come from various circles in the academic community. That challenge began on a serious note with the publication of David J. Garrow's *Bearing the Cross: Martin Luther King, Jr. and the Southern Christian Leadership Conference (1986)*, a Pulitzer Prize winning work replete with innuendoes, exaggerated claims, and questionable conclusions regarding King's vulnerabilities as a moral leader, thinker, and strategist. Garrow's portrayal of King as a womanizer, as a reluctant and often confused leader, and as one tormented by guilt and anxiety

150. "A National Holiday for King: But Not without Rancor," *Time* (October 31, 1983): 32; "Behind the King Debate," *Newsweek* (October 31, 1983): 32; Eric Breindel, "King's Communist Associates," *The New Republic* (January 30, 1984): 14; and David J. Garrow, "The Helms Attack on King," *Southern Exposure* 12, no. 2 (March–April 1984): 12–15.

151. "The Continuing Struggle for a National King Holiday," 27; "Arizona Governor's Stance on King Holiday May Cost State $18 Million Loss," *Jet* 72, no. 13 (June 22, 1987): 36; and "Arizona Finally Gets a M.L. King State Holiday," *Jet* 77, no. 1 (October 9, 1989): 18.

152. Young, "Martin Luther King, Jr.: The Legacy Lives," 531. In all fairness, Reagan was more generous in making positive comments about King's ideas, activities, and impact on the nation than conservatives like Helms and Mecham. See "President Reagan Declares Martin Luther King, Jr. Day," *Jet* 75, no. 16 (January 23, 1989): 6.

seriously undermined the man's role as a vital symbol of the civil rights movement and of the global human struggle.[153] Garrow's image of King was reinforced to some extent by Taylor Branch's *Parting the Water: America in the King Years, 1954-63* (1988), another Pulitzer Prize winning work. Ralph Abernathy offered support for disturbing rumors about King's lack of moral and intellectual integrity in his *And the Walls Came Tumbling Down: An Autobiography* (1989). Abernathy's claims about King's alleged womanizing struck at the heart of King's symbolism, especially since the two men were close friends and associates.[154] If King was guilty of such moral indiscretions, his meaning and significance for the global human family will undoubtedly be reassessed. Interestingly enough, the works by Garrow, Branch, and Abernathy appeared in the 1980s when efforts were under way to establish the King holiday throughout the nation. The revelations in these sources suggested that the authors were more concerned about diminishing than about enhancing King's symbolic importance.

The books by Garrow, Branch, and Abernathy have attracted a wide readership among the American public. Some conservative and racist elements in society have used the contents of these works to attack King's status as

153. Garrow's picture of King is strikingly different from that presented in the five chapters of Lewis V. Baldwin, *There Is a Balm in Gilead: The Cultural Roots of Martin Luther King, Jr.* (Minneapolis: Augsburg Fortress Publishers, 1991). King's tremendous intellect, his strong personality, his love of family, his devotion to spiritual values, and his love of wit and humor are traits that render questionable Garrow's portrait of the civil rights leader.

154. Steve Suitts, "Activist's Autobiography Betrays a Deep Sense of Sacrifice, Regret," *The Atlanta Constitution*, Atlanta, Georgia (October 11, 1989): 1ff.; Drew Jubera and Cynthia Durcanin, "Abernathy Book Called 'Criminally Irresponsible,'" *The Atlanta Constitution* (October 13, 1989): 1 and A-20; "Ralph Abernathy's Book Denounced for 'Painful Distortions' About King," *Jet* 77, no. 4 (October 30, 1989): 8–10; and Lewis V. Baldwin, "Abernathy Book Controversial, Marred by Claim," *Nashville Banner*, Nashville, Tennessee (November 18, 1989): D-15. For the most extensive and brilliant review of Abernathy's book, see Jimmie Lewis Franklin, "Review Essay: Autobiography, the Burden of Friendship, and Truth," *The Georgia Historical Quarterly* 74, no. 1 (Spring 1990): 83–98.

a national and world symbol. Such elements would undoubtedly agree with the conservative newspaper columnist and television personality, Patrick Buchanan, who, in an article entitled, "A Rascal's Bedroom Escapades Diminish His Status as a Saint," concluded unconvincingly that King, despite his achievements, "was not remotely so great a man or historic figure as George Washington, who led the army of independence, presided at our constitutional convention, and became our first president." "To raise Dr. King to a niche in the pantheon of American heroes alongside our founding father, as equally deserving of a national holiday," Buchanan continued, "is affirmative action at its most absurd."[155] These sentiments have obviously grown out of a failure to understand that King freed America in ways that George Washington and other founding fathers did not. Moreover, King is the only one, among a long list of great Americans, who symbolized the success of nonviolent strategy in addressing a multitude of ills that afflicted and continue to afflict American society and the world.[156] This has led Jesse Jackson to conclude that King's work will remain "untarnished" despite strong and consistent assaults on his moral integrity.[157]

Assaults on King's symbolic significance for America and the world have continued in the 1990s. Questions about the moral and intellectual integrity of King are still the basis for such assaults. Suggestions that he may have engaged in a homosexual relationship with Ralph Abernathy, his closest friend and confidante, remain unsubstantiated but nevertheless have damaged the perception of a name that has assumed heroic proportions

155. See Patrick Buchanan, "A Rascal's Bedroom Escapades Diminish His Status as a Saint," *The Tennessean*, (October 22, 1989): 5G.

156. Given King's uniqueness in this regard, it is strange that so little has been written about his symbolic meaning and significance. More studies need to be undertaken on this topic. Scholarly treatments might draw and build on Brown, "Grounds for American Loyalty," 1 ff.; and Lentz, *Symbols, the News Magazines, and Martin Luther King*, 113–42.

157. Jesse Jackson, "A Great Man's Work Remains Untarnished by Slanders," *The Tennessean*, (October 30, 1989): 9A.

and a mythic dimension for persons throughout the world.[158]

Even more damaging is the more convincing claim that King, from the time of his undergraduate studies at Morehouse, consistently appropriated words and ideas from other sources for his speeches and writings without giving proper acknowledgment and citations.[159] But there is a larger issue here that transcends that of intellectual or scholarly integrity. King's use of the words and ideas of others without proper documentation suggests that his academic training was essentially mechanical,

158. Richard Prince, "Abernathy, King Scandal: A New Twist," *The Tennessean* (September 21, 1990): 11A; and Carl T. Rowan, *Breaking Barriers: A Memoir* (Boston: Little, Brown and Company, 1991), 254–57. Rowan questions the charge about King's alleged homosexuality.

159. Stories about King's plagiarism were carried widely in the nation's newspapers and journals. For examples, see Peter Waldman, "To Their Dismay, King Scholars Find a Troubling Pattern: Civil Rights Leader Was Lax in Attributing Some Parts of His Academic Papers," *The Wall Street Journal* 72, no. 2 (November 9, 1990): 1 and A 6; Anthony De Palma, "Plagiarism Seen by Scholars in King's Ph.D. Dissertation," *The New York Times* (November 10, 1990): 1 and 10; Frances Schwartzkopff, "King's Plagiarism Rocks Scholars, Supporters: Academic Papers Failed to Credit Others," *The Atlanta Journal and Constitution* (November 10, 1990): A 1ff.; Cynthia Durcanin, "Plagiarism Revelation Splits King's Followers," *The Atlanta Journal and Constitution* (November 11, 1990): A 8; "Report: King Didn't Author Parts of His Writings," *The Macon Metro Times* (November 14, 1990): 5; David J. Garrow, "How King Borrowed: Reading the Truth Between Sermons and Footnotes," *The Washington Post* (November 18, 1990): C 1; Chris Raymond, "Discovery of Early Plagiarism by Martin Luther King Raises Troubling Questions for Scholars and Admirers," *The Chronicle of Higher Education* 37, no. 12 (November 21, 1990): 1 and A 8; "King's Plagiarism," *The Christian Century* (November 21–28, 1990): 1089–90; Clayborne Carson, "Documenting Martin Luther King's Importance—and His Flaws," *The Chronicle of Higher Education* 37, no. 18 (January 16, 1991): A 52; and Denton L. Watson, "Scholars' Focus on Martin Luther King Has Skewed Our Understanding of the Civil Rights Struggle," *The Chronicle of Higher Education* 37, no. 19 (January 23, 1991): A 44. A number of scholars addressed questions about King's plagiarism in *The Journal of American History* 78, no. 1 (June, 1991): 11–123. For interesting responses to the plagiarism charge by white neo-conservatives, see Patrick Buchanan, "Strip Plagiarizer of His Crown: Why Should a Nation Be Blackmailed over King?" *The Tennessean* (November 14, 1990): 11A; and Mark Silk, "King's Plagiarism Detracts from His Symbolic Importance," *The Atlanta Journal and Constitution* (November 15, 1990): A 23. For a liberal view by one of King's Boston professors, see "Conversation between S. Paul Schilling and David Thelen," *The Journal of American History* 78, no. 1 (June, 1991), 78–80.

and that his cultural background was eminently more important in shaping his life, thought, and vision.[160] King was steeped in cultural traditions that taught that ideas are not a private but a community resource, and, as such, they are for the free use of anyone in the community.[161] This has been especially true in the case of black preachers, who have always borrowed freely from each other. In this sense, black preaching has traditionally been an *imitative art.*[162] "King never quite accepted the fact," observes Wallace C. Smith, "that what works in the world of the black preacher does not work in the world of academia, where there are clearly defined canons of scholarship."[163]

Efforts to defend King from mounting charges of promiscuity and plagiarism have come from many circles, and particularly from his aides and advisors in the civil rights movement. Such efforts will undoubtedly

160. See Baldwin, *There Is a Balm in Gilead,* 1–336; and Garrow, "How King Borrowed," C 1. This thesis is strongly supported in "Conversation between Cornish Rogers and David Thelen," *The Journal of American History* 78, no. 1 (June, 1991): 41–62.

161. Waldman, "To Their Dismay, King Scholars Find a Troubling Pattern," A 6; and Keith D. Miller, *Voice of Deliverance: The Language of Martin Luther King, Jr. and Its Sources* (New York: The Free Press, 1991), 1 ff.

162. This is substantiated in Baldwin, *There Is a Balm in Gilead,* 273–336; Miller, *Voice of Deliverance,* 1ff.; and Keith D. Miller, "Martin Luther King, Jr., and the Black Folk Pulpit," *The Journal of American History* 78, no. 1 (June, 1991): 120–23. Questions about King's plagiarism should be raised in a sensitive and concerned manner, but not in such a way as to condone intellectual dishonesty. Many of the answers as to why the plagiarism occurred undoubtedly rest with Coretta Scott King, Dr. King's widow, and they will not be known until she tells her story. While explanations for the plagiarism may be offered, the act itself must be critically examined and solid conclusions must be drawn before we can get anything like a complete picture of King.

163. Lewis V. Baldwin, "A Conversation With Wallace C. Smith," First Baptist Church, Capitol Hill, Nashville, Tennessee (November 20, 1990). The tension suggested between King's tendency to embrace the ethos of the black preacher and his desire to follow the canons of scholarship as defined in the academic community was not always so evident, for at times he skillfully combined both. For other references to such tension, see "Conversation between Cornish Rogers and David Thelen," 49–62; Garrow, "How King Borrowed," C 1; Miller, *Voice of Deliverance,* 1ff.; and John Higham, "Habits of the Cloth and Standards of the Academy," *The Journal of American History* 78, no. 1 (June, 1991): 106–10.

prove futile for many King detractors. Even so, it is more important to focus on the good represented by King—the fact that he challenged the world with a greater or noble vision of what it means to be *human* and to live in *human* community. "Without narrow selfishness" and "meanness of spirit," writes the southern historian Jimmie L. Franklin, King "freed many citizens from narrow racial provincialism" and "provided a model for constructive social action here and abroad."[164] No American in history has done more than King to transform American values, institutions, and the general culture. Americans are a democratically stronger people because of what he said and did. King's flaws, whatever they may have been, do not undermine these outstanding contributions. They are simply a testimony to human fallibility—an indication that King, like every human being, was to some degree a creature of contradictions.[165] If King's flaws meant that he was characterless, then every human being with weaknesses or shortcomings is characterless. King was a great example of how God can use imperfect vessels to achieve a more human situation.

The black scholar William R. Jones has challenged King's symbolism at another level. He suggests that black America's fascination with King as a black messiah should not blind them to his shortcomings with regard to philosophy and tactics. "We must ruthlessly pinpoint the real defects in his thought," writes Jones, and recognize that white America desires to perpetuate this "nonviolent" leader as "a black hero who fits its special needs of oppression and not those of black liberation."

164. Ellen Goodman, "King Wasn't a Saint, But Really Tried," *The Tennessean* (November 18, 1990): 5D; "King Supporters Defend Allegations of Plagiarism," *The Atlanta Daily World* (November 13, 1990): 1 and 6; and Jimmie L. Franklin, "Still a Force for Much Good," an unpublished statement (November 19, 1990), 1–2.

165. Franklin, "Still a Force for Much Good," 1–2. Some scholars suggest that recent revelations about King's alleged moral and intellectual integrity lend support to the view that interpretations of the leadership of the civil rights movement should move beyond him to embrace other persons and groups that assumed leading roles. See Watson, "Scholars' Focus on Martin Luther King," A 44.

Jones insists that white America's "ideological abuse of King's thought," which includes its incessant pressing of King's philosophy on blacks to the exclusion of alternative philosophies such as that of Malcolm X, could make the civil rights leader a "guardian" of white values instead of a "black messiah" or a liberator of the oppressed.[166] Although Jones' concerns are well stated and justifiable, they do not detract from King's essential role as a vital symbol of hope and struggle for oppressed peoples everywhere.

As was the case during his lifetime, King will perhaps remain what Richard Lentz calls "a mutable symbol."[167] A fixed, one-dimensional image of him is highly unlikely in a world in which he is still viewed with a mixture of respect and disdain. Some will undoubtedly continue to worship him, while others question his moral and intellectual integrity. Whatever the case, no assessment of King's weaknesses as a symbol should occur without a recognition of his vast repertoire of virtues, the most important among which was his willingness to put human concerns and basic human values above personal fame and wealth. This is what ultimately made him such an important and powerful drum major for world peace, justice, and community.

KING AND THE CONTINUING QUEST FOR WORLD COMMUNITY

King's vision of a "world house" or a "world-wide neighborhood" in which people live together in peace and harmony is as far from reality today as it was in the 1960s. Even so, that vision is still unique and powerful—one that has relevance and implications for

---

166. William R. Jones, "Martin Luther King: Black Messiah or White Guardian?," a paper delivered at a meeting of the First Unitarian Society of Minneapolis, Minneapolis, Minn. (the personal collection of William R. Jones, Florida State University, Tallahassee, Fla., 6 April 1986), 1–10.

167. Lentz, *Symbols, the News Magazines, and Martin Luther King*, 237.

humankind's continuing quest for peace and community. Therefore, ethical dialogue with King concerning the meaning, character, and actualization of human community can be fruitful for humans everywhere as they seek to overcome the many barriers that prevent them from realizing their essential oneness as children of God.[168]

King's identification of racism, poverty, and war as major obstacles to peace and the unity of the human family is still accurate. Racism in particular has assumed a new intensity and sophistication in both covert and overt forms throughout the world. This is evident in the increasing number of racist attacks against American blacks by police, and in the physical and verbal abuse visited on blacks and other so-called minorities on predominantly white college and university campuses, on the dusty roads of Forsyth County, Georgia, and on the streets of Boston and New York.[169] One also detects this trend in the polarization and tensions that exist between the growing ethnic populations in the central cities of America's metropolitan areas. Relations between African-Americans and Jews, which were quite good during the King years, have declined significantly since

168. Baldwin, ed., *Toward the Beloved Community*, 1–20 and 260–80; and Fluker, *They Looked for a City*, 155–72.

169. Walter Leavy, "What's Behind the Resurgence of Racism in America?," *Ebony* 42, no. 6 (April 1987): 132–33, 136, and 138–39. The literature on what some social scientists call "academic racism" increased significantly in the 1980s, largely because of the rise of Skin Heads, Aryan youth groups, and other white racist elements on predominantly white college and university campuses. See Vernon E. McClean and Lois Lyles, " The Survival of Afro-American Studies," *The Chronicle of Higher Education* (March 6, 1985): 96; Brent Staples, "The Dwindling Black Presence on Campus," *The New York Times Magazine* (April 27, 1986): 46, 50–52, 54, and 62; Rob Levin, "Subtle Racism Colors Life at Vanderbilt," *The Atlanta Constitution* (February 12, 1987): 1-D ff.; "Students Challenge Campus Racism," *News and Letters* 32, no. 6 (April 10, 1987): 1 and 7; "Student, Faculty Rift Stirs Racism Charges," *The Tennessean* (April 11, 1988): 6A; Thomas Short, "A 'New Racism' on Campus?," *Commentary* (August, 1988): 46–50; Clarence E. Glover, Jr., "The Other Side of Racism: A Commentary," *NSBE Journal* (October 1988): 42–45; "Mary Berry Cites Racial Unrest on U. S. Campuses," *Jet* 75, no. 24 (March 20, 1989): 10; and "Professors' Race Ideas Stir Turmoil at College," *The New York Times* (April 20, 1990): A-13.

the 1970s because of differences over affirmative action, quotas, the crisis in the Middle East, big city election campaigns, and the bigoted remarks of black and Jewish leaders.[170] Equally disturbing is white America's fear and distrust of Asians, Hispanics, and other minorities whose numbers are increasing at a faster rate than those of whites. These realities, coupled with the spread of the Ku Klux Klan, the Skin Heads, the Aryan Nations, and Neo-Nazi groups, signal a continuation of the same racial nightmare that King and his followers struggled to overcome.[171]

The problem exists perhaps on the same level in other parts of the world. South Africa's white minority government is still oppressing and killing blacks and other people of color, and is destabilizing the entire region of Southern Africa.[172] Skin Heads, Neo-Nazi groups, and other racist elements are desecrating the burial grounds of Jews in various parts of the world.[173] Violent confrontations have been occurring recently between African and Chinese students at the Beijing Languages Institute and at other Chinese institutions of higher learning, and the Japanese business community is pandering to many of the same black stereotypes promoted

170. See Alvin F. Poussaint, "Blacks and Jews: An Appeal for Unity," *Ebony* 29, no. 9 (July 1974): 120–22, 124–26 and 128; Jack Newfield, "Blacks and Jews: The Tragedy of Jackson, the Logic of Coalition," *Voice: The Weekly Newspaper of New York* 29, no. 12 (March 20, 1984), 1 and 13; Robert G. Weisbord and Richard Kazarian, Jr., *Israel in the Black American Perspective* (Westport, Conn.: Greenwood Press, 1985), 1ff.; Henry Siegman, "Jews and Blacks: Reconciling the Differences," *The American Jewish Congress Monthly* 52, no. 1 (January 1985): 3–4; Michael Kramer, "Blacks and Jews: How Wide is the Rift?," *New York* (February 4, 1985): 26–32; Glenn C. Loury, "Behind the Black-Jewish Split," *Commentary* (January, 1986): 23–27; and Herb Boyd, "Blacks and Jews: Conflict on the Cultural Front," *Crisis* 96, no. 9 (November 1989): 34–36.

171. Leavy, "What's Behind the Resurgence of Racism in America?," 132–33; 136, and 138–39; and Charles Whitaker, "The New Mississippi: Is It Really Better than Up North?," *Ebony* 44, no. 10 (August, 1989): 30 and 32–37.

172. Margaret C. Lee, *Resource Guide to Information on Southern Africa* (Nashville: Winston-Derek Publishers, Inc., 1988): ix–x; and Margaret C. Lee, *SADCC: The Political Economy of Development in Southern Africa* (Nashville: Winston-Derek Publishers, Inc., 1989), 1–24.

173. *The Washington Post* (May 14, 1990): 1 and A-13.

for centuries by the white Western world.[174] These tragic occurrences suggest that one of the major problems of the twenty-first century may well be what King called "the color bar" and what W. E. B. Du Bois referred to as "the color line."[175] The lesson in the life, struggle, and death of King for people in America and abroad is that racism and discrimination must be rooted out at every level.[176]

It is significant that King's philosophy and methods still influence many who crusade against the global problem of racial discrimination. The S.C.L.C., under the leadership of Joseph E. Lowery, remains a force in this struggle.[177] This organization is devoting much time and energy to sensitizing the public worldwide to racism in the United States, South Africa, and other countries through workshops, boycotts, protest marches, sit-ins, and other nonviolent means. Its prophetic witness is nothing short of remarkable, especially considering its shortage of financial resources and its constant battle against conservative blacks and whites who claim that racism is not the major problem confronting blacks and other peoples of color.[178]

174. See A. B. Assensoh, "Oppression of African Students is Still Prevalent in China," *Times Tribune*, Stanford, Cal. (January 30, 1989): A-9; "Black Stereotypes Used to Market Products in Japan," *Jet* 74, no. 20 (August 15, 1988): 36–37; "Japanese Slurs on Blacks Causing Rift Between Them," *Jet* 75, no. 5 (October 31, 1988): 12; and "Japanese Family Fights to Remove Racially Offensive Products in Their Country," *Jet* 76, no. 22 (September 4, 1989): 37.

175. King, *Where Do We Go from Here?* 173–76.

176. George W. Shepherd, Jr., "Who Killed Martin Luther King's Dream?: An Afro-American Tragedy," *Africa Today* 15, no. 2 (April–May 1968): 2.

177. See *S.C.L.C.: The Southern Christian Leadership Conference National Magazine* 15, no. 1 (January–February 1986): 14–19; *S.C.L.C.: The Southern Christian Leadership Conference National Magazine* 16, no. 2 (March–April 1987): 18–31; a private interview with the Reverend Ralph D. Abernathy, Atlanta, Georgia, 17 March 1987; "Nation's Eyes Focus on the Poor, Jobless, Peace and Apartheid During D. C. March," *Jet* 74, no. 24 (September 12, 1988): 4–8 and 13; and Thomas R. Peake, *Keeping the Dream Alive: A History of the Southern Christian Leadership Conference from King to the Nineteen-Eighties* (New York: Peter Lang, 1987), 227–405.

178. Peake, *Keeping the Dream Alive*, 353 ff.; and a private interview with the Reverend Ralph D. Abernathy, Atlanta, Georgia, 7 May 1987.

The Atlanta-based Martin Luther King, Jr. Center for Nonviolent Social Change, Inc. is equally devoted to promoting nonviolently the elimination of racism on a global scale. The center's cultural affairs program, its National Hispanic Advisory Committee, its annual workshops, and its Chapel of All Faiths are among a range of programs and activities designed to help shape a world in which people of all races and ethnic backgrounds can co-exist on the basis of mutual respect.[179] Special attention is devoted to teaching young people about King's life and work so they can avoid the kind of racist attitudes that limit the advancement of humankind as a whole.[180] Coretta Scott King, as President of the King Center, is one of the world's most vital symbols in the struggle against racism—one who speaks out and demonstrates against racist oppression, especially in the United States and South Africa. Echoing the views of her late husband, she maintains, "The time has come for an international alliance of peoples of all nations against racism."[181]

Some alliances against racism are being formed in various parts of the world, inspired by the example and vision of Martin Luther King, Jr. In April, 1987, Bernard Lafayette and other black American religious leaders who worked with King joined the Reverend Raul Suarez and other Cuban Christians in inaugurating the Martin Luther King, Jr. Center in Havana's Marianao neighborhood, an effort geared primarily toward fighting racism. The effort created a certain consciousness, spirit, and

179. See *The Martin Luther King, Jr. Center for Nonviolent Social Change: State Historic Site* (a brochure issued by the King Center and the Georgia Department of Natural Resources, Atlanta, Ga., n.d.), 1 ff.; and Lynn Norment, "Coretta Scott King: The Woman Behind the King Anniversary," *Ebony* 45, no. 3 (January 1990): 116–18, 120, and 122.
180. Norment, "Coretta Scott King: The Woman Behind the King Anniversary," 116–18, 120, and 122.
181. *Four Decades of Concern: Martin Luther King, Jr.* (Atlanta: printed by the Martin Luther King, Jr. Center for Nonviolent Social Change, Inc., August 1, 1986), 27–35, 39–42, and 45–50; and Coretta Scott King, "The King Center and South Africa," *African Commentary* 2, no. 3 (March 1990): 40–42.

devotion to struggle among a broad spectrum of American and Cuban Protestants and Catholics which still exist.[182] Early in 1989, a similar alliance was formed between United States Congressional Black Caucus leaders and black political pioneers in Great Britain's Parliament. Meeting in London, the alliance, led by Congressman Ronald Dellums of California and Parliamentary Black Caucus Chairman Bernie Grant, promised to continue a dialogue about how to end racism as a threat to world peace and community.[183] This alliance bears a striking similarity to the one King helped organize in London in December, 1964, with persons from England, South Africa, Pakistan, and India.[184]

Developments of this nature are also occurring in Japan. Some Japanese, outraged by businesses in their country that distribute black sambo dolls and other racially offensive merchandise, have turned to antiracism coalitions for solutions to the problem. The most notable example is the Association to Stop Racism in Japan, organized by Hajime Arita, a ten-year-old Japanese boy who toured the United States in late 1989 at the expense of the Black Business Council (B.B.C.). Arita is among a growing number of Asians who realize the folly in perpetrating the same racist views that have victimized them and other so-called Third World peoples under systems of Western colonialism and imperialism for so long. Concerned about Japanese racial attitudes and about the conditions under which black people live in America and abroad, the young Arita is living proof of the vitality and durability of King's dream for humanity.[185]

182. *People's Daily World* (May 6, 1987): 5-A.
183. D. Michael Cheers, "Black U. S. Leaders Join Those in England to Start Parliament's Black Caucus," *Jet* 76, no. 3 (April 24, 1989): 28–31.
184. See "Transcript of a Radio Interview with Martin Luther King, Jr. Regarding Nobel Peace Prize," Oslo, Norway (The King Center Archives, 9 December 1964), 1–4.
185. "Black Stereotypes Used to Market Products in Japan," 36–37; "Japanese Family Fights to Remove Racially Offensive Products in Their Country," 37; and "Japanese Slurs on Blacks Causing Rift Between Them," 12.

The same can be said of the numerous coalitions against racism that are developing at Dartmouth College, the University of Michigan, and other institutions of higher learning in the United States, South Africa, and other countries. Many of these coalitions are sponsoring seminars and workshops on racism, and are employing protest marches, sit-ins, boycotts, and other nonviolent tactics used by King and other civil rights activists in the 1950s and 1960s. Such antiracism coalitions are consistent with King's prediction, made in the early 1960s, that college and university students will be "a part of a worldwide thrust in the future" to end racism.[186] They also reflect the wisdom of King's "thoughts about the role which our awakened youth—black and white— might play in the shaping of a new world."[187]

One of the greatest threats to the fulfillment of King's vision of world community lies in the failure of world leaders to consistently address the problem of racism. President George Bush and President Fredrick de Klerk of South Africa are among a very small group of world leaders who are vowing to use their influence to counter racial bigotry.[188] This is one of the most disturbing realities in the contemporary world. King often said that leaders of governments are in the position to add depth, integrity, and conviction to any struggle for racial harmony.[189] If world leaders do not take the kind of moral stand suggested and represented by King, the forces of racism will probably become even more comfortable in raising their ugly heads throughout North America, Europe, Africa, and Asia.

186. King, "After Desegregation—What?," 1–2.
187. King, *The Trumpet of Conscience*, xi.
188. "Bush Vows to Use the President's Office for a Pulpit Against Racism," *Jet* 75, no. 9 (November 28, 1988): 4; Patrick Laurence, "De Klerk's Rubicon," *Africa Report* 35, no. 1 (March–April 1990): 13–16; and Peter Tygesen, "Mandela's Mandate," *Africa Report* 35, no. 2 (May–June 1990): 32.
189. King, *The Trumpet of Conscience*, 3–17; and King, *Where Do We Go from Here?* 173–76.

Poverty remains as much a threat to world community as racism. Peoples of color are still, to a greater degree than whites, the victims of hunger, disease, and low levels of formal education. Homelessness and joblessness have reached frightening levels even in so-called developed nations such as the United States and Great Britain. Thirty of the forty-three poorest countries in the world are in Africa, and the remaining thirteen are in Asia, Latin America, and the Caribbean. The gap between the "haves" and "have-nots" is expanding daily, creating feelings of hopelessness, despair, and anger that, if continuously ignored, could lead to worldwide revolution. King warned of such a dangerous possibility almost thirty years ago, and his words still ring with a piercing sense of urgency in a world in which millions die each day of inadequate food, clothing, and health care.[190]

The tragedy is compounded by the fact that little is being done to mobilize and empower the poor across geographical boundaries. King's idea of a Poor People's Campaign that transcends racial and ethnic categories is virtually nonexistent. However, the homeless are beginning to organize and to demonstrate for better living conditions in the United States, a movement likely to spread throughout Europe in the future. In parts of Africa, Asia, and Latin America, one finds increased resistance among peasants and farmworkers, strong demands for agrarian reform, and the involvement of pastors, priests, and nuns in struggles for economic justice and equality. Many in these movements are driven by the same spirit of nonviolence and hope that inspired King.[191]

The S.C.L.C. and the Martin Luther King, Jr. Center for Nonviolent Social Change, organizations that claim a special devotion to the King legacy, are devoting very

190. King, *Where Do We Go from Here?* 176 and 189; and "King Accuses U.S.A. and Britain of Bolstering Racial Segregation in South Africa," *Relay News in English* (December 8, 1964): 4.

191. A serious study of King's influence on liberation movements around the world today is needed. A step in this direction is taken in Baldwin, ed., *Toward the Beloved Community*, Introduction and Concluding Essay.

little time, energy, and resources to global poverty. The struggle against racism has received most of their attention and resources. While both have a history of pushing for jobs, affordable housing, health care, and education for the poor in America, they have not yet developed the kind of programmatic thrust needed to address poverty on a global scale.[192] At the same time, the leadership of both organizations are now expressing a desire to study more carefully economic injustice as it affects the world's poor and to explore new and more vital ways of alleviating the problem within the framework of nonviolent strategy.[193]

Much of the responsibility for eliminating poverty and economic injustice still rests with the rich and so-called developed nations. King made this point consistently in the 1960s. As was the case in his day, the United States, Great Britain, Japan, and other countries are controlling and using an enormous, disproportionate share of the world's resources, and their economies are still being built and maintained in large measure through an exploitation of cheap labor. Their approaches to the world food crisis and the problem of poverty and economic justice in general are leading daily to a further victimization of the poor. They are

192. The failure of the S.C.L.C. to develop a strong action program that would have a decisive impact on the struggle against poverty at the national and international levels in the 1980s is evident from a reading of Peake, *Keeping the Dream Alive*, 353–414. However, issues of the S.C.L.C. National Magazine for the 1980s do reveal that the organization has staged boycotts in the interest of economic justice. The King Center has been criticized even by blacks as a middle class, elitist establishment, oriented more toward memorializing King than toward making his dream a reality for the poor. Coretta Scott King's assessment of the center's work challenges this view. The center, in her estimation, is promoting Dr. King's work against poverty through its general advocation of nonviolent social change and its educational programs. See *Four Decades of Concern*, 3–8; and Norment, "Coretta Scott King: The Woman Behind the King Anniversary," 117–18.

193. The leaders of both the S.C.L.C. and the King Center believe that the conditions of poverty will shape the next major social movement in America, a movement that will have global implications. See "A Poor People's Crusade Manifesto" and "Putting the Plight of the Poor in Plain View," *S.C.L.C.* 16, no. 2, 43–44; and Norment, "Coretta Scott King: The Woman Behind the King Anniversary," 118.

living proof of King's claim, made many years ago, that the existing global economic order is uncongenial to the pursuit of genuine and lasting human community. Most of the nations of the world still have not realized the truth implicit in King's contention that a solution to global poverty requires a fundamental shift in values, economic priorities, and a more democratic sharing of decision-making power.[194]

This point applies to the global problem of war and human destruction as well. At a time when nuclear weapons threaten the peace, survival, and well-being of the human family, few seem truly interested in recovering King's idea of a global application of nonviolent means.[195] The nations of the world are too inclined to rely on the sword rather than on diplomacy in their relations with one another. More than three hundred small wars have killed some thirty million people since the founding of the United Nations in 1945. Although the superpowers have transcended the Cold War and moved closer toward détente, global terrorism, the war between the Israelis and the Palestinians, and other forms of violence still haunt the global community. The world's poor are still being victimized by high levels of military spending, creating a situation in which bloated military budgets exist side by side with the bloated stomachs of undernourished and diseased men, women, and children. The antinuclear movement, which extends beyond North America to Europe, Asia, Africa, and other continents, is seemingly too weak and sporadic to break this disturbing cycle. It is virtually impossible to find a world figure of King's stature with the courage to challenge, vigorously and consistently, warfare and the building of weapon systems on the world stage.[196] Most peoples of

194. King, *Where Do We Go from Here?* 176–81; and King, *The Trumpet of Conscience,* 14 and 17.
195. King set forth this idea in King, *Where Do We Go from Here?* 184; and King, *The Trumpet of Conscience,* 64, 68 and 70.
196. Those leaders and thinkers in contemporary America who promote Christian nonviolence have not approached the fame and influence of King, nor have they practically applied nonviolence to the extent that

the world have seemingly succumbed to the belief that war is inevitable—that King's call for the employment of nonviolence to settle conflict between nations is even more unrealistic today than it was in his time. The S.C.L.C. and the King Center are among those establishments worldwide that are seeking ways to enhance global security through an advocacy of nonviolence.[197] They remain the main vehicles through which King's intellectual and moral influence on the current antinuclear movement is felt. Both Joseph Lowery and Coretta Scott King view creative nonviolent action as a global challenge for all people, especially given humanity's capacity for self-annihilation. They have offered numerous commentaries on the dangers of nuclear war and terrorism, have engaged in peace demonstrations, and have sponsored and continue to sponsor symposia, seminars, and workshops on the immorality and impracticality of violence as a means of addressing conflict between individuals as well as nations.[198]

Sexism is considered yet another threat to world community today. Although King never reached the point of addressing sexism as a global problem, his ideal of the beloved community still provides an inspiration and a model for millions who are struggling to resolve the problem.[199] The work of the National Organization of Women (N.O.W.), the National Council of Negro Women (N.C.N.W.), and other such organizations around the world testify to the power of that ideal. The involvement of Coretta King and the King Center in this protracted movement against the oppression of women is worthy of

---

King did. For important discussions of such figures, see Angie O'Gorman, ed., *The Universe Bends toward Justice: A Reader on Christian Nonviolence in the U.S.* (Philadelphia: New Society Publishers, 1990), 185 ff.

197. "S.C.L.C. Endorses International War Toy Boycott," *S.C.L.C.* 15, no. 1: 140–53; and *Four Decades of Concern*, 3–8, 27–35, and 39–41.

198. "S.C.L.C. Chairman Joins Peace Rally," *S.C.L.C.* 16, no. 2: 66; Peake, *Keeping the Dream Alive*, 353–414; *Four Decades of Concern*, 45–50; and Norment, "Coretta Scott King: The Woman Behind the King Anniversary," 116–18, 120, and 122.

199. Ansbro, *Martin Luther King, Jr.*, xiv–xv; and Young, "The Rich Legacy of Martin Luther King," 22.

special note. Coretta Scott King constantly urges women
throughout the world to approach sexism with the same
measure of concern and practical action as they approach racism.[200] She holds that "the full representation
of women" in issues of social justice and foreign policy
matters is "not only needed to rectify" centuries of discrimination but also to ensure the survival of humanity
"in the nuclear age."[201]

Although King would be disappointed with much of
what has transpired in the world since his death, he
would be pleased with some of the recent developments
in South Africa and parts of Eastern Europe. He would
value current talks between the United States and the
Soviet Union, and also their growing desire to reduce
nuclear weapons. This development is in tune with
proposals made by King. The recent release of Nelson
Mandela and the movement of black and white South
Africans toward a negotiated settlement coincide with
suggestions King made in the 1960s.[202] The same can be
said of the explosive changes in Eastern Europe. As the
people of Poland, Romania, Estonia, Latvia, Lithuania,
and other Eastern-bloc countries fight to break the
chains that bind them to the U.S.S.R. and Communism,
they add credence to King's contention: "Oppressed people cannot remain oppressed forever."[203]

The collapse of the Berlin Wall in late 1989 attests in a
special way to the vitality of King's vision and hope for
humanity. When King visited the Berlin Wall in 1964, he
preached in an East Berlin church, articulating a vision

200. *Four Decades of Concern*, 29–31.
201. Coretta Scott King, "U.S. Needs More Willing Women Participants in Foreign Policy," *The Tennessean* (March 1, 1988): 9A; and
Coretta Scott King, "Empowering Women Will Benefit Nation," *The Tennessean* (November 13, 1990): 9A.
202. Baldwin, ed., *Toward the Beloved Community*, Concluding
Essay; and Lewis V. Baldwin, "Martin Luther King, Jr.'s 'Beloved Community' Ideal and the Apartheid System in South Africa," *The Western
Journal of Black Studies* 10, no. 4 (Winter, 1986): 212–19.
203. "King Accuses U.S.A. and Britain of Bolstering Racial Segregation," 4.

that many in East and West Berlin today have come to see as true and attainable:

> I am honored to be in this city, which stands as a symbol of the division of men. Here on either side of the wall we are all God's children and no man can divide us. There is a common humanity which makes us sensitive to the sufferings of one another. There is one faith that binds us in a common baptism, a hope for the salvation of the world. Although there are man-made barriers and a man-made wall, there is something that unites us all as Christians. In Christ there is no East or West, in him no North or South; there is only one community. . . . Although we are separated through thousands of miles, we are one in our struggles together. In the very real sense, this is one world.[204]

King's ideal of world community may never be fully achieved in human history. Hatred, greed, and violence will continue to turn individuals against individuals and nations against nations. Even so, King's valor and his vision will continue to inspire millions the world over who cherish human freedom, just laws, and democratic institutions. The civil rights leader will always be remembered as "a man for all people"—as one who died believing in the ultimate redemption and transformation of human society.[205]

---

204. "Fall of the Berlin Wall Fits King's Dream," *Jet* 77, no. 8 (November 27, 1989): 53–54.
205. King, *The Trumpet of Conscience*, xii.

CONCLUSION

This book has shown how the South, the nation, and the world came together in King's consciousness to inform his vision and to shape his thought and activism. In this sense, *To Make the Wounded Whole* builds on the discussion afforded in my previous book, *There Is a Balm in Gilead: The Cultural Roots of Martin Luther King, Jr.* (1991). The two works together capture the complexity and uniqueness of King's personality and outlook, and reflect how the man moved from a little known southern black Baptist preacher to a recognized world figure. They prove that a genuine appreciation for King's significance as a national and international figure must begin with a consideration of his background in black southern culture.

Four objectives have been achieved in *To Make the Wounded Whole*. First, the study has demonstrated that King's absorption in the particularities of black life, thought, and culture determined his perspective on the black condition and on how that condition could best be improved. Chapters 1 and 2 are particularly important at this point. They show that a serious consideration of King's dialogues with black perspectives such as progressive accommodationism, redemptive nationalism, grassroots revivalism, and prosperity positivism, and of his legacy for contemporary black theology and ethics, can enrich and inform black America's continuing quest for freedom, justice, and equal opportunity.

Second, this work has suggested that King's global vision merits the attention and scrutiny of all moral and rational persons who seek to understand and improve the human condition as a whole. That vision was reflected in the positions King took on African independence, the Vietnam war, and other problems abroad. His metaphor of the "world house" or the "world-wide neighborhood," and his assessment of the major obstacles to world community, have significant implications for the shaping of a new humanity and a new world. His indomitable faith in God, his incurable optimism, his unwavering devotion to the democratic ideal, his skillful wedding of secular and sacred dimensions of life, his strong belief in the essential worth, dignity, and oneness of all humanity, and his willingness to suffer and die for a more just and moral social order—virtues and values that reflect both his cultural roots and his cultural legacy—contain invaluable lessons for humans struggling to overcome their alienation from themselves, other humans, and God. Thus, ethical and theological dialogue with King around the ideal of the beloved community must continue on the deepest possible level throughout the world.

Third, an appraisal of the importance of King's role as a world figure and as an international symbol of community has been made. It has been noted that King not only struggled and sacrificed his life for the realization of a more just, peaceful, and inclusive world, but has also become a symbol of the highest human values and virtues. His achievements on these levels are attested to by the landmarks established in his memory, and by the numerous honors given him annually around the world. Although such recognition is justified and laudable, it must not distort or minimize the importance of that which constituted the essential quality of King's soul. More specifically, it must portray him as one more concerned about the globalization of the ideal of human community than about statutes and monuments in his honor. Moreover, we would be untrue to King and to ourselves if we allow our recognition and celebration of him to become merely ways of absolving ourselves of the responsibility of fulfilling his dream.

Finally, careful attention has been given to King's legacy for humanity as a whole. That legacy can be aptly described as one of *hope* and *struggle*. *Hope* in this case implies the capacity to believe in the redemption and transformation of individuals and of human society, despite all of the ambiguities and vicissitudes of life. *Struggle* means that sense of moral obligation that compels one to suffer and even die nonviolently for that which is just and noble. Through his capacity to hope and his will to struggle, King provided an example for humanity that will withstand all challenges and tests of time.

INDEX